Chechn

CALIFORNIA SERIES IN PUBLIC ANTHROPOLOGY

The California Series in Public Anthropology emphasizes the anthropologist's role as an engaged intellectual. It continues anthropology's commitment to being an ethnographic witness, to describing, in human terms, how life is lived beyond the borders of many readers' experiences. But it also adds a commitment, through ethnography, to reframing the terms of public debate—transforming received, accepted understandings of social issues with new insights, new framings.

Series Editor: Robert Borofsky (Hawaii Pacific University)

Contributing Editors:
Philippe Bourgois (UC San Francisco),
Paul Farmer (Partners in Health),
Rayna Rapp (New York University),
and Nancy Scheper-Hughes (UC Berkeley)

University of California Press Editor: Naomi Schneider

1. *Twice Dead: Organ Transplants and the Reinvention of Death,* by Margaret Lock
2. *Birthing the Nation: Strategies of Palestinian Women in Israel,* by Rhoda Ann Kanaaneh (with a foreword by Hannan Ashrawi)
3. *Annihilating Difference: The Anthropology of Genocide,* edited by Alexander Laban Hinton (with a foreword by Kenneth Roth)
4. *Pathologies of Power: Structural Violence and the Assault on Health and Human Rights,* by Paul Farmer (with a foreword by Amartya Sen)
5. *Buddha Is Hiding: Refugees, Citizenship, and the New America,* by Aihwa Ong
6. *Chechnya: Life in a War-Torn Society,* by Valery Tishkov (with a foreword by Mikhail S. Gorbachev)
7. *Total Confinement: Madness and Reason in the Maximum Security Prison,* by Lorna A. Rhodes
8. *Paradise in Ashes: A Guatemalan Journey of Courage, Terror, and Hope,* by Beatriz Manz (with a foreword by Aryeh Neier)
9. *Laughter Out of Place: Race, Class, Violence, and Sexuality in a Rio Shantytown,* by Donna M. Goldstein
10. *Shadows of War: Violence, Power, and International Profiteering in the Twenty-First Century,* by Carolyn Nordstrom
11. *Why Did They Kill? Cambodia in the Shadow of Genocide,* by Alexander Laban Hinton

Chechnya

Life in a War-Torn Society

Valery Tishkov

With a foreword by Mikhail S. Gorbachev

UNIVERSITY OF CALIFORNIA PRESS

University of California Press
Berkeley and Los Angeles, California

University of California Press, Ltd.
London, England

Library of Congress Cataloging-in-Publication Data

Tishkov, Valerii Aleksandrovich.
Chechnya : Life in a war-torn society / Valery Tishkov.
p. cm. — (California series in public anthropology ; 6)
Includes bibliographical references and index.
ISBN 0-520-23887-7 (cloth : alk. paper)—
ISBN 0-520-23888-5 (pbk. : alk. paper)
1. Chechnya (Russia)—History—Civil War, 1994-
—Social aspects. 2. Chechnya (Russia)—History—Civil War, 1994-
—Personal narratives, Chechen. I. Title. II. Series.

DK511.C37 T572 2004
947.5'2—dc22 2003017330

Manufactured in the United States of America
13 12 11 10 09 08 07 06 05 04
11 10 9 8 7 6 5 4 3 2 1

The paper used in this publication is both acid-free and totally chlorine-free (TCF). It meets the minimum requirements of ANSI/NISO Z39.48-1992 (R 1997) (*Permanence of Paper*). ⊗

CONTENTS

FOREWORD

The war in Chechnya is a difficult trial for the new Russian state and for all its citizens, especially the Chechen people. The reasonable desire of the population of this former autonomous region of the Soviet Union to enjoy democratization and to correct the historical injustices done to the Chechen and Ingush peoples—the Stalin-era deportation and subsequent discrimination—have been misused to fuel nationalist hysteria and anti-Russian feeling.

In the prewar years, the socioeconomic and political situation in Checheno-Ingushetia was difficult. Many young men were without work, especially in the hill country. The leadership of the republic suffered deep corruption along clan lines. Murky ideas of creating an independent Islamic state in Chechnya spread among part of the intelligentsia and the Islamic religious leadership, although the religious issue was used from the very start primarily as a political slogan in support of a break with Russia.

The collapse of the Soviet Union had a particularly negative effect on Chechnya. Not content with the breakup of the fifteen former Soviet republics, which in and of itself was a huge historical shock, leaders and activists in several autonomous regions undertook the much more dangerous project of further disintegration of the country. In response, leaders of the fifteen republics who were involved in dismantling the central authority and the common state were setting a dangerous and often irresponsible course in regard to their own internal autonomous regions. Some promised the autonomous regions unlimited sovereignty, others tried to abolish them. Both approaches led to armed conflicts that resulted in ethnic cleansing and numerous casualties.

There was a chance to prevent violence and war in Chechnya. The thirst for power among those at the center and the lack of attention to what was happening at the periphery, as well as the ambitions of some Russian national leaders who came from the region, allowed a series of dangerous manipulations to unfold in Checheno-Ingushetia: the rise to power of General Dudayev, the destruction of the institutions of the state, the loss of control over arms stores, the appearance of armed groups among the civilian population, and the easy agreement to split the republic in two.

The illegitimate regime pushed the republic toward chaos and dangerous adventurism. The first victims were the non-Chechen population, who were robbed, pushed out of the republic, and sometimes killed. The helpless reaction of the Russian authorities and the silence of international human-rights organizations remain on their consciences. The slogan of self-determination turned out to be more important than human rights and elementary order in the country.

This was the time when supporters of further disintegration in Russia appeared in the outside world. If it had not been for their sympathy, financial subsidies, and secret instructions, events might have taken a different turn. There might have been talks with a peaceful outcome, as happened, for example, in Tatarstan. In the end, the ambitions, haughtiness, and arrogance of leaders—primarily Yeltsin and Dudayev—overpowered feelings of responsibility for the fates and lives of the citizens. Irresponsible improvisations led to war in 1994, which ended in August 1996 with a pseudo-peace, since no fundamental agreements were reached, except the proud but ahistorical claim to have brought about "the end of the 400-year conflict between Russia and Chechnya."

There were many guilty parties in this war, and history will put everything in its place. But the human lives lost cannot be brought back, and the destruction is difficult to reverse. But what happened after August 1996 has a somewhat different meaning. For three years, the destruction of the state and society in Chechnya proceeded apace. The militarization of the population, its ideological preparation in the spirit of Islam, the theft of the republic's resources, robbery, and murder, all fueled hatred and prepared the way for a new war, this time with the help of international terrorist forces.

All this led to the attack in the summer of 1999 on Dagestan, which raised the risk of a widening of the armed uprising into other regions of the North Caucasus and the destabilization of the south of Russia. The Russian state and its federal government could not ignore this challenge. The support from the Dagestani and Russian populations for decisive action against the Chechen separatists and foreign mercenaries speaks for itself.

That was followed by the shift of military action to Chechnya itself, with the aim of eliminating this international base of armed terrorism. By this time, a new generation had grown up in Chechnya, fully propagandized about the "great victory over Russia" and the extremist ideas of radical

Islam. Recruits from this generation preferred armed resistance to federal forces, and the local population lost control over it. Unfortunately, Russia's armed forces are not too well suited to such complex operations, leading to cruelty and civilian casualties. About half the population of Chechnya has left its small homeland and found refuge in other regions of Russia.

This volume, *Chechnya: Life in a War-Torn Society,* was written by a man well known in our country, whose works and speeches I consider well deserving of attention. Even before the era of perestroika, Valery Tishkov was a leading scholar on issues of nationality and the formation of a multinational state. In July 1990, he was a delegate to the Twenty-eighth Congress of the Communist Party of the Soviet Union, where he participated in the discussion of these issues and proposed adoption of the tenet that "individual rights are above those of the nation and that the party opposes special rights for so-called native nationalities in relation to the rest of the population of the republic," which was ultimately included in the congress's program statement. This principle had and continues to have many opponents, but if it had been implemented, we would not have suffered many conflicts, including the war in Chechnya.

All this makes the author not merely an ivory-tower academic but also an active citizen, a scholar-politician who through his scholarly works and his social activity has had a real influence on events in our country. Tishkov's new book is impressive for its materials, its approach to the problem, and its analysis. Much has been written about the Chechen war, and there have been many journalistic interpretations of it. Many of these works are politicized and amount to polemics, however, like the bullets that are fired in Chechnya.

Tishkov has written a different kind of book and offers a new view on the war in Chechnya. This is a book not about the war but about Chechen society, which has been forced into this war and cruelly traumatized by it. The firsthand accounts it contains from many Chechens in different areas, both fighters and those who stayed out of the fighting, both supporters of Dudayev and opponents, are the book's strength. The book exposes the deeper truth about people in time of war, in particular the Chechens.

The author's analysis of the situation in Chechnya, both before the war and during the conflict, contradicts the common view that the Chechens differ radically from the rest of the population of Russia. It is often forgotten that the Chechens and Ingush, especially the current generation, grew up in the Soviet era with their own autonomous republic and enjoyed diverse industrial and cultural outputs, a high proportion of educated people, and numerous outstanding citizens. The Chechens lived according to the same laws as the rest of the country, although they preserved their cultural uniqueness. The author has convincingly restored this forgotten picture, and this is very useful, since after all this destruction, more and more

Chechens are saying they had a perfectly good life. Until now, their propagandists and external advisers had continually harped on one theme: "genocide," "ethnocide," "ecocide," "national destruction."

This book confronts the difficult question of why such conflicts arise—why do people who have lived side by side start killing one another? Some explain this in terms of history, citing innate hatred, the incompatibility of civilizations, or the unusual social structure of the rival nationalities. Some say the war in Chechnya was bought and paid for. But the question remains of why it is so easy to lead a society into conflict: why people take up arms or find themselves unable to oppose the initiators and perpetrators of violence. Tishkov's explanation has important theoretical and political significance and deserves the attention of an international audience.

As a scholar and an ethnologist, Tishkov concludes that the past, especially that which has not been personally experienced, cannot be adduced as the reason for the Chechen conflict. History is mobilized by political leaders and social activists as an ideological argument and nothing more. The Chechens were not the only victims of Stalin's repression, but only for them did this trauma of the past become one of the main motives for an armed conflict. Social factors, such as unemployment among the male population, may create the conditions for them to take up arms, but not more. Other republics of the North Caucasus also have the same social problems, as do many countries of the world, but they do not inevitably lead to armed conflict. Neither do cultural traditions or particular family structures explain much, since most of this is artificially exaggerated by enthusiasts of ethnographic or militaristic romanticism. Finally, some argue that it is Islam, the religion of the Chechens, that makes them so steadfast and fierce, and that they have conducted a "holy war" against Russia and the Russians in the name of Islam and of the cleansing of the state of "infidels." But this is a false assertion. Islam contains a strong humanistic component, and religious leaders have never advocated a war with Russia.

In reality, things are at once much more complicated and yet simpler than in many of the explanations and apologies. People are inclined to abandon law and order and to resort to unlawful ways of reaching their utilitarian goals when coaxed along by high-sounding ideas and slogans, obeying those who put forward and inculcate such slogans. In societies that are little modernized or have just emerged from totalitarian rule, people may readily give up their individual civic responsibilities for an authoritarian collective idea, particularly if it is based on ethnic or religious sentiments. Having stolen or commandeered their Kalashnikov guns, the illegal groups or "guards" go on to grab property and resources belonging to others—property and resources they needed to work hard for in previous years. The temptations of chaos and lawlessness can be so great that many are overwhelmed by them. This logic of events is demonstrated in the stories

Chechens themselves tell, stories of how they found their way into the armed "battalions" and became involved in the senseless practices of war.

Another of the book's revelations is the state of a society immersed in bloodshed. People are subjected to an unprecedented flood of propaganda and to various external influences seeking not only to destroy the state control but to undermine an internal social order based on ancient moral principles and the authority of the elders. Ordinary people concerned above all with their own lives, with the welfare and safety of their families, find themselves victims of global ideological disputes and targets of rampant violence. Then the chaotic ruin of their homes and the death of their dear ones fall upon them and change their psychology: they are filled with despair and a lust for vengeance, they lose sight of what is happening in their land around them. They counter the situation by their own personal strategies for survival and the preservation of their families and property. They are numbed by the cruelty of war inflicted by both sides—including the destruction caused by the army in trying to cope with the insurgents.

In such conditions, the civilian population suffers more than the forces engaged in deadly combat. Civilian casualties in the Chechen war have exceeded those of both Russia's army and the insurgents' battalions and guerrillas. People are moved only by their desire to defend their homes and to take revenge. They have long forgotten the initial slogans of the conflict. Then various internal and external forces usurp the motives of war and take unspeakable profits from the chaos and the terror. The conflict is thus driv en out of control by the society immersed in it. The reigning ideology has become extremism and intolerance. Opponents, even in one's own ranks, are simply annihilated. Peace is perceived by some of the fighting men as a daunting prospect, one that calls for a resumption of responsibility and efforts to restore normal life, instead of toting an automatic weapon as a source of status and livelihood. Tishkov defines this state of society as demodernization and analyzes its features. What he finds is important for the understanding of all modern armed conflicts.

Of great value also is the author's conclusion that violent group conflicts are not so much preordained as constructed by interested forces in certain favorable conditions, particularly when the state is weakened in an underdeveloped civil society or during the crises of deep political transformations. The barrier between war and peace is then more fragile, and violence may break out even in previously more or less flourishing lands. That fact alone calls for greater responsibility than we have hitherto seen on the part of politicians and intellectuals. These actors often begin by favoring and supporting some unrealistic and dangerous geopolitical project and then end—while watching from the sidelines—by showing much concern over human rights violations or terrorism. That scenario played itself out after World War II in many regions of the world and then erupted again in

Chechnya. These are lessons to be learned by politicians, by public bodies, and by ordinary people. And this is the great contribution of this engaging and important book. Here social science demonstrates its potential as a field of knowledge with eminent relevance and significance—for society itself, for effective government in the interests of the people, and for protecting them from falling hostage to armed sects and indiscriminate violence.

This book is a warning, and I wish it numerous thoughtful readers.

Mikhail S. Gorbachev

PREFACE

If we talk of this war in detail—about this or that separate operation—it seems we understand it. But to put it all together, to show the links, so that each little thing falls in place—well, that's something only you scholars may be able to do. I wish to say just one thing: I had no heart to go to that war, and now it's over, I don't feel like a hero, though I have many decorations. Pointless business it is—I mean war.

TAUS A.

I am full of misgivings about having undertaken this study—in part because of my own lack of distance from the ongoing events in Chechnya. I initially started to write this book under the pressure of the evening news, which began every night by reporting on the Chechen war. And no final resolution of this conflict yet appears to be in sight. Indeed, just when I was completing the manuscript, a new cycle of violence commenced. Getting the book translated and published has taken three years, and even now that it is about to appear in English, Chechnya remains in a shambles; the postwar recovery is going slowly, violence still reigns, and the people of this war-torn land continue to despair.[1]

I cannot claim to have been able to "put it all together, to show the links" as a Chechen informant bade me do. On the contrary, my version and my conclusions differ so greatly from what others have written that I may only be adding to the emotional discord, political morass, and acrimonious debate surrounding this issue. My primary goal here is to present the voices of various participants in this drama—to allow them to give vent to their versions of the events—and to follow up on their views with my own understandings. This does not mean that I shall be glossing over my own political position, which will quickly become clear enough. In this regard, I should note the evaluation of my efforts by an intellectual guru of the Chechen militants, Movladi Udugov, who put the full text of my confidential proposals to the prime minister of Russia, Viktor Chernomyrdin, in my capacity as a member of the Russian governmental committee trying to work out a peace plan for Chechnya in 1995, on his Internet site, www.kavkaz.org. Udugov characterized the document as follows: "The following text by a Russian specialist in ethnography, Tishkov, is one of many proofs that practically all Russian politicians, public figures, and scholars, instead of promoting the natural right of all people for freedom, independence, and statehood, propagate scholarly-seeming recipes on how to keep freedom fighters in the imperial cage of Russia." I do not deny the politics that inform the writing of this book, but neither do I intend to "propagate scholarly-seeming recipes" in order to keep people in "the imperial cage of Russia." I intend to write about the war in Chechnya as I have known it, politics and all.

For years Chechnya has been one of the most painful problems facing Russia. It has drawn the attention of journalists, academics, international organizations, and world public opinion. Most academics have examined the problem from the perspective of history or political science. A few have dealt with it anthropologically. This study takes the latter approach. It is, however, less an anthropological analysis of the Chechen war than an anthropological study of *Chechen society at war.*

The war's background is briefly this. In 1991, the most militant faction of the nationalistic popular movement in the Checheno-Ingush Autonomous Republic, a constituent part of the Russian Federation, staged an armed rebellion and proclaimed its secession from Russia. At about the same time, there were similar efforts at armed separatism (or irredentism) in several regions of the former Soviet Union: in Nagorno-Karabakh in Azerbaijan, in Abkhazia and South Ossetia in Georgia, and in the Transnistrian region in Moldova (see Bremmer and Taras 1993; Chervonnaya 1994; Khazanov 1996; Suny 1998; Tishkov 1999; Beissinger 2002). Practically all of them have had some military successes, but complete political independence has so far eluded them. In Chechnya, Russia's efforts at armed suppression led to a destructive war, which ended with peace agreements being signed in August 1996 and May 1997 and the withdrawal of federal Russian troops. The 1994–96 conflict in Chechnya proved disastrous in human and material terms: approximately 35,000 people were killed; some 400,000, one-third of the territory's population, became refugees in their own country; and the capital city of Groznyy and dozens of smaller population centers suffered heavy destruction. It was a tragedy for the Chechen people and the worst crisis in the history of the new Russia.

The conflict remained unresolved. Warlordism, Islamic radicalism, and anarchy reigned in Chechnya for about three years. It also seriously affected Russian politics and society, especially after a series of terrorist acts (the blowing up of apartment houses) in Moscow and other cities. In 1999, with the goal of widening the area of armed separatism under "true Islam," Chechen rebels launched attacks on western Dagestan, a neighboring republic that is part of the Russian Federation. The "freedom" struggle became an "Islamic" war: "Chechnya, in fact, may have been the first war to be turned into part of the Wahhabi Islamist jihad that we see in Afghanistan, Central Asia and Kashmir" (Armstrong 2002: 15). This led to a new cycle of conflict.

In August 1999, under acting Prime Minister Vladimir Putin, the Russian federal government launched a military campaign to stop the spread of armed separatism and terrorism in the North Caucasus and to regain its control of Chechnya. By the end of 2001, the second war had cost 3,220 Russian military personnel killed and about 9,000 wounded; even more Chechen fighters had been killed, and another 100,000 refugees had fled Chechnya (see further Shenfield 2002).

After the federal army and loyal local militia had regained control of most of Chechnya, the Chechen rebels turned to guerrilla war, aided by a number of foreign mercenaries, committing ambush attacks and terrorist acts against the federals and local Chechens collaborating with the Russian authorities. As in the first Chechen war, outside financial and other support came mainly from Islamist terrorist networks like al-Qaeda. But it did not come only from such sources. Professional fighters from Arab and other countries launched their own personal "jihads" in this part of Russia, among them isolated adventurers like the U.S. citizen Aukai Collins.[2]

Tragically, however, the massive presence of federal troops in Chechnya was marked by atrocities and violations of the rights of the civilian population during what was officially categorized as an anti-terrorist campaign. At the same time, the Russian government and the Chechen provisional administration put a great deal of effort and material resources into restoring basic order and subsistence-level living standards in this cruelly afflicted land.

The events of September 11, 2001, in the United States greatly influenced both the dynamics of the Chechen conflict and perceptions of it.[3] Support from foreign Islamic radicals was minimized, and the neighboring countries of Azerbaijan and Georgia took steps to prevent their territory from being used for supplying armed groups in Chechnya. The authorities in Moscow and Groznyy sought to establish direct contact with Chechen field commanders willing to negotiate disarmament and a return to peaceful life. Massive financial and human resources have been allocated for the socioeconomic restoration of Chechnya and to reestablish the regional administration. In March 2003, in a referendum on a new constitution in Chechnya, 90 percent of the votes were in favor of federation with Russia. In June, following heated debate, the Russian parliament passed a law providing amnesty for Chechen fighters who had not committed serious crimes. New public initiatives to reach an accord and restore order in Chechnya have been launched by the Chechen community and nongovernmental organizations, among others. After presidential elections in October 2003 (Akhmad Kadrov was elected), Chechnya is moving toward the signing of a treaty with the Russian federal authorities on increased political autonomy and delimitation of power between Moscow and Groznyy.

. . .

Many people and institutions have lent assistance and support for this project. I must thank first the Harry Frank Guggenheim Foundation, which awarded me a grant for research, writing, and translation, and the Bellagio Research and Conference Center, where I set out on the long road to completing the book. I express my special gratitude as well to Professor Robert Borofsky of Hawaii Pacific University, who launched the University of California Press's California Series in Public Anthropology and invited me to publish in it. My deepest acknowledgments go to my partners in research—the Chechen scholars Dzhabrail Gakayev, Andarbek Yandarov, Galina Zaurbekova, and Vakhit Akaev—who played a double role as both informants and readers of my manuscript. I also want to thank other Chechen collaborators and critics, especially Kheda Abdullaeva, Ismail Munayev, Musa Yusupov, and Rustam Kaliv, a graduate student. Professors Sergei Arutuinov and Marina Martynova, my colleagues at the Institute of Ethnology and Anthropology of the Russian Academy of Sciences (IEA RAS), offered valuable criticism. Special thanks go to the original translator of the manuscript into English, Tatyana Sokolova, and copyeditor Peter Dreyer.

My greatest debt is, of course, to the many Chechen men and women who told me their life stories—some of whom I know have not survived the renewed fighting since 1999. The flamboyant Chechen nationalist activist Yusup Soslambekov, who was one of my informants, was assassinated near his Moscow flat in the summer of 2000, and here I can but offer my personal condolences to his family. The war destroys human lives and health far beyond the battlefield. A researcher studying the ongoing violence cannot fail to be affected by it, irrespective of the spatial and psychological distance one may seek to establish for oneself. I feel equal sorrow at the suffering and deaths of all my co-citizens, whatever their nationality or political position—be they federal soldiers and their relatives, civilians in Chechnya, or Chechen fighters, many of whom have nonetheless been guilty of ideological distortions and of contributing to the bloody spiral of violence. As one of my informants, the wounded and decorated Chechen "general" Taus A., put it: "I'm fed up to the teeth with Dudayev, but my soul is crushed by the atrocities of the Russian army as well."

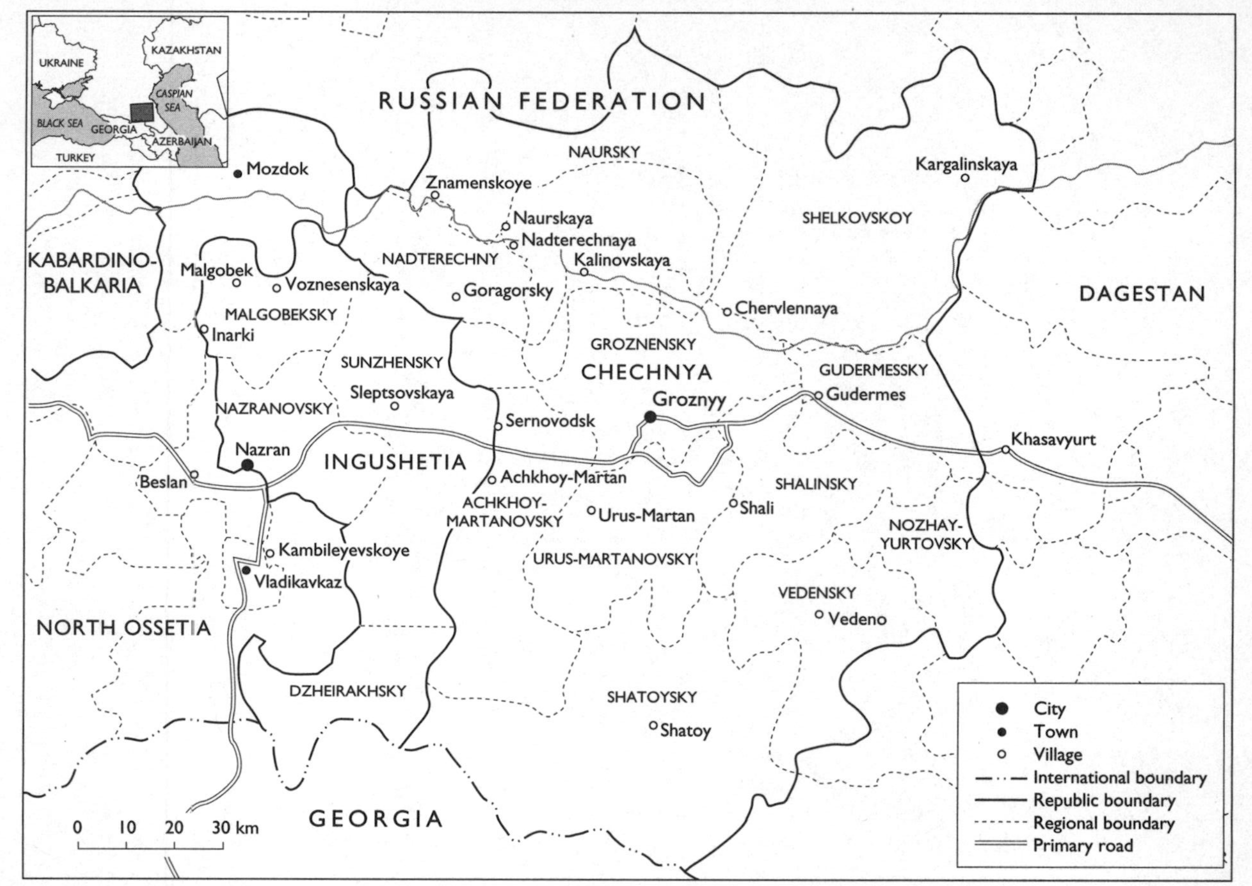

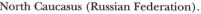

North Caucasus (Russian Federation).

ONE

Ethnography and Theory

A MORAL DILEMMA

Along the way, I found myself confronted by a moral dilemma not easy to explain. For eight years, Chechnya has been a part of my life: from my attempts to settle the conflict when I was federal minister of nationalities in 1992 under Boris Yeltsin to participation in Russia's delegation at the talks with the Chechens in December 1994; in my work on the Russian government's proposed peace plan in 1995–96; at disparate conferences and in publications of various sorts; and in backhanded remarks by my wife, Larisa, "Formulating the Chechen situation again, are you?" It was she, in fact, who first raised this moral problem: the danger of turning research into a war into a self-serving academic study.

Whatever sympathy and compassion writers may express about a society afflicted by war, they remain in some sense outsiders to it. Even if they are "participant observers" or committed ideologues, even if they experience suffering and danger firsthand, as journalists often do (and scholars less often), the war is still not *their* war. They are on the front lines, but not in the war; they are in the zone of conflict, but not in the conflict itself.

A sense of the wariness of those directly involved about outsiders exploiting the conflict for their own purposes, something I often saw, never left me in the course of my work on this study. Each time I met Chechens in Chechnya or received other informants (to use the technical term) at my Moscow office, I felt awkward about my professional distance. I knew that most of these people had suffered deep psychological traumas and irreparable losses. My partners in research (as I prefer to call them) would leave my office, but not for home. Kheda Abdullaeva returned to a one-room apartment in Moscow rented for a month by her uncle; at the end of the month her prospects were dim (at the close of 2001, she was still striving to find a decent job to cover her living expenses in Moscow). She subsequently married a Chechen living in Nal'chik, in the Kabardino-Balkar Republic in the northern Caucasus, and had a child. Vakhit Akaev walked to the Moscow University hostel where he lived while undergoing retraining. In 2000, he also moved to Nal'chik, but he asked me to get information about emigration to Western countries for him. I have since lost contact with Akaev. Dzhabrail Gakayev, who had lost a spacious apartment in Groznyy and his rich library of books in the social sciences and humanities, had bought a three-room apartment in Moscow, which he shared with his five grown children. Tragedy struck when his eldest son was killed in a car accident not far from his new home. Andarbek Yandarov and Galina Zaurbekova lived in several places in Moscow during the period in which we worked together and finally obtained a room in the student hostel of the Agricultural Academy, where they brought their two small children, aged three and five.

The contrast in lifestyles between "informants" and "anthropologist" struck me each time I raised my eyes from the painful stories before me to ponder the staggering beauty of Lake Como and the Italian Alps seen from the Villa Bellagio, where I began writing this book. My sense of my own good fortune was, however, somewhat diminished when, as a citizen of "a country with low living standards," I received additional "pocket money" from the Rockefeller Foundation. Indeed, compared to that of my Western colleagues, my Moscow prosperity seemed quite humble.

The moral dilemma that confronts me lies also in the obvious fact that, as a Russian living in Moscow, neither my cultural nor my geographic identity is neutral where Chechens and Chechnya are concerned. It is "Russia," "Moscow," "the Russians" that are simplistically projected by many participants in the Chechen discourse, both within and far beyond the country, as the cause of the recent tragedy. Kheda Abdullaeva told me that a colleague at the Chechen Republic's mission in Moscow once asked her: "Isn't he ashamed to write about it after what the Russians did to Chechnya?" Still, I have noticed that Chechens see most Russians as "passive culprits." In the words of one Chechen reviewer, Rustam Kaliyev, their guilt lies in the fact that "Russians did not protest actively enough and so failed to prevent the war."

Zalpa Bersanova, a Chechen sociologist, asked in a survey in 1995: "Do you regard the Russian people as guilty of the tragedy that befell the Chechens?" Among older people (60–80 years), 15 percent said "Yes" and 67 percent said "No" (18 percent were undecided); among young people (17–30 years), 32 percent said "Yes" and 46 percent said "No" (22 percent were undecided). "The Chechens distinguish Rossiya, its authorities, from Russians, the *Russkie;* and the very fact that, in spite of all its sufferings, the Chechen majority does not blame the Russian people speaks of the potential for tolerance," Bersanova concluded (1999: 247).

Only twice, while collecting material for this book, did I feel like an unwelcome outsider. In all other cases, I found open and sincere people of different ages and gender who shared their life stories or political visions of everything that had happened to their country and to their families. Many of them knew about my personal involvement in the case, as well as my political position and scholarly views. So as not to disturb the dialogue, and to keep myself from unwittingly influencing the results, I restrained myself from making public statements or contributing to conferences during the time I was writing the book.

But there were several exceptions to these policies after the new war began in the fall of 1999. On February 9, 2000, together with a small group of my academic colleagues, I met with President Vladimir Putin on the premises of the Presidium of the Russian Academy of Sciences. This was Putin's first visit as head of the Russian state to the central offices of the academy. And, as I understood it, this was to be a visit to talk about Chechnya—as such, quite an unusual type of briefing on the issues provoked by the publication of a report from the academy's Institute of Ethnology and Anthropology, "The Ways to Peace in the North Caucasus" (1999).

This book is densely populated with real people, and many Chechens know one another quite well. So as to avoid undue complications with the reception of the text, and for their own safety, I have decided to omit the last names of my informants, apart from those who are already well known in their fields.

WAR AS AN ETHNOGRAPHIC FIELD

This book offers no exciting moments of frontline ethnography drawn from the battlefield. The war and the postwar situation prevented me from following the most basic rule of an anthropological study: doing systematic fieldwork within the study locale itself. Since Chechnya was inaccessible, for reasons that will become clear below, I had to reassess the bounds of the ethnographic field confronting me. The work of Akhil Gupta and James Ferguson (1997) on "anthropological locations" raises a fundamental question: what constitutes a field in modern anthropological research? It is not, they argue, a geographic locality, but a construct created by the anthropologist, with both mental and spatial boundaries; it is a shifting locus within time and space. Their work thus raises an important issue: the linking of politics with anthropology. And in cases strongly tainted by both politics and violence, maintaining scholarly purity and ideological neutrality becomes all but impossible.

Uncritical loyalty to classical notions of ethnographic fieldwork divides the world neatly into the "home" of the anthropologist (a white European or American, presumably) and the "field," where the anthropologist studies the aborigines in their natural state. This understanding of the ethnographic field is less and less suitable for the analysis of nonterritorial cultural systems and their wider interactions. It is still less suitable when analyzing a society whose geographic and cultural identity has been ripped apart by intrinsic and external influences and can be described only as a result and a continuation of these impacts.

It is now clear that modern cultures and "anthropological events" are no longer rigidly tied to geographic localities: they travel just as much as, and often faster than, a professional ethnographer. When I was in Geneva at an international conference of nongovernmental organizations in June 1999, I talked for two nights in my hotel room with a Chechen, Umar Dzhavtayev. In Geneva in two nights I learned more about the Akkin Chechens of Dagestan and their attitude toward the Chechen war than if I had gone to Dzhavtayev's native Khasavyurt region myself. The reason for this is rather simple: being outside of a politicized and emotionally laden local milieu, my informant spoke more willingly and openly. In neutral Geneva, we developed close contact and straightforward dialogue that would be hard to imagine in another location. Umar argued passionately: "Don't you know that a big war will start in Dagestan no later than September? This is perfectly obvious." His bold prediction (or information?) was only slightly wrong: the war in Dagestan started a month earlier.

The field is complicated even more by the psychological effects of war. A researcher immersed in a society torn by war tends to lose the ability to understand the enveloping events clearly or to describe them adequately. Information obtained under such conditions is full of slogans, manifestos, and intense emotions absent in a calmer climate. Informants may be in such an agitated state that one can record only the background noise of an imposed reality that is often mistaken for "hard reality."

The fact is that audiotapes brought back from the field by my colleague the Russian ethnographer Yan Chesnov were useless: nearly all the questions, asked of both Russians and Chechens, were pointlessly stereotypic and superficial. "What are you fighting for?" "Why have you come to Chechnya?" "How do they treat you?" "Who is responsible for this and what is happening here?" This approach generated a standard repertoire of answers that turned a mass mentality into a mass media myth. "We don't know what we are fighting for," say federal army servicemen in the zone of a conflict. "Chechnya is not our land," say local ethnic Russians. "We are fighting for our mothers and our homes," "We have a right to self-determination," "Why is Russia bombing us?" say Chechen combatants. The ethnographic field shrinks to the scale of a newspaper page; reality is reduced to stilted or false propaganda; rumors and superficial accounts form and sustain the conflict-tainted mind.

And the responses are still further degraded when someone is interviewed by an external observer. The outsider nearly always fishes for his or her own preconceptions, hoping to fit them into a book or essay on the Chechen war. Most books on Chechnya share the same weakness: the "direct voices" in the text sound more like political declarations, and it is impossible to take them seriously as the position of "the Chechen people" as a whole. Books thus cobbled together are not about the conflict, but about the sweeping statements that swirl around it. Something is clearly amiss with politics and scholarship in conflict-rent societies. Both seem immoral in many respects, and both are unready to admit, "We were wrong," as Robert McNamara finally did about the Vietnam War twenty-five years after it ended. Is unbiased and self-reflective analysis possible with so many things at stake—including tens of thousands dead?

Out of all the conversations I recorded in 1994–96, I was unable at the time to construct even a fragmentary analysis: my attempts collapsed owing to the highly politicized nature and mythopoetic content of talk and the excessively dramatized nature of public discourse. Time was needed for at least a partial cooling of emotions. To me, the time seemed ripe three years later, though my Chechen cross-reviewer, Rustam Kaliyev, disagreed, saying: "I am not sure that your moment of partial cooling off three years later has really changed the basic rule you mentioned. Some of the political emotions have settled down, but others—no less acute or complicated—have come along to replace them. Just as before, willingly or not, an observer of Chechen reality risks getting bogged down in excessively politicized and emotional attitudes."

Rustam's analysis seems to me valid. No cooling off of political emotions has come about in the years since the first war ended in August 1996. The proof is that, for most observers, for security reasons, a trip to Chechnya in the postwar situation was impossible. I have been unable to visit the conflict zone since October 1995. It was necessary, therefore, that I seek a new mode of collecting material and access a different history.

THE METHOD OF THE DELEGATED INTERVIEW

What I employed in my work was the method of the delegated interview. I chose Chechen partners, Galina Zaurbekova and Andarbek Yandarov, as well as Kheda and Vakhid, to conduct interviews, in Chechen or in Russian. The questions or topics of conversation were simple: where were you during the war, what were you doing at the time, and how did you earn a living; what happened to your family; what did you think of the rulers and their aims; what has changed in Chechnya, and what can be expected in the future. I particularly asked my Chechen assistants to talk about what the war meant to the Chechen people they enlisted—men, women, old people, and teenagers.

I was struck by the sincerity and insight of the texts of the interviews that they brought back from Chechnya (done mainly in 1996–97), as well as by their imagery, their preciseness, and the refreshingly simple language that scholars forget how to use. These materials powerfully supplemented the interviews I had conducted in Moscow and elsewhere, particularly with political and intellectual leaders. The analysis is based on the evidence of fifty-four people, fifty of them Chechens, one Ingush, one Buryat, and two ethnic Russians.

But there are Chechens and there are Chechens. At one international conference, held in 1995 in Oslo, I overheard a participant say, during the speeches of two Chechen delegates, "These are the wrong Chechens!" The remark was a response to the fact that the two Chechen delegates at the conference condemned Dzhokhar Dudayev's regime, presenting a version of events different from what most participants had expected to hear. People promptly turned their attention, during informal meetings and in the corridors, to a third Chechen delegate, who figured as "Dudayev's representative" in the West. This delegate was well acquainted with the role expected by the audience.

So are the Chechen voices in my narrative those of the "right" or the "wrong" Chechens? My own interviewees, like those of my research partners, were not selected on the basis of any particular political preferences. It is true that I dealt more with those who opposed Dudayev's forces, owing partly to accessibility. But in Chechnya itself, the choice of respondents was wider, and to my satisfaction, quite a number of Dudayev's men were interviewed. In general, the political sympathies of our informants are varied: they range from firm supporters of Dudayev and Chechnya's independence to pro-Russian opponents of radical separatism and to others with no clear political orientation. Most often, there is a contradictory mix of convictions, strongly colored by condemnation of war, in a respondent's remarks. The fifty-four informants consisted of forty men and fourteen women; thirteen were elderly (fifty and over), twenty-one in middle age (from thirty to forty-nine), and twenty young (twenty-nine and under). Their professions varied, from statesman to housewife, and the geographical span was quite wide: eighteen people were from Groznyy and the rest from other places, including mountain villages.

Nearly all the younger men were combatants who had fought actively on the Chechen side. Of the ten young men, only two had not taken part in the fighting. Among the middle-aged group, seven men were active combatants, and five others were in the auxiliary services (reconnaissance, transport, and other). Among the elders, there were no combatants, although some Chechens over sixty are known to have fought. The combatants on our list included a couple of men who boasted the rank of "general," that is, field commanders. The rest were rank-and-file fighters, many of whom had been wounded or shell-shocked. The women were mostly housewives and mothers without permanent employment, some of them widowed or single. There were also some young unmarried women.

Another innovation emerged at the final stage of preparing the Russian-language text, when I presented a finished manuscript to my partners, Gakayev, Yandarov, Akaev, Abdullaeva, and Kaliyev, to be read for verification of their statements and for them to make such other comments as they might like. This process acquired its own meaning, and I decided to include some of their comments in footnotes as another "layer" of the text, one that originated from those whom I call "cross-informants." As I discovered later on, these footnote debates between informants became a hot issue after the book was published in Russian in the summer of 2001. The interesting reactions provided a good lesson about anthropological inquiry in cases where the author places his or her professional colleagues in the position of being themselves sources of ethnographic information.

Practically all of those who received a signed copy of the book were more concerned not with the holistic version of the conflict but with how they personally came across in the text. All of them resented being depicted as "nonscholarly" witnesses with everyday mentalities, not alien to stereotyping. "I am disappointed by the way you interpreted my remarks about Dagestanis' perceptions of the Chechens. The things I told you reflected not my personal vision but those of ordinary people, which I, as a professional sociologist, certainly do not share," complained Enver Kisriev, a scholar of penetrating mind and my good friend. For me, frankly, amid the flow of otherwise positive reactions to my book after it had been released, that was the most unpleasant moment of all. Maybe without these collisions of mutually unpleasant remarks, the book would not have been read so carefully by so many readers. But it is clear to me now that I would prefer to have had fewer readers rather than to have risked close friendships. Good anthropology cannot make people feel bad. No one should engage in the enterprise of writing at the cost of bringing people into conflict.

EXPLANATORY MODELS AND THEORIES OF RESEARCH

Social science literature has accumulated a great deal of research, undertaken from a variety of disciplinary approaches, to situations of armed separatist conflict, as well as on the more general issues of ethnic violence and war (see Alker et al. 2001; Beissinger 2002; Bocharov and Tishkov 2001; Brass 1997; Brubaker and Laitin 1998; Das 1990; Gurr and Harff 1994; Horowitz 2001; Ivekovic 2000; Kaldor 1999; Koehler and Zürcher 2003; Mekenkamp, van Tongeren, and van de Veen 1999; Petersen 2001; Premdas 1995a, 1995b; Stavenhagen 1996; Tambiah 1996; Tishkov 1997a; Vayrynen 1994). But despite considerable progress in understanding the range of problems presented by culturally/ethnically motivated covert wars, two main gaps remain. First, an insufficient number of sociocultural anthropologists have studied armed conflict, particularly in the former USSR and Yugoslavia, and there remains a serious lack of reliable ethnographic data amid an ocean of political science texts and enlightening journalism. Second, having become prominent, the business of conflict research often evinces a lack of theoretical concepts and a deliberate disregard of social theory. A striking example of shifting social science research from theory to "participation" can be found in the acclaimed and well-funded "War-Torn Society Project," with rather poor findings and recommendations (see Stiefel 1998).

As for analyses of the Chechen war, the list of publications is long, but the results are not very persuasive for a demanding (or even curious) reader. In Russia, among the more noteworthy publications are those of Dzhabrail Gakayev, who did substantial political science analysis of the 1990s events in Chechnya, with some historic background (Gakayev 1997, 1999), and D. E. Furman, who compiled a collection of well-written articles by both Russian (including Chechens) and Western experts (Furman 1999a). In Western literature, apart from journalistic texts (Gall and de Waal 1998) and secondary-source observation (Dunlop 1998), the most impressive research has been that of Anatol Lieven (1998). Lieven's writings and those of his referent authority in Chechen ethnography, Yan Chesnov (1994a, 1994b, 1995–96, 1996a, 1996b), have been the primary inspiration for the polemics in my own text, which, however, comes to conclusions quite opposite to theirs.

Let me offer a few words about "big theories" in conflict studies before moving on to explaining my own theoretical predispositions. In recent years, a number of authors, proceeding from a global vision, have written on how they see "peace by peaceful means" for the twenty-first century (Galtung 1996) or how one big fight should follow another for the dominance of the world. But as often happens, global concepts or theories, such as, for example, "basic human needs theory" and "group risk theory," do not meet the minimum definition of a theory as a reasoned proposition put forward to explain facts, events, or phenomena.

The basic human needs theory (Burton 1987, 1990) posits that groups (ethnic groups in particular) are collective bodies that have certain inborn needs, such as striving to preserve their identity and political self-determination. This proposition prompts the provocative conclusion that "people will aspire to meet their needs one way or another, even to the extent that they may be defined by others as 'deviant,' or even as 'criminal' (i.e., terrorist)" (Sandole 1992: 13). The ontologization of an ethnic group ignores the more modern view of ethnicity as a means of constructing cultural differences to meet the goals of human strategies arising out of specific contexts. The approach of Burton and Sandole fails to explain why the instigators of violent conflict are more often than not found among affluent groups in which a higher level of basic needs is met. It also ignores the fact that needs as a highly situational (relativist) category should first be explained and internalized before becoming an aspiration to be sought after and a slogan for combat.

More sophisticated but equally fragile in explaining conflict situations is risk theory, which attempts to identify minorities in a state of risk. When the proponents drew up a worldwide catalogue of such minorities (Gurr 1993), they knew nothing of such groups as Chechens, Ingush, Abkhaz, or Karabakh Armenians. The weakness of the theory is thus that the risk group is often unidentifiable, a priori. Risk theory explains a conflict only in retrospect—for only at this point can it qualify one or another group as "at risk." Another problem, one that affects both approaches, is the denial of "need" for majority groups, which invariably accords them a "no needs" and "non-risk" status. In the meantime, we can observe no less numerous cases in which representatives of minorities dominate and suppress "others," initiating and executing violence.

In general, the methodological weakness of holistic conflict theories lies in their obsession with the systemic and inability to see beyond groups as collective bodies with "will," "needs," and "universal motivations," which are more often than not invented, explained, and prescribed. They also ignore uncertainty and creativity, the role of human projects and their rational and irrational strategies, and people's often-mistaken decisions and choices. Even more serious is that in a highly interdependent and increasingly sophisticated international community of policymakers, scholarly theories can create (or destroy) reality. Predictions may be borne out as enforced realizations.

In many cases, academics have adopted a self-appointed advocacy for what they see as suppressed groups and through this engagement proceed to build their narratives and research methodology. The writings of such advocates are deadly, and the part they have played in the conflict in Chechnya is discussed below. Outside of their carefully selected data, the big theories fall short as regards case analysis. The general reader can find in scholarly literature such curious statements as "minorities at risk constitute one-sixth of the world's population. There are at least 47 violent conflicts in progress, generating about 50 million refugees" (Carment and James 1997: 206). One is given no chance to ask, how do these groups get counted and why are they so directly related to violent conflict? The statement quoted also ignores the fact that a number of conflicts have been initiated and pursued by minorities against majorities, or by minorities against other minorities (e.g., in post-Soviet states, Karabakh Armenians against Azeris and vice versa, Abkhazians against Georgians, Transnistrians against Moldovians, Ossets against Ingush).

Storytelling, or ethnography, is another aspect of information-gathering too often dismissed by analysts. For the purpose of presenting Chechnya and the Chechens as radically and culturally different from, and thus alien to, the rest of Russia's population, experts on the conflict prefer not to mention the basic commonalities among representatives of different ethnic groups, their modern sociocultural profiles, and the fact that Russian is the first language of the majority of Chechens. Academic and journalistic analyses tend to highlight cultural differences, so in the case of Chechnya, a civilizational watershed seems obvious: Orthodox Christian Russians are pitted against Muslim Chechens.

This book raises a number of issues that invalidate this assumption of difference. The Chechens' cultural similarity to the rest of Russia's population, to ethnic Russians and North Caucasians in particular, is far greater than their difference from them. First, the overwhelming majority of the post-Soviet populace, including those living in "Islamic republics," like the Chechens, are nonbelievers, even atheists. Second, a significant number of values, personal life strategies, and even standards of cultural behavior were held in common before the war and continue to be after the war.

Cultural differences resulting from "hard reality" have undoubtedly isolated members of this war-torn society from outsiders. The war itself drew a more rigid line of demarcation between Chechens and non-Chechens and heightened Chechens' sense of group solidarity. The warring parties in such a conflict start to "think" each other, and this thinking is intrinsically divisive. In a sense, *it is the conflict that constructs Chechens, not vice versa.*

SELF-DETERMINATION AS A POLITICAL PROJECT

The word "nation" is intimately related to the notions of statehood and political self-determination. As a result, immediate associations arise when the same word is used in its ethnic connotation; for the ethnic Abkhazians, Chechens, Kazakhs, Letts, Russians, Tatars, and Ukrainians, this means that they must seek national self-determination and possess their own states as nations. If they do not have their own national state, then they are a kind of semi-nation or incomplete nation. Equally, all ethnic Germans, Hungarians, Russians, and others who are outlanders from separate nations must reunite with, or return to, their "historic homeland."

As it had in the former USSR, scholarly rhetoric about ethno-nations as biosocial or ethnosocial organisms (e.g., Bromley 1983, 1987; Gumilev 1989) served as the basis for (post-)Soviet ethnic engineering. The words "ethnos" and "nation" came to be seen as totally synonymous, and in a time of painful transformations, provocative political projections were made about the "destroying" of small nations and the "dying out" of big nations as dangers in multinational states. There is no difference between the two—between concerns about "nations without [a] state" in a new Russia

(Bremmer and Taras 1993) and the rhetoric about "the tragedy of a great people," Russians allegedly being in danger of "dying out" (Kozlov 1995); the arguments and message are similar. They represent militant and exclusive—but politically unrealized—projects for usurping the state's power and resources on behalf of ethnic particularists. They tend to be projects of elite and armed sects determining for themselves (not necessarily for their constituents) what is and is not ethnic oppression.

A simplistic, monocultural image of the external world motivates the argument of ethnonationalists. Many domestic and outside experts on the former communist world believe that after the breakup of the USSR and Yugoslavia, the historic norm of nation-states has been (re)established for most of their constituent states, from the Baltic countries to Croatia, Slovenia, and Macedonia. For these experts, the sole remaining multinational state is Russia, only fourteen of whose nations have attained self-determination. Behind this rhetoric, there is a hidden political agenda, based on the assumption that in the post–Cold War world, the coalescence of "quasi-sovereign states" remains incomplete (Carment and James 1997: 205). The Russian Federation is perceived as a "mini-empire," an "improper Russia" (Brzezinski 1994) covering a huge territory spanning eight time zones.

The irony in all this is that the USSR fissured not along ethnic lines but between the existing multiethnic Soviet republics. Post-Soviet ethnonationalism thus emerged as a political and academic metaphor that provoked a serious reassessment of the idea of nationalism and the concept of self-determination. These changes in thinking seemingly came about as effects of new political agendas and ambitions, not as a result of new knowledge.

Many contemporary experts agree that the so-called Marxist-Leninist theory of the nation and the national question had unforeseen destructive political consequences (see, e.g., Brubaker 1996; Suny 1993), although these did not lead to serious revision of that decrepit ideology. The Soviet Constitution did not concern itself with the notion of multinationality or the concept of "self-determination up to cessation"—there were neither procedures for nor hope of implementing any such thing—but the 1993 Russian Constitution, devised by constitutional experts, begins: "We, the multinational people of the Russian Federation. . . ."

Western experts and politicians used the same self-destructive Soviet jargon to analyze the ongoing disintegration of their long-standing opponent. In "multinational" Russia, rather than ethnic minorities as a sociocultural issue, there are "non-status nations" or "nations without states" as an unrealized political agenda. Problems of minorities, of their cultural status, are ethnic problems (that is, in the West); but the trouble in the case of the Russian Federation is the "national problem" of self-determination in relation to the imperial system. As John Hall writes, "In retrospect, it is obvious that the Bolsheviks continued the work of the Tsars, thereby so delaying nation-building that its contemporary incidence is that much sharper and more determined. The peoples of the former Soviet Union itself were always likely to be attracted to nationalism, for the imperial system which dominated them was led by Russians—whose depredations were not merely political and economic but quite as much ecological" (Hall 1995: 25).

This stance ignores the point that it is precisely the Bolsheviks who constructed, institutionalized, and sponsored the pattern of ethnic nations that constituted the Soviet Union. It is also because of the Bolsheviks that all major non-Russian ethnic groups long ago had, and still possess today, a good measure of ethnoterritorial autonomy, each with its own constitution, state symbols, languages, legitimate government, and strong representation in the federal power structures.

The irony is that for Western social scientists, peoples like the Navajo, Ojibwa, and Hawaiians, each with its own long-established self-determination and first nations program, are not nations without states but just second-class minority citizens. It is not they but Chechens and Tatars, as linguistically nationalized groups, who deserve separate states. It seems to me that in the post-Soviet era, too much blood has already been spilled over these definitions, over constructs that become uncompromising political projects. The critical agenda for today is the *de-ethnicization* of the state and *de-etatization* of ethnicity. Ethnonationalism leaves little room for a peaceful transformation from an ethnos- to a demos-based polity.

The rhetoric of self-determination has been the chief legal and emotional argument underlying disintegration and violent conflict. In Chechnya, that rhetoric pervaded the entire ideological space: it was the main argument advanced by the leaders of the Chechen resistance, and it was talked about by common Chechen people, at least before the war. Not everything, however, is a hopeless morass, at least as regards understanding European nationalism. Rogers Brubaker argues that the upsurge in nationalism need not lead to the reification of nations: for him, nationalism can and should be understood without invoking nations as actual entities. Instead of focusing on nations as real groups, we should focus on nationhood, on "nation" as a practical category, an institutionalized form, a contingent event. "Nation" is a category of practice, not (in the first instance) a category of analysis. To understand nationalism, we have to understand the practical use of the category "nation," the ways in which it can come to structure perceptions, to inform thought and experience, and to organize discourse and political actions (Brubaker 1996: 7; see also Tishkov 2000).

THE DEMODERNIZATION PHENOMENON

The various theories of modernization proceed from the common epistemology of society's physical and intellectual progress. But the Chechen situation does not reflect this context. In Chechnya, change tumbles forward too swiftly for society to cope. The state order falls into anomie, beset by such violently imposed dynamics as to fall into social disintegration. It is not a situation of organized anarchy, so long seen as an intrinsic feature of the Chechen tradition, that makes order and governance impossible in Chechnya today. Comparing it with Afghanistan, Anatol Lieven writes: "The same in Chechnya, ancient traditions of 'Vainakh democracy' did not prove more capable of creating a contemporary democratic state than [had] other similar tribal traditions" (Lieven 1999: 283).

What I call the "demodern phenomenon" better fits this context. Our analysis shows that the Chechen people, or Chechen society as a collective body, no longer exists as an agent or locus of social action. Since 1991, Chechnya has been torn apart by various violent contradictions, notwithstanding that the most widespread external image of Chechnya is that of a rare ethnic group in solidarity. In a book by one of the chief ideologues of Chechen secession, Zelimkhan Yandarbiyev, we are told that "only the Chechen people can stage major events and determine their choice" (Yandarbiyev 1996: 15). This is a figment of his imagination. If one discounts all those so disdainfully treated by the author—the "com-bureaucrats," "rotten suit-and-tie intellectuals," "Zavgayev's accomplices," "Moscow's stooges," "empire's minions," all those "cowards," "treacherous fellow-travelers," "provocateurs," and others he excludes from the "history-forging Chechen people"—what remains is a rather narrow, ragtag group described as "We." In fact, "We" was an armed group that throughout the war did not exceed three to five thousand people.

In the course of the war and its aftermath, people's minds became inflamed with massive doses of propaganda inherited from Soviet ideology or borrowed from national liberation rhetoric. The impoverished stock of ideas bearing on political life had narrowed down to a single solution, one brooking no alternative—an armed fight. "The result of the struggle for independence is preordained," Yandarbiyev asserts. "The people know what they are doing. . . . A people wishing to be free and to build its independent state should be able to act resolutely and be ready for sacrifices. Each father and each mother should be prepared, as in our epic songs, to give their sons for the cause of the people" (Yandarbiyev 1996: 43).

In the analysis of real-life stories, neither my partners nor I came across Chechen combatants' parents holding to that view. The phenomenon of people dying for their nation is explained by the psychologist Paul Stern as resulting from limited information about possible alternatives, or variants of action, rather than as a basic instinct or human need. In certain situations, emotional links to a core group, as well as socially transmitted norms and rules, may be more powerful than individual interests and calculations, because "it is easier to follow rules than to make utility calculations" (Stern

1995: 227). It is extremely difficult for an individual to escape this outcome.

The salient characteristic of demodernization is a mental world usurped by simplified and limited versions of events, past and present, and of individual decisions pursued under pressure of limited information about available choices and under acute pressure of time. There is little time for debating when tanks are lumbering along the streets and bombs are falling.

Another characteristic of demodernization is an exodus of those people capable of implementing the agenda of modern life through society's key institutional structures—such as economic and political administration, education and culture, and social security. The first to flee from Chechnya were those who were not ethnic Chechens. These were followed soon by Chechen intellectuals and professionals. The conflict then ousted great numbers of urban and rural dwellers who had suffered ruin and devastation, as well as those who did not wish to stay and see their children living in a society torn by conflict. Finally, after the war of 1994–96, Chechnya was abandoned by those who could not or would not link their lives to building the new kind of social order that emerged. In the end, more than half the population of Chechnya (its best half, in the sense of education and professional qualification) had left the ruined republic.

An exodus of that depth and breadth changes the very nature of a society. In place of the Chechen people as a distinct entity in a complex dialogue with its multiethnic environment, we have an ethnically "clean" Chechen population controlled either by an armed fraction of that population or, after the fall of 1999, by the federal army and provisional administration.

Demodernization is thus a radical transformation of social links and institutions that undermines the otherwise universal capacity of human communities for self-organization. But it does not pitch society into a state of complete chaos. Rather, it retains the basic institutions of family and even local quasi-administration, though the latter is left severely eroded. Family links are weakened through death and departure; the established norms of family relations are altered; and the psychological climate is distorted by devastating trauma. Local administrations, usually run by appointed leaders, are invaded by interlopers who dictate their will at the point of a gun. At a higher level, the government is built on military rule. The "nation" has become a "Kalashnikov [or gun] culture."

What emerge, as ways of rescuing the territory from chaos, are false coalitions and mythical social structures. In Chechnya, such coalitions, brought about through the war, often consist of groups of battlefront warriors camouflaged as "traditional" Chechen clans (*teips*). Our analysis shows that these armed coalitions are extremely volatile, that their members' solidarity is limited to microgroups of men coming from the same village, most likely with a more informed city man as their commander.

Another feature of the Chechen society in conflict is the habit of turning to the abused past for arguments applicable to the present. The argument for the Chechen militants rested on a dramatic representation of the past—of the nineteenth century's Caucasian war and the deportation trauma suffered under Stalin. The search for a lost ideal (which never existed) is still the driving force of intellectual debate in Chechnya.

Chechen society also borrowed foreign models, before, during, and after the war. First, the resistance copied the texts of the Lithuanian and Estonian People's Fronts, in the course of piecing together its own political platforms; emulated the activities and symbols of armed combatants in other Islamic (and non-Islamic) regions of the world; and, finally, drew upon Sudan's harsh Shari'a Code in establishing a similar rule in Chechnya. Such eclectic borrowing of ideas that differ sharply from long-adopted norms and values may also be seen as demodernization. In fact, European norms of life had long been adopted in Chechnya, though often in forms distorted by the Soviet regime, and co-existed with so-called traditional institutions and cultural values.

Still another feature of demodernization is the state of apathy, as well as disregard for human life and common decency, that so easily develops. Despair becomes the dominant mood. In the spring of 1992, I observed it in Tskhinvali (South Ossetia, Georgia), and in October 1995, I saw it in Chechnya. The evidence collected in this book suggests the many forms despair takes. Social psychologists, focused on individuals within larger groups, know this phenomenon as postconflict trauma or post-traumatic stress. In this study we look at the phenomenon in a wider social context.

What all these factors yield is such a deep exhaustion of society's resources that it can neither restore the former status quo nor develop efficacious new structures. Escaping demodernization is extremely difficult, for it has never been proved that social evolution always moves in a progressive direction. War and political violence have never been put in the category of progress, unless, of course, defined a posteriori, for the purposes of historical legitimacy, as liberating, revolutionary, or just.

What external recommendations might reasonably be made by a scholar studying the phenomena of war and conflict? To what end and for whom is such a study undertaken in the genre ambitiously designated "public anthropology"—that is, anthropology addressing urgent social needs and seeking, from the perspective of certain political positions, the ways and allies whereby a society might emerge from the abyss of crisis? By the time we reach the last chapter, this study will have attempted to answer that question.

TWO

Indigenization, Deportation, and Return

They forgot the people who live in that country, who make it up. I noticed when I received letters from abroad that they were sent to the address beginning with your name, then the street, the city, and finally the country. We begin with the country, then the city and the street, and last comes your name.

KHAZHBIKAR BOKOV

Evidence from Chechen citizens, mainly those from ethnic Chechen backgrounds, makes clear that strides were made toward modernization during the Soviet period. Though the regime's repression, particularly the 1944 deportation, dealt a heavy blow to the social and demographic structure of Chechnya, it was preceded and followed by a policy of encouraging Chechen culture and the economic potential of the Checheno-Ingush Autonomous Republic as a constituent unit of the Russian Federation under the USSR. But while Chechnya remained a dynamic society moving at the pace of the modern world, contradictory state policies would eventually contribute to the outbreak of war.

ON THE USE AND MISUSE OF HISTORY AND ETHNOGRAPHY

A cherished Russian tradition in the social sciences, including anthropology, is to explain modern problems by invoking history. In academic jargon, this is called "historicism"—the deeper the historic arguments, the more convincing the conclusion. "Just as the general Marxist outlook is that of historical materialism, the basic principle of Soviet ethnographers is that of historicism," the Soviet ethnographer S. A. Tokarev observed (1958: 8). Cultural phenomena are explained as part of a historical continuum, and the Chechen "national revolution" and war elicited a plethora of interpretations involving the entire recorded and mythic history of Chechens and their relationship to Russia and the rest of the USSR. Not by chance, when signing the treaty with Aslan Maskhadov in the Kremlin in May 1997, Boris Yeltsin pronounced, "We are ending four hundred years of enmity." The two leaders and their advisers seemingly regarded the conflict more as a product of a long, turbulent history than the complex sociopolitical dynamic it was.

The historical discourse can get so thick that one is hard-pressed to penetrate it and arrive at the war's contemporary context. I participated in dozens of conferences on Chechnya that debated its history vis-à-vis Russia in relation to the roots and nature of the conflict. Even when the organizers of one meeting formulated its theme as "Chechnya: What Is the Next Step and Where Are the Keys to the Solution," the speakers continued to focus on historical analyses. My own methodological position is grounded in the premise that historical and ethnic factors were not the basis for such conflicts in the former USSR, including Chechnya, and that history cannot serve as an argument for today's political events and decisions. Rather, these conflicts have contemporary actors who deal with contemporary problems and objectives. Can't we use history as a tool for understanding a conflict, rather than seeing it as a primordial force predetermining it? Just how much is the past needed if we are to understand the essence and dynamics of the Chechen conflict? Thus, although historical explanation is not an objective of this study, we need to understand these arguments in order to understand the fallacy of relying too heavily on them to explain the recent crises.

Before the birth of Russian anthropology in the late eighteenth and early nineteenth centuries, the territory of what is now Chechnya had not been a field for intensive discoveries. One of the first descriptions was that by the Russian academician Petr Pallas (1799–1801), who made a journey to the Caucasus in 1793–94 and left ethnographic observations of the "Circassians" and "Tatars" living in the northeastern part of the Caucasus. At the outset of the nineteenth century, Julius von Klaproth (1812–14) visited territories occupied by Chechens and Ingush to study their languages, everyday life, and settlement patterns, and in 1859, the head of the Caucasus Department of the Imperial Russian Geographic Society, the historian Adolf Berzhe, wrote the first summary study of Chechnya and the Chechens. Later in the century, the Russian archaeologist Vsevolod Miller (1888) brought to the eyes of the outside world the unique masonry architecture of Chechnya and Ingushetiya. About the same time, the first ethnographic descriptions by the indigenous writers and scholars Chakh Akhriyev (1875) and Umalat Laudayev (1872) were published.

Of the early evidence left by foreign travelers, missionaries, writers, and scholars, I shall cite only one of the more interesting examples here: the *Report of the Edinburg Missionary Society for 1817, with an appendix, containing a geographical and historical account of the society missionary stations in Asian Russia.* Apart from the above-mentioned two groups (Circassians and Tatars), this source described a group of Kisti, a people different from the Circassians: "The Kisti, or Kistins, though called by the general name of Circassians, speak a different language from any other of the mountain tribes. They occupy an extensive tract of the north of Caucasus, to the south-west and south of Kitzlyar. They are an extremely powerful tribe, and are divided into three stems—Tschetchens, Karabulaks, and Ingushes, who all speak the same language, though with some variety of dialect. The Tschechens are among the most troublesome, thievish, and desperate enemies with whom the Russians have to encounter on the Lines; and are so situated among the debris of the mountains, and possess such strong holds in them, that every attempt to reduce them fails of success" (*Report* 1817: 45).

At the outset of the twentieth century, the prominent Russian scholar Leo Shternberg wrote an article on "Chechens" for an encyclopedia (Shternberg 1903: 785–86). His text reflected the typical Eurocentric stereotypes embedded in the available ethnographic material at the time. He defined the Chechens as a Caucasian *narodnost*—a term widely used for ethnic groups (and later nationalities)—of the eastern highlands that constitute the territory between the rivers Aksai and Sunzha and the main Caucasus mountain range before the mid-nineteenth-century Caucasian war (more on which below). Later, the Chechen narodnost settled there, mixing with Russians and Kumyks (the Turkish-speaking group) between the river Terek and the southern border of the region.

The Chechens, not including the closely related Ingush people, numbered 195,000 in 1887. Their name was taken from the large settlement called the Bolshoi Chechen—"a center where they used to hold their assemblies, discussing war plans against Russia," Shternberg wrote. Not much is known of the ancient history of the Chechens, though legends mention Arab ancestors, and before 1840, the Chechens had more or less peaceful relations with Russia. "But in that year they abandoned their neutrality and, incensed by the Russian demand that they give up their weapons, they joined the well-known leader Shamil, under whom they waged a desperate struggle against Russia for nearly twenty years, at a heavy cost to the latter." After that war, some of the Chechens emigrated to Turkey, and others came down from the mountains to the flatlands.

In the following passage, Shternberg mixes stereotypes and facts freely and fancifully:

> Chechens are tall and well-built. Their women are beautiful. Anthropologically, they are a mixed type . . . [anthropometric data are quoted]. They are considered to be gay, witty ("the Frenchmen of the Caucasus") and impressionable, but they are less liked than the Circassians, owing to their suspicious, treacherous, and harsh nature—probably resulting from ages of armed struggle. They are known for dauntless bravery, deftness, and hardiness, [and are] cool-headed in a fight—qualities long recognized even by their enemies. In time of peace, they rob. Cattle rustling and abducting women and children—even if it be at the risk of their lives or having to crawl for miles—are their favorite occupations. . . . In the period of independence the Chechens, unlike the Circassians, had no feudal system or class divisions. They lived in free com-

> munities governed by people's assemblies. "We are all *uzdeni*," they explained, that is, free and equal. Only some of their tribes had khans, whose hereditary power originated from the Mohammedan conquest. . . . The absence of aristocracy and equality explain their exceptionally tough resistance to the Russians. . . . The only element of inequality among them was [their habit of] making their captives into personal slaves. (Shternberg 1903: 786)

For nearly a hundred years, scholars accepted Shternberg's description of the Chechens as canonic. His article became a point of reference for generations of researchers studying the Caucasus in general and Chechnya in particular. In the years 1920–30, new research on Checheno-Ingushetiya was published by linguists, archaeologists, ethnographers, and historians of art. The well-known Chechen scholar and writer Khalid Oshayev (1928) published popular essays on his native country. The leading local linguist Nikolai Yakovlev (1927, 1939, 1940) wrote the first descriptions of the morphology and syntax of the Chechen language, together with some historic ethnographic observations.

In 1935, the North Caucasian archaeological expedition of the Institute of Archaeology, USSR Academy of Sciences, began its excavations under the distinguished archaeologist Eugenii Krupnov, who, after several decades of research, published seminal works on the ancient history of the North Caucasus (1960, 1971), and who played an outstanding role in training many young Chechen and Ingush scholars after their return from deportation. Professor Rauf Munchayev, director of the Institute of Archaeology, Russian Academy of Sciences, and an active participants in the North Caucasian expedition of 1950–60, shared with me the following reflections on the study of history and culture of the region:

> The very name of Eugenii Krupnov was linked with the emergence of the humanities in Checheno-Ingushetiya. He made important discoveries of ancient and medieval sites in the region. All of his works were organized with the active participation of local specialists and young people. Then the war came, and Krupnov later told of how he had wept to see his Chechen and Ingush comrades in arms sent into exile straight from the front line.
>
> After the war, Krupnov resumed his excavations in Chechnya. He taught us that we are all in debt to this people and urged us to liquidate the gaps in the study of the Chechen past and culture. But the task was not so simple, because even a mention of the Chechens and Ingush was a rare occurrence in those years. Krupnov nonetheless continued his research on the Chechen lands for another twenty years, making important new discoveries in the area of Bamut village.
>
> In 1957, the year of return from the exile, with our assistance, the Checheno-Ingush Research Institute of History, Language, and Literature was established in Groznyy, with Akhmad Salamov as director and the Chechen scholar and writer Khalid Oshayev as deputy director. Apart from serious

> research publications, Oshayev wrote a remarkable book, *The End of Vendetta.* There being no academic history text on Checheno-Ingushetiya at the time, Krupnov invited other scholars to prepare an outline for the first text on the ancient history of this region.[1]

Rauf Munchayev has been cautious about reaching any firm conclusions regarding so-called ethnogenetic links and cultural-linguistic parallels between the local cultures revealed by archaeology and great centers of ancient human civilization in Mesopotamia like Babylon, where he made his later excavations. But it is precisely on these supposed links and parallels that contemporary Chechen radicals founded their constructions of "Chechen uniqueness." Strangely, more has been written about Chechnya in the past ten years than in all previous years combined. Much of the newer material involves colorful and highly politicized writings about the "Frenchmen of the Caucasus," a new version of (anti)colonialist ethnography, now leveled at a diminished but still "imperial" Russia.

A common historical analysis, and the one most attractive to the general reader, offers a historical reconstruction of Chechen society as a group with a specific social structure and a unique system of values. The social structure (to be precise, extended kinship lineage *teips* and Sufi brotherhoods), with its custom of blood revenge, supposedly produced a society that, according to D. E. Furman, editor of an interesting collection of essays on Chechnya published in Russian, "on the one hand, cultivates freedom and equality, unwillingness and even inability to bow to any external coercion, and, on the other, a strong competitive spirit (within its own social environment) and a sense of honor." Furman concludes that "the system of values largely surviving to this day—the Chechen love of freedom and their dynamic blend of 'anarchic' individualism with solidarity—is the main factor differentiating the contemporary Chechen way from other nationalities and has nothing in common with the late Soviet and post-Soviet model of development" (Furman 1999b: 8–9).

But this interpretation presents a problem. Social anthropology has trouble finding societies that epitomize complete "freedom and equality" and/or human "honor and dignity" outside the European and American literary tradition of the "noble savage" (as depicted in the writings of such authors as James Fenimore Cooper and Leo Tolstoy). Among advocates of "minorities" and "aborigines," there is admiration for "a self-sufficient society," such as the Chechens, who, "if left alone, would live long in their *teips*" (Furman 1999b: 9). This perspective often carries an underlying political message—that "the terrible external threat of Russian conquest" (quoting Furman again) is to be condemned, that the path of Chechen history was distorted and these "historical injustices" should be corrected.

The chapter of Chechen history that *is* of enormous significance to the Chechen conflict is the period of Stalin's deportation of them, and this is where history essentially begins for the modern generations of Chechens, though there are some family memories of the prerevolutionary period (before 1917) and the early Soviet period. Some of my Chechen friends' parents remembered the years just before and after the 1917 Russian Revolution, and the unfounded accusations leveled against Chechens who had faithfully served the revolution, only to have someone inform on them or testify against them, are a theme in these old memories. Zhovzan Zainalabdieva said:

> My paternal grandfather was also a victim of such repression. . . . My grandfather, who supported the Reds . . . was accused of saying, "We must keep Arabic writing at school until things settle down, and we'd better wait a little with collectivization." A court brought a case against him for it, and two Chechens put their fingerprints to the testimony.
>
> My father didn't remember his father. He only remembered that he had patted his head before leaving and forbade anyone to shave the boy's head before he returned. And so no one ever shaved his head, just cut his hair, though the Chechens have a custom of shaving the heads of boys and girls at a certain age.

On the whole, modern Chechens' historical memories convey the impression that their great-grandfathers were loyal subjects of Russia. After the 1917 Revolution, many supported the Bolsheviks, even serving in the Red Army, only to suffer later in the repression under Stalin's regime. It was only during the recent conflict that "new genealogies" were unearthed that traced families back to Chechen *abrek*s—a traditional word for Caucasian Robin Hoods—who had resisted tsarist and Soviet authorities in the region, raiding and plundering. Along with those of various Soviet generals and artists, Musa Geshayev includes portraits of the abreks Zelimkhan Kharachoevski and Khasu Shatoiyevski in his book *Znamenitye chechntsy* (Famous Chechens), published in Belgium in 1999. The existence of such heroes supposedly proves that the Chechens never obeyed any authority, including that of the Soviet Union. If they "assisted in the victory of the Bolsheviks," Geshayev asserts, they were "trapped" into doing so. This radical double negation of the past—not only the dominant politics and ideology but also everyday realities are delegitimized—is an interesting example of the climate of demodernization in which abuse of history gives scope to irrational perceptions of contemporaneity and self-destructive political projects.

THE SOVIET POLICY OF INDIGENIZATION

In the 1920s and 1930s, the Soviet government pursued a policy of encouraging cultural development among ethnic minorities and helped establish local institutions of state power, one of the results of which was the establishment of an ethnoterritorial autonomous region of the Chechen and

Ingush people, as well as the promotion of literacy programs and the training of intellectuals and professionals. Part of the program included organizing education in a cultural group's mother tongue, which in turn entailed creating writing systems for several languages.[2]

In 1914, Chechnya had 154 schools, and some of the primers were in Arabic. Most of these schools were located in Groznyy, then a growing center of Russia's petroleum industry, but there were others in some mountain villages. Still, less than 1 percent of Chechens could read and write at the time. The Chechen researcher Zulai Khamidova explains that because Islam dominated Chechen social life in the eighteenth and nineteenth centuries, Arabic was used for religious writings, official documents, and even private correspondence. Along the way, the Chechen language borrowed many Arabic words. The speech of the Chechen people in Groznyy and the neighboring villages determined the literary norm for the region. Written Chechen, based on a number of so-called dialects, used the Arabic alphabet. Teachers at Muslim schools actively promoted the spread of literacy, and a new Chechen primer was printed in 1921. By 1923, fifty teachers had been trained to carry out a literacy campaign in the countryside. Between 1924 and 1932, they succeeded in teaching 69,333 adults, including 2,120 women, to read and write (Khamidova 1999: 134–35).

Soon, however, Soviet cultural policy changed in favor of the Roman alphabet. As one communist leader, Anastas Mikoyan, put it, the change would "break down the wall between the European and Muslim cultures, and bring the East and West closer." In 1925, despite strong opposition from Muslim clergy, Chechnya switched over to the Latin alphabet. In 1927, the first Chechen-language newspaper, *Serlo* (*Light*), appeared, in Latin script. In 1928, the first Chechen-language radio station began broadcasting, and in 1929, Chechen writers formed a union. In 1930, the USSR introduced universal compulsory primary education and launched a campaign to implement the law in Chechnya, despite teacher shortages and difficulties in reaching remote mountain villages.

In these years, Chechen culture and language blossomed. Chechen dictionaries, readers, and schoolbooks were published, as were collections of Chechen folklore. A college of "national culture," two primary-education teachers' colleges, two vocational schools for the oil industry, two agricultural colleges, a medical school for trained nurses, a petroleum-industry polytechnic, and a higher-level teachers' college all opened in Groznyy. Chechen writers could now publish their works in the Chechen language.

After Chechnya and Ingushetiya were united into a single autonomous region in 1934 (their languages are almost dialects of each other), they adopted a single alphabet based on the Latin script. Local authorities energetically pursued a policy of "indigenization," and in February 1936, the regional soviet issued a decree that concluded: "Ignoring or opposing measures for conducting official business in the native language shall be seen as counterrevolutionary acts by the class enemies." Under this decree, by the end of 1936, soviets at all levels aimed to provide instruction in the native language in all country schools and teach the native language in secondary and vocational schools as well as at colleges in the towns. The Soviet government also organized the study of Chechen language for people of other nationalities (first of all, Russians) living in the region (Khamidova 1999: 138).

By 1937, the proportion of indigenous people in the autonomous region's bureaucracy had reached 70 percent, but on August 1, 1937, the NKVD (the police and security service, later known as the KGB) staged a purge of "anti-Soviet elements" and arrested 14,000 people in Checheno-Ingushetiya. Some of them were summarily executed; others were sent to concentration camps. Arrests continued until November 1938: 137 people were seized from among the autonomous region's bureaucracy alone, nearly all of them Chechens or Ingush. Some Chechen writers suggest that perhaps 200,000 people suffered in Checheno-Ingushetiya during the repression of the 1930s (Abumuslimov 1995: 59).

Although it is hard to gauge the accuracy of these figures, it is well known that great numbers of Chechens holding prestigious posts were arrested, from the head of government to the staffs of rural councils. To prevent the various governmental programs in the region from grinding to a halt, the arrested officials were quickly replaced by others.[3] In 1938, the National Theater of Folk Music and Dance opened, as well as an elementary and secondary music school. Writers, artists, architects, and composers set up unions; a museum of fine arts was founded; and a club of amateur artists was established. Before World War II, the republic had 16 newspapers, 408 schools, 5 theaters, 248 libraries, and 212 rural reading rooms, and the literacy rate had risen to roughly 75 percent (*Kulturnoe stroitelstvo* 1979: 20–24).

In Zulai Khamidova's estimate, "the progress of the cultural revolution was great in spite of the terror. As a part of the USSR and the RSFSR, Checheno-Ingushetiya's development depended wholly on the ideology and policies of Russia, particularly Moscow. . . . But the Chechen language fell victim to Russia's changes of policy" (Khamidova 1999: 140). In 1938, the USSR decided to switch all newly written languages to the Cyrillic alphabet, a decision that affected seventy ethnic groups, including the peoples of the North Caucasus, and caused great difficulty. It meant teaching a new alphabet, publishing new textbooks, producing new printers' type, devising new spellings and terminology, and even devising new translations for words in the fields of science, medicine, and architecture. After this "reform," the indigenous languages were taught as special subjects, and all other subjects were taught in Russian. Still, scholarly work on the Chechen language, Chechen folklore, and the history of Chechen literature continued (Desheriev 1960, 1963).

The collectivization project produced limited results. The local Cossack communities opposed it, and, tired of the Bolsheviks' cruel repression from the 1920s onward, many Chechens met collectivization with protests and sometimes open rebellion. Eventually, the so-called *kolkhozi* and *sovkhozi*—collective and state farms—were established, but they existed alongside traditional Chechen farms and communal organizations. By the time of the deportations in 1944, the republic had 146 large rural settlements (not counting small villages, particularly those in the mountains), 137 collective farms, 14 state farms, 24 farm-machinery shops, and 439 industrial enterprises. Individual farming was common (and remained so even after the return from exile). In 1943, the Itumkalin *raion,* for example, had a total of 15,000 cattle and 28,000 sheep, 800 (13 percent) and 1,800 (6 percent) of them, respectively, on the collective farms; the Shatoysky *raion,* 7,600 cattle, 332 (4 percent) on the collectives; and the Galanchozh *raion,* 13,700 sheep, 2,637 (19 percent) on the collectives (Bugai 1994: 213).

Before World War II, most ordinary Chechens and Ingush carried on their lives without actively supporting or opposing the Soviet regime; as in so many other societies, they were busy just trying to get by. With the outbreak of war with Nazi Germany in 1941, however, 29,000 Chechens left to defend the Soviet Union. To some contemporary Chechen authors, the notion of the Soviet Union as "their country" belongs in quotation marks (Khamidova 1999: 141), but that was not true of this earlier generation. In a letter to K. Ye. Voroshilov, the chairman of the Presidium of the Supreme Soviet of the USSR, V. A. Aliyev, writing from Magadan, the "capital" of the Gulag Archipelago, wrote the following preface to his dramatic story of how he was arrested following his service in the war, made to confess to a crime he had never committed under threat of a firing squad, and imprisoned. Nonetheless, he remained a staunch supporter of communism and his country.

> I was born 1924 in Chechen-Aul [a village] of the Ataghi *raion,* in the former Checheno-Ingush Autonomous Republic. My father, Amethaji Aliyev, a shoemaker, actively participated in the Civil War and was crippled during the 100-day battle in Groznyy against the White Army Cossacks. My mother was a peasant woman, a housewife who could neither read nor write. I went to a Russian school: I finished the first form and then went on to a college. Thanks to the Communist Party, I, a member of an ignorant family and a backward nationality, received an education and a broad perspective. As a child I was an October kid [member of a children's organization], and before my arrest in 1944, I had planned to join the Communist Party. In the years in between, I was brought up by the Pioneers and Comsomol [Young Communist League]. I was an activist, a secretary of the regional Comsomol committee for propaganda. In 1943, fighting on the Dnieper river for the city of Kanev, I was twice decorated. (Bugai 1994: 244–46)

Evidence of this sort of allegiance to the Soviet Union runs contrary to the stereotype of Chechens refusing to obey authority. Not all Chechen and Ingush men volunteered for the army, but only a few refused to serve or deserted. There are few data to support the image of Chechens as "eternal rebels" in the period before or during World War II. Even throughout the much later Afghan war, Ruslan Aushev, president of Ingushetiya and an Afghan veteran, told me, there was no case of a Chechen defecting or surrendering to the mudjaheddin. "The Chechens were the best soldiers in the Soviet Army of that time," he said.[4]

THE TRAUMA OF DEPORTATION

The history of Stalin's deportations of entire ethnic groups (Koreans, Volga Germans, Crimean Tatars, Kalmyks, Karachai, Balkars, Ingush, and Chechens) just before and during World War II has been the subject of many scholarly investigations (see Conquest 1960; Nekrich 1978; Aliyeva 1993; Polyan 2001). No one author has offered persuasive answers to the question of why the Soviet regime embarked on this extraordinarily brutal policy. Certainly, it was a paranoiac Joseph Stalin who was the key figure in executing such massive crimes against whole peoples without rational arguments or it making good political sense. For the Stalinist totalitarian machine, it was simply one episode among many other crimes (for comprehensive accounts of the "Great Terror" in the USSR, see Service 1998; Suny 1998).

The deportation of Chechens and Ingush began on February 23, 1944, and was completed in only a few days. "I report the results of the operation of resettling Chechens and Ingushi," Lavrenty Beria wrote in a telegram to Stalin dated February 29, 1944. "The resettlement was begun on February 23 in the majority of *raions*, with the exception of the high-mountain settlements. By February 29, 478,479 persons were evicted and loaded onto special railway cars, including 91,250 Ingush. One hundred eighty special trains were loaded, of which 159 were sent to the new designated place" (Bugai 1994: 51). In July 1944, Beria reported to the Kremlin that "in February and March 1944, 602,193 residents of the North Caucasus were moved to the Kazakh and Kirghiz SSRs, including 496,460 Chechens and Ingush, 68,327 Karachai, and 37,406 Balkars" (ibid.: 85). Chechens and Ingush were also moved to Kazakhstan (400,600) and to Kirghizia (88,300) (ibid.: 59).

Chechen attitudes toward Stalin's deportation can be divided into two distinct periods: before and after the liberalization of the late 1980s. During the Soviet period, people kept quiet, as if the tragedy were some sort of collective stigma for which they had to pay, an attitude common among many deported or otherwise victimized peoples. Kheda Abdulayeva told me:

> The deportation was hardly ever mentioned, only as an abstract point of reference: this or that happened before or after the *aardakh* (the Chechen word for "lead out"). Mother often used it in her stories. I never understood: where was this? I think they should have explained to us what it meant. I remember that when I was in the fifth form at school, we had a history lesson with a Russian teacher, and I asked her about it. She threw me such a glare and asked: where did you read about this? I said that I'd just heard it, that I could not have read about it anywhere. She told me to ask my father. I assailed my parents: You say you lived in Kazakhstan. Why? Didn't you want to live at home? The answer: we had to. What do you mean, you moved there of your own free will, didn't you? No, we were asked to, we were told to leave. And it was in the eighth form at school that I understood at last that we had been deported, all of us exiled!

Middle-aged Chechens, particularly those who had attained prominent administrative posts, curiously referred to their exile period as work on the "virgin lands." Thus, they associated themselves with one of the most widely publicized economic campaigns under Khrushchev: cultivating the vast virgin lands in northern Kazakhstan. This is what I was told by Khazhbikar Bokov, about his relationship with the regional Communist Party secretary in Kazakhstan:

> I'd been through the school [that prepared us] for working on the *tselina* [the virgin lands]. It wasn't enough to obey orders from above, you had to act on your own and be your own man. It was the Comsomol [Young Communist League] School of Selfless Patriotic Labor for the Motherland. I was highly regarded by the first secretary of the regional [Communist] party committee, Prokopii Ivanovich Chernyak. He was the classic party functionary: always working hard, always clad in work clothes and hip boots. He tried to gain me a promotion to first secretary of the district party committee, and recommended me as the best Comsomol leader. He did all this through the regional party committee without telling me anything. It was true, I was a good worker: since I'd been deported there at the age of eight, I'd worked hard—plowing, sowing, herding cattle, then managing the local club. I'd been brought up doing constant labor. He told me, "Wait, I'll get you sent to the high party school [postgraduate training institutions for party officials]."

After the liberalization of the 1980s, attitudes changed. The deportation of the Chechen and Ingush people became the subject of many dramatic, literary, and poetic narratives. The current version is that the deportation amounted to genocide. It was the most horrible crime of Stalin's regime. It ruined the lives of several generations of Chechens. When the Chechen war began, I heard this assertion from nearly all the Chechen delegates at the December 11–13, 1994, Vladikavkaz talks. Whatever question was under discussion, Chechen delegates would remind Moscow's delegates that the Chechens had suffered mass deportation. Yet although most of these delegates had spent their childhoods in Kazakhstan or Kirghizia, as they grew up they moved to the larger Russian cities, where they studied at various institutions, such as Moscow University, Sverdlovsk Law School, or the Tula Tank Troops Academy.

Literary and historical writings and political rhetoric alike tend to concentrate on the initial stage of the deportation of the Chechen and Ingush people: the painful journey in overcrowded cattle cars, where many Chechens died of cold, starvation, or disease, or were murdered by guards. Dzhabrail Gakayev, in his political history of twentieth-century Chechnya, writes:

> Upon their arrival in the areas allotted for them, the deportees were distributed for work on the local collective and state farms. The special commandant's office, headed by an NKVD officer, exercised direct control. He held in his hands the lives of hundreds of thousands of defenseless people who had been denied any rights. All of the able-bodied among the exiled population were forced to work for no other remuneration than food ration coupons. Traveling more than three kilometers from the place to which one had been assigned was strictly forbidden. Each deportee reported to the commandant's office twice a month to confirm his presence. A breach of the rules was punished by twenty years' hard labor without trial. . . . Famine, disease, and harsh treatment brought the Chechen and Ingush people to the brink of survival. (Gakayev 1997: 104)

Even by the most conservative estimate, the Chechen and Ingush people lost, across the years of exile, over a third of their total number, but the most horrific memories come from the initial act of deportation and the first years of exile. The stories that follow were told me by members of the present generation, as told to them by their parents:

> My name is Zhovzan. I was born in Kirghizia, in the village of Novopalovka (near Frunze), in 1954. Our family—my father, Said, my mother, Kuku, my grandmother, Amanat, my younger brother, Umar, and my elder sister, Sulai—moved back to Chechnya in May 1957. My mother was from the well-known "progressive" Saikhanov family (her grandfather was killed by the White Guards during the Civil War, and later a street in Groznyy was named after him); her father perished in the repression. At the time of the deportation, my mother, Kuku, was eight. She had been sent to the village to see if their flour had been milled, so she lost her family and was sent to Kazakhstan with another family that picked her up. In Kazakhstan, they were starving, so they were about to leave Kuku in an orphanage. My grandmother, Marshan, however, searched for Kuku all over Kazakhstan and Kirghizia. She asked around for her everywhere. She could speak Russian because she had lived in the Vedeno fortress, where her father had worked with the military before he was killed. The Kirghiz officials even thought she could read, so they covered the documents with their hands when they talked to her. Finally, she found

> Kuku, who was by that time thirteen or fourteen. She gave her a boy's haircut, which made it safer to bring her to the place where they were settled. . . . When we returned to Chechnya, we found our house occupied by an Avar family. We shared the house with them for several years, for they had nowhere to go. Granny saw her Singer sewing machine being used by them, and she bought it back from them. Our house wasn't large. We divided it and lived as separate households, but we never quarreled. We talked Russian with them and Chechen among ourselves. Later, my father built a separate house for us. And much later the Avar family often visited us in our village, because their relatives had been buried next to our Enghinoi *taip*'s cemetery.

THE DAILY EXPERIENCE OF DEPORTATION

Many Chechen families were separated during the trip to Central Asia, but as Dzhabrail told me:

> You should know the Chechen word *khabar*—a kind of oral telegraph, which worked efficiently across any barriers. There were special people who took on the mission of traveling all over Kazakhstan and Kirghizia, from village to village, collecting and spreading the information on the missing members of families. There were quite a number of them, volunteers who received no other reward but a meal where they stopped and a bed to spend the night. It was a rather dangerous thing to be doing. The deported people weren't supposed to leave the places they had been assigned to. They risked arrest or even a prison term if caught. People were afraid to visit even a neighboring village for fear of being caught by bad weather or for some other reason forced to stay. Still, after a few years of this, the Chechens and Ingush had found nearly all the missing relatives.
>
> The first years were hard, for lack of housing (some of the deported people were just dumped in the open steppe), as well as food (the local Kazakhs were also starving). My father had about forty people in his charge: his own children and several relatives. He was a very strong man, with the look of authority. His name was Dzhokalu. . . . The situation was desperate: our men had to steal livestock from the Kazakhs, mostly their sheep. Father told us once that a group of Kazakhs riding on horseback had caught up with him as he was driving away their sheep. He drew a circle round himself with his knife and said, "Don't cross the line. I'm starving, and I'll fight to the death." They thought about that a little and rode off.

Shamsuddin Umarov offered these childhood impressions of the evenings when Chechens would gather together: "In the first years, we had no electricity, we had the light from a candle or a splinter torch. We met to play the balalaika and sing. We shared jokes and laughter in the semi-darkness. We had almost nothing to eat, just some potatoes fried on the stove. I remember around 1948, the first time Mother put up curtains on the window, that it was taken as a sign of a better life to come."

Nearly all adult Chechens eventually found jobs, many of them in towns and cities. "Former deportees recall that some time after their arrival, the Kazakh markets, which had earlier had little to offer, were graced with a choice of vegetables and fruit, meat, and milk."[5] Photographs from this time in Chechen family albums suggest that things were not so bleak. We see in these pictures well-dressed men in the quasi-military outfits typical of the time: leather hip boots and woolen service jackets. The exiles kept many of their customs and observed religious rites. In personal family relations, they spoke Chechen or Ingush; outside the home, they used Russian (Pohl 2002).

Some archival documents reflect the social and demographic circumstances of the Chechens in exile. In his report to Moscow dated April 8, 1957, at the time of restoring the Checheno-Ingush Autonomous Republic, the chairman of the planning department, A. Platonov, noted that the total number of Chechens and Ingush living in Kazakhstan and Kirghizia was 415,000, in 90,000 families; people over sixteen made up 244,000 of the total. Of that number, 38,500 were employed in industry, 91,500 in agriculture, and 25,000 in various organizations and offices—a total of 155,000 (Bugai 1994: 212).

We can draw two conclusions from these data. First, that the Chechen and Ingush population was young, which means that the birthrate in exile was high—about 150,000 children were born during the thirteen years of exile. Second, that people were for the most part employed, and the proportion between industry and agriculture was close to the USSR average. The period in exile actually promoted Chechen urbanization. Even with all the bans on moving, people flocked to the towns and cities for a more comfortable lifestyle than they had found in the countryside. After Stalin's death, a Chechen and Ingush newspaper was published in Frunze, the capital of Kirghizia, a radio program in the two languages was inaugurated, and a music and dance ensemble offering public concerts was organized. Nevertheless, most Chechens in exile, even the elderly, had to learn Russian to get by.

SEARCHING FOR ANSWERS

Khazhbikar Bokov, a Chechen teenager in Kazakhstan, attended the party's Marxist schools. Tired of the silence and suffering, he went looking for answers to the mystery of deportation. This is his story, told to me much later:

> At first there were no thoughts in my mind about the guilt of our people. I knew I wasn't guilty. But in time I came to feel a great urge to learn more. I heard some of our people deny the guilt, while others admitted they'd betrayed our country. If so, I asked myself, why do they love their land so

much? Why do they cry for it, dream of returning to it? You wouldn't pine for something you'd betrayed. All talk on any public occasion—like a wedding or a funeral—was about our native land (to me it was Checheno-Ingushetiya; I had no broader idea of a Chechen motherland).

In Pavlodar I rented a room in order to attend high school. In the village where my parents lived, there was no secondary school. I made a living by working as a loader in the evenings. I didn't really pay rent, because I lived with distant relatives. My parents were unable to support me.

At some point, a librarian advised me to find answers to my questions at the Marxist-Leninist University. So I went to the Marxist class at the MLU. When they asked me who I was, I replied that I was an eighth-form school student. They told me they did not admit minors, but I refused to leave. They tried to turn me out, but I held onto a desk. Since I was a burly lad, from lots of farmwork, they failed to budge me. They sent for the headmaster, who came, looked at me, thought a little, and allowed me to stay. Still, he indicated he would discuss the situation with the party secretary. When I came next time, the secretary called me in. When he asked me why I wanted to join the class, I explained I wanted to get a clear answer to the question of why the Chechen people had been deported by the authorities. He looked at me attentively and asked, "What is your fault in all of this?" He obviously knew nothing about the deportation. I said it was no fault of mine, I was eight when we were deported. So the party secretary allowed me to attend the MLU.

These questions torment you until you get answers. When I grew up, I went on looking for the answers, and when I became secretary of a regional Communist Party committee, I found them. It involved a social system in which a human individual meant nothing, and a group of individuals meant just as little: all was sacrificed for the common goal. "Let our country live," as the song goes. They forgot the people who live in that country, who make it up. I noticed when I received letters from abroad that they were sent to the address beginning with your name, then the street, the city, and finally the country. We begin with the country, then the city and the street, and last comes your name.

A resurgence of interest in, even a preoccupation with, the deportation developed in the late 1980s within Soviet and, particularly, Chechen, society. This renewed focus on the period most commonly took the form of literary, poetic, and musical works, and a perception of the deportation as genocide arose often in our interviews after the 1994–96 Chechen war. Naturally, it was linked with strongly anti-Russian sentiments, although—curiously enough—both Stalin and Beria, the main instigators of the action, were ethnic Georgians. Here is a statement from Khizir I., one of the Chechen combatants:

I, for one, never liked Russians, for as long as I can remember. Many of our people told us how terribly they had treated Chechens in 1944, and even later, after their return from exile. My father and grandfather were both deported. My father, then a young boy, grew up in Kazakhstan. But he always remembered their village, their house in the mountains. When we returned to Chechnya, the exile was still not over. At first they allowed us to return to our village; some of our people even managed to restore their old houses. Then an order was issued for us to move down to the flatlands. They feared that bands might spring up in the mountains again, or that people would keep unregistered herds of cattle. Now our people are scattered in Samashki, in Yermolovka, and other places. My grandfather dreamed of returning to his native village, but only got back there in time to be buried in our cemetery.

THREE

Contradictory Modernization

We were proud, and can still be so, of the great political, economic, and social changes in the life our small nation, of the rising material well-being of our people. But we close our eyes to the fact that much material success is achieved through other than honest labor, and this does not improve morals, but brings out the worst side of human nature. Our republic gives all sorts of shady dealers, profiteers, and corrupters a free hand.

KHAZHBIKAR BOKOV TO THE POLITBURO OF THE CPSU CENTRAL COMMITTEE, 1987

In the fire of war, after human beings, printed materials, especially books, are the next to perish, and writing this chapter brought this forcefully home to me. Few written sources had survived. I asked many of those to whom I spoke to lend me some local publications containing material about Chechnya before 1991, but the answer was always, "All that burned up in Groznyy during the war." So I turned to whatever was available: publications from the Soviet period; oral evidence from informants; the material on the Checheno-Ingush Autonomous Republic in *The Great Soviet Encyclopedia,* written mostly by Chechen and Ingush authors; and several hundred publications kept in Moscow's National Library on the nature, history, economy, and culture of the land. The work of colleagues at the Russian Academy of Sciences on Chechen history and ethnography published in 1960–90 became valuable material for historical-anthropological reconstruction (Kaloyev 1960; Pchelintseva and Solovieva 1996; Smirnova 1983). Chechen social scientists have also published a number of serious investigations of local society (e.g., Khasbulatova 1985, 1986; Madayeva 1985, 1986; Zaurbekova 1986). All these sources, along with my own observations, helped me to write about Chechnya and the Chechens after their return from deportation in 1957.

THE RETURN HOME

On January 9, 1957, the presidium of the USSR supreme soviet passed a decree "On reconstituting [reestablishing] the Checheno-Ingush Autonomous Soviet Socialist Republic within the Russian Soviet Federative Socialist Republic." All previous decrees on liquidating Checheno-Ingush autonomy

(March 7, 1944) and on restrictions against Chechens and Ingush living in their homeland (June 16, 1956) were abrogated. In February 1957, the USSR supreme soviet considered the question of resettlement. The report on this issue stated:

> The practical measures necessary for restoring the national autonomies of these peoples will take a long time, as well as a great organizational effort in preparing the needed housing, production, and living and cultural conditions in the old homeland. It will require considerable material and financial means. Therefore, the resettlement of the citizens of the said nationalities wishing to return to their former places of residence should be carried out in an orderly manner, in limited groups, on appointed dates, and according to waiting lists. (Bugai 1994: 211)

The process extended from 1957 to 1960, with only 17,000 families assigned to return in the first year. The great majority of deportees were impatient to return, however, and they did so en masse. Over 50,000 families returned in 1957.

Upon the return of the Chechen and Ingush people, a new chapter in their history began. In terms of social relations, settling down again, and procuring life's basic necessities, it was a difficult period. Many of the old Chechen houses were now occupied by other people. In the villages, many abandoned farmsteads and their infrastructure (sheds, fields, wells, roads, and mountain paths) had deteriorated. It was also necessary to resettle the thousands of ethnic Avars, Darghins, and Laks who had replaced the exiled Chechens and Ingush back to their native Dagestan. Substantial mountainous regions were closed to new arrivals for reasons that were not clear: either fear of inadequate political control or as a part of a general campaign to modernize the mountaineers by settling them in the lowlands. Part of the territory (978 square kilometers) formerly occupied by Ingush (the Prigorodny *raion*) stayed within the jurisdiction of North Ossetia, and its authorities did not allow Ingush to settle there. As Gakayev recalls,

> In Kazakhstan, my father got permission for just one family to return, but he managed to include ten families on this list! We traveled two weeks on a freight train without fresh air, food, or water. We returned to Chechnya on September 13, 1958. By that time, instead of the planned 50,000, 200,000 had arrived. Tragedies befell them immediately.
>
> "This is our house," say the Chechens.
>
> "But where should I go with my kids?" reply the Russians.

Some people negotiated peacefully, some got furious, especially those from the devastated Belgorod, Kursk, Smolensk, and Voronezh regions. In 1958, Russian-speaking citizens in Groznyy protested the return of the Chechens and Ingush but were ruthlessly suppressed by the authorities. On the whole, the attitude in the republic was "that it was understood that the Chechen and Ingush people had been pardoned rather than politically rehabilitated" (Gakayev 1997: 107).

The restoration of the Checheno-Ingush Republic (in terms of resettlement, economic life, administration, culture, and education) was carried out fairly quickly, and in many respects, it became a different place. Two large areas of the Stavropol Region—the Naursky and Shelkovskoy *raions*—were included to increase the territorial resources and stimulate the resettlement of Chechen highlanders to the flatlands.

In December 1961, the republic's Communist Party leadership issued a report on the work completed since 1957. Of the total number of 524,000 Vainakhs who had lived in Kazakhstan and Kirghizia, 432,000 resettled in the republic; 28,000 (mostly Chechens) in Dagestan; and 8,000 Ingush in North Ossetia. The republic's population had now reached 892,400, including the 432,000 Chechens and Ingush. Of the original 496,000 deportees, some 34,000 Chechens and 22,000 Ingush remained in Kazakhstan. And of the total number of arrivals in the republic, 118,000 were able-bodied citizens: in 1961, 112,223 of them were employed, including 19,000 in industry (compared to just 1,077 in 1944). As for housing, 10,000 lived in communal apartments; 73,000 had built or bought houses; 10,400 families were finishing their houses; and 1,600 were renting housing in the private sector. Moreover, by 1961, forty-nine industrial enterprises had been built: a sugar plant, a milk plant, a chemical plant, a plant manufacturing prefabricated reinforced-concrete items, and a thermal energy plant. The collective and state farms had enlarged their cultivated lands, and many of them also kept cattle. At this time, the Chechen and Ingush peoples were represented in the power structures at all levels: by 3,997 (55.3 percent) out of the 7,222 deputies elected in Checheno-Ingushetiya to the USSR, the Russian Federation, and local soviets, as well as by 1,182 (19.7 percent) of the 5,982 communists elected to the district, city, and regional CPSU committees. Among 995 secretaries of the local party divisions, 122 (12.3 percent) were Chechen or Ingush, and at all levels of the soviets, 42 percent of the deputies were women. Over 41,000 Chechens and Ingush belonged to the Young Communist League.

From 1957 to 1961, the number of schools in Chechnya rose from 365 to 414, the number of schoolchildren attending rose from 80,000 to 150,000, and 1,056 schoolteachers had been trained. The republic had four central and seventeen local newspapers, and a Research Institute of History had been founded (Bugai 1994: 234–35).

Popular mythology contends that the Chechens and Ingush harbor an exceptional devotion to their primordial homeland and the graves of their ancestors, and the process of return often took on an almost sacred character. One story, told to me by an Ingush, Isa Buzurtanov, applies in equal measure to Chechens. After the dissolution of the regime of special settlement in Kazakhstan, Isa, having graduated from a technical secondary school for construction workers, settled in Abakan (Khakassia, southern Siberia) with his wife and four children. He held a good position, got an apartment, built a dacha, and was generally satisfied with his life. At home his family spoke their native language, although they all knew Russian well, and they kept up certain Muslim customs as well. They then returned to Nazran, in Ingushetiya, for family reasons: a younger brother living with his parents had almost completed the construction of a spacious house intended for his future family, but he was killed in an automobile accident. It was Isa's obligation to his parents, and the inheritance of a prime piece of property, rather than the pull of the homeland, that made him leave Abakan. "For the first few years in Nazran, I found it difficult to become accustomed to the local norms and conditions of life. I had to submit to many community demands and traditions, whereas back in Siberia I had been more free. Most important, our children do not receive a tenth of the education here that they could get in Abakan schools. Now, because of the conflict, they are hardly studying at all."[1]

A logic of collective behavior worked well in the time of mass resettlement in the late 1950s, but it ceased to be an argument for many thousands of those who integrated themselves into the new environment and achieved a certain social status. Later appeals on the part of the new leaders in "revolutionary" and "independent" Chechnya failed to draw these people back to their homeland. A number of Chechens preferred to return to Kazakhstan and other places of their former exile to avoid the hardships of war.

POLITICAL STATUS AND LOCAL ELITES

Checheno-Ingushetiya gained its status as an autonomous territory within the Russian Federation in 1934, first as an autonomous *oblast,* then, in 1936, as an autonomous republic. It had its own constitution, which, although modified when the USSR constitution underwent certain changes, was generally well preserved until 1991. Under the constitution, Chechnya had a one-chamber legislature (supreme soviet), whose deputies were elected by popular vote to five-year terms, one deputy per 6,000 people. The legislature had a presidium and a chairman. Khazhbikar Bokov, of Ingush nationality, held the latter post for seventeen years, but in 1990, he moved to Moscow, because, he says, "Rallies against and attacks on the authorities began, including against me personally. The Chechens wanted to take over for themselves, leaving no place for me." Bokov is now an editor of the journal *Zhizn Natsionalnostei* (Life of Nationalities) published by the federal Ministry of Nationalities.

The government of the Checheno-Ingush Republic consisted of the republican supreme soviet and the soviet of ministers (the cabinet), which managed the economy and other vital spheres (social security, law and order, education, medical service, and culture). There were about fifteen ministers in the cabinet, and the republic was represented both in the supreme soviet of the Russian Federation and in the supreme soviet of the USSR. One of the latter's chambers, the soviet of nationalities, had eleven deputies from the republic in 1970. In *raions*, towns, and villages, there were local councils where members were elected by popular vote for two and a half years. The republic also had a supreme court consisting of two collegia, for criminal and civil cases. Judges at all levels, as well as people's jurors, were elected by popular vote. The republic's prosecutor was appointed by the USSR's prosecutor general for five years, as were prosecutors in towns and districts.

But to what extent did Chechens have real power in Chechnya? In pursuing this question, we must bear in mind two things. First, the Soviet regime rested on the singular institution of the Communist Party and its special services, mainly the KGB. The overarching nature of the Soviet political structure determined the nature of politics in Chechnya, as it did everywhere else. Second, local peculiarities, particularly in the so-called "national autonomous territories," lent the Soviet authorities there a uniquely Chechen influence.

The real power in Checheno-Ingushetiya belonged to the republican committee of the Communist Party. Its first secretary, who was "number one" in the republic, was followed by the chairman of the republic's supreme soviet. Above all, power lay in Moscow—the secretary-general of the Communist Party, the politburo, and the organizational department of the party's central committee. The highest Communist Party functionaries—the actual rulers of the USSR—seldom visited Checheno-Ingushetiya, and when they did, their arrival constituted an important occasion for the local authorities. Visits signaled attention, support, and a chance to obtain financing for local development projects. Khazhbikar Bokov gives a vivid description of Leonid Brezhnev's visit in 1981:

> We waited three days for Brezhnev to make a stop in Groznyy on his way from Azerbaijan. We didn't know with any certainty where he'd stay, in Beslan [North Ossetia] or with us in Chechnya. We had been told from Moscow to be ready—"Maybe on your territory, somewhere at that railway siding. If his retinue, his guards, permit it, you may meet him. You may then enter his special railway carriage, and have something with you, just in case. We can't tell you more exactly."
>
> For those three days we had these files with us, "just in case." We didn't sleep: we'd just drop in to have a drink and then go back on watch again. We felt a bit hazy when his train from Baku [in Azerbaijan] finally stopped. It was seven in the morning. The leaders of Kabardino-Balkaria and North Ossetia quickly joined us at the Groznyy railway station. No one from Dagestan came, because he had already stopped there.

Brezhnev came to the door of the carriage, and even before he alighted he called out to us, "How are you, comrades, how's life?"

"Fine, Leonid Ilyich!"

"Any problems? Shortages of meat?"

"Yes, we are short of meat."

"What, do your people eat that much?"

"Yes, Leonid Ilyich, they do like eating meat."

Then, when he'd stepped down on the platform, [First Party Secretary A. V.] Vlasov [of Checheno-Ingushetiya], and [First Party Secretary T. K.] Malbakhov [of Kabardino-Balkaria] flanked him on both sides, supporting him under his arms. [A.] Chernenko [head of the USSR supreme soviet] was walking behind, and I joined him as one of the hosts. As we walked on, Brezhnev was telling us how [First Party Secretary G.] Aliyev [of Azerbaijan] had shown him around Baku: "When I saw the same monument a third time, I asked him, why are you taking us around and around? It was a tiring trip: we worked our way there, and we worked our way back. And then they made me play that favorite game of theirs (with his hands he demonstrated the moving of chips on a checkerboard). Then I had to answer phone calls from other leaders—Hussein called me and invited me to come hunting."

There was an awkward pause. To fill it I said, "It's an invitation worth accepting; he once invited me too. The hunting is good there." Chernenko looked at me sideways as if to ask, who is this man, unintroduced to him, to make such impertinent remarks? Vlasov turned back and I read in his eyes the question, are you out of your mind, Bokov? But I didn't mean the king of Jordan. I was talking of Hussein Zalikhanov, a friend of mine, the senior gamekeeper in Kabarda's wildlife and hunting reserve. If I'd had a clearer head that morning, I would've thought better of it—my Hussein Zalikhanov could not have been esteemed enough to invite Brezhnev.

Later, for a couple of years, I would turn away from Chernenko when I chanced to be in the presidium with him and other chairmen of local supreme soviets; everyone applauded him and looked him in the eye, and I looked away, so that he wouldn't recall the strange fellow who got phone calls from foreign kings.

Three hours after Brezhnev left us, we held a plenary session of the regional Communist Party committee, with all local bosses and dignitaries invited, to discuss "measures for implementing the directives that the secretary-general, L. I. Brezhnev, had discussed, measures aimed toward economic growth and higher living standards in Checheno-Ingushetiya." The report on the issue had been prepared in advance and took an hour and a half to read. In reality, Brezhnev had never said a word about any of it.

In fact, during the 1970s and 1980s, Checheno-Ingushetiya received no special attention from the Kremlin or the Russian Federation. Chechnya was among the autonomous republics developing fast enough, economically and culturally, with a sufficiently stable political and interethnic climate, that Moscow felt no need to worry about it excessively. The USSR had many other, more problematic, regions to be concerned about. Trips to Moscow by the local leaders—to Communist Party congresses, sessions of the supreme soviet, and various conferences—were frequent and useful in establishing formal and informal links. In Moscow, they relaxed a little and felt more aware of their ethnicity, that is, being "others." Here are a few stories from Bokov:

> Our "First" [the first secretary of the regional Communist Party committee] once called me up to say, "Don't leave tonight until I call you." He called me to his office about nine in the evening. I was then twenty-eight, administrator of the committee's ideological department. He gave me a sealed envelope, "Take this to Moscow tonight. It is a recommendation for your promotion to our regional committee's post of secretary for ideology. Tell your wife you have to go on an urgent business trip, but don't tell her the purpose."
>
> "But it's only an hour and a half before the train leaves."
>
> "Never mind, you don't need any preparation. Get a car and go."
>
> I went with Mahomed Abubakarov, who was being installed as our committee's secretary for agriculture. He was a fine specialist, a good-natured, inoffensive man, but not a politician. He would talk innocently, in detail, about cattle cross-breeding in front of women; our strictly brought-up women were embarrassed, but interested. Once in Moscow, I dropped by his hotel room: he was watching a ballet on TV with the sound off, listening instead to the sound of funeral music from the radio. I increased the volume on the TV set. He reacted calmly, "Yes, that's jollier."
>
> Soon some of our countrymen dropped in on us with a few bottles of vodka to celebrate our Moscow reunion. We were all young, and drank a bottle each without much consequence. Then, after ten in the evening, we received a phone call from Staraya Ploschad ["Old Square," the famous address of the central committee of the Communist Party of the USSR]. We were called immediately to Kapitonov [the all-powerful secretary for organizational matters]. No excuse was possible. We put our heads under the cold-water tap and filled our mouths with peppermint breath mints. We didn't call a car but walked in order to get some fresh air. In front of Kapitonov's door, we sniffed each other's breath—did it smell of vodka? We were still quite drunk, of course.

During the late Brezhnev era and the beginning of Mikhail Gorbachev's perestroika, nepotism and corruption had become the norm for the central and periphery elites, and still more for those in the provinces, as was the case in Checheno-Ingushetiya and in other autonomous republics (see Fairbanks 1993). Some members of the local administration tried to protest the corruption. On July 15, 1987, Bokov wrote in frustration to the politburo of the CPSU central committee, even though it was extremely rare for the chairman of a republic's supreme soviet to write such a letter without the knowledge of the first secretary of its Communist Party committee. Bokov wrote, not a personal complaint, but of his outrage at the existing political and moral climate. Here is the abridged text of the letter:

At the presidium of the autonomous republic's supreme soviet, . . . I found it my duty to point out specific examples and to state frankly that with each passing year, more and more economic inequality emerges in the republic. The good fortune of the few is not based on honest labor and fair remuneration. A whole social stratum has developed for sponging on the public.

I expected the first secretary of the regional Communist Party committee, Comrade V. K. Foteyev, to render an appropriate political assessment. . . . I was, however, bitterly disappointed by his response: he remarked that we must eventually get into these matters, but that I had exaggerated and overdramatized the situation. No one else spoke of the matter, as if it were a minor issue. I do not exaggerate or overdramatize, but speak the bitter truth. The republic's leaders, visiting our settlements, fail to see the two-story mansions with underground garages, fenced with metal gratings or stone walls; they proliferate with each year [that passes]. Who are the owners of these mansions? . . . They are usually persons engaged in trade, in distribution, party leaders, or holders of important posts in the economy. In short, persons not at all engaged in production for the common good. How could it happen that, with our order of stringent control over social processes, such obvious social distortions occur? We were proud, and can still be so, of the great political, economic, and social changes in the life of our small nation, of the rising material well-being of our people. But we close our eyes to the fact that much material success is achieved through other than honest labor, and this does not improve morals, but brings out the worst side of human nature. Our republic gives all sorts of shady dealers, profiteers, and corrupters a free hand. They even flaunt their ability to make money. With money, they circumvent the law in many ways: they bribe "needed" officials with lavish gifts and great sums of money, under the guise of Caucasian hospitality; they buy a way of life for their children—from inflated school grades through college entrance exams and unearned diplomas and on to cozy official posts. All this is common practice, indulged in without fear of punishment.

And despite all this, I am told "not to exaggerate or overdramatize." The question of more active resistance to unearned incomes was to be raised at the session of our republic's supreme soviet. I was asked to make a report, and, being aware of the situation, I called for a principled critical assessment. I handed a copy of my report to Comrade Foteyev ten days in advance. He made no critical remarks, but on the eve of the session he called me up and said, "I don't recommend you make such an overly critical report. I advise you to read out the decision by the [USSR supreme soviet's] commissions and follow it with ten minutes of "comments." I went to talk to him personally: I asked him about his reason for rejecting the report just a few hours before the session. The only reason he gave was the critical tone of the report and its criticism of certain officials who tolerate embezzlement in their organizations. "It looks like what we say about ourselves is worse than what outsiders think of us," he said with indignation. He had put me in the role of a slanderer of my own people. . . .

I must also express my thoughts on the sensitive issue of intra- and interethnic relations. There is a simplistic approach toward the selection and appoint-

> ment of cadres that offends our national dignity. Instead of being guided by the personal worth of candidates, the appointments follow the rigid principle of ethnic quota: 5:4:1, that is, five Chechens, four Russians, and one Ingush. Appointments also, depending on their importance, follow a certain ethnic pattern. That infringes on the basic principle of the equality of all citizens, irrespective of nationality.[2]

Upon receipt of this letter, Staraya Ploschad sent its inspector to the Checheno-Ingush Autonomous Republic, and Foteyev called a closed meeting of the regional party committee's bureau. The inspector remarked after the meeting that he felt like washing his hands after greeting these people. The central committee could hardly change anything in the republic. Late in 1989, a rally of "national democrats" demanding the return of the Prigorodny *raion* to Ingushetiya was held in Nazran and lasted for seventeen days. The activists asked why Bokov would not join his Ingush people at the rally, and he replied that he was responsible for the entire autonomous republic, not only the Ingush people. "Where are the people?" he asked. "Here? No, this is just a crowd. The people are working in the fields and in the factories." In March 1990, Bokov left for Moscow, and was soon transferred to the Federal Ministry for Nationalities, where he worked as deputy minister while I served as minister.

In 1990, the Chechen Doku Zavgayev became the "number one" official in the republic. Many stories about Zavgayev suggest that he was an energetic, strong-willed leader, though he also did many things that alarmed and upset people in the republic. Partly owing to the political liberalization under Gorbachev, a struggle for power arose. With the old party *nomenklatura* system (see Voslenski 1991) dead (under the old system, Moscow had appointed a Russian to the post of first secretary of the republic's Communist Party, never trusting such a position to a member of the local ethnic elite), Zavgayev proceeded to delegate all prestigious posts to his relatives and protégés, and conflicts and rivalry among the Chechen elite grew increasingly vicious.

THE CONTRADICTIONS OF MODERNIZATION AND CHECHEN DISLOYALTY

The decades of the 1960s through the 1980s saw the formation of a new society in Checheno-Ingushetiya. The demographic balance among the main ethnic groups had now radically changed, and after the exiles returned to the restored Chechen-Ingush Republic, its population increased by 46.3 percent in eleven years (arguably because the majority of those who returned were young and of reproductive age; see *Chechnya Report* 1992: 26).

Given their high birthrate, the Chechens and Ingush in the republic increased in number from roughly half of the population to a substantial majority, becoming one of the largest groups in the North Caucasus, second only to the total number of ethnic Russians in the area. The degree of urbanization was noticeably lower, however, compared to the Russian Federation's average: in the 1989 census, it was 73 percent in the Russian Federation, 57 percent in the North Caucasus as a whole, and just 41 percent in Checheno-Ingushetiya. Chechens in the urban centers of Checheno-Ingushetiya numbered roughly 25 percent of the total population.

These years saw a rise in modern industry within the republic, particularly in the oil, gas, energy, and engineering industries. Nearly all the oil and gas extracted in the North Caucasus regions was processed in Groznyy's refineries. Groznyy became a principal supplier of high-quality motor fuel for aviation and other equipment, such as machinery for the oil industry, pumps, tractor trailers, electrographic machines, bottling lines, and medical instruments. Up to 90 percent of all aviation lubricants in the USSR were produced in Checheno-Ingushetiya. Some light industries (knitwear, footwear, ready-made clothes) were also centered in Groznyy and Nazran. The republic seemed "an industrial giant" in relation to its neighbors in the North Caucasus, comparable only to North Ossetia, where defense industries were based. Because the republic's industries were 95 percent affiliated with the USSR's central government, profits from oil extraction and refineries went directly to the USSR central budget. This was also the case in many other regions, including Bashkiria, Tataria, and Yakutia.

Industrialization in Checheno-Ingushetiya had a curious ethnic dimension. The republic's economy fell primarily into two sectors: the "Russian" (oil, engineering, infrastructure, vital services) and the "indigenous" (low-productivity agriculture, migrant labor, and the criminal sphere). The indigenous sector tended to absorb new generations entering the labor market. The paradox was that the industry and transport sectors badly needed more workers, particularly trained specialists, but because of ethnic discrimination, little was done to engage Chechen and Ingush youths in these fields. In the late 1980s, the largest petrochemical companies, Grozneft and Orgsynthez, employed 50,000 workers and engineers, only a few hundred of whom were Chechen or Ingush. Dzabrail told me that even though he held a high post at Groznyy University and was well known in the republic, he had great difficulty in helping one of his nephews obtain a job at the Groznyy plant, Krasny Molot, where they preferred not to employ Chechens.

Since agriculture could not provide employment for the growing numbers of people, many young Chechens, particularly educated ones, left for other regions, and some joined criminal gangs. It is estimated that the labor surplus reached perhaps 100,000 to 200,000, or 20–30 percent of the able-bodied population. Later, these people became the main reserve for the armed struggle. Gakayev writes:

> The work of the petrochemical complex left the indigenous people of the republic with nothing but a polluted environment and gutted resources. The social infrastructure was not developed, particularly in rural areas. Although the migrant Chechen and Ingush workers built sumptuous houses with their earnings, many of their settlements had no hospitals, schools, roads, or other social services. Unemployment resulted in increases in migrant labor and profiteering and a rise in criminality. (Gakayev 1997: 109)

The number of migrant workers leaving Chechnya seasonally reached 100,000, and they often took along their school-age children as help, which disrupted schooling. Gakayev notes another significant aspect of the social situation in those years:

> Most of the migrant workers earned their bread from hard toil under terrible conditions that caused health problems. Some Chechen "entrepreneurial mediators" skimmed profits from these activities by arranging false papers, and by thefts of building materials (in cahoots with the local administration), thereby exploiting tens of thousands of their own countrymen. These men brought home not only huge windfall profits obtained illegally but also narcotics, and this marginal culture undermined the traditional values of Vainakh society. (Gakayev 1997: 109–10)

These circumstances explain the high level of crime among Chechens in comparison to other groups, and about 4,000 to 5,000 Chechens and Ingush were annually sentenced to long prison terms in the republic. Until recently, KGB surveillance and informants were common in the region, and some experts assert that the local justice system was ethnically biased against Chechens.

After their return from exile, the Chechens, along with the Ingush, remained the object of special attention by local party organs, as well as by the KGB and the Ministry of Internal Affairs (MVD) of the USSR, which continued to consider them insufficiently "loyal" to the regime and prone to "nationalistic prejudices." For example, on April 30, 1966, the chairman of the KGB, Vladimir Semichastny, submitted a document to the central committee of the CPSU concerning "the revival of nationalistic and chauvinistic manifestations" among the intelligentsia and young people of the Checheno-Ingush ASSR, as well as the increase in interethnic dissent, which "frequently grew into group incidents and excesses." This document notes several examples of the "dissemination of anti-Soviet slanders against the Communist Party and the nationality policy within the Soviet Union." The KGB chairman reported that among Chechens and Ingush, there were "hostile attitudes toward people of other nationalities living in the republic, especially Russians." He further noted the tendency of "nationalistically inclined persons" to focus on recruiting young people.

In the republic, interethnic tension manifested itself in forms that were rare elsewhere in the USSR; group clashes were frequently accompanied by murders. According to KGB data on the Checheno-Ingush Republic, in 1965 alone, there were sixteen group clashes and a total of 185 severe bodily injuries from gun and knife wounds, 19 of them fatal. Among the reasons cited by the state security apparatus for the violence were the influence of "anti-Soviet propaganda by foreign radio stations broadcasting in the Chechen and Ingush languages" and the harmful activity of "people of the older generation, including part of the creative intelligentsia." Finally, it noted that "nationalistic and other harmful phenomena arise out of religious and clan memories. . . . Individual authorities, taking advantage of the dogma of Islam, preach hatred toward 'unbelievers,' prophesy the destruction of Soviet power, exert a harmful influence on believers, incite fanaticism, and attempt to preserve and support obsolete traditions and morals."[3]

The MVD of the USSR sent information to the central committee of the CPSU during the same years, on the same themes. On May 7, 1971, Minister N. M. Shchelokov reported that

> In 1969–71, the MVD implemented various measures, including an "army operation" in December 1969, for "the full liquidation of the criminal gangs." As Minister Shchelokov reported, in the past eighteen months alone, 347 criminals from among the Chechens and Ingush had been discovered. Information about the confiscation of firearms from the population in the republics of the North Caucasus, Kazakhstan, and Kirghizia was sensational for such seemingly "stagnant" times of totalitarian control over society: in 1968, 6,704 firearms were confiscated or voluntarily surrendered; in 1969, the number was 7,039; and in 1970, the total reached 6,787, including 4 machine guns, 54 automatics, and 2,105 pistols and revolvers.[4]

Throughout these years, analyses of the problems were limited to ideological pronouncements and are thus not grist for scientific study. The actual social and psychological reasons for "Chechen criminality" or "disloyalty" were never investigated. In propaganda literature, platitudes about the Checheno-Ingush Republic successfully developing within "the fraternal family of the peoples of the USSR" predominated. This policy of denial and "congratulatory toasts" (to use Gorbachev's expression) contained a certain positive element in that its very silence dampened ethnic conflicts among Soviet citizens.

It would be misleading, of course, to judge the general situation in the republic and the social behavior of the Chechens solely on the basis of KGB and MVD documents. The mass return of Chechens and Ingush after 1957 was a complicated process, entailing significant social and psychological tensions. After 1944, about 77,000 new settlers from various regions of Russia settled on land vacated by the Chechens and Ingush—most of them with special orders from the authorities. Some of these settlers came from regions devastated by the war, and some came from nearby Ossetia and Dagestan. When work on reconstituting the republic got under way, there were 540,000 persons in the Groznenskay *oblast.* Many occupied the houses and urban apartments once lived in by deported persons, and this could not help but invite conflict. The chickens had come home to roost, and in 1958, there were open clashes between Chechens and Russians in Groznyy.

In rural areas, people constantly disputed land held by the *kolkhozy* and state farms. Much of the land formerly held was inaccessible to the returnees: several mountain areas were closed to habitation, and their former residents had to settle in lowland *aul* (villages) and Cossack *stanitsy* (settlements). The Akkintsy Chechens who returned to Dagestan could not resume life in their native villages, because these lands had been settled by the Laks—people from the mountain *auls.*

The central authorities tried to resolve the problems attendant upon reestablishing the republic by granting Chechnya control of two *raions* of Stavropol *krai*—Naurskii and Shelkovskoi (5,200 square kilometers)—chiefly inhabited by Russians, Kumyks, and Nogais. Some assert that this was done to prevent the Chechens from predominating in the new republic (*Chechnia Report* 1992: 16), but documentation does not support this. On the contrary, the government appears to have implemented several measures to help the returnees: Chechens and Ingush received substantial credits and financial aid (including subsidies for building new homes and buying livestock), tax breaks, and special supplies of agricultural equipment and seed. There were also programs of social support for pensioners and speedy construction of schools, hospitals, and cultural institutions (Bugai 1994: 213–33).

Our information also does not support the high level of "Chechen criminality" and "Chechen clashes with Russians" that the KGB reports suggest. One informant, Shamsuddin Umarov, whom I met during Alexander Lebed's peacekeeping mission in the North Caucasus, had worked for a long time (some of it under Dudayev's government) in Chechnya's Interior Department, holding such posts as deputy interior minister and head of Groznyy's Interior Department. He told me that in the 1980s, there had been from 300 to 600 criminal cases in Groznyy annually:

> I am absolutely sure all was done in strict conformity with the law. We didn't care what nationality the offender was. Not more than 5 percent of cases resulted from conflicts or crimes colored with ethnic friction. We dealt mostly with street brawls, hooliganism, theft, robberies, and murders, crimes in which people of all nationalities were involved. The only preference we had was for Russian witnesses, who seemed neutral and disinterested. A Chechen witness would be likely to withdraw or change his evidence in order not to testify against other Chechens.

EDUCATION AND THE NEW GENERATION

The Great Soviet Encyclopedia (1978), in its article on the Checheno-Ingush Autonomous Republic (in vol. 29), contains extensive information on education and culture. The reconstituted republic experienced not only a demographic but an educational boom: it now had 569 secondary schools, with 288,000 students; 29 vocational schools, with 15,000 students; 12 specialized secondary-level colleges, with 15,000 students; and two institutes of higher education—the Checheno-Ingush University and the Petroleum Industry College—with 12,000 students between them. In 1980, the republic had a rather modern cultural infrastructure. Apart from three professional drama theaters, a musical theater, and two museums of fine arts, there were about 400 culture houses and clubs, 484 public libraries, and 300 cinemas in cities and rural areas. Checheno-Ingushetiya had developed a mass-media industry, with republican TV and four newspapers, fourteen *raion* newspapers, and two literary journals. The total daily periodical circulation reached one million copies (Ovkhadov 1983: 26). There were also several active professional unions (writers, composers, journalists, etc.).

These encouraging figures, however, concealed some serious problems. Gakayev evaluated the situation as follows:

> Teaching at the schools in the rural areas, where 70 percent of the indigenous population lived, remained at a very low level for decades. Schools had a shortage of financing, teachers, infrastructure, and books. Many children didn't attend school because of their families' poverty and the seasonal migratory work their parents asked them to do. At college entrance exams, those from village schools, mostly of Chechen and Ingush nationality, could not compete with the Russian-speaking city youth. In consequence, local colleges failed to train Chechen or Ingush specialists. The percentage of Vainakh students (particularly at the Petroleum Industry College) was low. Since Vainakh college applicants were at a disadvantage, they often had to pay bribes to gain admission. Russia's colleges had a system of reserving quotas for applicants from ethnic autonomous regions, but the republic's Communist Party committee began admitting Russian-speaking applicants among the indigenous candidates in these reserved quotas. Those from city schools—Russians, Armenians, Jews—received more opportunities. These policies prevented the Vainakhs from bridging the cultural gap caused by the years of exile. (Gakayev 1997: 112)

Thus, in the period 1957–85, the Chechen and Ingush people nursed a sense of wounded pride. They had limited rights and opportunities compared with the Russian-speaking part of the republic's population, as well as the indigenous people in the neighboring republics. I asked Kheda about her studies at the secondary school in her large rural settlement of Benoi-Yurt, to see how education operated at the grassroots level:

> We had one large school for boys and girls. Girls shared desks with boys. From the third to the tenth form, we had the same class mistress, a Russian woman. She had a strong character and an organizational talent. She always arranged something interesting for us—outings, parties, and so on. All the parents respected her for setting high standards. She told us we were one large family. She was very strict about young love: if a boy and a girl were caught kissing, she put her foot down. Or once, when a birthday party was held in the woods for all the March kids in our class, some kids drank a bottle of champagne and some of the boys smoked. She called a parents' meeting and made a great fuss. She would sometimes hit the boys on the hands with a ruler, but they took it patiently. She even forbade champagne for our school-leaving party, but the boys smuggled it in and added it to the soft drinks surreptitiously. So, we had no real romances at school, but once our girls left, many of them got married right away. As it happened, few in our class went on to study at college.

I asked Kheda how she, a girl from a Chechen village, had managed to receive a college education and take a postgraduate course at one of Moscow's prestigious research institutes. Her story is quite illuminating for its responsive answer to why and how so many researchers and college teachers in Checheno-Ingushetiya took postgraduate courses or pursued special studies in Moscow:

> I took entrance examinations at Groznyy University and passed them all but wasn't admitted. My family did not offer a bribe, because I would not let them. I was so hurt and upset that I felt like drowning myself in the Sunzha [a river in Groznyy]. It was a good thing that my father came with me. After we returned to our village, I received a telegram inviting me, as one of those applicants who had failed the Russian exam, to join the Vainakh department. In fact, I was particularly good at Russian, and had written a good essay for the written exam (they tried to accuse me of cribbing). I knew that the girl near me during the exam had made a mistake every other word but had still been admitted. They must have had a secret list in advance of those they would admit. I said I would never go near the university as long as I lived. I stayed in our village for three years working in the public library and reading books. Eventually, I joined the Literature Department of the Groznyy Teachers' College. Much later I met the man who hadn't given me the passing grade in the oral Russian entrance exam for the university. I reminded him of it, and he remembered me. "You behaved too independently for your age at sixteen," he explained, "I was about to give you an even lower grade, but that would have been awkward, given your good performance."
>
> For postgraduate studies, my good schooling stood me in good stead. I had always done more at school than the basic curriculum required—I knew a lot of Russian poetry by heart, for example. After graduating from the teachers' college I found a job at a research institute in Groznyy. It was both prestigious and interesting. They sent me to Moscow for a six-month study period, and I found out that I would be able to take a postgraduate course there. I felt good among colleagues in Moscow, which gave me confidence. Yuri Barabash [a famous

> Russian literary critic and philologist] treated me especially warmly. When the war began, I don't know what I would have done without their support. Barabash procured a map of Chechnya and traced the fighting on it. "Here's another village we have taken." He meant *us,* the Chechens—how grateful I was for that! Each of them offered to help, asked if I had any problems, invited me to their "dachas," and said encouraging things to me. Later, I compared this with other Chechens' experience. None of them had had it so good.

The corruption of the late Brezhnev period was indeed a major cause for mass dissatisfaction. The dominant feeling was disgust with the party *nomenklatura* (or bureaucratic) system, the paucity of educational opportunities, and the low living standards. Most people supported the changes proclaimed by Gorbachev, both glasnost (i.e., bringing real facts into the open) and democratization.

ON LANGUAGE AND HISTORY

In one of my conversations with Kheda, I asked her to tell me about her "romance" with the Chechen language:

> The Chechen language has always been with me. I had an excellent grade in it at school. It rose to new heights for me when I first heard a song written for lyrics by Bisultanov. Those were philosophical verses; I tried to translate them into Russian, but found it too difficult. The music was by Betilghiriyev; it's close to Okudzhava's with similar variations. When I met the poet, I understood him, and myself, better. With all his marked Chechen identity, he is, I think, one of the universal men of genius of our time. Once I picked up his book, I did not sleep until morning, reading it straight through.
>
> At college, we had Russian and Vainakh departments, the latter for those who didn't know Russian well enough. It was not then in fashion to study the Chechen language. Some people said that soon we wouldn't have a nationality written in our passports, so it seemed irrelevant.
>
> In my uncle's family one of my cousins—she was five years older than me—knew the Chechen language very well. She could recite poems by heart. All the old women in our street came to hear her. She would stand on a stool and recite them as they sat around and wept. They always made her repeat "In the Mountains" by Mamakayev. I wondered at them—what, weep over the same poem night after night?
>
> At home, our family spoke Chechen, but my father, who taught Chechen language and literature at school, never insisted on it. He approached it as a teacher. My uncle's family saw it differently. They reproached my parents for giving up traditions and bringing me up in the wrong way. Still, my first language is Russian. I understand Chechen perfectly, but when I talk, I have to resort to some of the Russian lexicon.

As the story suggests, a number of Chechens lost the use of their mother tongue or became bilingual. Today, a pidgin Russian mixed with Chechen words predominates, though more than once, Vainakh intellectuals raised the question of teaching Chechen in the city schools. Zulai Khamidova recounted her struggle to include the Chechen and Ingush languages in the city schools' curriculum. In 1989, Khamidova organized courses on the Chechen language for people of different nationalities living in Groznyy, which were a great success: 200 people enrolled. A half-hour program was launched on television once a week, "We Study the Chechen Language." The children's "Good Night" program, which ran for fifteen minutes each week, included animated cartoons in Chechen. Another program was called "What Do You Know of Your Mother Tongue?" For the first time in many years, conversation books and self-teaching manuals were published in Chechen.

Along with the interest in language came a new focus on Chechen history. Chechen and Ingush intellectuals rejected the accepted notion of Soviet historiography that Chechnya's peoples and territories had joined Russia voluntarily (in fact, only some did). Hot debates arose from study of the works of the local historian and archaeologist V. B. Vinogradov, who championed the official (but discredited) version of Chechnya's "voluntarily joining Russia," with the support of the regional Communist Party committee. By that time, new interpretations had already become available, including studies by Western authors of Imam Shamil's war on Islam in Chechnya and Dagestan (Bennigsen and Wimbush 1985; Gammer 1994), and the Chechen emigrant Abdurahman Avtorkhanov's important works *Imperia Kremlya* (The Kremlin Empire) and *Ubiistvo checheno-ingushskogo naroda: Narodoubiistvo v SSSR* (The Killing of Checheno-Ingush People: The People-Killing in the USSR) have been translated into Russian (Avtorkhanov 1991a, 1991b).

The intellectual climate of perestroika opened up possibilities in Checheno-Ingushetiya for more varied viewpoints and for works contesting the received judgments of the past. This marked the beginning of a new period: Chechen ethnic nationalism gradually began to emerge as a foundation for a political platform. The filling of an ideological vacuum has manifested itself in repudiations of the past and rejections of the existing order—without constructive scenarios for future responses.

FOUR

Chechen Images

First, I am a Chechen, but I am a Rossiyanin too.*

BAGAUDI M.

It seems that with one foot I am among Chechens, but my other foot is somewhere in Dagestan, or perhaps in Russia. It is hard for me to define who I am. My family suffered many reproaches for not being pure Chechens.

SHAMIL A.

In examining how violent conflict has reshaped the Chechen identity, the question arises of whether identity emerges within changing forms of organization, politics, and external influences or is transmitted through early childhood, internal collective narrative, and sociobiological mechanisms. If the Chechens profess a self-image centered on a rigid set of cultural characteristics, how might war affect such an image? In part, war encourages the emergence of uncritical self-perceptions, self-proclamations, external borrowings, and fantasies reflecting the absurdity of violence and the impasse confronting efforts to explain it with rational arguments. These fantasies around group identity constitute a message to the outside world about a suffering human collective.

But this is not the whole story. Though it may seem absurd to speak of Chechens as an imagined community in a time of savage fighting, a constructivist approach is absolutely timely for this research. Conflict and its extreme form—war—should apparently strengthen the primordial vision of ethnicity, embellishing it with rainbows of attributes and historic citations. But the theoretical intrigue lies in these very fantasies about the "primordial Chechen nation" (Anatol Lieven's words), and it is in them that we find most spectacular proof of ethnicity's constructivist nature. Who the authors of these fantasies are—politicians, political analysts, anthropologists, or their informants—makes no difference. Conflict produces a thick discourse where differentiation between actors has no particular meaning. In some respect, it is not Chechens who author the conflict, it is the conflict that produces Chechens in their contemporary perceptions of themselves.

**Rossiyanin* (cf. *Rossiya* and *Rossiyskaya Federatsiya,*) an exact transliteration of the Russian term for a citizen of the country irrespective of ethnic origin, has increasingly been used since the disappearance of "Soviet people." Unfortunately, English and other foreign languages lack equivalent terms for citizens of the Russian Federation in general, as distinct from ethnic Russians *(Russkie).*

THE CHANGING CONCEPT OF THE PEOPLE

There are descriptions of the Chechens in the native Chechen ethnography that has long been integrated into the context of Russia's social sciences. There is an article on "Chechens" by Chechen authors from Groznyy in the 1994 *Narody Rossii* (Peoples of Russia) encyclopedia that gives what might be termed a standard academic account of any ethnic group before calamities like the recent events. It affirms the relative antiquity, cultural uniqueness, and rigid boundaries of the Chechen ethnos (a dominant category of analysis and practice in late Soviet and post-Soviet ethnography; see, e.g., Bromley 1983, 1987; Semenov 1999). This article contains all the features of a primordial approach: ethnogenesis, ethnic history, information on the group's material and spiritual culture, its "ethnic subdivisions," and so on. It admits no doubts about the relative antiquity, cultural uniqueness, and distinct mentality of the Chechen ethnos.

It is only since the late 1980s that the local ideologues have been fundamentally emending the historical myth of the Chechens and, in the process, current Chechen identity. In this construction of new Chechen identity, two rival trends can be observed. One includes as many historic communities as possible in the Chechen entity in order to widen its geographic span and deepen its cultural legacy. The other, born out of competition for resources and power, focuses on narrower group boundaries based on locality and "clan" ties. My informant and cross-reviewer Rustam told me:

> When Dudayev came to power in Chechnya, we heard of the Melkhistins, Orstkhoy, and Akkin as separate nationalities for the first time. Some Melkhistins even tried to enter this nationality on their passports. In the past, those groups may have rated as separate *teip*s, but they can scarcely be described as present-day nationalities. In 1988–94, they gained much stronger standing among the Chechens. They began their rise by accumulating capital through control of the Groznyy oil refinery. Later, when their "representative" Dzhokhar Dudayev rose to power, they brought the republic's entire petroleum industry under their control. That is why they wanted sovereignty for their *teip* above all others![1]

What was Dudayev's own concept of the Chechen people? He had not lived in Chechnya and knew little of his own people when called upon to participate in the nationalist movement. In 1991, upon proclaiming the sovereignty of what was still the Checheno-Ingush Republic, he said, "There is a single and indivisible Vainakh people with a place of honor for each of its five member-nationalities: Chechen, Ingush, Orstkhoy, Melkhistin, and Akkin. Today, history gives us a unique chance to establish that fact by creating a single Vainakh statehood" (Dudayev 1992: 32).

In an appeal to the Ingush people at a meeting of Ingush elders in December 1991, Dudayev not only expressed his concept of a single

Vainakh people but proclaimed the utopian idea of a "Greater Chechnya" that would include both the Akkin Chechens, most of whom live in Dagestan, and the Melkhistins, some of whom live in Georgia.[2] In 1992, he published an essay entitled "A Slave Resigned to His Slavery Deserves Double Slavery":

> The [Russian] "divide and rule" policy has certainly played its role. The Chechen tribes were divided into two ethnic groups: the Chechens and the Ingush. But all the Chechen tribes are united under the name "Vainakh," meaning literally "our people": the Chechens and Ingush (here in the Checheno-Ingush Republic), the Akkins or Aukhovtsy (in Dagestan), and the Kisty or Kistins (in Georgia). We are all indivisible. Nor were we divided by our enemies during the genocide: we were deported together and fought for our independence together. (Dudayev 1992: 31)

Dudayev, like other Chechen leaders and activists, praised the heroic and romantic qualities of the Chechens, saying:

> You could scarcely find a more patient people on the Earth, never mind our occasional aggressiveness and quick temper. . . .
>
> . . . Chechnya was never part of Russia, and the Chechens never thought of themselves as citizens of Russia. . . .
>
> . . . We are Chechens, and that can be a heavy burden. By the law of the mountains and our ancestors' custom, we are obliged to help people who need shelter and protection. In such cases, even the law of blood vengeance loses its importance. (Dudayev 1992: 14, 54, 57)

Chechen leaders endorsed the idea of the Chechens as a people with deep, ancient roots. Many, certainly including President Dudayev, sincerely believed this. The Chechen minister of economics and finance, Taimaz Abubakarov, tells the story of Dudayev's visit to Lebanon in the summer of 1993: "In Baalbek, Dudayev saw an ancient stone structure with giant columns resembling the masonry of the medieval towers in the mountains of Chechnya and Ingushetiya. The sight led him to assert that both were built by the same tribe—namely, the Vainakhs" (Abubakarov 1998: 17). Dudayev came to a new version of Islam's origin, which he did not hesitate to proclaim. According to Dudayev, the great religion of Islam must have emerged, not in the lifeless desert of Arabia among nomadic tribes, but in the earthly paradise among peoples of high culture and mutual respect. That garden of Eden was Chechnya, and its people, the Vainakhs, must have been the founders of the Islamic faith. According to Abubakarov, "Hearing this proclamation, Chechnya's mufti, M. Kh. Alsabekov, was greatly embarrassed, particularly when he was told to adopt . . . this new view of the ethnic and geographic origins of Islam. The mufti did not quarrel with this revisionist history, but he declined to give his support" (Abubakarov 1998: 17).

On another occasion, on a visit to France, Dudayev amazed his hosts with a new version of the story of Noah's Ark, in which the Ark landed in the mountains of Chechnya and Noah and his family were the direct ancestors of the Vainakhs. Mankind, therefore, owed its salvation from the Flood to the Chechens. "I can't say how much he believed it himself, but he spoke with the conviction of a man who knows mysteries that are concealed from others," Abubakarov says (1998: 17).

One day in 1993 I was talking with Yusup Soslambekov, one of the "fathers" of the "Chechen revolution," in my office. By this time Chechnya had come to be dominated by a radical nationalism, and Moscow was dismayed. Yusup explained it to me this way: "We have a new generation, one that covets power, prestige, and money. The Chechens don't like being poor, and they are ready to go to any lengths to grab power from the *nomenklatura* [long-standing Soviet jargon for Communist Party apparatchiks], hence the revolution. And it didn't take us long to learn how to write various declarations and proclamations. We had some foreign help—the Baltic countries were willing to oblige."

The period following 1991 was filled with the rhetoric of Vainakh self-determination, with ritual incantations about perestroika's democratic ideology, and with promises of postcommunist sovereignty for the autonomous republics. At that time, Chechen radical nationalism was based on the negation of the former regime and on the political doctrine of a secular Chechen state. The texts of the Sovereignty Declaration passed in November 1990, under the government of Doku Zavgayev, which was then still communist, and of the Declaration of the Chechen People of July 1991 contain key features of the new Chechen identity, one based on the image of a "banished and fighting people."

Stress was laid on "historical injustices" that had to be set right. A fact-finding mission from International Alert, a UK-based nongovernmental organization devoted to conflict resolution, which visited Chechnya in 1992, reported: "The highest official of the executive branch who received us was Arslanbek Akbulatov, chief of the presidential staff, who gave us a carefully articulated account of Chechen history, concluding with an account of ways in which Chechens continued to suffer discrimination in employment, education, and allocation of resources until 1987: 'We were treated like the Untermenschen of the Nazis!'" he declared (Chechnya Report 1992: 52).

The theme of deportation and its untold suffering dominated Chechen political discourse, both in the literary efforts of local writers and, later, in youth pop songs. Many young Chechens were influenced by pop songs whose theme was the 1944 deportation. Musa Geshayev describes the impact of having a song use his lyrics: "It had the effect of a bomb blast. I felt proud that one of the hits on our local TV channel was 'The Dark Days,' a song incorporating my lyrics. Thus,"

Of our dark days the mountains told me,
A darker story no highlander ever heard,
No time can heal the pain felt in the Vainakh land
When it saw its people rounded up
And banished from their homes in contempt
By a cruel order they couldn't understand.
We were like cattle driven into freight trains—
What had we done that we were punished so
By our country in that wartime year?
We passed through horrors and starvation,
We prayed, and we heaped our curses on Stalin's head,
He paid no heed, wading knee-deep in blood
Toward his pinnacle over the frightened crowd.
We were like cogs in that well-oiled machine,
What woeful time we had to live through,
Torn from our dear mountains of the Caucasus!
Once on my way back there I met a friend:
I asked him what he carried in his bag.
He said he'd dug out his mother's ashes
To take them home to be buried in our land.
Our train arrived at dawn, and as we got off
We saw an old man in a worn beshmet [wool placket]
Alight and fall down upon his knees
To touch his native land and give it a kiss.

People began to believe that to end any continuing discrimination against them, the Chechens had to assume control over the republic. Chechen activists continually called for measures to unify their nation and for the return of all Chechens living outside Chechnya. (As regards the latter, it would be interesting to speculate about what had motivated many Chechens and Ingush to remain in other lands after their exile. At least 50,000 of them had stayed in Kazakhstan and Kirghizia or had moved to other areas beyond Chechnya.)

Religion played little part in the forming of the new Chechen identity during perestroika (i.e., before the first Chechen war). Apart from some ritual mentions of Islam, the Chechens did not identify themselves as an "Islamic people." I agree with G. Derluguian that "there is no ground for using the Islamic religion to explain the extremely strong and often painful national consciousness among the Chechens" (1999: 210). Furthermore, the religious factor bore little connection to the original Chechen "national revolution." Collective suffering, rather than religion, culture, or language, cemented Chechen identity. Only after 1991 did the Chechens begin to call themselves *nokhchi,* meaning "Caucasian peoples" (in the plural).

Yan Chesnov came to the same conclusion: "This ethnic name has only very recently established itself as a common identification among all

Chechens, in spite of [the term's] deep historical roots, going back to the seventh century's Armenian chronicles" (Chesnov 1999: 67). In many people's memory, this was the term that mountain groups applied to those who lived on the "flat lands" (the *ploskosti*). Along with *nokhchi,* a new, politically colored identity had emerged in the form of *Ichekeriitsy,* especially when Chechnya had been renamed the Chechen Republic (Ichkeria) under Dudayev. "I am a real *Ichkeriika,*" Malika Salgiriyeva told me. The term implies a certain political agenda—the imposition of a new pan-Chechen identity in order to minimize the significance of the Russian-ordained word "Chechen," which has more recent roots. Eighteenth-century Russian sources called these people the *okochany,* and the territory where they lived, Okotzkaya Zemlya (Kusheva 1997).

On the whole, "Chechen" became a political identification, a metaphoric category linked to the tragic past, which encouraged Chechens to believe that in "their own" state everything would be set right. In some ways, the "revolution" and the Chechen war created a new group identity—an identity based on both historic and invented precedents. This is a widespread phenomenon among ethnic groups in the North Caucasus (see Shnirelman 2001).

DIFFERENTIATING AMONG CHECHENS

Interviews demonstrate that grassroots self-perceptions can change with time. After the war, some of the historical themes and subjects, such as the historical discrimination against Chechens, were replaced by internal distinctions and contradictions. Most discussed was the distinction between highland and lowland Chechens *(gornye* and *ploskostnye).* The following interviews suggest some of the forms the tension took:

> I have lived in Kazakhstan longer than in Chechnya. Half my children stayed there, and half have moved to Groznyy. So I can compare life here and there; I know lots of different people. And I can tell you this: for some reason, all the highlanders supported Dudayev. Even in Kazakhstan, where there's no war, the Chechens split into two factions—the highlanders there are all for Dudayev. Those with more understanding and conscience keep silent, but in their hearts they are against him.
>
> That's how it is: the highlanders are brazen folk, always trying to bully you, to shout you down. We keep apart from them, we don't talk back, but they're out to provoke us. They envy us. But why should they? Whatever I have, I've earned it by working hard since my childhood. I remember when I was a little girl, before the deportation, they would bring cheese or lard down from the mountains to the market—and they would look like wolves, hating you. I think it was a mistake for the Russian authorities to resettle them from the highlands down here. They'd be better off left up there with their herds, instead of getting the upper hand here with their numbers. Now they show their hatred. (Zura M.)

What do the highlanders, in turn, think of lowlanders and themselves? Here is an interview with a highland Chechen:

> I have been farming for forty-eight years, since I first went out to work in the fields with my father when I was twelve, back in Kazakhstan. Ever since then I have been farming, and I have taught my children to do it. So this war is to me like a comb for a bald man. And so are all Dudayev's doings. But when the lowlanders badmouth him, I take offense. I was taken to Kazakhstan as a lad, and when I returned, they didn't let me settle in the mountains, so I've lived forty years here in Zakan-Yurt. I have forgotten the highland speech, and all my children have the lowland dialect. You might think that we have all become one, but no! There's always someone to sneer at my highland talk—meaning we're illiterate, less cultured than they are. So I was proud of Dudayev—for once, we had our highlander president. They said on television that he came of Jewish stock—we call them *tati.* I don't care. There are all sorts of people among the Chechens: Turks, Arabs, Nogai, Azeris. . . . We are all pilgrims in this world. But when they speak against us highlanders, I bristle. I've sent all my children to colleges. My youngest daughter is now at college. Are we any worse than the lowlanders? (Isa I.)

At least one cause of this differentiation is the highlanders' resentment of the historical intra-Chechen perception of them as inferior. Not allowed to settle in their old mountain villages upon returning from exile, they were forced to find their bearings in the lowland communities, where they were "aliens." This led, in turn, to the dispute over who the more genuine Chechens are, the highlanders or the lowlanders.

But this bifurcation is far from straightforward. On the one hand, there is no *teip* that is settled exclusively in the mountains, and on the other all Chechens, even lowland Chechens, have links with origins in the mountains.

The term "highlander" *(gornye)* in fact has little historical grounding. It is a modern intra-Chechen stereotype of the village bumpkin—uncouth, unshaven, aggressive, and pro-Dudayev. Lowlanders tend to exaggerate the highlanders' numbers, although even before the war only a small part of the population lived in the mountains. The ethnographer Yan Chesnov is right in insisting that a division of Chechens into two groups—flatlanders and mountain folk—is a mistaken and historically unfounded dichotomy (Chesnov 1999: 68–69). What is missing in his analysis is how this dichotomy managed to become an issue in a war-torn society when practically all non-Chechens had left the territory and in-group dispositions became no less earnest than those observed between groups. This is in fact a more general phenomenon for the post-Soviet regions where ethnic Russians or other "non-natives" have left local societies and this absence of "outsiders" has helped precipitate tensions within an indigenous group itself based on small perceived cultural differences.

In conclusion, I want to make the following generalization based on my

Chechen research: whether in conflict or not, a group or institution often tends to produce its own image of unity, notwithstanding that its members live in a social reality of great diversity. I have tried to give a brief sense of the changing Chechen identities and selective self-images generated by the crude realities of deportation and war, as well as by the cacophony of the failed communist order. During the conflict, Chechen perceptions and loyalties were never one-dimensional. Amid the violence and destruction, Chechens were often torn between painful polemics and options.

FIVE

The Road to War

The idea of Chechen self-determination as a form of nonnegotiable secession first arose under Mikhail Gorbachev's policy of perestroika, when nationalism on the periphery overpowered the process of democratization pursued by both reformist communists and their radical-democratic opposition. Ethnic nationalism demonstrated a great mobilizing power, and the granting every Soviet ethno-nation its own state was viewed as natural, desirable, and democratic. Seemingly, all the necessary preconditions for putting this idea into practice existed. Fifty-three autonomous ethno-territorial entities nurtured by the Soviet system, and above all, the fifteen union republics—with a variety of state institutions, ambitious bureaucrats, and intellectual elites hungering for the supreme power that had hitherto belonged exclusively to the Kremlin—aspired to sovereign statehood.

The rising radical Soviet/Russian democrats preached the virtue of ethno-national self-determination as a basis for building "normal" states, and to that extent they encouraged and supported nationalist movements in the Soviet autonomous territories. It was the Moscow radicals who first publicized a draft of the so-called Sakharov Constitution, which sought to proclaim a "United States of Europe and Asia" through granting full independence to all fifty-three Soviet "nation-state formations" (there was a four-tier hierarchy of ethno-territorial autonomous entities: the union republics, the autonomous republics, the autonomous *oblasts*, and the autonomous *okrugs* (see further Suny 1993, 1998; Tishkov 1997a). As with all utopian projects, self-determination for every Soviet ethno-nation seemed at the time both appealing and likely to be easily realized.[1]

Not only representatives of top-ranking union republics like Estonia, Latvia, and Lithuania but also leaders of "double minority" territories (notably Abkhazia and South Ossetia in Georgia and Tatarstan and Bashkiria in the Russian Federation) were enthusiastic about this program. The Checheno-Ingush Republic was not the first to engage in a political clash with the authorities of the USSR and the Russian Federation on this topic, but neither was it among the last. The old political elite of Chechnya, led by the ethnic Chechen Doka Zavgayev, first secretary of the republic's Communist Party since 1988, preferred to move more cautiously than had more radical leaders in other republics, such as Vladislav Ardzinba in Abkhazia, Mintimer Shaimiev in Tatarstan, and Murtaza Rakhimov in Bashkiria. On November 27, 1990, the Supreme Soviet of the Checheno-Ingush ASSR adopted a declaration on sovereignty and established the conditions under which the republic would agree to sign Gorbachev's new Union Treaty. The declaration aimed to transfer the North Ossetia territory of the Prigorodny *raion* "back to the Ingush people." It is worth noting that this declaration was promulgated under Zavgayev's rule and under his personal control. The dangerous game of challenging the status quo had thus begun before General Dudayev came to power in Chechnya.

Within the republic and among influential Moscow Chechens, a still more radical political scenario took root with the creation of the Vainakh Democratic Party, and on November 25, 1990, a National Congress of the Chechen People (OKChN) was convened under the leadership of Zelimkhan Yandarbiev, Yusup Soslambekov, Beslan Gantemirov, and Yaragi Mamodayev. The OKChN aimed both to bring about a democratic transformation in the republic and to protect the "national rights" of the Chechen people. According to the chairman, Soslambekov, the Congress of the Chechen People was formed as a result of "local surveys." One thousand delegates attended, along with invited guests such as Dzhokhar Dudayev. The resolution adopted by the Congress focused on ways to help ameliorate "a whole range of specific national problems that have come to confront the Chechen people, and must be resolved to secure Chechnya's further development as a nation." These included eliminating discrimination against Chechens in general and against Chechen representation in the organs of federal power. Also noted were "delays by the central government in resolving the problems of Aukhov Chechens [Akkin Chechens living in Dagestan], the need to restore the Ingush Autonomous Republic, and the plight of more than 230,000 Chechens compelled to live beyond the boundaries of their national state."[2] The Chechen nationalists thus sought to unite the Chechen nation (*ethnos*) on "their own" territory. They saw expanding the territory and returning those "forced" to live outside of it as a natural condition of appropriate political development.

The November 1990 resolution declared the Chechen Republic to exist within the borders of the entire Checheno-Ingush ASSR, with the exception of two western sections, which were "assigned" to the Ingush (who would supposedly return to their 1934 boundaries). In Dagestan, the Akkin Chechens would have their former lands returned, and in Chechnya itself, the influx of immigrants from outside was to be limited, "with the exception of persons of Chechen nationality." The Congress approved measures supporting the Chechen language and culture, the Muslim religion, and restitution of their losses for those previously deported.

But nationalism, in asserting itself, relies on its own version of "national history." Because the works of the local historian V. B. Vinogradov on Chechnya's "voluntary merger with Russia" did not reflect the dominant consensus on the subject of the allegedly deeply rooted autonomous nature of the Chechen people, the Congress deprived him of all his awards and professional titles, as well as of his citizenship in the republic.[3] Furthermore, it resolved to introduce nationwide censure of any Chechen who supported the "propaganda of Vinogradov's pseudoscientific conceptions." The Congress also passed a set of proscriptive ethnic rules, for example, making "persons of non-native nationality" ineligible for the posts of chairman of the KGB, minister of internal affairs, or procurator of the republic. Clearly, the Congress envisioned ethnic Chechens as politically dominating the republic and as the exclusive owners of its resources.

Dzhokhar Dudayev became the leader of this new "Chechen nation." Born in 1944, only a few weeks before Stalin's Chechen deportation, Dudayev spent his first thirteen years in Kazakhstan. After graduating from night school, he enrolled in flight school, and then at the Tambov Military College. He served in the military as a pilot in Siberia, Ukraine, Afghanistan, and Estonia, and later held a high command post in the long-range strategic air forces. His life exemplified the career of a successful Soviet military officer. Married to a Russian, and having almost never lived in Chechnya, Dudayev had little connection with the republic. Nonetheless, he maintained a working knowledge of the native language and possessed a strong sense of Chechen identity.

Chechens in successful administrative posts in the Soviet Union held special significance for Chechens in the republic, since they bore testimony to the possibility of upward mobility in Soviet society. In Soviet times, members of non-Russian nationalities often competed to be "heroes of the Soviet Union" (the highest decoration in the USSR) and sought to promote "native sons" (i.e., non-Russians) to federal administrative positions. Thus it was that influential Chechens, including Doka Zavgayev, beseeched the Russian leadership to make "just one Chechen a Soviet general," and in 1990 Dudayev received that rank. That summer, Dudayev visited the republic, where his relatives held a bountiful feast in honor of "our own general." It was then that Yandarbiev, Mamodayev, Soslambekov, and other activists invited him to play a leadership role in the burgeoning national movement.

"NATIONAL REVOLUTION"

When the second National Congress of the Chechen People (OKChN) was held in July 1991, Dudayev acted as its leader. The OKChN adopted a declaration proclaiming Chechnya separate from both the USSR and the RSFSR (Russian Soviet Federal Socialist Republic), and the executive committee of OKChN, headed by Dudayev and named Nokhchi-Cho, was declared the sole legal organ of power in the new republic. Radical democrats in Moscow were sympathetic, thus strengthening the OKChN's position and exacerbating the political tensions in the republic. Local "informal" leaders in Groznyy soon began engineering demonstrations against the acting authorities. Tainted money from nouveau riche Chechens like Mamadayev paid for impressive meetings in Groznyy. Participants in the Sheik Mansur Square demonstrations, for example, received up to 100 rubles a day (at that time a rather significant sum). Livestock was specially slaughtered and meat prepared in the square for the demonstrators. Most participants were elderly males demonstrating the strength of their spirit through the traditional warrior dance—the *zikr.* Some Chechen elders came to resemble TV celebrities, appearing on many national and international channels.

The post-Soviet collective manifestation is an interesting anthropological phenomenon: it was not a political outpouring in the usual sense; rather, it was a demonstration of group solidarity, a liberated spirit, and a provocative militancy, all of it mobilized and directed by a small circle of activists. I had observed similar demonstrations in South and North Ossetia, Ingushetiya, and Kabardino-Balkaria in situations where violence had either already taken place or was threatened. In September 1992, in the role of federal minister, I personally negotiated a serious crisis of power in the Kabardino-Balkar Republic when the local government building came under siege by demonstrators, the situation verging on open violence. In that case, an agreement on power-sharing reached with "informal" public groups saved the day.

So what is the mechanism of public mobilization, and why did order in Chechnya collapse so easily? According to Igor Kochubei, the chief of the Checheno-Ingush republican KGB at that time, the organs of state security constantly monitored the situation and attempted to control it. Yandarbiev, a writer and one of the Chechen activists, was called into the local state security headquarters for a "prevention talk" and pledged that OKChN would not break the law. Soon after the meeting, however, the KGB headquarters in Groznyy would surrender to Yandarbiev's militant followers after telephone instructions arrived from the federal KGB's deputy head, Viktor Ivanenko, in Moscow. Zavgayev demanded that Moscow take stern measures to disperse the demonstrators, but it was not until September 3, two months after OKChN's pivotal meeting, that the presidium of the Supreme Soviet of the Russian Federation adopted a resolution declaring a state of emergency in the republic. That same day, Dudayev declared the overthrow of the local supreme soviet a symbolic retaliation against pressure from Moscow. The following day, Moscow revoked its declaration of a state of emergency, being unable to implement it in any case amid the political infighting between Yeltsin and Gorbachev. On September 7, a delegation representing various nationalities in Checheno-Ingushetiya arrived in Moscow seeking support for a legitimate government and ways to negotiate the escalating conflict in a more peaceful manner, but it was not received by the chairman of Russia's supreme soviet, Ruslan Khasbulatov, himself a Chechen. Instead, he made an unambiguous choice in favor of Dudayev and against the "procommunist" Zavgayev, who had supported Gorbachev against Yeltsin in the August 1991 putsch.

Igor Kochubei's testimony on March 31, 1995, before the Investigating Commission of Russia's security council, on the causes of the events in Chechnya, confirms this:

> On August 26, Chief Procurator Zemlyanushina arrived in Groznyy. The curators in Moscow did not allow the local KGB to undertake any serious measures. Moscow demanded that the guard be removed from Zavgayev and that support for the local supreme soviet by MVD and KGB structures in this republic be stopped. From August 17 until September 6, when I was relieved of my position, not a single written instruction came from Moscow. We knew that Dudayev had had telephone conversations with Khasbulatov and Aslakhanov [another influential Muscovite Chechen, who headed the committee on legislation and criminal affairs of the Supreme Soviet of the Russian Federation]. On August 25, Yandarbiev, making reference to Moscow sources, reported that Khasbulatov and Aslakhanov had discussed removing Zavgayev from power. People carrying weapons then appeared among the demonstrators for the first time. It would have been easy to confiscate these weapons, but there were no instructions to do so. Besides, this was not a direct function of the KGB. (Author's files)

Dudayev's armed followers then forcibly seized the buildings that housed the government of the republic and the main radio and television center. On September 6, they entered the building where the Chechen supreme soviet was in session. The chairman of the Groznyy city soviet, Vitalii Kutsenko, a Russian by nationality—was thrown from a window to his death.

With Dudayev's sudden ascendance, and in the face of a lack of support from Moscow, the current leaders were demoralized. Khasbulatov and Aslakhanov demanded that the Checheno-Ingush supreme soviet disband itself. After Dudayev seized the government building in Groznyy, representatives of the federal authorities—Gennadii Burbulis, Mikhail Poltoranin, and Galina Starovoitova, later joined by Ruslan Khasbulatov—made a brief trip to Chechnya to finish their business with the old authorities. Too late, they discovered that although Dudayev's forces had dismantled Zavgayev's government, the center had not acquired a new democratic ally. During a public appearance, Dudayev took the microphone after Khasbulatov to say that "no one is going to determine how Chechnya is ruled any more."

Moscow had thus played a decisive role in the overthrow of its own control. According to Kochubei, the KGB had 700 active operatives in Groznyy who, along with MVD forces, were capable of "neutralizing the radicals." There was no mass theft of federal weapons until mid September (Dudayev had previously received weapons from Zviad Gamsakhurdia, the president of Georgia, by way of the territory bordering the Akhmetovskii *raion* of Georgia, which is peopled by Kistins, a kin group of Chechens). Misgivings had only slowly begun to arise among the Muscovite initiators of Chechnya's "decommunization" regarding Dudayev's increasingly independent behavior. As Khasbulatov later admitted, he had spoken "with Yeltsin about adding one more star to Dudayev's shoulder-strap and returning him to the army."

On October 8, 1991, OKChN declared itself the only power in the republic, and on October 27, it held elections for president and parliament. OKChN also declared the mobilization of all able-bodied males between fifteen and fifty-five years of age, and branded all opponents of an independent Chechnya "enemies of the nation." Election turnout was estimated at only 10–12 percent, and voting took place in only 70 of 360 election districts. General Dudayev nonetheless received more votes than any of the three other candidates and became president. On November 1, he issued a decree declaring the sovereignty of the Chechen Republic. This decree created a new state entity within the boundaries of the former Checheno-Ingush ASSR, one that excluded only two of the fourteen administrative regions, which remained part of the Ingush state. Dudayev placed even the Sunzhenskii *raion,* where the majority of the population was Ingush and only a few villages were Chechen, under the control of Chechnya. The Chechen leaders concluded that if the Ingush so desired, they could create their own national movement and take territory from North Ossetia. In an interview with Russian television, Dudayev declared, "The Ingush must travel their own path of hardships in the struggle for their statehood."

The Russian authorities finally began acknowledging that they had lost control of Chechnya, realizing that Dudayev was in no way inclined to consider Moscow's wishes. On November 2, 1991, the Congress of People's Deputies of the RSFSR declared the elections in Chechnya illegal; five days later, the president of the RSFSR issued a decree declaring a state of emergency in Chechnya. In the turmoil that accompanied the dissolution of the USSR, Moscow was not prepared to send troops into Chechnya, however, and the decree was set aside by Russia's supreme soviet on November 11. In Chechnya, this decision was interpreted as a significant victory over Russia and a de facto recognition of the republic's independence.

The Yeltsin-Gorbachev rivalry had paralyzed the operations of government in Moscow and indirectly contributed to Chechen separatism. Vice President Alexander Rutskoi reported at hearings before the State Duma's (federal parliament) investigation of the events in Chechnya that, toward the end of August or the beginning of September, he had questioned whether various activists were acting illegally in Chechnya, but President Yeltsin had told him not to interfere. When attacks on the state authorities and seizures of weapons began, a proposal was drafted for Soviet troops to blockade Chechnya, and for special forces to be dispatched if necessary. "The appropriate draft of the decree was prepared, but the president then disappeared for five days, and there was no contact with him whatsoever."[4] The confusion within Moscow's leadership also affected the republics. On November 7, a reconnaissance group from the Soviet army was sent to Groznyy Airport. They did not use force, however, because someone, "possibly Gorbachev, gave the command to break off the operation. The military hardware was sent to Mozdok [a city and military base with an airport in North Ossetia], and the personnel to Vladikavkaz [the capital city of North Ossetia]." Vadim Bakatin, head of the Soviet Union's KGB, and Viktor Barannikov, minister of internal affairs, refused to undertake any measures involving force in Chechnya, because the orders to do so had been issued by Yeltsin, and not by Gorbachev, who formally retained power in the Soviet Union, which had not yet been dissolved. For Gorbachev, Yeltsin was his own Dudayev. Khasbulatov, in hearings in the State Duma in February 1995, stated: "In order to thumb their noses at Yeltsin, on Gorbachev's behalf, none of the Union ministers wanted to implement the decree of the president of the Russian Federation." Instead, Dudayev and his supporters were permitted to take charge in the Checheno-Ingush Republic.

THE FAILURES AND MISCALCULATIONS OF CHECHEN SECESSION

By the end of 1991, the "Chechen revolution" had assumed its own independent character. Local residents attacked various military installations, where Russian troops were facing their own problems. According to General P. A. Sokolov, commander of the 173rd Training Center of the North Caucasus Military District in Groznyy, there were 653 officers and only about 300 enlisted men in his center. In February 1992, Dudayev's armed personnel moved into the military settlement. "Shamil Basayev sat constantly in my office, a real bandit who kept asking me to give him a machine gun," General Sokolov recalled at a session of the commission of the security council on March 31, 1995.[5]

At the beginning of June 1992, Dudayev decided to expel federal troops from Chechnya and delivered an ultimatum to the local commander to leave, sending women and children to blockade the military barracks. On June 6, the commander of the North Caucasus military district ordered General Sokolov (by telephone from Vladikavkaz!) to leave the territory of Chechnya. But only part of the enormous military arsenal there was carried away; the rest was mined and left under light guard. Using the civilian population as a shield, Dudayev managed to seize most of these weapons as the troops withdrew. This amounted to 40,000 automatic weapons and machine guns, 153 cannons and mortars, 42 tanks, 18 "Grad" vehicle-mounted rocket launchers, 55 armored personnel carriers, and 130,000 hand grenades. Dudayev also gained control of 240 training airplanes, five fighters, and two military helicopters, which had been left at local airfields. Alexander Rutskoi, at the hearings of the State Duma, offers another version of how Chechnya successfully armed itself: "Weapons were sold to the Chechens by the local military. Even some of the weapons of the Trans-Baikal Military District were sold to Dudayev at clearance prices."[6] A report in the press stated that General Sokolov himself had been involved in the sale of weapons: "Thank you, you have made me rich," were his farewell words to Dudayev.

The possession of an enormous military arsenal radically changed the internal dynamics in the republic. Local military groupings emerged, headed by charismatic leaders, and an emotionally charged climate of insurgency and of "the people's war" took hold in Chechnya. Individual warriors, some of whom had a criminal past, soon acquired a Robin Hood–like fame among the people. Their first "military successes" came in Abkhazia, where their "Abkhazian battalion" headed by Shamil Basayev supported the Abkhazian separatists in their fight against Georgia.

A second important step in the formation of the self-proclaimed state was the framing of new political and legal structures for governing public life. Local intellectuals prepared a constitution for the Chechen Republic (Ichkeria) imbued with a spirit of representative democracy and secular law. Islam was relegated to a minor ritual role; the constitution made no mention of Islam or Allah, and religious liberty was recognized for all citizens. The constitution placed no restrictions on its citizenry on the basis of ethnicity or religion.

From the very beginning, however, the erection of the new state faced serious problems. In the first place, the constitution called for a tripartite division of state power into legislative, executive, and judicial branches, but President Dudayev soon violated this arrangement, totally dominating the political arena. The initial euphoria from the presidential elections quickly evaporated, and opposition to Dudayev and his policies grew. The parliament of the Chechen Republic set the date of June 5, 1992, for a referendum on the question of the form of power in the republic, aiming for the dissolution of Dudayev's presidential style of administration. In response, Dudayev simply dissolved parliament and introduced direct presidential rule. His armed soldiers took over the parliament building, killing several opposition deputies and arresting others. Opposition parties and newspapers were simply outlawed.

The 1992 fact-finding mission of the London-based NGO International Alert summarized the dissatisfaction with Dudayev as follows:

1. Dudayev has done little to consolidate Chechen statehood, and has been very slow to implement economic reform. His military background has not equipped him to develop a clear concept of political leadership or an understanding of the complexities of forging a democratic government.
2. He has gathered a small clique of followers around him and governs arbitrarily and secretively. As a result he has fallen increasingly under the influence of corrupt "mafia" types and political adventurers.
3. Dudayev's response to any form of opposition criticism has been to stir up fears of Russian intervention, which frustrates efforts to initiate a rational negotiation process with Russia. He thus plays into the hands of conservative party and military elements in Russia who advocate "settling" all Caucasian problems by force. (Chechnya Report 1992: 50)

From the very beginning of the "national revolution," violence and social disruption increased in Chechnya, as did the militarization of marginal social groups, especially unemployed young men from the countryside. The aggression targeted ethnic "aliens," particularly Russians, most of whom lived in Groznyy. According to data of the MVD of Russia, in 1992–93, perhaps 600 premeditated murders were committed in Chechnya per year—seven times more than for 1990 (Gorlov 1995). Many well-known residents of Russian origin in Chechnya were victims of the violence. As Dzhabrail Gakavev explained, "Chechen marginals were ready to rob everybody, irrespective of their nationality, but Russians were an easier target, since they could not defend themselves, unlike Chechens, who have many relatives."[7]

These actions, taken collectively, generated a profound economic crisis in Chechnya. Although once a reasonably prosperous region, within two years, the republic had been transformed into one of the most socioeconomically crisis-ridden regions in Russia. Overall production fell by about 60 percent per year in 1992 and 1993. More than two-thirds of Chechnya's industrial production came from the oil and gas industries, which were heavily dependent on suppliers and consumers in other regions of the former USSR. Concurrently, there was a mass exodus of the Russian population. These were generally the most qualified professionals in Chechnya, those on whom the republic's oil and gas enterprises depended. According to the Federal Migration Service of Russia, from 1991 to 1993, more than 90,000 people left the republic.

But the departure of the Russians did nothing to improve the local employment situation. Unemployment was about 33 percent before Dudayev came to power and grew rapidly with the economic crisis. Groznyy filled with crowds of angry young people for whom participation in the revolution became the only "worthy" and reasonable occupation. Public health and education collapsed. Many schools closed, and most retirees ceased receiving pensions and social assistance in spite of ongoing transfers of funds from the federal budget for salary and social payments. Small elite groups, on the other hand, enriched themselves easily in this atmosphere of disorganization. Data on the capital assets held by Dudayev or others are unavailable, but tales of corruption and plundering certainly circulated among Chechens. When I asked in 1995 why Dudayev did not want to end the war, a field commander answered:

> Dzhokhar [Dudayev] and others like him are bound together. . . . With the pension and oil [money] that his circle has gobbled up, you could build a republic like Kuwait! If even 5 percent of the sale of oil were given to the needs of the population, how we could live! . . . The children would not starve, and our parents would not have to go to Ingushetiya and Dagestan to get their pensions. . . . They've swallowed up the oil together: he gobbled it, Gantemirov gobbled it, Mamodayev gobbled it, and now they sit there as a government of popular trust.[8]

This Chechen fighter's words reveal one of the characteristic threads of the poetics of self-proclaimed secession: the hope of a more prosperous life. Throughout the former USSR, this perception is prevalent among nationalist movements, together with the idea, nourished by the dominant public discourse, that one or another region or ethnic group is the object of repression and theft on the part of the government or of the people.

For the initiators of independence and certain other segments of the population, establishing a "free state" can bring quick rewards. Beginning in 1992, Chechnya paid no taxes to the federal budget, but in that same year the republic received more than 4 billion rubles in the form of various subsidies. According to Yegor Gaidar, economic and financial relations with the separatist regime represented a complicated problem for the federal government:

> The government continued to ship crude oil to the Groznyy oil refinery from other regions of Russia, although in 1992 delivery was curtailed by one-third (from 14 to 9 million tons) and another cut of 5 million tons was planned for 1993. . . . On May 10, 1993, Dudayev asked me to set an export quota at 2.5 million tons, but the Ministry of Fuel and Energy, which was the patron of the plant in Groznyy, set an export quota of just 230,000 tons. . . . Until March 1993, Chechnya received money from the federal pension fund, which was controlled by the Supreme Soviet [of the Russian Federation].[9]

Dudayev did make some attempts at reaching a compromise. His appeal to the first vice premier of the government of the Russian Federation, dated May 10, 1992, deals with the problem of 1992 export quotas for oil products. Dudayev proposed drawing up an intergovernmental agreement on this question in order to lay down "good-neighborly relations between the Chechen Republic and Russia" and to provide the "necessary financial basis for resolving the most pressing socioeconomic and ecological problems." Federal authorities could not, however, accept Dudayev's formulation of the problem to be addressed, because it presumed that Chechnya was no longer part of Russia. Dudayev perceived the problem quite differently:

> Let us remember that in the Chechen Republic there developed a situation that was in clear contradiction with common sense: although possessing vast stores of the highest-quality oil in the territory of the countries of the CIS [Commonwealth of Independent States—the title of the alliance of twelve post-Soviet states], processing yearly up to 15 million tons of crude oil, entering the republic from Russia, the Chechen Republic is nonetheless the poorest region of the former USSR, ranks lowest in social security, has the highest indices for infant mortality, unemployment, environmental pollution, cancer, and tuberculosis. At the same time, the funds coming into the republican budget from the activity of the oil-extracting and processing complexes are unsatisfactorily (not to say offensively) small, which does not allow placing the solution of a single national problem of Chechnya on the agenda.[10]

There can be no doubt that maintaining the freedom to export petroleum products throughout Russia brought solid personal rewards to certain leaders, including Dudayev. But there were hundreds and possibly thousands of young male Chechens who exchanged the longtime practice of seasonal "moonlighting" for making shopping trips to Turkey and other countries, thus providing themselves with a reasonable means of subsistence. Every month, 100 to 150 Russian airline flights flew out of Groznyy to foreign destinations. A small-scale but energetic barter trade stimulated economic activity and gave the appearance of a market saturated with goods, chiefly at the level of street trade. The portrait of a typical Chechen fighter painted by a journalist in December 1994 illustrates this:

> He is twenty-five, wears a black leather jacket and blue jeans, and carries a Kalashnikov automatic. In peacetime he flies regularly to Iraq and buys clothes, shoes, kitchen appliances, TV stands, and other things. Thus, his main "military profession" is as a middle-level wholesale trader bringing in middle-level revenues. Dudayev, as president of an independent Chechnya, is completely irrelevant to him. What are not irrelevant are his business, his wife and children, and his house, which he is ready to defend by force of arms. (*Izvestiia,* January 6, 1995, 2)

The lack of federal control in Chechnya made it possible to transform it into a base of operations for Russia's wider criminal community. As early as 1992, Chechnya became a center of counterfeiting and the production of false documents. In 1993 alone, approximately 4 billion counterfeit bills of Chechen manufacture were confiscated throughout Russia. Russian banks lost some 4 trillion rubles through forged letters of credit involving Chechen criminal groups. The North Caucasian nationalist organization Confederation of the Peoples of the Caucasus (KNK) made Chechnya its military and political base. One of its leaders, Yusup Soslambekov, was also Dudayev's closest advisor and a leader of OKChN, and the leaders of military KNK detachments were always Chechens. This was also when the first Arab and Turkish adventurers, mercenaries, and special envoys began arriving in Chechnya, representatives of Osama bin Laden's business groups from Saudi Arabia among them.

Thus, over the course of three years, an illegitimate, unconstitutional regime, backed by force, imposed itself on Chechnya as the result of an armed coup d'état. What kind of politics was pursued by the federal authorities in response to this challenge, especially after Yeltsin ousted Gorbachev from the Kremlin and the political chaos that immediately followed brought about the end of the USSR in December 1991?

THE RESPONSE FROM THE CENTER

As I have made clear, to a considerable extent the so-called Chechen national revolution took its material and moral support from Moscow's intellectual and political circles, including federal policymakers of Chechen origin, like the head of the first Russian parliament, Ruslan Khasbulatov, and General Aslambek Aslakhanov, as well as other federal actors from the North Caucasus. The hard reality of a self-proclaimed independent Chechnya under Dudayev and the swiftly developing crisis in the republic took the federal authorities and Russian society by surprise. Even up to the summer of 1991, none of the experts listed Chechnya among potential candidates for secession. The idea of independence from Russia was perceived as a Chechen extravagance, and even after Dudayev's seizure of power in Groznyy, many believed that sooner or later Chechens would realize the absurdity of secession.

In 1992, the members of Gaidar's government thought food shortages, economic reforms, the growing rivalry among political forces in Moscow, and hard dialogue with Tatarstan to be the most pressing issues. Moscow continued to maintain the necessary ties with Chechnya in the socioeconomic and humanitarian spheres. The Checheno-Ingush Republic, and later the Chechen Republic (after June 1992, when the Ingush Republic was constituted by Russia's supreme soviet), appeared in all state plans and programs. Anatoli Chubais's privatization program of 1992 described in detail the privatization enterprises planned for Chechnya. Only a few factories and the oil pipelines were to remain under the control of the federal authorities. Against this wishful thinking in Moscow, corruption and nepotism back up by Kalashnikovs (or military violence) made privatization in Chechnya a quick reality. Private citizens even tapped oil pipelines. "If something is on your territory, that means it's yours, even if it's a pipeline," the "field commander" Ballaudi Movsaev remarked.

In many other aspects of its public life, apart from economics and federal financial transfers, Chechnya remained in Russia. Moscow newspapers and TV broadcasts were received in Groznyy. Migrations of Chechens from and to other regions of Russia, especially of young entrepreneurs and members of their families, continued on an unprecedented scale: by some estimates, in Moscow alone, the Chechen community had grown to 40,000 (it had numbered 8,000 in 1989). Not by any means did all of these Chechens belong to the criminal world: many were successful businessmen and academic or cultural figures, as well as those pursuing diasporic activities through the respectable Association of Rossiyan Chechens and Chechen Cultural Center. In spite of shortages of resources in Chechnya and in the country at large, scholars and humanitarian intellectuals tried to maintain professional ties as well.

Moscow did make several attempts to normalize the situation in Chechnya. The sessions of the government of the Russian Federation, in the period from February to October 1992, did not specifically discuss Chechnya, but as Yegor Gaidar reported, "at the sessions of the security council, the question of Chechnya was discussed many times, and we tried to avoid the implementation of forceful measures. . . . The Ministry of Security spoke against the adoption of force."[11] Moscow knew that although Chechnya possessed an enormous arsenal of weapons, no units aside from the so-called presidential guard stood ready for battle. What Moscow did not understand was that because the civilian population, too, possessed a multitude of weapons, they could quickly be mobilized for combat, especially under the pretext of fending off "external aggression."

The first real attempt to employ the Russian army against Chechnya occurred in the fall of 1992, during the Ingush-Ossetian conflict in North Ossetia (see Tishkov 1997a: 155–82). Large army units, including tanks, were deployed in North Ossetia with no military justification. Yegor Gaidar arrived in Vladikavkaz, visited Nazran, inspected the Russian military regiments deployed short of the border with Chechnya, and, as he himself admitted, "was convinced of the low morale and other aspects of preparedness of the [Russian] troops." He invited Yaragi Mamodayev, deputy chairman of the cabinet of ministers of the Chechen Republic, to a meeting and reached an agreement with him on the withdrawal of troops, later noting,

"I persuaded Boris Nikolayevich Yeltsin to make good on this agreement."[12] On November 13, 1992, Sergei Shakhrai, who succeeded to my ministerial position and who was also the head of the provisional administration for the territories of North Ossetia and Ingushetiya (an agency established after the Checheno-Ingush violent conflict took place late October 1992), met with representatives of Chechnya and agreed to the protocol, which was signed two days later by the deputy head of the provisional administration, Alexander Kotenkov, and by Mamodayev.

January 1993 saw negotiations in Groznyy between the Russian delegation, headed by Shakhrai and Ramasan Abdulatipov, chair of the chamber of nationalities of the Russian parliament, and representatives of the parliament of the Chechen Republic, headed by its chairman, Khalil Akhmadov. They agreed to prepare a treaty between the Russian Federation and the Chechen Republic on the delimitation and mutual delegation of powers. The following day, Dudayev dismissed the talks, however, stating that "no political agreements with Russia are possible." This generated serious disagreement between the president and the parliament, whereupon Dudayev dissolved parliament by force and sent the head of the government, Mamodayev, into retirement. Dudayev would agree only to talks with Yeltsin personally, and only on the topic of Moscow's recognition of Chechen independence. On March 30, 1993, he sent Yeltsin a letter stating,

> Dear Mr. President! I express my deep respects, I wish health and good fortune to you and your family, peace and prosperity to the people of the Russian state. I appeal to you in the name of all the Chechen people on a question that has a fateful significance for mutual relations between our states. . . . I appeal to you . . . to discuss the question of recognition by the Russian Federation of the sovereign Chechen Republic. Resolution of this question would remove all barriers in the path to overcoming the many problems in the mutual relations of our states. The Russian Federation would acquire in the Chechen Republic a reliable partner and a guarantee of political stability in the entire Caucasus. I am sure that you, as president of a great power, will show the political wisdom characteristic of you and do everything possible to resolve the question of recognition of the Chechen Republic by the Russian Federation. Our consciences will be clean, both before history and before future generations, if we can smooth out relations between our peoples and guarantee equality and mutually advantageous cooperation between our states.[13]

General Dudayev thus chose to adopt a personal style, not so much to achieve resolution of the conflict as to obtain a meeting with Yeltsin and thereby strengthen his own hand. Several days later, he wrote yet another letter to the president of the Russian Federation, a letter of an even more "personal character," which was not even on official stationery. This letter, rather pretentious in tone, set forth Dudayev's thoughts on the political situation in Russia on the eve of the referendum of April 25, 1993, on constitutional matters:

> Being in possession of vast and, believe me, highly reliable information about the work of the opponents . . . of executive power in Russia and also of those historical reforms for which you so selflessly battle, I would like to protect you from the possibility of further growth of opposition in the Russian Federation, which could lead to unpredictable and irreparable consequences. I would like to direct your attention toward serious analysis of the prognosticated results of the referendum and the postreferendum strategy of action.[14]

Dudayev recommended that Yeltsin settle for the dissolution of the supreme soviet, the calling of elections for a new parliament, and the adoption of a new constitution in September 1993. "In jurisprudence there is justification for a less severe crime that does not entail judicial consequences if it is committed with the aim of preventing a more serious crime. It's the way things are done with the troops: as long as a decision has been made—even if it is incorrect—it is wiser and more expedient to carry it out to the end than to stop halfway and adopt a new decision."[15] Ironically, the similar political stances and levels of concern for civic responsibility of the two leaders led to Yeltsin's prescribing activities along the lines of Dudayev's recipes: Yeltsin dissolved the Russian parliament in October 1993 and then, as "things are done with the troops," took the recommended stance in the course of war in Chechnya.

But Moscow did not awaken to the situation in the Chechen Republic until the winter of 1994. The catalyst was the signing of a treaty between Russia and Tatarstan in February. This peaceful resolution created the opportunity for Russia to propose a similar treaty with Chechnya, one that would divide the plenary power between Moscow and Groznyy and set the boundaries of Chechnya's sovereignty. The proposal, however, came too late. Sergei Filatov, head of the presidential administration of the Russian Federation, defined the "three stages" of the Chechen crisis: "The first stage was winter–spring of 1994, when negotiations and the meeting of Boris Nikolayevich [Yeltsin] with Dudayev were being prepared. The second stage was June–July, when the internal settling of scores and the mass annihilation of people by Dudayev began; by this alone, he crushed all hopes for a meeting. Everyone understood that he thirsted for a meeting to bolster his authority, which had been shaken and was perhaps already undermined. At this stage, the Kremlin gave its support to the provisional council formed at the Congress of the Chechen People, which stood in opposition to Dudayev. . . . The third stage was the summer and autumn, when Dudayev began to shift the terms of conflict from political confrontation to military action."[16]

Throughout these stages, the internal dynamics of political leadership in

Moscow had played a major role. After the adoption of the new constitution in December 1993, the elected parliament was less compromising on the issue of separatism in the republics and the preservation of Russia's territorial integrity. As to ratification of the Tatarstan treaty, the federation council, in the opinion of the then presidential adviser Emil Pain, would "certainly reject it."[17] In March 1995, the State Duma adopted a new resolution (proposed by Sergei Shakhrai) concerning the Chechen Republic, one that excluded the possibility of direct negotiations with Dudayev. The Duma required that before negotiations for a treaty with Chechnya could be undertaken, new elections would have to be held. It also recommended that in preparing the treaty, the central government should establish political contacts with forces opposed to Dudayev.

Despite the Duma resolution, on April 14, Yeltsin officially instructed his government to hold consultations with Groznyy and to prepare a treaty with the Chechen Republic. This approach, which recognized Dudayev's legitimacy, provoked mixed responses. Emil Pain notes "several obvious peculiarities," such as the three-month delay in forming the delegation for the negotiations, as well as the appointment at its head of Shakhrai, a person Dudayev had called "an enemy of the Chechen people." Shakhrai opposed the use of force but was unable to resolve the crisis, and therefore stepped down. Proponents of the use of force against Dudayev's regime replaced him. We can only agree with Pain's conclusion that "Russian political reality at that time was such that the president was forced to create the appearance of negotiations."[18]

AN EARLY EVALUATION

The Chechen crisis can be described as an intrastate conflict, with one side striving to secede from the other so as to build a new state structure under the claim of ethnic nationalism. Dan Smith, director of the International Peace Research Institute in Oslo (PRIO), has calculated that of the fifty-two armed conflicts of various sizes that took place in forty-two states in 1993, thirty-six, in thirty states, had ethno-national characteristics; that is, at least one side could be identified as belonging to a distinct ethnic group. So it was with the Chechen crisis.

Many representatives of the intellectual and political elite in Russia supported the "Chechen revolution" in the autumn of 1991. In a doctrinal and political sense, Chechnya's "national independence" was legitimated by both Russian ideology and political practice—especially the belief, in the early years, that democratic transformations would naturally be realized by establishing sovereignty on an ethnic basis.

For many reasons, Chechnya was the first to fully implement this radical view of sovereignty. First, the Chechens, although one of the largest minority groups in the Russian state, were also one of the least assimilated into Russian culture and felt a historical sense of injured collective dignity. Neither the Russian state nor Russian society in general understood this. None of the programs of liberalization and social transformation begun under Gorbachev allowed for even symbolic gestures toward healing the profound trauma of deportation.

Second, Chechnya had suffered from many social problems, including high unemployment, a relatively low standard of living, and a general lack of modernization. This proved to be fertile ground for the rise of both criminal activity and armed militias. Chechens saw many of these social, political, and cultural inequalities as following ethnic lines and deeply resented it.

Third, from the 1960s through the 1980s, some Chechens, especially townspeople, had been on a fast track to modernization. They acquired higher education and became politicians, scholars, soldiers, and administrators of the economy. Under the collapse of the unitary Soviet system and the weakening of the Communist Party *nomenklatura,* this new elite formulated claims "in the name of the people" for more equitable redistribution of power and greater priority in access to resources. Independence from the federal center, as they practiced it, meant more rewards for local leaders than for the general populace. Some Chechen leaders, with the support of certain politicians at the Russian center, as well as in diaspora communities, mobilized part of the population around the slogan of ethnic self-determination. Dudayev's accession to power, which began as part of the decommunization conducted by the center, took the form and rhetoric of popular revolution.

Fourth, what was decisive for the insurrection's success was the transfer of weapons to Dudayev from the arsenals of the Russian army, which allowed him to mobilize an impressive resistance to federal armed forces.

Various means were available to resolve the Chechen crisis without resorting to armed force, and such possibilities existed right up to December 1994. I find it impossible to agree with the opinion of the president of the Russian Federation that "state coercion was used in Chechnya [only] when the federal regime had exhausted all other means of influence." As far back as the autumn of 1991, the federal regime had left much undone that ought to have been done. Throughout the crisis, not a single top government leader contacted President Dudayev directly to listen to his position and propose ways of resolving the conflict. Emotionally charged arrogance and a lack of skilled political diplomacy on many sides helped aggravate the crisis. A political double standard also existed: the Russian armed forces acted quite differently when dealing with analogous events in the Republic of Georgia, and the participation of Russian citizens in the so-called Abkhazian battalion on the side of the secessionist Ardzinba government was permitted.

In reviewing my manuscript, David Laitin raised an important point concerning the character of the war. At some stage in the handling of the rebellion, Moscow lost sight of the important distinction between seeking to impose legality and undermining it. The Russian authorities seriously subverted their own claim to legality when they started to rely on the same tactics as the rebels. The behavior of Yeltsin, Yegorov, Grachev, Barsukov, and many other top politicians and military, not to speak of the rank and file, was incomprehensible from the point of view of a legal modern state. They opted for atrocities, revenge, and other ugly tactics, not only against Chechen fighters, but also against sympathizers and neutral civilians in Chechnya, who were in fact their own compatriots. There are many factors explaining this misbehavior, but in principle it was criminal.

Russian society at large paid dearly for Boris Yeltsin's poorly managed ego. After two years of war in Chechnya, some 35,000 to 40,000 lives were lost. Dzhokhar Dudayev was killed, but he was succeeded by the even more nationalistic Zelimkhan Yandarbiev and his partner Aslan Maskhadov—a military mastermind in command of Chechen guerrillas. Finally, on May 2, 1996, Yeltsin announced his intention to visit Chechnya and meet the separatist leaders, saying, "I could not negotiate with Dudayev. Dudayev was a man the president could not meet."

These miscalculations and blunders can be explained in part by the complexity of the situation in Russia and by lack of experience on the part of the new generation of Russian politicians. Still, the crisis could have been played out at a lower level of confrontation. Indeed, it could even have been resolved within Chechnya itself. No fatal threat to the territorial integrity of Russia existed, but the myth that it did went hand in glove with the myth of Chechen independence. Those who believed in (or exploited) these myths and made decisions on the basis of them were the chief culprits in the profound tragedy that befell the country.

SIX

Dzhokhar

Hero and Devil

It seems to me that the war couldn't have been avoided, no matter what figures were in power. I think of Dudayev as a national hero. It's just that so far, his role hasn't been appreciated by everybody. That will come with time.

KHAVA ISMAILOVA

The people go on listening with the same indifferent humility and still pretend that Dzhokhar [Dudayev] and his ideas mean something to them. The only ones who derive a sincere satisfaction out of this talk and fiction are some old men. It seems they see it as moral vengeance against Russia for the past suffering in their lives.

RUSTAM KALIYEV

Academics rarely give enough attention to the role of charismatic leaders in a conflict, and in Chechnya, the war was a highly personal struggle in which charismatic leaders strongly affected the flow of events. Dzhokhar Dudayev, formerly a general in the army of the USSR, and president of the self-proclaimed republic, stands out as its preeminent hero. In order to understand the emergence of such leaders in the post-Soviet context, the following questions need to be addressed: How did a new breed of "national leaders" emerge from liberalization? How did the post-Soviet populace perceive them, and why did the masses follow such leaders? It is on this last question that we shall focus most closely, since the impact of Dudayev's leadership role in determining the events in Chechnya cannot be overestimated.

THE MEDIA IMAGE OF DUDAYEV

A commonly heard idea in Russia's academic and public discourse is that when civilizations are in conflict, in the natural course of things, the ethnic groups, or peoples, of which they are composed throw up leaders who express their collective will to realize a historically predestined outcome. In other words, if Dudayev had not risen to power, someone else would have, and everything would have played out in similar fashion. As Dudayev's former fellow serviceman General A. N. Osipenko remarked, "He did not choose the national idea, that idea chose him" (*Izvestia*, November 2, 1991). Russian political writers and academics still tend to think in the old Soviet categories of "popular movements" and "revolutions." They believe that states are always built on an ethnic basis, that a forceful dismantling of an existing order is just, and that armed secession is moral when it is justified in terms of "national" (read ethnic) self-determination. It is rarely admitted that a leader creates, or at the very least significantly affects, the so-called "revolutionary movement" on his own. There is a deep-seated belief that tectonic societal shifts cannot be explained by small things like individual or tiny group ambitions and interests.

The Russian journalist Irina Dementieva described her impressions of Groznyy in 1991 in the following romantic and heroic terms:

> Stretched across the pediment of the government house in Groznyy is a poster with a quotation from the Koran: "Sow peace among you—Mohammed." And just below: "Fatherland or Death!" One translated from Arabic; the other, from Spanish. Ancient wisdom and youthful impatience. At the rally, sedate old men wearing high fur caps sit in the front row on chairs. Milling about behind their backs are youths who have yet to have their first shave with starry eyes and [their] grandfathers' guns on their shoulders. (*Izvestia*, November 2, 1991)

In reality, the picture was much more complicated. The middle-aged generation striving for limited resources and available power positions formulated the unrealizable agenda of "national liberation." The older generation brought about the climate of anger and gave the struggle their symbolic blessing. Not all were united in their vision and actions, but the majority hoped to benefit from change, some hoped to make big money challenging the status quo, and a handful dreamed of acquiring the power to rule "their own people." As to the younger generation, they were armed, not with their grandfathers' ancient guns, but with modern weapons from the arsenal left unguarded by the Soviet army, and they became the primary culprits and victims of the violence. Eventually, however, violent conflict affected men and women of all ages; everyone was bound to suffer in a war. Those who perhaps suffered least were the leaders, notwithstanding that some of them, even at the top, may have endured the hardships and wounds of war.

The British journalist and scholar Anatol Lieven offers a frank portrait of Dudayev. Lieven, like others, was struck by the element of acting and posturing in Dudayev's behavior:

> His speech was exaggeratedly clipped, emphatic, martial, and authoritarian. When speaking in public, he combined this with a heavy stress on the last syllables of words. . . .
>
> What part exactly he thought he was playing I've never quite been able to determine, but it was probably a fairly hackneyed version of national hero/wise ruler/visionary/prophet. That aside, an element of play-acting was perhaps also intrinsic to his position. He was, after all, a Soviet general, a man who had spent by far the greater part of his life in the Soviet armed forces, and

there may well have been moments when he wondered what the hell he had got himself into by joining the Chechen revolution. (Lieven 1998: 66)

These aspects of the actor in Dudayev were noted by other observers as well. One interviewee told me that when asked about his health, the general responded by quickly pushing his chair from the table and turning a back somersault. Landing on his feet, he said, "That's the state of my health!" Lieven believes that Dudayev was a "non-Chechen" in many respects and felt awkward in his new Chechen national identity

> because of a personal feeling of insecurity, a feeling that because of his long service in the Soviet military, away from Chechnya and Chechen society, and because of his Russian wife (who never even pretended to convert to Islam) and half-Russian children, and his initially poor grasp of the Chechen language, he was not really a Chechen in the full sense and therefore had to present himself as a 200 percent Chechen nationalist by way of compensation. (Lieven 1998: 66)

To outsiders, particularly Western observers, Dudayev's style strongly suggested the stilted image of a third-world dictator. It was only his anti-Russian stance that elevated him in Western eyes to the status of a hero. Still, Lieven's observations concerning Dudayev's personality give one pause:

> There were indeed moments when I thought Dudayev was mad—or, shall we say, psychologically unstable, with strong features of both paranoia and megalomania, in the clinical sense (this is also the private view of two Western diplomats from the Organisation for Security and Cooperation in Europe (OSCE) who met with Dudayev in 1995, and with whom I have spoken—and this man once commanded a wing of nuclear bombers!). Nothing else, it seemed, could explain his reckless and totally unnecessary verbal provocation of Yeltsin and Russia on several occasions. In one of his first speeches as President on Chechen TV, he accused the Russian secret services of preparing to attack Chechnya with an artificial earthquake—when I visited Chechnya in February 1992 people were still talking about this supposed threat. (Lieven 1998: 67)

A PROUD AND COMPLICATED MAN

Dzhokhar Dudayev came of highland Chechen stock. He never mentioned his *teip* (clan), and in that respect he was similar to many other modern Chechens. The Dudayevs lived in the settlement of Tashkala, on Shakespeare Street. His parents died leaving ten children, of whom Dzhokhar was the youngest. Rising to the rank of major general was a major feat for a Chechen boy who grew up in exile in Kazakhstan and then passed through the grueling mill of military service and study. In fact, prior to his spectacular leadership, he had never lived in Chechnya, had known little of the Chechen language, had learned Chechen history haphazardly from random texts, and had never been a Muslim. But at the same time, people in the Checheno-Ingush Republic whose relatives had attained prominent positions in Russia followed his life with rapt attention. "Their" general's marriage to a Russian woman was a matter of pride, a contribution to the so-called "united family of the Soviet peoples." When journalists congratulated Dudayev on his rank, he replied, "I can tell my compatriots, and all other young people, that nothing is more honorable than the defense of your country."

When he visited his relatives he said, "What do I remember most often? My childhood, of course, the warmth of our family hearth; I will be faithful to it all my life. I remember the hard years of my youth. The years of service and studies in Tambov. I have had ups and downs in my life, but the main thing I learned is the love of my work. I think there is no higher calling than to be a professional defender of our Fatherland" (by "your country" and "Fatherland," Dudayev then meant the Soviet Union, in whose armed forces he served) (Dudayev 1992: 36). By the spring of 1991, however, Dudayev was a Chechen nationalist.

> All my life I've dreamt of seeing my Chechen people independent. When I made statements about it, it was not by chance or on the spur of the moment—I was expressing my faith. I have acquired sufficient knowledge and experience. For years I worked in three possible directions toward solving the problem. I shall not talk about two of them, for they were discarded as needless, but the third direction is open now: it is the way of an open political struggle based on the international norms of statehood and independence accepted by all mankind and won by the peoples. The first two directions are not for the press, but people who are close to me know that they were real. I needed two or three reliable supporters, and I was convinced that we could set our cause in motion. The mechanism for it had been prepared, but now conditions are ripe for an open political fight. (*Kavkaz,* November 3, 1991; Dudayev 1992: 40)

We shall never know the two other ways of reaching independence that Dudayev was not prepared to explain. One might be a terrorist attack. We do know that while possessing access to atomic weaponry as the commander of a long-range strategic aircraft regiment, he was preoccupied with conspiracy and danger, and one of his close associates later witnessed his deep distrust and suspicion of people around him (Abubakarov 1998). In August 1991, he claimed to be able to "foresee" that the anti-Gorbachev push threatened "a repeated deportation of the Chechens," and he later explained all crime in Chechnya in terms of provocation by Russia's secret services (Dudayev 1995: 41, 45).

Rustam Kaliyev told me that Dudayev's suspicions grew increasingly intolerable for the Chechen leaders, including district and municipal administrators. In 1993, when an explosion twenty kilometers from Groznyy killed the Chechen interior minister and his driver, Dudayev claimed that it was an attempt on his own life. He attacked the local prefect and ordered the State Security Department to arrest him. The prefect's relatives defended him at gunpoint, and the order was not carried out. But the next day, the Security Department abducted R. B. Ezerkhanov, head of the administration of Alkhan-Kala (a village six kilometers from the site of the assassination), whom Dudayev suspected of complicity because he had been seen to glance at his watch fifteen minutes before the explosion. A warrant was issued for the arrest of Ch. R. Vakhidov, an Interior Ministry department head, on suspicion of his involvement because he had gone on holiday a week earlier.

Throughout the years of the Chechen revolution, Dudayev made incongruous statements, which were nonetheless approved by the many Chechens who were inclined to trust him rather than their own reason. He told a journalist, for instance, that he had been offered a promotion in the armed forces, "but I chose rather to tell the esteemed Deinekin [commander of the Russian air force] that the highest rank as far as I am concerned is that of an ordinary Chechen" (*Stolitsa* 1992, no. 15: 3). Dudayev may have believed what he was saying at the time, but it would be naïve to think that he acted on it. Yusup Soslambekov told me in private conversation that in the autumn of 1991, Dudayev had asked Zavgayev to make him head of the republic's KGB or the Interior Ministry (see also Soslambekov 1996: 10). After he became president, he expressed his readiness to give up that post "to another citizen" if he were "preferable to the people," even naming the Chechen émigré Abdurakhman Avtorkhanov for consideration. Few of his listeners took him seriously, but it implied that Dudayev had the courage to step down if his people denied him support.

Dudayev invited the well-known and influential Islamic leader Abdul-Baki to Chechnya in hopes of making him the spiritual pillar of his power. Abdul-Baki, an ethnic Chechen, accepted the invitation in 1993, and after having been in the republic a few days criticized the situation there, including the regime and president, on local television, saying: "A state in which even one child, or an adult, is starving while the rulers are well fed cannot be called Islamic. Even less so, if in that country Islam and the Chechen *'adats* [customary law] are used, not for constructive purposes, but for the destruction of society, law, and order. This is dangerous and ruinous for the Chechen people themselves." The next day Abdul-Baki was branded by Dudayev "a spy of Russia's secret services," "vice president of the world's mafia organizations," and a "traitor of the faith." Dudayev stripped him of the title "honorary citizen of the Chechen Republic," awarded to him only a month before, and it was no longer safe even to mention his name in Chechnya. Another spiritual leader, the former mufti of Chechnya Mukhamedbashir-Hadji, when asked why he had left Chechnya, replied, "If I tell the truth, I fear Dudayev; if I don't, I fear Allah." Dudayev listed him as a traitor and infidel too.

To support his positions, Dudayev drew on a treasure trove of writings by ethnic radicals in Russia, the Baltic states, and Ukraine and hired "minority freedom fighters" from other states as advisers. A proud and complicated man, he presented himself and his vision for Chechnya in contradictory ways; he was adamant, fierce, and psychologically unstable. New materials confirm that despite his aggressive nature, he was prepared for a peace agreement with Yeltsin. It is tragic that neither Dudayev nor Yeltsin was politically or emotionally prepared to work together toward a solution while they still had the opportunity to do so.

MASS PERCEPTIONS

Dudayev used simple and emotional themes like freedom, fatherland, and resistance to mobilize people. The following account by an 18-year-old villager from the Vedenski *raion* illustrates his ability to capture people's imagination:

> When Dudayev came to power, I was a student of a *khyvzhar* [Islamic school]. Our teacher told us that Dudayev had been sent to us from heaven, that his real name was Dzhovkhar ("pearls" in Chechen), and that his advent had been predicted in ancient lore. We had many rallies at that time, and all shouted "Allah akbar." Then we chanted "Dzhovkhar! Dzhovkhar!" Our teacher, who was the mullah of our school, also came to the rallies. When I asked him who our enemies were, he answered *gyaurs* [infidels]. He also said that in a dream he had seen Dudayev descending from heaven on wings. "With such a leader we are invincible!" he said. All that people talked about, more and more often, was the war. I also wanted to go to war. (Said-Selim G.)

In war, however, Dudayev's power had its limitations. Chechen combatants were more apt to follow their field commanders than the commander-in-chief. One commander said to me during the war, "I will lay down arms if Maskhadov gives the order. The rest of them, including Dudayev, are nobody to me!"

Some compared Dudayev to other world leaders, as in this conversation overheard by the journalist Irina Dementieva. Two young women—Chechens, to judge from their head scarves—were talking in a bus, "Did you see General Dudayev last night talking on TV? Latin American moustache, dark glasses for some reason—a kind of Pinochet, you know!" Kheda Abdullaeva reminisced about Dudayev's inauguration day:

> I remember the day of Dudayev's inauguration. It wasn't known in Russia then how many people attended it. He was sworn in at the theater and then walked to the Government House among the people, in a huge crowd. It was extraordinary, I felt that something important was happening. I can't say that I

> became devoted to Dudayev right there, but something turned for me then. He was so handsome in his splendid general's uniform. I had the impression that I was seeing so many beautiful faces around me for the first time, and I never really again experienced that. Let's go and see it, we'll never forgive ourselves if we miss it, I told friends.

Though he was widely popular, some refused to accept this charismatic image. Some men, particularly in the military, did not share this glorified opinion of Dudayev:

> You ask me how I came to support Dudayev? Frankly, he made me sick from the start. Dudayev is a clown, and self-important. . . . Only it's not a joke, but a tragedy for the people. I always knew it would be like that. When I first saw him, I immediately sensed the grief he would bring us. He was never himself, always acting someone else. To this day I can't understand how it was that people didn't see that he wasn't even a Chechen like us. He hadn't lived in Chechnya. But he swindled the people all right. It is not for me to solve the puzzle. (Taus A.)

. . .

> At first I thought: here's a man who has become a general, he must have deserved it, he does honor to our people. Besides, I liked the way he looked, always clean shaven, spruced up as an officer should be, whether in uniform or in a civilian suit. I'm also a military man, after all, have served for ten years. . . . [Then] I met the commander of the special unit [i.e., KGB supervision] of the division in which I had served, near Minsk. . . . I won't name him, he's a good man and I don't want him to have any trouble. He told me that after Dudayev ejected [from his plane] when he was shot down several times in Afghanistan and had his brain frostbitten in the low stratospheric air pressure, he was to have been dismissed from the forces. He'd also had some other trouble with his head. Then, instead of dismissal, he was suddenly promoted to general. Normally, there can't be such career leaps in the armed forces, not to a general's rank anyway. Clearly, there was some other service for which Dudayev was so honored. Well, here my old friend suggested to me the answer: Dudayev had long worked for the special services. Otherwise, he could never have had a chance to obtain a general's shoulder straps, no more than any other Chechen serviceman in those years.
>
> I couldn't figure out, though, who he was working for after the KGB was split up in 1991. But my friend was right in saying that special services are as eternal as mankind. And believe me or not, I understood that there was some dirty game going on with the destiny of our people, that we were facing some grave danger. (Kyura A.)

In these recollections, we see different myths about Dudayev's image: (1) the conspiracy version: he wasn't a real Chechen but an outsider sent by the KGB or some other force to do the Chechens harm; (2) the trickster version: *shaitan* [the devil] lives inside him and he is not a real human being; and (3) the insanity version: his brain was frostbitten, resulting in partial insanity, but nobody sees it, or, seeing it, wants to recognize it. All the versions of the Dudayev image, both positive and negative, have this fairy-tale character. It is impossible to pinpoint when these different images gained ground, but they arise frequently in conversations with Chechens and Ingush. The negative view was never due to what he said about Chechen "national independence." The reasons for doubting him included the overthrow of Zavgayev, as well as the profiteering of many in Dudayev's regime. One of my Chechen acquaintances, a modest and timid man, asked me back in 1992, "Why should we have ousted Zavgayev, tell me? He had already done well for himself and all his relatives. And a new leader will come along, hungry for all that, and we'll have to fatten him and his gang up anew. What a burden on the people!"

DUDAYEV AND WAR

Dudayev knew his military trade well and, as many witnesses have pointed out, he viewed war as his primary occupation. When having to live as a civilian, he found his emotional life difficult, by his own admission. In early March 1992, when Dudayev was already president, he lived in a fairly dark, otherwise deserted street of one-story houses in a Groznyy suburb, with guards wearing uniform raincoats, armed with short-barreled automatic weapons of local production. Here is an excerpt from an interview with Gagik Karapetyan:

Dudayev: I come home very seldom. At first glance I have now what may seem like a strange way of life—I can't go to sleep till five or six o'clock in the morning because I constantly mull over variants of this or that decision in my head.

Karapetyan: And what problems don't let you sleep now?

Dudayev: Many problems. The main one is our resistance to the aggression and provocation ordered by Russia's leadership. We have to be on guard every day, every hour. They can't understand the meaning of democracy there. In Ostankino [the Moscow TV tower and studio building], a whole team of journalists is working—on *someone's* orders—to find ways to blacken my image.[1]

Dudayev treated politics and government as a sort of quasi-military game. It became clear with time that he was prepared to risk his own and other people's lives amazingly casually. In his speeches, Dudayev always spoke of the Chechens' singular audacity, their superiority in battle, their supreme morale and other martial virtues, and warned of the Chechen temper and readiness to fight: "I wouldn't advise anyone to anger Chechens—this is extremely dangerous. Our compatriots were dispersed all over the world, after finding no place in the former empire in which they were not branded as 'criminals.' In that long confrontation we have acquired such strength that in any part of the world and at any time, our people can cause great disruption."[2]

Dudayev was convinced, as were some of his close followers, that the achievements of the Chechen revolution were evident in all spheres of life, in the economic as well as the political and military: "Recently, Groznyy was visited by a group of our Estonian friends, who carried out an expert assessment of the work we do. Those doctors of economics reported unreservedly that they were amazed by what we had accomplished over the past period. It would have taken Estonia some three and a half years, they said, to solve so many problems."[3]

More remote sources also offered high praise. Paul Henze, a longtime member of the RAND Corporation, for example, who led the mission to Chechnya by the nongovernmental organization International Alert, wrote a report with two younger authors on "the amazing progress made by the Chechen revolution." Even this sympathetic text, however, gives us pause:

> Dudayev has done little to consolidate Chechen statehood and has been very slow to implement economic reform. His military background has not equipped him to develop a clear concept of political leadership or an understanding of the complexities of forging a democratic government. He has gathered a small clique of followers around him and governs arbitrarily and secretively. As a result he has fallen increasingly under the influence of corrupt "mafia" types and political adventurers. (Chechnya Report 1992: 50)

Preoccupation with external danger was Dudayev's constant theme:

> Dudayev's response to any form of opposition or criticism has been to stir up fears of Russian intervention, which frustrates efforts to initiate a rational negotiation process with Russia. He thus plays into the hands of the conservative party and military elements in Russia who advocate "settling" all Caucasian problems by force. (Ibid.)

In the following account, Alik A., a 35-year-old schoolmaster from Groznyy, describes how Dudayev vacillated between war and peace, finally deciding on war:

> I didn't take part in combat, but I was in the midst of war, both in Groznyy and in the countryside. Shortly before the war, I had been offered a job at the mayor's office. Though my post wasn't a high one, I often met Dudayev and his stooges. I can tell you with confidence that Dudayev wanted war—he craved it, cherished it. In September and October of 1994, several peacekeeping missions came to Groznyy from different regions of the CIS. I was present at all those meetings, and I can bear witness that during his meeting with the

> Chechen delegation from Kazakhstan and in meeting with religious leaders, including the head of Chechnya's muftiyat, Alsabekov, who recently resettled from Kazakhstan, General Dudayev was quite ready to accept Moscow's conditions and prevent the war. . . . Quite suddenly, however, he left the room and went to telephone someone. (I was told this by his secretary. I had to go out to the anteroom and ask her what the matter was, since there was an awkward pause at the meeting. Its participants were exchanging puzzled glances, since it seemed that Dudayev wouldn't be coming back for some time.)
>
> When Dudayev returned, his face was set—nothing human left in his expression, no regret that he was changing his mind and making a decision that would lead to war. He abandoned the almost completed peace settlement with unconcealed pleasure. . . . He rubbed his hands with glee; his eyes, rather dull and uneven in size, were now gleaming, his cheeks were flushed. Can you believe that Dudayev's rise to power was all by chance? No, as with Hamlet, there's method in this madness.

People's perceptions continued to vary: some venerated Dudayev, others despised him. The following statements express some of the range of these views:

> This is what I can tell you, my girl. This Dudayev is of no more use to me than last year's snow. They keep blabbering on television that he is a hero, that he wished his people well. Look out the window: What's left of our city? Dust and wormwood. Is that what he wished us? You needn't go far to see it, no village now, just dozens of poles in the graveyard, or iron pipes decorated on top, standing taller than all the other tombstones. They are in memory of ghazis [Muslim soldiers]. See how many have fallen, and for what? That's the good of your Dudayev. There's never before been a worse enemy to Chechens—a man who would ruin his own people. Now look around—want and misery everywhere. They tell us on television that we have freedom now. What kind of freedom is it if people are starving? There's no freedom if we are so poor and our children can't go to school. The teachers and doctors have all left, and those few who stayed are trying to sell something on the market . . . to keep from dying of hunger. (Zura M.)

. . .

> I don't think we can blame Dudayev for all this. He was a military man, he didn't understand political intrigues or the wily people surrounding him. He was a good, honest man, but not a statesman. He should have chosen intelligent, competent men as his aides and set them to work. He should have given directions, and they would have carried them out. But in reality it was the other way around. His close circle dictated to him what to do. The result was large-scale theft and embezzlement. All state property was stolen: the oil, the museums, everything in the government stores. And Dudayev, the blunt-speaking military man that he was, said when it turned out that the 1991 crops had all been pilfered on the state farms, "Right! It should all belong to the people, not

fatten the state at the people's expense." In such talk, both the state and the people are beggars. But what can you expect from a military man? Another time he said, "He who dares—let him grab; he who is a coward—let him shut up." On the whole, Dudayev was a creature of his retinue. They gave him a lot of money when he was struggling to gain power. And then the same people robbed the state. We know their names. I think they are chiefly to blame for the republic's present poverty. Dudayev wished the people well, but he was surrounded by thieves. (Visit M.)

. . .

Many people think that if Dzhokhar were still in power, everything would be different. He has become a mythological hero. There's a slogan pinned up in Groznyy, "Dzhokhar, come back—these bastards are the limit!" I didn't take him seriously. I thought he'd been in cahoots with Russia, but then . . . he talked of war. . . . I agree the war couldn't be avoided; if not Dudayev, someone else would have been in his place. But whoever that is, nobody gives a thought to the people. The authorities just do nothing. Maskhadov is busy with palace intrigues, he has no time to think of the people. None of them will be able to raise the republic out of this ruin. Someone from outside will have to do it. It's not by chance that in the past the Chechens called for rulers from Dagestan or Kabarda. An outsider could be thanked and sent packing. It's more difficult with local leaders. (Natasha A.)

. . .

I was given some special missions by Dzhokhar, but most of the time I handled the supplies of arms and provisions. More than once I spent the night at his place. He was frank with me. We talked a lot about the future. Dzhokhar thought that the oil fields in Chechnya had not yet been fully prospected, that our land holds untold riches. Kuwait, he would say, can't stand comparison with Chechnya—it has no water, no timber. We can sell water from our springs and drink camel's milk. We could acclimatize camels from Saudi Arabia, they have lots of them there. We could have intellectuals trained in the best universities of the world, and they would gradually oust the Jews. The Jews are a talented nation, but the Chechens have more audacity. We could become the leading intellectual force of the world. I believed all these things that Dzhokhar said. We had long talks about it all. He wished to make his people happy; he was a real patriot. He was an extremely brave person, he knew no fear.

Maybe there was something between Dudayev and Yeltsin. But still, Dzhokhar was tops—he swindled Yeltsin. One man told me that they had quarreled over oil, that Russia was charging Dudayev too high a percentage. I don't think that was important. The main thing is that Dzhokhar won our independence for us. In politics, if you don't cheat, you don't drink champagne. Dzhokhar was tops anyway! (Akhyad Kh.)

POSTWAR GLORIFICATION

After Dudayev's death on April 21, 1996 (his car was hit by an air-to-ground missile), and the Chechen fighters' victory against the Russian army, critical analysis of him ceased. Russian authors took an uncritical attitude toward Dudayev, Chechen writers and propagandists canonized him, and poets preached his virtues. The following poem, "The Great Chechen," by Musa Geshayev (a Chechen poet who lives lavishly in Moscow) is an example:

He was forged by the time, born of the age,
Nurtured by a highlander mother,
Imbued with her warmth,
Unvanquished by enemies.
The great Chechen, the dreamer Dzhokhar
Never sought easy ways,
To the Vainakhs, the children of nature,
He first gave the taste,
The bittersweet taste of freedom!

Similar panegyrics and eulogies abound in Chechnya, particularly in the newspapers. The local press was full of glorified quotations about him. Since March 1997, a daily political newspaper has been published in Groznyy entitled *Put' Dzhokhara* (Dzhokhar's Way) with Dudayev's words taken as the epigraph: "A slave who does not try to shake off his fetters deserves double slavery!" The paper belongs to the national political movement Dzoxaran neq, and its editor, Raisa Dadayeva, and leading journalists are Chechen women fanatically devoted to Dzhokhar's memory.

Any newspaper you happen to pick up extols Dudayev. An editorial entitled "DZHOKHAR: The Hero Never Dies, the Hero Lives Forever" in *Phyarmat* (Prometheus) reads:

"Bring our cause to its completion." That was the last will of the immortal son of the Caucasus who paved the way to victory for the age-old hopes of peoples suffering under imperial oppression. The citadel of that empire—Groznyy—is no more, replaced by a city of your name—Dzhokhar.

You dared challenge the evil empire to whose might and power the whole world bowed—Dzhokhar.

You, like the peaks of the Caucasus, symbolize the reserve and patience on the thorny way toward freedom—Dzhokhar.

You gave us our motto "War in the name of peace," for only war could lead us to peace in the end—Dzhokhar.

You called yourself "a sacrifice of history" and, like Prometheus, you stole the fire to give it to the people—Dzhokhar.

You followed the Nakh proverb, "The stone is left, the water runs off," so you remain forever in the hearts of the people—Dzhokhar.

You rose like a brilliant star to join the constellation of the stars of Islam in the fathomless universe—Dzhokhar.

> Come back to us from heaven on a snow-white steed with the sword of the *turpal* [hero] Ali in your hand—Dzhokhar.

At a ceremony celebrating the 200th anniversary of the birth of Imam Shamil, the journalist G. Esenbayeva wrote:

> As if to remind us that before the war, Ichkeria had had its own aviation, and [that it] should have it again, a Chechen youth was flying in circles above the crowd in a delta-wing plane. He kept zooming down and rising again and waving his hand to the people, who looked up at him smiling and asked, "Isn't that Dzhokhar?" Whatever some of our leaders tell us about his death, the people don't believe it. They are waiting for him to come back, and will wait forever![4]

Even Dudayev's son contributed to the myth. At the founding congress of a military-patriotic union, Dzhokhar's younger son, the 14-year-old Lieutenant Deghi Dudayev, was invited as a guest of honor.

> "What do you think of all that's happening here?" he was asked by a correspondent.
>
> "I think all will be well. Dzhokhar will come back and things will settle into their proper places," he replied.
>
> "Deghi, you are the son of a singular, legendary great man, Dzhokhar Dudayev. How do you feel in that role?"
>
> "I find it very hard."
>
> "You are still so young. Have you any plans concerning Dzhokhar's Way? Do you link your life with that way?"
>
> "I want to go into military service. I will be a flyer. It's my duty, as it is of any Chechen, to follow the way started by my president. Ichkeria should be a sovereign state."[5]

The myth of Dudayev is also used to demean Maskhadov's regime, which is criticized for abandoning Dudayev's ideas. Some of the most radical fighters, acting in the name of the dead hero, have moved outside of Chechnya. The so-called "representative of President Dudayev in Poland," Movsud Dudayev, declared that no one could equal what had been done by Dzhokhar, and newspapers ran headlines like "DZHOKHAR'S WAY COULD BE BLAZED ONLY BY DZHOKHAR!"[6]

Rustam Kaliev noted in spring 1999 that

> Even to discuss the problems created by Dudayev is considered a crime now. Not only to criticize, but even to discuss them is dangerous. At the beginning of 1997, I tried to publish my version of the 1995 events. It was to be a feature article, including bits of an interview with Salambek N. Khajiyev. No paper even dared to show any interest in the material. It was never published. But a file with my photo was opened by the Chechen Security Service. Only the solid support of my relatives prevented them from laying hands on me. Since his death he has been canonized, nearly deified. A type of Lenin, Stalin, and Saddam Hussein rolled into one! "That's what Dudayev thought," "That's what

Dzhokhar wanted" are expressions that have the ring of law, to be neglected by no one, not even Maskhadov.

POST-TOTALITARIAN CHARISMATIC LEADERS

In spite of florid rhetoric about "the people," the Chechen war was a highly personalized conflict. Each region of conflict in the former USSR in fact produced its own warrior-politician. This new cohort of leaders emerged in the institutional and ideological vacuum that prevailed after the collapse of the strict selection and control system that had functioned under the communist regime. Used to one-dimensional thinking and to the one version of events depicted "on TV" or "in the newspapers," these leaders initiated mass-mobilization projects without resources or expertise.

The great men came from a wide range of previous professions: a plant director in Transnistria, a philologist in Abkhazia, an expert on ancient manuscripts in Nagorno-Karabakh, and a schoolteacher in South Ossetia stepped forward to play the part. Chechnya was unlucky, however: it got a real military general.

Gorbachev's liberalization opened the door to many new would-be architects of social space, but it did not change the nature of the available human materials, and it did not increase the expertise capacities of the decision-makers or of those who found themselves in power. Dudayev was a typical "nonsystemic" charismatic whose power lay precisely in putting forth unrealizable projects, in defiance of rational governance and order, in ignoring solutions to practical problems. As M. A. Sivertsev writes, "the charismatic leader seeking a response to the challenges of a transitional and unstable time must find it in a visionary horizon: he must restore the long-lost links with the idealized basics of life. This capacity (his charisma) for restoration of sacral experience gives a leader legitimization of his actions. His malfunctioning and his trivial shortcomings in the formalized-rational sphere are pardoned and even considered as additional evidence of charismatic strength allowing him 'power negligence'" (Sivertsev 1997: 26–27).

Addressing myths of struggle and victory, animosity and revenge, the charismatic leader shapes the perceptions of his followers, and from that success, his personal heroic image acquires needed stability. Thus, he constructs a closed subculture that develops its own language, its own code, and its own practices, with minimal connections to the outside world. It seems to me that it is precisely this irrational, closed subculture of charismatic leader, in constant conflict with the dominant milieu, that so effectively provokes the demodernization phenomenon.

This attractive charisma concept introduced by Sivertsev for explaining the post-Soviet leadership contradicts some hidden realities, like hard bargaining for corrupt cash money extracted from the state in times of liberalization and of the Kremlin's weakening power. Some experts on the war provide a version and evidence that Dudayev and his immediate circle had an undislosed agreement with Russian oil industry barons and top leaders (such as the Russian ministers of the oil industry Mikhail Shafrannik and Ruslan Khasbulatov) to transfer to Moscow only 80 percent of the money from Groznyy oil and keep the remaining 20 percent.

The real conflict became unavoidable when Dudayev violated the rule and established a 50–50 split between Moscow and Groznyy (see further Gakayev 1999). Most Chechens believe that Dudayev's involvement derived from corrupt Moscow partners in the oil business. "Look what the Russians bombed first: the bank, the archives, and other buildings with documents on money transfers," informants often said.

SEVEN

The Sons of War

I enjoyed fighting. It was a risk, of course, but I knew no other trade.
SHAMIL A.

Maskhadov, as president, must declare war on Russia. We must initiate this war ourselves in retaliation for the intervention against us.
SHAMIL BASAYEV

In my work, I have to rely on informants from the ranks of Chechen fighters to write about those who are actively involved in the war. Many Chechens shared their information readily. The Chechen separatist leader Aslan Maskhadov, for example, lectured in the United States on the experience of fighting in urban conditions, and there are numerous reports, videotapes, songs, and poems about the actions of these freewheeling insurgents, their fighting efficiency, and the atrocities they committed. It is known that Chechens often delayed their military operations until somebody in the group found a camera. As Dzhabrail Gakayev remarked, "They will not fight and die until a camera observes them doing it." This important feature of staged or performative violence, as a kind of message and as an account, has become a particularly striking issue for research analysis since the world watched the televised tragedy of the World Trade Center attack in September 2001. By the time of my investigation, this sort of exhibitionist behavior had become daily fare among the Chechen *boyeviki* (fighters).

THE *BOYEVIKI*

When I first met Beslan Gantemirov, leader of the anti-Dudayev armed group in Chechnya and former mayor of Groznyy, I was struck by the ironic defiance with which he introduced himself. He held out his hand and said, "Gantemirov, *boyevik.*" It is hard to pinpoint the moment when the word *boyevik* entered the post-Soviet lexicon, but in time it became inseparable from the ethnic conflicts in Nagorno-Karabakh, Abkhazia, and Tajikistan. It corresponds more or less to the English words "insurgent," "combatant," "militant," or "freedom fighter," but it eventually lost any political neutrality it might once have had. In Russian, it literally means "fighter," but in its new form it has a connotation close to "commando," "mercenary," or "paramilitary."

Novels, journals, and academic texts are filled with images of these Chechen fighters, images that greatly color people's perceptions of the Chechen war. One of the more serious studies, written by the Western observer Anatol Lieven, reflects an image of "primitive fighters" defeating a totalitarian monster:

> The Chechen forces in the latest war have been "primitive" in the sense that the great majority of them have been spontaneously generated on the basis of informal social groups and traditions, and not through action by the state; that they lack a military hierarchy and organization, formal training, formal commanders and tactical doctrine, and also lack most of what are considered essential arms for modern war: air-power, armour, heavy artillery, electronic intelligence. In terms of their lack of capacity for state military organization and mobilization, one would almost have described the Chechens of 1994 as a semi-tribal, loosely "anarchistic" people. (Lieven 1998: 325)

Lieven also writes that "the unwillingness and restraint shown" by Dudayev's troops was "an unwillingness to kill *other Chechens*" (ibid.), but he is mistaken; like any other people, Chechens did kill Chechens. The early victims of the Chechen "national revolution"—Russians living in the city of Groznyy—were victims not because of their ethnicity but because they had attractive possessions (apartments, cars, etc.) but not enough armed relatives for self-defense.

The facts of the Dudayev regime's brutal assaults and the killings it inflicted on Chechens who did not share his ultraradical platform of militant secession are not mentioned often enough. Yavus Akhmadov and Dzhabrail Gakayev, both of them participants in anti-Dudayev meetings on Theater Square (April–June 1993), witnessed Dudayev's death squads shoot people on the square, kill members of parliament inside the parliament building, and, finally, shoot a dozen disloyal policemen at the city's police headquarters. Akhmadov assured me that Minister of Economics and Oil Taimaz Abubakarov had personally paid the killers for this dirty work—the killing of Chechens by Chechens.

Chechens thus committed violence against one another (killing, hostage-taking, robbing, etc.) as well as against non-Chechens, and by most estimates, each of the Chechen sides had lost about 1,500 people in such internecine fighting before and after the first war. In August 1996, for example, Chechen combatants retook Groznyy from the federal troops and hunted for all those who had collaborated with pro-Russian authorities. In front of video cameras, Shamil Basayev executed an old man who had been a local administrator in his native village of Vedeno. Galina Zaurbekova told me a story of losing her 31-year-old younger brother, who was killed by Vakha Arsanov's guard without any reason: "It was just a little street quarrel, and he pulled out his handgun and critically wounded my brother. It was my greatest loss in this war, and now I understand the Chechen saying that to lose a brother is harder than to lose one's parents." During the second campaign in Chechnya, the federal soldiers, loyal Chechens, and especially local administrators, militiamen, and religious authorities became the main targets of irreconcilable militants. Over seventy Chechen officials have been killed by armed *boyeviki* since the end of 1999.

In his book on Chechnya, Anatol Lieven quotes the Russian anthropologist Sergei Arutiunov:

> Chechnya was and is a society of military democracy. Chechnya never had any kings, emirs, princes or barons. Unlike other Caucasian nations, there was never feudalism in Chechnya. Traditionally, it was governed by a council of elders on the basis of consensus, but like all military democracies—like the Iroquois in America or the Zulu in southern Africa—Chechens retain the institution of military chief. In peacetime, they recognise no sovereign authority and may be fragmented into a hundred rival clans. However, in time of danger, when faced with aggression, the rival clans unite and elect a military leader. This leader may be known to everyone as an unpleasant personality, but is elected nonetheless for being a good general. While the war is on, this leader is obeyed. (Arutiunov 1995: 17)

Lieven calls this "a striking passage" supporting the suggestion that the "Russian invasion" of December 1994 was such a "releasing stimulus" (1998: 329). Together with Georgi Derguluian (1997) he develops a unique assessment of Chechen warfare:

> The Chechens then are archaic warriors schooled and trained in centuries-long influences of ethnic and/or tribal solidarity and duty, to which over the past two hundred years have also been added religious unity and national suffering and resistance. Rather than as the vainglorious, individualistic, aristocratic, and unreliable Achilles, they have appeared as Hector, dying in defence of his family and homeland—or even more aptly as Aeneas, a hero adopted by Virgil, given a set of Roman virtues of fortitude and stoicism, and sent out into an epic of duty, carrying his father on his back like the burden of his national tradition and its iron demands. Rather than archaic Greek heroes, the Chechens are classical Greek hoplites, held in the line of battle not just by loyalty to the *polis,* but by ties of family and neighborhood to the next man in the line—and held there very firmly indeed. (Lieven 1998: 330)

As we shall see later, my ethnographic material does not square with this.

JOINING THE RANKS

Initially, Chechen armed resistance consisted of two main groups: on the one hand, the regular rank-and-file fighters and a number of field commanders under the supreme command of Dudayev and Maskhadov, and, on the other, the so-called Indians or wild fighters, who had no organized structure of command. Since my collaborators and I were unable to trace or analyze this second group of fighters, we talked with members of the organized resistance about its membership and structure. Contrary to widespread assertions that the "highlanders" had always been armed, the citizens of the Checheno-Ingush Republic had no arms to speak of before 1991. The first young men with submachine guns appeared in Groznyy's central square in September 1991. As Igor Kochubei, then head of the local KGB, testified later, "We could easily have arrested all those lads, for they were obviously wary of the authorities' reaction. But we had no instructions from above to restore order or in any way interfere with the ongoing demonstrations."[1] The first armed groups were organized in Groznyy in response to the decree by Russia's president proclaiming an emergency situation in Chechnya in November 1991.

Zelimkhan Yandarbiyev says of the initial stages of the rebellion, as the masses moved openly toward violence:

> I remember those days clearly enough to be able to describe the heroic enthusiasm we felt. The days when the people had not yet cooled off after the storm of passions brought on by the putsch [August 1991], but also the times when things took on a more legal character, in the period of the election campaign. After Dzhokhar Dudayev was elected president, the storm was transformed into a stable public mood. Patriotic zeal, civic spirit, revolutionary elation, love of adventure, of gain, both egoism and altruism, and many other elements were entwined in the character of the time and the people. . . .
>
> The process could not be stopped even if all the empire's millions-strong army came to crush the Chechen people. . . . It was the logical stage in the historical law of national revival. . . . But not all were able or ready to understand the situation from the philosophical and psychological points of view, least of all those who saw themselves as the nation's intellectual elite, but who nevertheless found no better use for their intellect than simply observing events in cowardly fashion, instead of joining the front ranks, or who even indulged in panicky pro-Russian democratic demagogy. . . . But it did not matter much in that situation, for the people knew what to do without their "intellect." That knowledge came from the long experience of our fathers' struggle for independence against, above all, the Russian empire. That experience awoke in the Chechens' blood, stirring them up for battle. (Yandarbiyev 1996: 89–90, 94)

Intellectuals and dissidents clearly had no place in the ranks.

The first group of Chechen fighters was organized and armed in Groznyy on November 8, 1991, the day after Yandarbiyev's appeal to the public to rally against the "problems of the Interior Ministry." "The people moved to besiege the main stronghold of opposition to independence." In the forefront were the Mehk-Khel, or council of elders, led by Said-Akhmad Adizov, who stormed into the office of the interior minister threatening to blow up all those present there with grenades if they dared order suppression of the action. "From all sides, streams of people, walking or driving their cars, some of them armed, converged on Groznyy. They were ready to fight for freedom. They arrived, formed groups or squads, and got themselves registered in Freedom Square as to where they had come from, how many of them there were, and whom they had selected as their commander" (Yandarbiyev 1996: 92).

Yandarbiyev suggests that armed groups or squads of Chechen resistance fighters were organized on a territorial basis throughout the war. People coming from the same village or settlement formed the core of each battle group. It was important that they knew and trusted one another, felt secure in the same circle, and were confident that they would not be abandoned in an emergency. I did not trace any special *teip* connections or solidarity in these critical moments of the armed uprising.[2]

Leadership within the units varied. Commanders were not assigned on any consistent basis; the choice could be an older man, one with greater physical strength, reputed superior intelligence, or army service experience, or simply the man who had brought the heaviest weapon. Akhyad D., who fought throughout the war alongside his buddy Lom-Ali, has this to say about the commanders:

> In January I was always in the president's palace, under the bombs. We had our own group without any commanders. Though I saluted top leaders, I had no one directly above me to give me orders, nor did I give orders to anyone. We trusted each other without any orders, and it may happen that orders are given by men who do not really know what to do. We were about a hundred men defending the palace—all mixed up together. . . . And who was to give orders? Let's say a team leader on a vegetable farm is made a commander. What does he know of military strategy? So, it is up to you whether to hold out or to run. In war no commanders are needed. Your friend is next to you, and the two of you are out for yourselves.

In February 1995, I talked with Ballaudi Movsaev, the "field commander" (who sometimes called himself "chief of staff") of the Afghan battalion, from Samashki. Ballaudi told me that he had bought a tank with his own money and kept it under his command. I do not know the real strength of these battalions and other units, but in most cases it appears the groups numbered from fifteen to twenty men. While watching numerous videotapes of the fighting, I never noticed larger groups of combatants (of course, the parades held before and particularly after the war involved much larger groups).

Small independent bands of fighters that acted on their own, without commanders, came to be called "Indians." As Akhyad D. noted, "Why give orders to others if you don't know what to do yourself? Most of our people were Indians. Only the president's guard was a regular force, but almost nothing is left of it now. Indians obey no one and give battle of their own volition, as they see fit."

FEAR AND BRAVERY

An amazing aspect of the armed conflict was the Chechen participants' ability to overcome the psychological barrier of fear and master the techniques of guerrilla warfare. Many external observers, even some Chechens, did not expect Dudayev's troops to be so effective, and their skepticism was expressed in some of our interviews:

> When the federal troops entered Chechnya, I expected Dudayev's circus to scatter, because his army was nothing but a clownish force: strutting about, berets pulled to one side, looking important. I knew that those who put on airs and posed on television were nothing but windbags. And I was right. Those who fawned on Dudayev were never in action. The war was won by the common people, by the volunteers. (Taus A.)

. . .

> War is a serious matter. For a long time after it began, we could not believe that it was in earnest. We thought: they will shoot a little, the criminals released from prison will scatter, and things will settle down. But no! The Russian side, they say, sent into the first battle young conscripts with no skills or experience—those who had never smelt powder, as the saying goes. So the bandits on our side cut them to pieces, like so many chickens. And what was the best place for criminals to hide? Many of them were [among] the police's most wanted men, from all over the former Soviet Union. Here in Chechnya they were lying low. Besides, Dudayev released the local thugs from prison to keep them company. (Said M.)

What also amazed the world of politicians and experts in the Chechen conflict was the tenacity and effectiveness of the Chechen armed resistance. Various explanations are usually offered: the extreme unpreparedness of the federal troops and their self-destructive tactics; the military talents of the Chechen leaders, Maskhadov above all; and the incomparable courage and valor of the Chechen fighters. Each of these factors did play a part, and they are justifiably emphasized in some studies (e.g., Lieven 1998).[3]

The arguments over valor and courage miss a serious point, however: how did a small and badly organized part of the Chechen male population triumph in what logically appeared to be a hopeless fight? Faith, fanaticism, tradition, and romantic clichés fail to explain the mass mobilization. I believe the crucial point was when somebody fired the first Grad missile launcher at the column of federal troops marching on Groznyy and somebody else began turning heavy tanks onto their side and setting them ablaze in huge bonfires. The euphoria and publicity attending this seemingly impossible feat went to many Chechens' heads. "To think that Russia had sent more tanks against us than against Hitler's troops in the Kursk battle, and we began to shoot them down!" was the dazed impression shared with me by a member of Dudayev's delegation in the Vladikavkaz negotiations.

In October 1995, when I was accompanied to Groznyy by Vakhid Akayev and Ismail Munayev, they could not help but tell me, right away, about how the Chechen youths had burnt armored vehicles. This initial success set the moral and political tone for the combatants; it gave them a great emotional boost and a feeling of triumph. Thus, the emotions underscored by most analysts were seen to be more important than the archaic values handed down to contemporary Chechens from the dawn of history.

This initial success was coupled with indoctrination about the "holy war" (*ghazavat*) against "interventionists," "occupants," and "colonialists." Akhyad told me that before the war, the mullahs (religious leaders) in each settlement chose young men worthy of service in the president's guard. Akhyad was among them.

> I was never paid, and I had nothing of my own before or during the war. I even borrowed my submachine gun. Some of our marauders grabbed all they could, they rushed under the bullets to get their automatics and other weapons, even their clothes. The Russian soldiers hastened to finish us off. They would drive their tanks over the dead bodies. We would ask for a halt to pick up our dead, but they would not let us. Still, I managed to pick up some bodies, both ours and theirs.
>
> We never drank vodka in action, but Russians were always drunk to ward off fear. I had fear only in the first week, then I became hardened. The main thing is to move at a run, because then you are not such an easy target. But I was hit three times. I still have a splinter in my head and another in my side.

Rustam Kaliyev pointed out that to some extent, the Chechens' readiness to fight was rooted in a mood of despair and hopelessness shared by many:

> I am quite sure that no such tenacious and successful resistance would have followed if from the start the Russian troops had not molested and killed the civilian population. The reason for the effective Chechen resistance was not in the military talent of one side and the incompetence of the other. By their actions, the Russians turned our people against them. The young Chechens had to resist. I seldom heard anyone shout: "For motherland, for freedom!" but I often heard people say, "We are doomed all the same—all the people of Chechnya. They are out to exterminate us. But they will find it hard to do. The main thing is to kill as many of them as possible." Many fighters hardly ever believed that they could win.

THE KALASHNIKOV CULTURE

One myth about Dudayev's troops is that they were well armed from the beginning of the war, and that a great number of them engaged in active fighting. By all my estimates, the real number did not exceed three or four thousand. It was only in August 1996, when the federal troops began to leave Chechnya, that Groznyy was invaded by three or four times as many men, and still more took part in the victory celebrations that followed. As for arms and ammunition, Dudayev and other paramilitary commanders (such as the opposition leaders Beslan Gantemirov and Ruslan Labazanov) had a good stock of arms as their personal repository, but rank-and-file Chechen recruits did not. Only with great effort could one procure a personal weapon. A Kalashnikov automatic rifle or a grenade launcher was the most desired acquisition. A "Kalash" was a cherished possession, sometimes decorated with ribbons, and always handled with care. Ordinary fighters talked about the scramble for weapons:

> The city was being bombed, dead bodies lay everywhere. But people were more interested in the weapons than in the dead. They would crawl under fire to get a gun. I also learned how to do it by trying to notice the direction of the sharpshooters' fire. But each time I dashed out to get a gun from a dead man, somebody else was ahead of me. They said that an automatic cost more than a cow. When after heavy fighting our troops were routed from the trolley depot, the federals left their blockhouses near the overpass. I watched them and saw that many of them were drunk and would often stray away alone. Still, I had little chance to grab a weapon. Then, in the daytime, I hid a piece of rail on the overpass and came back in the dusk to wait. I was in luck—I heard a drunken brawl: two soldiers came out of the blockhouse and, grappling with each other, drifted toward my hiding place. I dropped my bit of rail on one of them. He was hit on the head and sank without a sound. The other looked around and ran off without a word. That was enough; I slipped down the bank, grabbed the gun, and was off. (Makhdi B.)

. . .

> Right before the war, I left my squad. I had quarreled with the commander because he felt I had taken on too much responsibility. So I returned to my village. I wanted to start my own business, but had not enough money—I'd thrown it about too much. Then the war began, and I had not even a Kalashnikov, so I went back to town. I managed to get around for a while but could not find a gun. Once I saw some of our fighters closing in on a sniper in a ruined house. When they discovered him, he began running from one window to another—he was a skilled son of a bitch and hit two of our guys. Finally they got him with a grenade rifle shot. When the flame flared up in the window, they paused a moment—they did not see at once that they had hit him.

Otherwise they would have got there first; a sniper's gun is valuable. But I saw my chance and rushed in from the other side through a gap in the wall. They were still running up the stairs when I got there ahead of them. The sniper was still alive, it seemed. I grabbed the gun and also his money and leapt out through the same gap. Our guys must have been surprised to find that there was no gun there. Served them right for dawdling. That is the law of wartime. (Khalid)

. . .

I have been fighting since the day Dzhokhar arrived. For some time I served in the president's palace guard, though I had not been picked out for his personal guard. But Dzhokhar noticed me. He sometimes called me to his office to talk, and I helped him when he fell out with Labazanov. You think the war began in 1994? That's for the birds. We had had a lot on our hands ever since Dzhokhar came here, and we showed the old supreme soviet what we were made of. Dzhokhar thanked me in person, shook my hand. So I have never parted with this Kalashnikov since I got it from the garrison store. I have had many other weapons since then, but I will never exchange this one [fondling the butt with his hand] for anything else. How many enemies I have got with it is between the two of us. (Chinghiz A.)

WHY FIGHT?

Most of our interviews with *boyeviki,* concerning their motives for fighting, differ from those mentioned by political leaders. The image of the Chechen warrior as strong and humane was carefully molded by political leaders and propaganda experts. Yandarbiyev, for example, speaks of Chechen fighters as "ordinary Chechen guys, great warriors of independence." "Their secret was simple: the Chechens knew what they were fighting and dying for, but the Russian soldiers couldn't feel such a connection, because they'd been sent by aging and ailing leaders to die for the sake of the empire's political ambitions. Yesterday's Chechen civilians proved to be more 'professional' than the Russian military commanders" (Yandarbiyev 1996: 358).

In interviews, I noticed other motives: (1) fighting for fighting's sake and/or the lure of danger, (2) defense of home and family or revenge for losses, and (3) competition for status or material rewards, always a factor during a war. The first motive is rarely discussed in the literature, but it has really deep cultural roots. In all known societies, young men are predisposed to demonstrate physical superiority and fighting prowess. In different cultures and in different epochs, they often go through all kinds of "fights" (both in war games and in real wars) as a kind of ritual initiation. "Young people always fight," the iconoclastic anthropologist Eric Wolf remarked when I asked him about the issue. In the Chechnya of the early 1990s, there had been an explosion of interest in traditional "highlanders' weapons." In 1992, for example, a book entitled *Sabli raya: Gorskoe oruzhie v Kavkazskoi voine* (The Sabres of Paradise: The Mountaineers' Weaponry in the Caucasus War) sold 10,000 copies. Not only did Dudayev thus want to fight, thousands of young men did too. Many rural Chechens who were not considered "of good birth" in the status hierarchy saw combat as a means of achieving upward mobility.

The Russian anthropologist Viktor Bocharov has traced such youthful aggressiveness back to a tradition in premodern societies of raiding against outsiders, thus neutralizing psycho-biological aggressiveness by institutionalizing it and expelling youth violence from the core social collectivity to make it more stable. "At the same time as they encourage fighting by the young, the older people strictly control it" (Bocharov and Tishkov 2001: 507). In traditional cultures, there were a variety of mechanisms limiting the upward social mobility of young people and allowing adults to control resources seized by young males in raiding (cattle, women, etc.). There was a certain ethics that condemned bravura for the sake of material rewards.

The Soviet system encouraged militancy and war games among young people and at the same time severely limited their social mobility. Encouraged both "traditionally" by heroic mythology and "officially" (by everything from sport competitions to patriotic agitation), the younger generation of Chechens were ready to fight. They needed both to let out their aggressiveness and to replace the older *nomenklatura* and win higher status and rewards for themselves.

The next motive involved "home defense" and revenging relatives who had been killed. This was not only a component of the drive for higher status but also legitimized violence in terms of procreation. Explanations such as "for our girls" and "for our children"—this is not pointing to the real causes of fights: societies approve violence signaled by the reproductive sphere. All this signifies one of the main conditions allowing violence: it is acceptable when used in defense of the procreative sphere ("women and children"). This complex combination can be observed through the following testimonies:

> I began fighting at sixteen. My father had been shot dead from a helicopter, my older brother had been blown up by a land mine. It was my duty to take revenge or I would lose my honor before my neighbors. If not, how could I look them in the eyes? Most of the time, we stayed in the Nozhai-Yurt *raion* [region]—now making a truce, now going to war again. And I did not feel I was doing the right thing. Yes, we fought together, we risked our lives together. Still, I felt as if I did not belong, as if I was not quite a Chechen. Of course, I hated Russians, I took revenge on them, and I will go on doing so because of the deaths of my father and brother—that is my duty. I followed the ancestors' custom, but I no longer felt I was fully Chechen. I have one foot among the

Chechens, and the other? It may be in Dagestan, maybe even in Russia. It is hard for me to say what I am. Then I heard talk on TV that Dudayev was not a real Chechen, that he came of highlander Jews— *"tati nekyi."* To tell you the truth, we were glad to hear that—I mean my mother, my sister, and me. If our president is not a pure Chechen, then we are not alone in this. And it is a question of who is better. My mother and sister became active supporters of Dudayev, never missed a rally in his favor. We hoped Dudayev, our president, thought the same as we did. And our family had long suffered from being reproached that we were not pure Chechens. When we learned that Dudayev was like us, a load was lifted off our shoulders and we breathed freely. Dudayev said that all our woes had come from Russians who had oppressed the Chechens for 400 years, that to win we had to unite, no matter who was among our ancestors or when they mixed with other Caucasian peoples. We are all one people in the Caucasus. He called for a Caucasian war with Russia, and I liked it. I enjoyed fighting. It was a risk, of course, but I knew no other trade. (Shamil A.)

. . .

Then I joined the *boyeviki.* Many of them still had no automatic weapons, they were armed with whatever came to hand. And I had my Kalashnikov and could hold my own, no worse than anyone else. I burnt six tanks, I blew up stores. Then we retreated into the mountains. It was cold and we were starving. Lots of times I joined sorties into town. In all that time I saw so many deaths, so many atrocities, that it will last me to the end of my days. I was sixteen when the war was at its height, and I felt like an old man. At first I enjoyed the risk, the heat of battle—after all, I was in more danger of being killed than the enemy. In war, I saw, things are not always decided by strength, but by spirit. I had no personal rancor or malice against the Russians—they were lads like me, just a little older. If not for that war, we would have served in the same army with them, would very likely be friends. But in those days there were many things I did not understand. It is only now that I can say that those who initiated this war are the real culprits. (Mahdi B.)

"RENEGADES, IDLERS, AND PARASITES"

Despite the military and political triumph of the Chechen militants, the *boyeviki* in postwar Chechnya acquired a negative image. Some Chechens perceived them as ignorant rural marginals—cruel, grasping, and ready to kill anyone, including other Chechens. This change of mood toward *boyeviki* came about in August 1996, when armed "war veterans" took control of Chechnya. Civilians, and some militants, felt nervous and hesitant about military rule. And, true enough, some "veterans" prospered from assuming high posts and profiting financially, while others received little recognition.

Alik, a teacher, speaks of his bitterness about the *boyeviki* and the crimes they committed:

> I retain no illusions about Dudayev's forces. Every eighth Chechen was killed in the war, but the field commanders of Dudayev's close circle were not among those who died. Their methods of warfare were dirty and provocative. A *boyevik* would fire on federal troops from behind a fence or the wall of somebody's house, drawing return fire, and in seconds the house would be aflame and full of charred bodies. Most ordinary people were against the war, but they were forced to take part in it because of these tactics. Everything was done to fan the people's hatred and [desire for] vengeance. Dudayev's force was made up largely of criminals who recognized no law, divine or human. They were capable of horrible cruelty and sadism.
>
> For example, a colleague of mine lived in a cottage in a suburb of Groznyy. When he heard *boyeviki* shooting near his house—he was already familiar with their trademark methods—he went out and asked them to move farther away from his home. He had children in his house and a sick old mother. Or, he said, they could go and shoot from behind their own homes. They seized him, subjected him to inhuman torture, and shot him point-blank. The height of their sadism was that after killing him on that first day, for a week they wheedled a ransom from his relatives to let him come home. When the *boyeviki* left the area, the family found his body slightly covered with earth.
>
> What broke my heart was the fate of my senior in the service at the mayor's office. His name was Tashtamirov. He was not a professional civil servant, but he was a modest, accessible, friendly man doing his best to help as many people as he could, to save lives. After their mutual double-dealing, the federals threw the city open to the *boyeviki* in August 1996, and the Zavgayev administration disbanded. Some of the *boyeviki* came to Tashtamirov and asked to borrow his car to take a wounded man to the hospital. He did so, but they failed to return the car. Out of Chechen etiquette he refrained from reminding them of it, thinking they probably needed it for some more wounded. After a week, in the early hours of morning, they burst into his house and seized him and some of his relatives who had found shelter under his roof. He had never thought of hiding or avoiding the *boyeviki*, for he had done them no harm, but had saved dozens of lives. They took Tashtamirov and his young relatives away and tortured them all atrociously. They tied him to their armored vehicle and dragged him until he was torn to pieces. . . .
>
> As a teacher and a witness of the events, believe me, I can tell you that the *boyeviki* are far from representative of the Chechen people. That tragic war did not all boil down to the outrages committed by Dudayev's daredevils, criminals, and other outcasts. The Chechen people themselves rose to defend their lives, honor, and dignity and produced some honest and worthy leaders. The curious thing is that after the war those leaders all disappeared from public view. Instead, we see in the streets and on television a parade of those dirty, unshaven, insolent bandits wearing combat fatigues, passing themselves off as heroes of the people's resistance. There is another story, too—of those honest God-fearing people who always bore the brunt of war and who brought it

to an end. But that story needs a different state of mind. My mind is all burnt out.

. . .

Speaking of the war, I am against all violence. When the Russian troops serving under contract violated our peaceful people, I was against them and helped the *boyeviki* with provisions. But then I saw for myself that those *boyeviki* were scoundrels and not at all the good guys we saw on television. There were many thieves among them. When the *boyeviki* killed Russian soldiers—those incompetent young lads in the first months of the war who had never smelt powder—I was against the *boyeviki.* To my mind, the war was waged by unscrupulous people on both sides. I think it was a dirty, criminal war. Only when people defended their families, their homes, the graves of their ancestors, from the brutalized soldiers was the fighting a just war. And honest, sincere people did this. The *boyeviki* were mostly renegades, idlers, and parasites. They were well known in each of the villages they had come from. They were the idle ne'er-do-wells who envied hard-working people who were earning their well-being, trying to live decently and in comfort. Now they grabbed lots of other people's property and made fortunes from it. I am sure they will squander all that booty very soon and will be just as needy as they were before the war.

I saw marauding and robbery that I will never forget in my life. I think that the democrats [a widely employed connotation that covers those in Russia, including Chechnya, who were active in all of the recent decade of transformation] unleashed that war on purpose to stir up the lowest instincts and to ruin the country through it. Now I am for sovereignty, though, frankly, like most other Chechens, I don't really know what it is. But when I recall what torture Chechens were subjected to in the filtration camps, how they were dropped alive from helicopters, I do not want Chechnya to remain part of Russia. But maybe that's what the democrats counted on: setting peoples against each other, to make them unwilling to live again within one single state. (Timur)

. . .

I was never one of the *boyeviki,* and I do not know to this day what they are. During the war some of them posed as some kind of macho men—like cowboys or Latin American guerrillas. Others tried to look like Amir Shamil's naibs. True, there were some serious fellows among them, but just a few. They defended their homes, but on the whole, it was a kind of show. Many of them carried guitars and tape-recorders. And all of them were play-acting, role-playing—artistes, you might say. But I never heard then that they were defending sovereignty or fighting for freedom. All that was invented later to justify what had happened. The only ones I respected were those who took revenge for their smashed homes and their lost families. They were not playing theatrical roles, they were silent and serious. (Said M.)

A WAVE OF GREED

Evidence of robbery and of destroying or damaging the property of civilians by the federal forces is presented in the report by the "Memorial" Human Rights Center (Orlov and Cherkasov 1998: 250–59) and in other publications. There is less recorded evidence of similar actions by the Chechen combatants, but it is important to note that for some of them, material gain was the main incentive. The following statements by Chechens show how common this was:

> At first my buddy and I rode in to see the city being bombed. Once we saw a helicopter shot down over the Shatoi road. The pilot must have been killed at once because the helicopter fell like a heavy sack, but it did not catch fire, and we were the first to get to it. We stripped the pilot of his suit, its pockets stuffed full of tapes, and we took his earphones too. I had never seen such things before. I liked his jacket best of all—soft leather like a woman's skin. After that, we went foraging in the city more often. We had the pistol we had picked up from that dead pilot, and later we procured a grenade-thrower. We liked that sort of life. War was a jolly business—eat and drink as you please, have a good time, lots of nice things to pick up. Many Chechens had become rich, and we made quite a bit for ourselves during the war.
>
> And why not? The federals were taking out booty by trainloads. The officers sometimes did not have enough trucks for it all, so they sent whole squads to requisition private transport to haul it. As to spare parts, I saw heaps of them stacked up by the Atashin crossroads. Tell you the truth, we too got bold and grabbed everything we could get hold of. And when we couldn't carry it, we set fire to it so as not to leave it for the federal troops. And so did the soldiers. They would muck up the property so that their officers couldn't benefit by it. Just pop into a rich man's house after they had been there, and you would see that all the carpets, the bedding, were covered with shit; the lamps, the furniture, the glass had been smashed by gunfire. I know the soldiers hated their officers. . . .
>
> Then soldiers learned to make traps for us. They would let us get into an unrobbed house or street, and then cut off the retreat, encircle it—and level it entirely to the ground with heavy guns. Many of our lads died in such traps. But then we got wise to it. We would fake our entry into a trap like that and quickly get away through a prepared escape route, most often down the Sunzha River, which for some reason was never guarded. Then the soldiers would mistake their own fellows for us and exchange fire. In the dark they would kill each other by the dozen, maybe by the hundred. And we would add to that from outside, so that the officers would hang out the white flag. A rotten kind of army it was, I can tell you; I'm glad I never served in it. Our elders told us it used to be a strong army when they served. I knew one who had been in the Damansky battle [a reference to a Soviet-Chinese border war skirmish in the early 1960s], and he said it had been the strongest army in the world. I think the officers ruined it. Soldiers need no commands in action, they know what to do, and commands only confuse them. Just tell the men: all you can

get by the force of arms will be yours, and that is better than any command. I know that from my own experience. I brought home so many goods, we did not have enough places to keep them. So I began to make caches in the mountains behind the village. So many of them, particularly of weapons, that I cannot remember where some of them are. I'll be rich to the end of my days. (Masud)

Masud and Kyura talk about this wave of greed that swept over people:

After my father was killed, I lost interest in everything. During the August war, after I was eighteen, I was made a colonel. But it was no joy to me. I went on waging war unwillingly, out of habit. I understood that the federals had to be made to leave Chechnya after what they had done here, so I went on. Everyone around me tried to grab as much as they could—cars, apartments, other things. I had a lad in my battalion, younger than me, who bought two apartments in Argun and still it wasn't enough for him. So he got two more in Groznyy. To tell you the truth, he had just thrown an old Russian woman out of the last one. But it was all the same to me after my father's death. In August, I remember, my battalion captured the huge government stores opposite the Karpin Hill. The guards had surrendered them to save their lives, and the stores contained every type of goods I could think of. I told the locals nearby to come and pick up as much clothing and food as they could. Some people came again and again. One man, a former trade official, hid himself there for the night to find the consignment of French-made sheepskin coats that he knew from the shipping documents must be there. We caught him in the morning and wanted to throw him out at first, but he tried to escape from us and hide again. When he offered to share the goods with us, I ordered him to be shot, but then I felt how futile that was.

We waited for orders from our headquarters about what to do with the remaining stores, but then the federals began a counterattack from the airport. We beat them off, though we lost several of our best fighters. And as we turned back, we found that the stores had been captured by Vakha Arsanov's [later Maskhadov's vice president] force, who had driven my guards out of there. To recover the stores, we would have had to attack him this time, and I would have done so, for Vakha had more than once foraged in my wake, but the usual headquarters confusion prevented me from doing it. Vakha had the people from the 15th State Dairy Farm [a type of Soviet kolkhoz] in his unit—tenacious fellows, greedy for rich pickings. But my battalion consisted of aces who were expert fighters, who never cringed at the worst moments. Now Vakha is among our VIPs, but the time will come when I'll settle with him. Never mind that he is my senior. In battle we were all equal, no matter what age. (Masud)

. . .

In August 1996 I guarded the stores of our firm. The things I saw then do not let me sleep to this day. To begin with, how did the *boyeviki* get into town? Do you think the Russian forces had not seen them? I am a devout Muslim, and I

> can swear by doomsday that Dudayev was a Russian agent, that in summer 1996 the *boyeviki* captured Groznyy with the connivance of the Russian troops. I swear I witnessed Russian guards—some of them mercenaries—stop everyone at their roadblocks to search their bags for vodka and grub, but turn their backs on *boyeviki* who passed it. And what began after that?! At times the Russians and the *boyeviki* would hold different sides of the same street, with the civilian population between them. They would visit each other amicably and share tobacco and liquor, and they would shoot the civilian population from both sides. How can you understand such a war?
>
> Then they began ransacking our stores. The director had bid me stand guard, and I buried the keys where they could not be found, thinking, let them beat me all they like, I would not betray that secret place. They robbed the stores all the same, but how? First, the Russians would come—eat, drink, and be off. Then the *boyeviki* would follow, eating and drinking and grabbing what they could. When they had taken everything that wasn't nailed down, they began to saw off the pipes, as if they could eat them up in their mountains.
>
> Not that all Chechen fighters were thieves. There was a group of *medrese* [religious school] students who came through once, inexperienced boys who were sent to contain the federals' breakthrough at the Krasny Molot plant. They slept on the floor beneath newspapers, refusing to touch the blankets nearby in the store. I was told later that they had all been killed.
>
> Finally, our heroic *boyeviki* got down to the great government stores. The doors were of armored steel, so they bashed them point-blank with heavy guns till the locks came off, and then they sacked the stores like a Tartar horde. Local women, too, grabbed bags of sugar or flour behind their backs and ran off with them—all the time under fire from the direction of Krasny Molot. When I tried to stop the marauding, one of the women called some *boyeviki* and demanded they shoot me on the spot. They refused to do that. They said I was a Muslim, and they did not want to face blood vengeance on my account. The woman grabbed a gun from one of them to shoot me, but she did not know how to use it. (Kyura)

The existing literature on the conflict and riots undoubtedly underestimates a powerful drive of certain people to capitalize on the war, not only through upward mobility and the expression of aggression but also in pursuit of material rewards through robbery and stealing. As for the leaders, such material rewards took an additional form: through shifting money into foreign bank accounts and through acquiring a well-paid celebrity profile.

THE VETERANS OF WAR

The end of the war was followed by apathy and internal division, rather than the expected enthusiasm and solidarity. The split could be seen in several directions: between the commanders and the rank and file, the war veterans and the new recruits, the highland (red-haired) and lowland (city) Chechens. The entry of the *boyeviki* into towns instituted a change in

Chechen society. Instead of showing generosity, the victors began violently to persecute other Chechens, particularly those who did not cooperate with them. A scramble for posts, awards, and property followed, particularly on the part of those who had not yet acquired a car or an apartment in Groznyy. One of those who had assisted the *boyeviki* during the war ("served in the reconnaissance") told of his disappointment:

> Two or three days after victory, all the people from the mountains were down here: Cheberloy, Sharoy, Galanzhoy, wearing rawhide gaiters, old men with staffs, old and young women with children, like a Tartar horde. It was sickening to see that craze. Do they call themselves Muslims after that? I've had enough of it; when I recall all that horror, I am ashamed. And I find it harder and harder to live. War is a dirty and villainous business. It stirs up the worst in people. The only thing that supports me in life is my faith in divine justice. (Kyura)

Some of those who had fought in the war found themselves elbowed aside in its final stage, reduced by Maskhadov to "unruly Indians." Akhyad told me about his postwar experience with great bitterness:

> We did all the fighting, some fifteen hundred of us. Then, when we had done the job, lots of *boyeviki* came by—Basayev and all the others. We had been in many more dangerous situations than his Budyonnovsk feat, but he reaped all the glory. Well, people flocked around Maskhadov like that after he had disbanded the guards. Our commander was from the village of Samashki, and we needed no other. We left the city and settled in a former children's summer camp, but we had no source of livelihood with so many other war veterans all around. We had not asked for much when we were fighting, but many people supported us then. Now Maskhadov stopped paying us, but he did manage to pay all those who had joined the war at the end.

We see, then, that these Chechen sons of war were not only the young men; as the war escalated, both the age limits and the geography and manner of participation widened. The goals of the Chechen resistance leaders were largely different from the interests of rank-and-file fighters. War meant more than "motherland and freedom," it meant protecting home and family, exacting vengeance for their loss, a certain satisfaction in wreaking violence on others, and/or a consuming pleasure in plundering. Many of the fighters were unable to escape the cycle of violence they had embarked upon, and what ensued was chaos and demodernization.

The war became a giant sea change for most of the active fighters. After losing sight of the declared goal, or in some cases even having reached it, they found themselves outcasts from peace and its values. They capitalized on the violence of combat and could not escape its trap. The postconflict reconstruction after the second war will be extremely difficult, even impossible, without therapy and the social rehabilitation of the military segment of this war-torn society. How to accomplish all that will be a staggering challenge.

EIGHT

The Culture of Hostage-Taking

Each hostage fears two things if they come for him during the night: they will kill him, but if they bring a video camera, that means beating, maiming, or raping.
DMITRII BALBUROV

Father, I feel very bad, please give them money now. I feel very sick here. There is a very bad man. Please, please, give money now, and I shall go home.
ADI SHARON

The lucrative business of holding hostages for ransom developed among Chechens during the first war and after the peace agreement escalated into a full-fledged crisis by 1999. It graphically illustrates the progression from the initial cycle of violence to the outbreak of new hostilities three years later, as Chechen military groups gained a powerful economic and political tool for leveraging their aims. In outlining the problem, Sanobar Shermatova and Leonid Nikitinskii (2000) write:

> In the "period between the two wars," hostage-taking developed into a branch of Chechnya's economy. Business flourished because trading partners were found on the other side of the Chechen borders. The number of hostages who were being consistently exchanged reached the hundreds, and the total turnover of that industry ran into tens of millions of dollars. It was precisely this economic activity (aided by drug trafficking, shadow oil trade, and other criminal pursuits) that permitted the Chechen rebel formations to obtain modern arms for continuing the war. According to the mathematics of hostage-taking, each redeemed hostage cost the Russian side many times more than the sum of the ransom paid. The money was used for purchasing new means for abductions, robberies, murders, and war.

Although the collection of information on hostage-taking in Chechnya had been ongoing since the outset of research related to this book, my initial sources were still reluctant to talk about the practice. Their principal assessments were that: (1) the federals initiated the practice by making Chechens pay ransoms for their arrested relatives, sometimes even for the bodies of their dead, in order for them to be given a decent funeral; (2) the hostage-taking industry is perpetuated by criminals, who abduct Chechens too, causing suffering to all; and (3) reliable information on this topic is inaccessible, since it is carefully kept secret. Even asking questions can be dangerous. By way of explanation, some of my informants referred to a "centuries-old" tradition in Chechnya of abducting people, holding them prisoner, and trading them for captives held by other forces.

THE POLITICAL AND PSYCHOLOGICAL OBSTACLES

Submitting the subject of hostage-taking to social and cultural analysis has proved difficult, for a number of reasons. First, it was necessary to sweep aside certain popular myths that had been generated around this theme during the Chechen war. Second, the perpetrators of such deeds were not accessible for direct interviews. Third, their victims were often far from ideal sources of accurate information, owing to the intense physical and psychological traumas they had suffered. Finally, the people who liberated the hostages were so biased, both politically and personally, that they were also not very helpful in illuminating the character of the phenomenon. Just as some Chechen combatants had claimed responsibility out of vanity or self-aggrandizement for sensational terrorist actions or abductions they had never performed, the liberation process was colored by politics and group rivalries so intense as to sometimes result in the failure of their operations. To illustrate the political complexity of some of these cases, here is an excerpt from my conversation with Alexander Mukomolov, a member of Alexander Lebed's peacemaking mission who was making courageous efforts to free hostages in Chechnya. I began by asking him, "Were large sums paid for the release of, say, the group of NTV journalists or Valentin Vlasov?" He replied,

> Not by us! We never had that kind of money. But cases where large ransoms had been paid were widely acknowledged. I don't know about Vlasov. I had no part in that, but I don't think they literally paid them. But I did take part in liberating the NTV journalists when Gusinsky [the director of Media-MOST] asked us to help. At first, we went to Chechnya to try to arrange the release without paying money, but then we took $2 million. For a week I traveled all over Chechnya, but [in the end] I had to come back with the money. Evidently, the people who accompanied us had been given orders not to release the captives for $2 million. Actually, it was a game between B. [Boris Berezovsky, a Russian oligarch] and G. [Vladimir Gusinsky, Russian media magnate]. It's a terrible thing when big bugs, important people, are mixed up in such cases and exploit [the cases] for their own interests, [people] including high-ranking police officers, and, pardon me, even the president, publicly shook hands with the liberated French press photographer [Brice] Fleutiaux before the president's visit to the West. That reporter had entered Chechnya through Georgia and was actually an illegal immigrant. Any country would punish him for crossing its border illegally.[1]

Mukomolov did not reveal all the details, but the article by Shermatova and Nikitinskii (2000) illustrates how complicated, chaotic, and personally motivated the actions of the "big bugs" were in that infamous case. They quote Alexander Komarov's account of the release at some length. Komarov was the security chief of Media-MOST, the corporation headed by Vladimir Gusinsky.

> I conducted talks about liberating the NTV cameramen with some dubious people, many of them involved not only in politics and business but also in the criminal world. As a former police officer, I understood, of course, that by discussing a ransom with dubious characters, I was embarking on a slippery slope, but we were in an extreme situation. After a month of official talks, including those between Gusinsky and Movladi Udugov [minister of information under Dudayev], and other high dignitaries in Chechnya, we hadn't progressed a step, and we were already being given hints that it was time to pay up. . . . At the end of July, I was advised to call on Alexander Mukomolov. We met in an apartment he was renting in Kolpachny Lane in Moscow. Also present were Sharpuddin Lorsanov, the Chechen interior minister in Dudayev's government, and Sasha Lyubimov, of another TV channel, who wanted to liberate a group of their journalists [who had been] captured at the same time. At first the sum of $2 million was mentioned. Lyubimov said he didn't have that kind of money and would have to consult others. After that we held talks separately.
>
> Lorsanov told us he was interior minister in Chechnya, and before that he had been head of the Interior Department in Shali—in short, a man of authority. At the beginning of August, Gusinsky met with Lorsanov and Mukomolov to discuss the terms [of the operation]. He asked them directly what motives they had in taking up the liberation of the NTV journalists' group. Mukomolov said he was working with Alexander Lebed. . . . The talks went quickly, and the whole process took about a week, in August 1997. Then Lorsanov's younger brother Nazhmuddin entered the picture: he had spoken with the people who were holding our press photographers in Chechnya, and this was confirmed by the MVD people I was in contact with. From the same source, I learned that in Chechnya they were counting on getting $1 million for our three hostages, whereas Lorsanov and Mukomolov were talking about $2 million.
>
> . . . Nazhmuddin Lorsanov unexpectedly arrived in Moscow and said that we had to fly out immediately. Since we been given no guarantees, we asked the elder Lorsanov to stay in Moscow, at the Ukraine Hotel, under our guard. Gusinsky called an urgent meeting with the NTV corporate owners, at which they passed a resolution to ask the MOST group for the ransom money. I received $2 million in cash from the MOST Bank, and in my application for it, I wrote "to pay a ransom for hostages," in addition to $50,000 for redeeming soldiers. . . . We bought three oilskin bags, prepared a written description of each one, wrote down the numbers of the banknotes, and packed them in the bags. On August 8 at 10 A.M. we left for Beslan [airport

in North Ossetia] on a TU-134 [aircraft] rented by the NTV. We arrived in Beslan at 12:00, and within an hour the younger Lorsanov and Mukomolov joined us. On the plane we bargained; they demanded $2 million at once, but I wanted to give them $1.5 million at first, and then $500,000 after the hostages had been handed over. Finally, they agreed, got into the car, and drove off. The local police saw them to the Chermen block post but couldn't accompany them. We were preparing to seize those who would come for the money, but nobody returned—either after two hours, as they had promised, or after four hours.

The next day at 7 A.M., yet another Lorsanov brother came, bearing a note from Mukomolov: "The goods are in order, but we have problems with transport." I told him that though we had no blood-vengeance tradition, they would never see their older brother again should the operation fall through. Since nothing had transpired, on August 9, at 3 P.M., Gusinsky ordered us to return to Moscow. As soon as we got back, telephone calls began coming in from Chechnya. Mukomolov called several times to say all was well, the commitments were assured. A little earlier, we had received a cassette, with the hostages' [voices] on tape, for which we paid $30,000. After that Tolboyev [a well-known Dagestani public figure involved in releasing hostages in Chechnya] called, asking why we had let them raise the price—it seems they now wanted $3 million. This clearly meant that they had all known, back in Chechnya, what had happened, since the news of the money arriving instantly had reached Makhachkala [the capital of Dagestan].

We returned to Moscow on August 9, and the younger Lorsanov and Mukomolov flew back on August 12. They brought back the $1.5 million in the same bags, with the same banknotes. When they had returned the money to us, we led them out to the older Lorsanov. The brothers met and talked in high-pitched tones, and during that heated debate I heard for the first time the names Arbi Barayev, Vakha Arsanov [vice president under Maskhadov], and others. According to the Lorsanov brothers, [the journalist] Elena Masyuk and the press photographers were being held by "eight shareholders," who had held a meeting in a cafe in central Groznyy, where they had come to blows over the situation.

I continued my talks with Mukomolov, trying not to let him escape the game, but on August 17, I was told to get in touch with Gusinsky, who was then abroad. Gusinsky told me on the phone to take the $2 million and call up one Badri Patarkatsishvili [Berezovsky's business partner]. I did that, and Badri told me to take the money to the Logovaz Company [company owned by Berezovsky] and hand the money over to "Ivan," who would meet me. When I asked how we could record handing over the money, he said that there would be no formalities. I called my bodyguards, took the money, and went to the Logovaz facility. I was met outside by a man aged about thirty. "Are you Ivan?" I asked.

"Yes." I opened the bag and showed him the money. We went into the building, and judging from Ivan's behavior, I understood he was a kind of boss there. I gave him the money.

The first time the ransom had not been accepted, because when we had

> offered it we had bypassed Logovaz. And through Logovaz the connection was made, but this is only my personal impression. If I were facing an investigator or a prosecutor, I wouldn't risk writing this in the indictment. (Shermatova and Nikitinskii 2000)

Millions of dollars were paid by Berezovsky and Gusinsky as ransoms for their journalists, thereby contributing to the flourishing criminal business of hostage-taking in Chechnya. Such huge gains turned the heads of many Chechen criminal bosses and small-time bandits. President Maskhadov repeatedly declared campaigns against the practice, while some of his closest allies continued to play this game with people's lives. By chance, the names of some top Chechen leaders—Udugov and Arsanov—were mentioned in that story. The name of Shamil Basayev, who made a frank confession to Mukomolov concerning the distribution and use of funds raised by extorting ransoms, could also be added to that list.

I asked Mukomolov, "How was the ransom money distributed?" He replied:

> There may be a certain system of distributing that money. I talked with Basayev about kidnapping when he was a deputy premier in Maskhadov's government, and though he condemned it in principle, he also said, "I know by whom and where that business is being done, but try to understand that 40 percent of it is used for disabled war veterans, a certain percentage goes to army needs and armaments, and some of it is paid for the work done." The common way of dividing the money, as far as I know, is that five or six men get together and argue over it, since each had counted on getting more than he did get. That happens because the ransom has to be scaled down, particularly when you tell them that their demand is unrealistic. They sometimes hardly know the difference between a billion and a million. It also happens that in the course of the talks, one of them will say, "Let's agree to that," and the others object. There's no single group or center, still less a fixed tariff. The group is led by one man, who is led by another; when they have a division of labor, single leadership is altogether impossible.[2]

We may never know the whole truth about the involvement of Chechen leadership in the hostage-taking, which was indirectly encouraged, not only by important politicians and some of Russia's business tycoons, but also by the foreign media. The most barbaric terrorist acts and murders of hostages in Chechnya failed to rouse indignation in the outside world. The foreign media never used words like "terrorism" or "massacre" in describing the Arab mercenary Ibn Khattab's attack on a federal convoy, in which over one hundred soldiers were killed—it was instead reported as a great military success for the Chechen fighters.

Some foreign journalists, experts, and politicians, as well as some Russian human rights activists, tried to justify the terrorism and kidnapping in Chechnya in a variety of ways. Yury Zakharovich, the Moscow correspondent for *Time* magazine, explains that many American journalists "did not search for an excuse for terrorism, but they tried to show how this terrorism was provoked by the war. Violence gave birth to new violence" (Zakharovich 1999: 302). As an example, Zakharovich cites a story in *Newsweek* about the attack on the provincial Russian town of Budyonnovsk in June 1995 by a Chechen force led by Shamil Basayev, in which almost 100 people died. "We are not bandits," Basayev was quoted as saying. "We are a country at war with another state. They have taken our families, our land and our freedom."[3]

In the days following the ghastly murder of three Britons, Darren Hickey, Peter Kennedy, and Rudolph Petschi, and a New Zealander, Stan Shaw, who were working for Surrey-based Granger Telecom to install a cellular phone system for Chechen Telecom, in Chechnya in December 1998, followed by the display of their severed heads, I looked through dozens of Western press commentaries on that event. I was amazed: even in this case, Western journalists and politicians showed their support for the "Chechen resistance." This stands in stark contrast to much of the Western reaction to the discovery of the bodies of forty-five ethnic Albanians in a ravine outside the village of Racak in Kosovo in January 1999 shortly before the NATO operation was launched against Serbia. Many Chechen combatants were aware of these encouraging, or at least noncondemning, attitudes on the part of the international community.

Given much of the silence surrounding hostage-taking, then, I am grateful to Dmitrii Balburov for his frank conversation with me on July 20, 2000. We met in the evening at my office, over a cup of tea and a cigarette. Balburov is a soft-spoken, shy young man with a capacity for self-reflection. I had glimpsed some of his emotional and psychological reactions to captivity in his published "Diary of a Chechen Captive." It contained more than just the routine description of being held hostage, including "the hatred that floods you upon your liberation." He concluded with the words, "With these notes I'd like to close the gloomiest page in my life and never return to it again, either in thoughts, or words, or deeds" (Balburov 2000: 95).

If I had read only his diary, however, I would have missed much of what interested me in my research. He talked into my tape recorder for more than two hours. His voice and eyes betrayed the fact that it wasn't easy for him. He was living at the time in his Moscow apartment with the support of his colleagues on the newspaper staff, and I thought he needed counseling even now, six months after the trauma. Apart from a two-week stay in a sanatorium upon his release, he had received no therapy. Here is an excerpt from our conversation. When I asked him if being taken hostage had affected his health, he replied:

> Upon my return, I was sent to a sanatorium in the Kashira region. I stayed there with my mother. I had pains in my back between the shoulder blades,

and they treated me for that. But I didn't go to a psychiatrist or a psychologist; in that sense I recovered on my own, though for two or three months I wasn't myself. Everything seemed strange and scary to me. I often had nightmares, as in Lermontov's poem, "Help, mates! they're hauling me to the mountains. . . ." I had them every night, and I still sometimes have them. I talked about that with Ilyas Bogatyryov [another journalist who had been taken hostage], a fellow student, one year my senior. We had lived in the same Moscow State University student dormitory. He said, "How could it be otherwise? It took me six months just to come to my senses, and a year to return to normal." Frankly though, I don't think he's the same man he used to be. He had been held hostage for slightly over two months.

Your first feeling after it's over is resentment: good God, how could it happen? You feel hurt. About a month later I had hallucinations. Once I went to do some shopping at a little street market [in Moscow]. It was a fine spring day. I'm walking along, then I turn my head—a car's after me, that same white Volga, crawling at low speed, the license number beginning with 06, from Ingushetiya, and in the backseat was the mother of that Judas Mogushkov, looking at me with her wily smile. I rushed to mix with the market crowd. Then I stopped, telling myself, stop, wait! There can't be a car with an 06 number here, and Mogushkova is under arrest for investigation. She can't pop up here, so calm down. But I saw it with my own eyes, sober, in broad daylight.

Then I thought that all the Mogushkovs had sworn to take revenge on me, so I would do what Hadji-Beck of Dagestan did in his time. He had been taken prisoner, and his cell mate was paid to hang him. Not wanting to give them that pleasure, he hanged himself instead. So I wrote a farewell letter before planning to commit suicide. This was two or three months after my return. I apologized to everyone in my letter and started planning how to do it. I live on the sixteenth floor, so if I jump out the window, I'll die instantly. As probably often happens in such cases, some trivial thought stopped me. I live in a housing cooperative, with journalists of *Izvestiia* and *Moskovskie novosti* in the same block. There's a pretty lawn below, so why mess it up? I imagined the public scandal, the press coming, so awkward for my neighbors, and that stopped me. It seems funny now, but it was serious then.

I tried to numb myself with work, to write, but nothing came out well—you need the right frame of mind for it. If I did manual labor—as a garbageman, for instance—that might've been better. But my colleagues were very helpful, and they gradually got me involved back in work. I asked Ilyas about that, and he said he couldn't work properly for a long time. So it's only recently that I started really working. I also feared people would be sorry for me and treat me like a lame duck, but no one reminds me of anything. Who I feel sorry for is my mother. She came to look after me for some time and heard my screams at night. She suffered more than anyone.[4]

Balburov's story touches on the strategy of establishing tactful relations with one's captors. His main advantage was his ethnic origin, specifically his Asiatic looks, and he did not hesitate to use them.

> My guard told me later that I had drawn a lucky ticket. When they were told a Russian journalist was to be brought to them as hostage, they were all bloody-minded because, after the attack on Dagestan, bombing had begun in Chechnya, with severe casualties. "Now we'll press him for the full program," they said, meaning torture or even murder. "But when they pulled you out of the car and took off the hood and the ropes and we saw your face, we lost all such thoughts. Look, he's not Russian! Are you a Kalmyk?" Yes, I said, I'm a Kalmyk. "But you Kalmyks were also deported, why don't you fight the Russians, why don't you rise against them?"
>
> Later, that guard told me they would have killed me if I had been Russian; they had already decided to cut off my head and display it as a threat, as had been done with the Englishmen. Then the bombing got worse, and one of them lost his home and family. My life, he said, had often hung by a thread, but each time they changed their minds.[5]

WHY ABDUCTIONS?

Over a few years, abductions in Chechnya reached astonishing proportions and took on sophisticated forms. None of my informants could recall any such cases before 1991, although it had been common, in previous decades, to lure social outcasts into semi-slavery and indentured servitude. These people often lived unpaid with a Chechen family and in most cases were unable to leave. This is what Mukomolov told me about the practice:

> I must say that since old times, households in Chechnya have used workmen of the beachcomber or tramp type. In each village, you see some Petya, Yura, Vasya who has lived five, ten, or more years with Chechen families. They are usually loners without family connections or friends, mostly drug addicts or alcoholics. They are not missed by anyone, and they don't even try to escape. I remember once visiting friends in a Chechen village and seeing a man of Slavic appearance in their yard. I asked who he was, and they replied, "That's Yura, he's lived with us about fifteen years. We sent him packing to Kharkov twice, but he would just get off at the station and spend all his money on drink. Then somebody would bring him back, or he would return himself."[6]

Similar practices have been observed in other North Caucasian republics, particularly in Dagestan. During recent military activities in this area, a village was found where nearly every household, including that of the local schoolmaster, had so-called "workmen" *(rabotniki)*, or domestic slaves, from the lowest social category of destitute people brought from far-off regions.

In fall 1999, there were still 851 people missing and/or detained in Chechnya out of the 1,843 cases that have been monitored by the Russian Ministry of the Interior. About fifty foreigners have been liberated so far. Some experts estimate that the total income gained by this abduction activity has reached $200 million, more than the sale of oil or the allocations from Russia's federal budget. The largest hostage markets functioned in

Urus-Martan and in Groznyy, where it was always possible to buy or even place an order for a captive, pay an advance, and name the category you wanted—businessman, officer, civil servant. Lists of categories on offer were then passed from hand to hand until someone or some group decided to take one up. According to Mukomolov,

> [Abductions] were perpetrated solely for the ransoms. We must trace the history of this business back to the federals' filtration camps. Though abducting people has been known in the Caucasus since Tolstoy's time, it's the recent war that generated kidnappings on a mass scale. In the filtration camps they did the same thing: relatives of Chechen missing people came, paid the money demanded, and took their men away. [The Chechens] were missing about 1,400 men; they knew them all by name, and they often knew which personnel carriers had picked them up, but they had to search for further links in the chain. If they could trace them quickly, they would usually succeed in buying the prisoners' freedom. But there was also a practice of exchange. Let's say some federal soldiers had been captured in action—if they were not all killed out of hand. Then the field commander keeps maybe five soldiers who can be exchanged or sold. That becomes his exchange fund, and it can be used for freeing some of the Chechens serving terms in Russian prisons. Their relatives can buy a captive from the bandits for themselves and exchange him later for their own jailbird. We once had to deal with a case like that where a Chechen woman bought a federal soldier from the bandits and kept him working at her house for some time while she conducted talks on a possible exchange. When we learned that her man was serving a prison term for murder, we refused outright to take part in the deal, but after spending nine months trying to get her to agree to some other option, we finally liberated that lad anyway.
>
> Rich people, particularly businessmen or Jews, are also abducted for the ransoms they might command. The hostage-takers would ask the Jewish hostages to appeal to Berezovsky or Gusinsky if they had no money of their own.[7]

As the war continued to undermine people's moral values, many things that had earlier been condemned became increasingly acceptable. In a situation where armed groups and government militias dominated the civilian population, it was impossible to take effective measures against the abductions, although most Chechens condemned the practice. The number of people who were involved in kidnapping or who had important information about it, though significant, remains open to speculation. I asked Mukomolov, "How wide was the circle of people who knew what was going on?" He replied:

> Many people knew a good bit, but few had exact information on who held whom, and where. And less and less information has been reaching the federal side lately. Now, bandits have begun killing those who help the federals, so people are afraid to cooperate with them. On Monday, a group came here

> from Chechnya and told us that in Yermolovka a militiaman had been shot down for siding with the federals. When a purge was staged there, they arrested two close accomplices of Barayev—one of the most notorious kidnappers—but released them after two hours.[8]

Hostages were sometimes taken for construction labor, especially if the work required special skills. This is what Mukomolov told me about it: "Abductions of workmen are widespread. When the first teams of construction workers were sent to restore Chechnya, particularly Groznyy, many of their members were lost, particularly masons, carpenters, and brick and tile layers. They were passed from home to home for small sums of money until some family released them, or until we found them and arranged their release."[9]

Sometimes, relatives of hostages organized their own armed groups to make independent raids, and in several cases hostage-taking provoked a chain reaction of reciprocity. When several Ossetians were kidnapped in Chechnya and Ingushetiya, the Ossetians took a group of Chechens hostage and demanded an exchange. This almost brought on a serious crisis after a large meeting of armed Chechens gathered at the Groznyy stadium and passed a resolution to attack Vladikavkaz, the capital of North Ossetia.

WHO MIGHT BE KIDNAPPED—AND HOW

Most abductions appear to have been carefully planned several months in advance, from choosing the victims to identifying methods for their seizure to ensuring delivery to the place of detention. The system is more complicated for operations in large cities outside Chechnya, owing to the police presence and the numerous traffic checkpoints that must be passed. Many precautions, such as frequently changing the location of detention, are taken. The French photographer Brice Fleutiaux was moved eleven times in nine months.

Abductions could be staged anywhere, even in Moscow. Twenty-two-year-old Kirill Perchenko was abducted near the Kantemirovskaya metro station.

> First they shoved me into the van of a big truck. The back part, partitioned off with glass, included an electric light and even a bio-toilet. In that cell, with two guards, I was taken to a suburb of Groznyy, where they stopped in a field, put me into a jeep, and took me to an apartment in the city center. There they played a videotape for me, depicting how Chechens execute hostages. They told me they could hand me over to those cruel men at once or, if I obeyed them, they would place me with a normal Chechen family. Then they took me to Urus-Martan, where they put me into a cellar with eleven other men from Moscow, Dagestan, and Ingushetiya. From there we were taken to different places in the mountains.

> There was a cheerful old man among us who'd had two fingers cut off. There were two young men who were later killed—one was from a rescue team of the federal Ministry for Emergencies; the other, who was from the Russian Intelligence Service, was clubbed to death. The man from the rescue team attacked a Chechen guard with a knife, but only wounded him. Had he killed him, we would've all been dead. As it was, they executed that man in front of us by cutting his head off with a saw.
>
> Later, they took me and another prisoner, a young Kazakh, down from the mountains to exchange us for money. They handed us over to Wahhabites, who left us for some time in a room with a boarded-up window. We tore off the boards and escaped. Soon, we met a venerable-looking old Chechen in a tall fur cap, with a mouth full of gold teeth, and thought he looked like a symbol of Caucasian respectability. He turned out to be one of the local elders, and took us to the federal commandant's office. The riot police stationed there searched us and questioned us. Then they gave us several cans of corned beef and condensed milk, and we wolfed it all down.[10]

Small children were often kidnapped to extract ransoms from their parents; and young women were taken to perform various services for armed groups.

> I was taking my two kids home from the playground, and when we entered our doorway, several men who had been waiting there stunned Yana and me by hitting us over the head, and took off our little Denis. I can't tell you how many tears we shed and what we had to do to get him back! When I saw him get out of the car I didn't recognize him for a moment; his hair had been cut off and he was all swollen and pale bluish.[11]

The usual method of pressuring the relatives is to keep them aware of the hostage's suffering and to threaten his death if they fail to pay up. Various ways were used to transmit this information. Victim's letters and calls from a mobile telephone were the most common. Among the documents in Mukomolov's dossier, I saw a note written in pencil in English by Adi Sharon, the 14-year-old Israeli boy whose finger was cut off. It read: "Father, I feel very bad, please give them money now. I feel very sick here. There is a very bad man. Please, please, give money now, and I shall go home."

The bandits often tortured or maimed their hostages on video. They cut off ears or fingers, or beat the victims, making them beg their relatives to pay the ransom. The cassettes were delivered to the families, and the bargaining would begin. One businessman whose child was kidnapped said later that at first the bandits demanded $1.5 million, then gradually lowered their demand to $50,000, though even that was very difficult to find.

One horrifying story is that of a group of construction workers from the Stavropol region. In October 1997, five of them were captured. One, Victor Zinchenko, was beheaded with an axe, and a videotape of the execution was sent to the relatives of the others. Zinchenko had been chosen because he had no relatives. The ransom demanded for the rest of the group was $1.5 million. Mukomolov explained the logic of this case:

> Such demonstrations are needed as a persuasive tool. They would get together to discuss the situation. "Nobody is bothering to ransom the hostages. Let's show them all that we mean business." And they cut off Zinchenko's head. We had long tried to liberate that group, and even got one of them out when they were in Ingushetiya, but they kept the other four and gave us two months to pay. Still, nothing doing. Then they executed Zinchenko, recorded it on videotape and sent out the cassettes to put on the pressure. It was barbaric, of course. Typically, they would kill only when their own relatives had died in the course of war, when they are under stress or the influence of narcotics. That's when they beat their captives badly or even killed them. Executions might follow instances of the prisoners' open defiance or escape attempts, but in most cases they beat the hostages rather than killing them.

Next to businessmen and well-known officials or journalists, Jews were the preferred victims of kidnappers. Many bandits were anti-Semitic, and treated Jews with particular cruelty. Barayev even declared he would kill all captured Jews.

Mukomolov explains why there were many Jewish people among the captives:

> I would rather point out that Jews are often placed in prominent positions in Chechen firms because they are perceived to be "men with brains." The victims of abductions are often chosen from that circle in the expectation that they or their relatives must have a lot of money. That was the fate of a man with the family name Fradkin (he is actually called Kurnosov, his mother's maiden name). He was on holiday near Nalchik [in the republic of Kabardino-Balkaria], throwing money around and bragging quite a lot. As a consequence, he was kidnapped, not even by Chechens, but was taken to Chechnya. On the strength of his own words, the kidnappers demanded a huge ransom—$2 million. They telephoned his parents every day demanding payment. According to our usual practice, we got in touch with Fradkin's company and obtained its financial balance. We found evidence that his parents were elderly pensioners, war veterans, retired teachers, and contrived to get those documents to his captors. When they receive such information, they usually begin to see that it's hopeless to expect so much money. But they still kept phoning, and insisted the parents should go to Berezovsky or Gusinsky or Jewish bankers and ask them for money. That young man perished. We can't provide such great sums, of course. Still, one of our goals is to get realistic information to the kidnappers, so that they at least don't count on getting what people don't have.[12]

Mukomolov also recounts the story of the Israeli boy Adi Sharon, although the Lebed mission was not directly involved in his release (he was liberated by the Russian police):

> Adi Sharon and his father, Joseph, were captured in Moscow, in August 1999. The kidnappers stopped them by showing police credentials, then pulled sacks over their heads and spirited them off. The next day they released the father but took the boy away. I have Joseph Sharon's letter to Lebed in which he puts the ransom figure at $170,000. . . . Sharon started by finding an intermediary from Ingushetiya and giving him $50,000, but that man died and the money was lost. Then he wrote letters to various officials, and a criminal investigation was started. At the end of March 2000, he telephoned me and came to see me.
>
> Our rule is that if we take up a case, we inform the appropriate official services, because it's no good to poke one's nose into an investigation that is already under way. So I phoned the Central Department for Combating Organized Crime, and they asked us to help, but that department has different branches, and one of them was actually investigating the case, though they didn't tell us about it at the time. We took it up, established the necessary contacts, and obtained a recent photograph of the boy through intermediaries. This is a must—you've got to have a photo or a letter, or some other confirmation that the hostage is alive. Now it's possible to use a mobile phone. Sometimes they send you a videotape.

The boy was eventually freed in May 2000. Though he had not been kidnapped by Chechens, the abduction had been planned in Chechnya, and some of the men involved were from Chechnya and Ingushetiya. It was a Chechen who led the operation and who cut off two phalanges of one of the boy's fingers, and sent them to his father.

In another case, Savi Azariyev, a Jew from Volgograd, told me, "Arbi Barayev's men said their task was to shake Jews down for money and then annihilate them all. Our family had scraped together $300,000, but it wasn't enough for them and they refused to release me."

Another person, named Alla Geifman, recalled, "On July 1, they cut off one of my fingers and sent it to my parents. On August 1, another finger. One of my fellow prisoners had the tip of his tongue cut off, then an ear, then a finger. To intimidate us, they brought out a man and beheaded him before us."

ORGANIZERS AND EXECUTORS

The hostage-taking business was shared among several armed groups. The important zones of influence in the business were controlled by the best-known field commanders: Gudermes by Salman Raduyev, the Shatoi region by Abu Movsayev, and Urus-Martan by the eight Akhmadov brothers. Ramzan, the oldest of the brothers, was the boss, and Uvays provided cover as a head of the local police. One of the most notorious and brutal of the hostage-takers was the Chechen commander Arbi Barayev, who reportedly tortured captured soldiers and hostages and personally finished off many wounded. When the first Chechen war came to a close in 1996, he began specializing in abductions and turned hostage-taking into a highly lucrative business.

Barayev evidently established close links with powerful figures in Moscow and became the partner of several top Russian politicians and businessmen—all of them profiting from the trade in hostages.[13] Barayev's people abducted Valentin Vlasov, the Russian president's envoy in Chechnya, who was eventually released for the fabulous sum of $7 million. They also kidnapped two officers of the Russian Federal Security Service (FSB), Gribov and Lebedinsky, from Ingushetiya and held them for an $800,000 ransom.

In July 1998, Barayev tried to take control of Gudermes and establish a radical Islamic regime there. The local population put up resistance, and Aslan Maskhadov ordered the disbanding of Barayev's Special Islamic Regiment, stripping him of his rank and awards. Maskhadov's order was not obeyed, however, and there is reason to believe that Barayev was subsequently involved in the attempt on Maskhadov's life. In 1998, Barayev was hunted by a number of his enemies seeking blood vengeance. The relatives of an Ingush police officer he captured in 1997 made several attacks on his life. Taking hostages among Chechen or Ingush people had apparently become a rather tricky business by 1998.

This is the story of certain "slave-trading generals":

> At the "slave market" it was possible, not only to negotiate the sale, purchase, and exchange operations, but also to secure a so-called "trademark." Well-known group leaders and field commanders accepted responsibility for abductions that might be committed a thousand kilometers from Chechnya. All the subsequent talks were conducted in that commander's name, and should the operation be successful, he would take a percentage of the ransom "for lending his trademark." By using the name of a field commander notorious for his cruelty, a kidnapper of lesser renown could cover his tracks and also demand a larger ransom.
>
> The best-known "trademarks" were often used by groups within Chechnya. The most notorious case culminated in the murder of four engineers, three Britons and one New Zealander, in 1998 as a result of clashes between Chechen groups over a "trademark." The kidnappers had used Arbi Barayev's name in a prior operation, obtained the ransom, and returned the hostage to his family. Barayev, who had consented to the use of his name in the talks, demanded his share of the ransom for the use of his "trademark" but never got it. Barayev's group then abducted the four foreigners and claimed a ransom of $10 million for them. Chechen Telecom, the organization that had invited the foreign engineers to Chechnya, agreed to pay, but Barayev unexpectedly refused to release them and beheaded them instead. There's a popular version that some third party had interfered and paid Barayev more for the heads of the engineers.

Arbi Barayev had claimed credit for such widely publicized operations as the abduction of journalists such as the NTV group, with Elena Masyuk, and the ORT group. Barayev's "star" rose then. During the first Chechen campaign, he was just over twenty and served as a bodyguard for the Chechen vice president, Zelimkhan Yandarbiyev. Barayev never took part in any fighting, nor could he claim any combat record. But through Yandarbiyev, large sums of money came from abroad, as *Moskovskie novosti* reported in its issue No. 36, 1997. It was rumored that part of that money was used after the war for setting up the "Shari'a regiment" commanded by Barayev. That provided Yandarbiyev, who had lost the 1997 presidential election to Maskhadov, with a formidable guard. Barayev then assumed the title of general, and both of them became known in Chechnya as Wahhabites [Islamic extremists].

In the short period of peace between the two Chechen campaigns, Barayev got into many scrapes: he was officially charged with kidnapping in a public statement made by the deputy premier, Turpal Atgeriyev, in March 1999; he took part in the attempt on Aslan Maskhadov's life in 1999; he and his "Shari'a regiment" were nearly wiped out by the field commander Sulim Yamadayev in Gudermes during the summer of 1998; and he was wounded twice during the course of Chechen infighting, the latter time quite seriously, in June 1999. But he survived, and in the early hours of January 5, 2000, his group safely withdrew from Groznyy to Alkhankala, rumor has it, by paying their way with $100,000, half of which was found to be counterfeit. That same passage became a death trap to other groups later on.

The Akhmadov brothers of Urus-Martan stand second only to Barayev in hostage-taking and also enjoyed good luck, though one of them was killed in December 1999. They miraculously escaped the federals and fled to the mountains from Urus-Martan. In Chechnya they say that the Akhmadovs had promised to cease their resistance in exchange for a safe passage. It's also possible that they paid for their passage by surrendering two Polish women who had been taken hostage in Dagestan and kept in Urus-Martan. The women were released in the mountains and walked fifteen kilometers under crossfire to the federals' positions.

Also notable among kidnappers is Baudi Bakuyev, who is little known outside Chechnya. Nonetheless, we have information that it was he who held the presidential envoy Valentin Vlasov. It is said that, unlike Barayev and the Akhmadovs, Bakuyev and his people didn't molest their captives. After gaining a ransom for Vlasov (different sums have been unofficially named, from $3 to $7 million), they handed out $100 to each family in Petropavlovskoye, Ilyinka, and Dolinsk. Nobody claimed this was the money received for Vlasov, but the people in those three villages noted the link between the date of his release and the timing of these unexpected gifts. Baudi Bakuyev is thirty-four and he, unlike the others, fought in the first Chechen campaign. At the beginning of the first war, Dzhokhar Dudayev, by secret decree, set up a special squad for capturing Russian officers, the plan being to obtain information of value. He entrusted the task to a former traffic policeman, Vakha Arsanov, and Baudi Bakuyev was in that squad.

. . . Each of the hostage-takers had a well-outlined sphere of influence.

> After collecting capital and making a name for themselves, commanders like Barayev or the Akhmadovs rarely performed abductions themselves. They accepted goods and sold their "trademark" to small-time kidnappers within and outside Chechnya. (Shermatova and Nikitinskii 2000)

Kidnapping in Chechnya was increasingly a story of big traders, but there were many who played minor roles in seeking and delivering hostages to central dealers. Balburov told me he had been kidnapped through a chain of hostage-takers. The first one, Ingush Mogushkov, received only 500 rubles for informing another group in Ingushetiya that he was holding a journalist from Moscow. Those who took him from Mogushkov's car and delivered him to Chechnya were not Chechens, but Ingush. They received their payment from the Chechens, who then became the "owners" of the Moscow journalist. They hid their prize carefully, especially when transferring him from one place to another.

DOMESTIC PRISONS

In both the business of hostage-taking and the practice of forced labor, it is essential that the victims be held in secret detention for long periods of time. The humane treatment of captives was comparatively rare. Hostages were normally hidden in secret locations called *zindan,* which could range from an abandoned garage to a carefully concealed pit in the ground, safely locked and camouflaged. In the mountains, hostages lived with their guards in special dugouts made in the woods. Balburov was kept in such a *zindan* for more than two months.

> It was a small wooden hut, recently constructed in the bush near a mountain stream, with a stove and two sleeping berths built from wooden planks. I slept on a floor between them. There was a toilet area outside, a freshly dug pit surrounded with tree branches. They brought food, blankets, and the same heavy metal chain and lock they had used to hold me in the previous place, but this time they left it outside and didn't use it. In any case, I could not have escaped this remote and abandoned place.

The most common places for detaining groups of hostages over long periods of time were specially constructed prisons. Mukomolov describes them as follows:

> It was only later that they built special places for detention, called *zindan.* Earlier, hostages had been kept in any suitable room. Once we freed a man who had been locked up for eighteen months in an apartment in Groznyy, in the bathroom. Later they began to concentrate captives from different places in special prisons, with proper guards and services.
>
> These prisons are managed by specially assigned people, and each prison might be different. In Achkhoi-Martan, prisoners were forced to dig their own pits in a former pencil factory, which had in its time been the first in the USSR

> to produce ballpoint pens. All that was left of the building was a concrete frame and floor. The prisoners dug out pits and connected them with passages. Above, they made manholes, which were covered up with rubbish, and nothing was seen or heard from below. The guards lowered food and drink in a pail on a rope—one meal a day. At night they sometimes took the prisoners out for a walk. In case of trouble, they could summon help immediately. They kept about twenty men there in Achkhoi-Martan.

The hostage-taking gave rise to a particular style of architecture for private houses owned by men engaged in the business: two- or three-storied mansions with vast, specially equipped cellars, surrounded by impenetrable brick walls up to three meters high. Groznyy had dozens of these domestic prisons, particularly in the Tashkala and Katoyama quarters of the Staropromyslovsky district—the so-called "Santa Barbara" of the Chechen hostage trade. On one street, six such cellars were later discovered—complete with bolted doors and instruments of torture. These were fortresses equipped for defense as well as detention.

During the second Chechen campaign, one such house, owned by Dzhokhar Dudayev's nephew Tukhan, survived the bombing of Groznyy intact. The *Komsomolskaya pravda* journalist Sergei Gerasimenko described the house as having a cast-iron gate on which somebody had written in white chalk and with some black humor, "PRISON: 'BLOOD FROM GOLD TAPS.'" I don't know what these words really mean.

> Behind a formidable wall we see a spacious yard. The house has on its roof a damaged radio retransmitter, and judging from its size, the radio station could well reach from Tukhan Dudayev's place to Dagestan and Georgia. In the backyard we found a space reserved for the prisoners' walks and a special toilet for them. The house had been designed and built with care in order to give the owners no more trouble than would a hen coop.
>
> The entrance to the cellar is from the façade—a heavy door made of a thick metal sheet with a heavily barred window. Steep stairs lead to a wide corridor with four prison cells on each side, behind more heavy doors complete with peepholes and numbers. The brick walls inside are smeared with dried blood. Blood-stained sweaters were left on the bunks. On the floor lies a textbook, *The Basic Shari'a Law.* The cell at the back must have been a torture chamber, with chains heaped in the corner and handcuffs fixed in the wall. . . . More instruments of torture are laid out on a special table—some type of pincers, surgical lancets. Tukhan's people had crammed up to thirty hostages and POWs in the other eight cells, never fewer than twelve since the house was first built. The last prisoners kept here were Russian army officers, a Chechen and two Dagestanis. The meals were irregular bread and water, soup on holidays.[14]

Movladi Udugov had a one-story house built on a lavish scale with a spacious hall and small rooms around it. A hatchway in the living room led to the basement.

> "Climb down!" invited my guide Vakha Khurtsiyev, a middle-aged Chechen from the Stariye Promysli, not far from here. "This was made for Russians like you. Who would have a hatchway into the cellar in his living room? Would you sit about with your friends and have your wife darting in and out all the while?" True to his words, behind some dusty glass jars, we saw a narrow passage that led us into an enormous basement. It was a prison, with wooden bunks on metal frames and a narrow window up under the ceiling. The brick walls were covered with rows of crosses—the prison calendars, seven crosses in each row.
>
> "This is where your millionaires were held," Vakha told me, "those for whom Udugov's men demanded millions of dollars in ransom. You can see from those crosses on the walls that they were kept a long time and were well guarded. I remember seeing some thirty men armed with automatic weapons loitering in the yard, and about the same number in the house. They would pump themselves full of drugs and shoot all night. More prisoners were brought into the house all the time, but few of them got out again—I didn't see much of that."

In the cellars of the Ministry for Shari'a Security, Lecha Saifutdinn's people kept about fifty hostages, periodically replenishing their number from the hostage market in Groznyy's Friendship of the Peoples Square.

Many Chechens were abducted as well. Abuzar Sumbulatov, a lecturer from Groznyy University, was abducted from his home by masked men on April 28, 1999. His colleagues published an open letter to President Maskhadov stating: "We have known Abuzar Sumbulatov for many years as a highly educated, decent man who was never mixed up in any political intrigues. . . . We hope that you will take time from your important state duties to consider our request and instruct the appropriate structures and agencies to increase their search for our abducted colleague and their efforts to liberate him."[15] The president could do little about such crimes.

ABDUCTIONS AND HIGHER POLITICS

The motive behind abducting Chechens was usually ransom money. Only once was a hostage taken to make somebody pay a debt, and that hostage was a three-year-old child. In addition to commercial gain, hostage-taking was linked to political maneuvering. High-ranking officials or foreigners were sometimes abducted to influence political and economic decisions, such as preventing Maskhadov from holding talks with Russia's federal government, or Chechnya's participation in constructing a pipeline for Caspian Sea oil. On July 3, 1997, in Moscow, the president of Azerbaijan, Geidar Aliyev, signed a treaty governing the transit of oil through Chechnya. British Petroleum took part in the consortium involved. On the same day, two British charity workers, Jon James and Camilla Carr, were abducted in

Groznyy. When Maskhadov visited London in March 1998, he was personally informed by Margaret Thatcher that British investments in Chechnya were directly contingent on the release of the two British subjects. After Maskhadov's return to Chechnya, his "anti-terrorist brigade" attempted to seize the military enlistment office in Urus-Martan where Arbi Barayev was holding the British captives. Barayev, supported by Raduyev's men, put up formidable resistance, and Maskhadov backed off, fearing a civil war.

A month later, in April 1998, Maskhadov convened a meeting between the heads of the North Caucasian republics and representatives of Georgia and Azerbaijan, at which he presented his ambitious proposal for an all-Caucasian common market based on the transport of Caspian oil to world markets. It was necessary, however, to have the project approved by the Russian federal government, and it was precisely at that time that "anonymous terrorists" gunned down a convoy of trucks sent by Russia's General Staff to the Chechen border. Unknown armed people abducted Valentin Vlasov the moment he arrived by plane in Groznyy.

In October, Maskhadov met with Russia's then–Prime Minister Yevgeni Primakov in Vladikavkaz. On the same day six Russian citizens were abducted in Chechnya, considerably souring the meeting. In March 1999, General Gennady Shpigun of Russia's Interior Ministry, who had been dispatched to work with Maskhadov's government, was abducted upon his arrival at the Groznyy airport (his body was later found in a mass grave). After that the federal government and various Russian organizations dropped all contacts with Chechnya's leadership.

Hostage-taking and terrorist actions had thus run their course, from a means of addressing hostilities during the first Chechen war to an obstacle to the republic's normalization, provoking a new cycle of violence. Maskhadov's government understood the gravity of the situation, but was unable to deal with it. Any actions against hostage-takers triggered harsh retaliation. After the liberation of the two Britons, Barayev's people captured the four foreign engineers working for Chechen Telecom, whose severed heads were later found by a roadside on the Chechen-Ingush border.

Although hostage-taking had begun in Chechnya in the early 1990s, initially as a means of settling debts and other business relations, it eventually became fully integrated into the war and its economy. With the end of the first war in 1996, and the installation of a new regime in Groznyy, an organized system of kidnapping civilians arose, and abductions escalated soon after the Khasavyurt cease-fire agreements, which had been interpreted in Chechnya as a great victory. Some observers interpreted terrorist attacks and hostage-taking as resulting from senseless spirals of action and reaction. Seen from close up, the terrorism in question looked much more like a combination of political bargaining and racketeering. As Charles Tilly has noted on this specific case, "Chechen captors regularly mutilated their hostages, sometimes subjected them to lingering, spectacular deaths, and usually made sure other people learned about their cruelty. They certainly practiced terror. But they used terror to extort revenue and concessions from their enemies. Not all users of terror, by any means, bargain coolly over the lives of their victims. Some do. That is the point: terror is a strategy, not a creed" (Tilly 2002: 13).

The Russian and Chechen authorities had made only a weak response to the continued civilian abductions. Often the only source of protection and aid for targeted individuals was offered by the relatives and friends of the victims. It was therefore with them, and not with the state authorities, that kidnappers usually established communications for extorting ransoms. The state "woke up" only when senior officials or foreign citizens began to be captured. Even then, efforts to obtain their release were made not by special service operations or negotiations, but merely by paying the ransoms. The state's failure to take a tough, principled position only encouraged the bandits. The proliferation of hostage-taking was indisputable evidence of the independence movement's failure. It had enabled the various Chechen military factions—and not the rule of law—to gain control of the region for more than three years. It was thus a failure of the state as well.

NINE

Violence in Secessionist Warfare

I envied the dead. But I didn't want to die.

ZARETA

This war brought all sorts of scum and vermin out of the mire, and it will take a huge effort to force them back into the pit. Evil lurks in all men, and any mutiny or armed clash will loosen their moral restraints. The result is a fiendish maelstrom that's hard to control.

MUSA P.

War, death, and ruin—those horrors are right under our feet, so close to us that a man can sink into the abyss at any time. The very foundations of human life are insecure. We all tread on a thin crust, as it were, and might at any moment plunge through into the depths.

SAID M.

If we reject simplistic and politically influenced notions of "inherent" Chechen or Russian cruelty, what is the sociocultural basis for the widespread violence that surfaced in the Chechen conflict and in Chechen society as a whole? More important, what happens to society and to an individual in a context of secessionist warfare? The Chechen war was neither a conflict between two ethnic groups nor one between two states. It was a group-*versus*-state conflict. The fact that President Yeltsin launched a military invasion into the breakaway region without the necessary technical and logistical preparation complicated matters immediately and substantially. Why was that decision made, what were the army's marching orders, and how did they set the moral and political tone for the Russian forces' brutal conduct within their own country? As the State Duma Deputy Sergei Yushenkov commented, Oleg Lobov (secretary of the Security Council) told him cynically, "We need a small victorious war, as in Haiti, to raise the president's ratings."[1] The "small victorious war" turned into a large-scale conflagration, triggered not only by the Chechen separatists' armed resistance and ferocious ambush attacks on the troops but by the army and internal security troops' cruelty to Chechens.

The Chechen war was unusual in how vaguely the enemy was identified and in the exceptional brutality of the participants. These factors characterize what I call "demodern" phenomena: accepted limitations on violence are abandoned and society increasingly lapses into anarchy and chaos. Andrei Kamenshikov, an early supporter of peacemaking in Chechnya through the NGO Nonviolence International, complained to me:

> During the first few weeks I brought knapsacks from Moscow to Chechnya full of brochures on humane principles of warfare and peacekeeping. I handed them out to soldiers and Chechen fighters, but soon realized it was useless: nobody wanted to read them or to listen to me, let alone follow such norms. I even experienced a sort of mental crisis over my inability to influence the situation, and saw myself as a naïve idealist. . . . I therefore withdrew myself from all that madness.[2]

No war is unremittingly violent. The ethnographer soon discovers a striking combination of paralysis in the face of violence and incredible reserves of inventiveness and adaptation under the endless pressure of daily needs: which way to run, from whence to expect danger, where to hide, where to get food, when to attack, where to shoot. This situation does not change when violence is no longer imminent and people find themselves muddling through a post- or interwar period. One informant told me:

> My attitude toward any war is negative. There are no issues that can't be settled over the negotiating table. The war was a great tragedy. I had hoped that after passing through that hell, people would come out morally purified, with better values. But when I was in Groznyy in February 1995, I was surprised to hear my neighbors talk, not of the ruined city, but only of what had been stolen from them. It made me sick to hear that. The war hadn't changed people. (Ramzan Dzh.)

The Chechen conflict shows how war can be conceived of, not only as death and destruction, but as an extreme and dramatic form of life. Air raids, artillery bombardments, battles, torture, executions, fears, and grieving merge with human experiences like peace, victory, joy, songs, humor, and boredom. Seen from this perspective, the disasters of war engender a culture of survival, which manifests itself not only in the trenches and on the battlefield but also, for example, among people hiding in cellars fearing that they may not be able to dart out for drinking water fast enough to escape death. It is seen in a mother's horror when her teenage son disappears, or when her daughter catches the attention of a squad of soldiers. Here are two glimpses of life under wartime conditions:

> I stayed in the president's palace until the end. It had been held mainly by guys from Dudayev's guard, not more than one or two hundred of them. I had a sore throat, couldn't talk, and my bones ached from a high fever. I found a fancy bottle of French cognac in a cupboard, probably left by one of the former officials. I wanted to open it, but the guys tried to stop me. They said I shouldn't drink, since if I was killed, I'd go to hell instead of heaven. I told them I wasn't going anywhere yet, and I needed something for my cold. I

opened it, took a drink, and felt better immediately. Then I picked up the grenade launcher to try to get a Russian sniper on the second floor of the opposite building—he'd held the corridor for days and nobody could do anything about him. He shot at me, but missed, so I got closer to his window and blasted his spot. No more was heard from him. I went back to have another drink, but by then the bottle was empty. My throat was better the next day. (Akhyad)

. . .

I went to Chechnya in the summer of 1995 to visit a cousin in the Staropromyslovsky *rayon* [the administrative neighborhood of Groznyy]. When I arrived at her place, I was told she wouldn't be home until six, so I decided to go to the ruined center of town—after all, what could happen to me there? It was all fenced off. I stopped where a garden used to be in the central square and sat down on a bench, trying to remember what it had looked like before. It was a very hot day, and I was lost in thought. Suddenly I felt somebody standing over me, a Russian soldier from an armored vehicle on the other side of the street. He demanded my documents. I rummaged through my bag but couldn't find my passport, so I handed him my student card. He asked me where the college was, and I said in Moscow. Still he decided to bring me in for an identity check. I refused to go with him. I searched my bag again and found my passport with the $600 that my relatives had inserted in it. I was about to remove the money, but he grabbed it, counted it, and put it in his pocket.

"You look suspicious," he said.

"Why?" I asked.

"You were in one place too long." Then he looked so hard at me that I felt uncomfortable and wished I hadn't dressed so brightly. His companions yelled, "Leave her, let's go!" There was no one else around except an old Russian woman, who also said, "Leave her, son, what are you doing?" He told her to mind her own business. At that moment some Chechen youths drove up in a black jeep, all of them dressed in black denim. "What's going on?" one of them asked in Chechen. I could hardly answer. I was on the verge of tears. "I'm taking her away," he told the Russian soldier. "I won't let you," was the answer. The Chechen boy saw my passport and the money in the soldier's pocket. "Is this yours?" he asked and took it back. He told me to get into the jeep. I walked over, hunched down, but the soldier shot at me from behind. The bullet struck the jeep; it would've hit me if I hadn't ducked. The two groups got into a brawl, but there was no more shooting. Finally, the Chechens took me off and returned my passport and money. I never saw them again. (Kheda)

IMAGING AND TARGETING THE ENEMY

Our data show that the atrocities blamed on "historically rooted," "ethnically coded" group animosities, which are often cited and said to be "in their blood," are frequently postfactual rationalizations based on superficial observations. I asked Mikhail Piotrovski, director of the Hermitage Museum in Saint Petersburg, and Rauf Munchayev, director of the Institute of Archaeology in Moscow, who had spent many months in rural mountain areas of Checheno-Ingushetiya in the 1960s working together with young male Chechens at archaeological sites, about any evidence of enemy perceptions and aggression on the part of the Chechens toward the others. "No, not at all," they exclaimed. Nevertheless, it is imperative in warfare that an image of "the enemy," whether a group, a stereotype, or an institution, be cultivated as a means of mass mobilization. In the conflict—which of course straddled both Russian (more precisely, non-Chechen) and Chechen ethnic lines and political allegiances—such distinctions were vague. For Chechens, the enemy were defined as "federals," "Russians," "occupants," "aggressors," or *gyaours* (infidels). To Russian soldiers, the enemy were "bandits," *doukhi* (from the Afghan *douchemans*), *nokhchi* (the Chechens' own name for themselves), *boyeviki* (fighters), or "terrorists." They were "not of us," even if they were technically compatriots.

I was astonished at how from the outset of the first military operation, many commentators, including the leading journalists Eugenii Kiselev, Pavel Felgengauer, and others, started stereotyping the Chechens as "enemies" and speaking of "our troops" and "enemy forces." Both sides started to do this extremely quickly, with scant reflection, showing that "inherited" enmity can be quickly established. "How could I have served in the same army with them yesterday!?" one Chechen exclaimed.

The violence in Chechnya had become widespread even before the onset of full-scale war. What had the enthusiasts of Chechen independence employed as targets in these early years? Said-Selim, an 18-year-old from a village called Makhety, in the Vedensky *raion,* said in the summer of 1998:

> The central square [in Groznyy] was full of benches collected from the public gardens, and people were coming from the most remote mountain villages. Men formed circles to dance the *zikr* [a sacred war dance], something I'd never seen before. Great drums made you feel alive, so that your feet would carry you into the round—the dance prepared us all to meet the enemy. What enemy? Nobody knew exactly, yet we all felt a need to unite against it, whether it was Zavgayev or the Russians. It didn't matter very much then. In the face of that common enemy, all Chechens became as one.

To the question "Who did you think were your enemies?" another informant, Chingiz Z., a 36-year-old from the village of Dubai-Yurt, replied in October 1997:

> Ah, who knows! I couldn't figure it out. At first it was the opposition—Dzhokhar's enemies, and therefore mine too. Then Labazanov and I made it our business to collect debts by intimidation. The debtors also became

> Dzhokhar's enemies. When they were given oil to sell on commission, they would keep all the money and lie low. We would find them and call them on it, even if they put up resistance. Then there were other opposition guys—they had no guts: officials, intellectual college teachers, artists. They would speak at rallies and thought highly of themselves . . . but when you shook one of those guys, he would turn to jelly. Then we were up against the Terek Chechens [a name for lowland Chechens]. Though Chechens, they were also part of the opposition. We placed several artillery pieces up in the hills. One of our guys argued that he didn't want to fire on Chechens, that we'd be cursed for it. But we reasoned with him. It wasn't a big clash. We knocked a couple off their posts, and they scattered. Later, in November, they marched on the city in tanks. We prepared an ambush in Petropavlovskaya.

Local Russians or other people of non-Chechen origin, particularly "city people" with apartments and cars, became popular targets for violence. Dudayev's government didn't specifically brand local Russians as enemies of the Chechen revolution; and in fact there were many Chechens who opposed a rift with Russia, but everyday participants in the conflict made their own, often more utilitarian decisions, such as taking the property and lives of those who were vulnerable or had no part in the new Chechen order.

I did not interview local Russians who suffered during those years. But the violence meted out to them is well known and resulted in the near-total exodus of the Russian population from the republic.[3] This side of the Chechen conflict is often ignored, especially in accounts by Westerners, because discussion of it is seen as politically incorrect, but it is essential to understand it, because many similar cases show that "selective targeting" with no retaliation creates a feeling of impunity and excitement that leads to more violence against "weak targets" (Horowitz 2001: 124–50). If Dudayev's government had given more thought to protecting the Russian population within Chechnya, the conflict might never have escalated into a full-scale war. And this was not because of the overall indignation on the part of the country's dominant ethnic Russian population. It was because the political economy of antipathy evolves into the imperatives of violence. To seize an apartment or to point to someone as guilty of "nation-killing" is not enough. The owner of the property should be expelled from the territory or killed.

The image of the enemy crystallized, and violence erupted to new heights, when federal forces began a campaign of destruction in Groznyy, later repeated in other parts of the republic. The events of December 1994 and January 1995 have been described many times, although little is known about what ordinary citizens and fighters on the two sides experienced and felt. Not enough is known about nationalist mobilization and secessionist warfare, in spite of a number of excellent studies done on this topic

(Alker et al. 2001; Beissinger 2002; Brass 1997; Horowitz 2001; Kalyvas 2002; Petersen 2001; Tilly 2002). Among these unpredictable things are the timing of actions and scenarios chosen by those who represent the legal order against those fighting an irregular war. The rebels' likely response is no more predictable. Many things depend on the outcomes of the first major strikes marking either the end or the further escalation of violence into a war.

DISBELIEF AND SHOCK AT THE OUTSET OF THE WAR

There is an element of disbelief in nearly all the stories about the war's beginning. Despite the ardent propaganda coming out of Groznyy during the rule of Dudayev and Maskhadov, most Chechens saw themselves as Russian citizens and weren't ready to reject federal authority. Many, therefore, reacted to the Russian army's march into Chechnya with shock and horror.

> At first I failed to recognize the war for what it was. I thought for a long time that it was some kind of misunderstanding. It never occurred to me that such a thing was possible. Soviet power had given us a kind of security; we felt that, for all its defects, it was still our own state and would never turn against us. It was unthinkable that our country's authorities would kill their own people. My mind was turned upside down; the whole world was overturned. (Mudar K.)

. . .

> Until 1993, I'd worked on the state farm. Then it all fell to pieces. There was no work and no pay. My parents had no wages either: Mother had worked on the state farm, and my father had been a schoolmaster. I now had to make trips to Georgiyevsk to sell our home produce in the town market. It was a bad situation. But nobody suspected that still worse horrors were in store for us. On December 11, 1994, my friend and I went to Malgobek [a neighboring Ingush city]. On our way there we saw armored vehicles riding over the fields and along the roads, with planes circling overhead. Some Ingush people tried to stop them at the border, and a tank rode right over three of them. Anyone passing along the road or near it was held, their documents checked, their bags searched. It was a horrible scene. They were coming in such numbers that there seemed to be ten soldiers and one tank for each Chechen man or woman. We understood that something awful had begun, and we feared we wouldn't be able to get back home. When we finally got back in the evening, our whole village was in a state of alarm, because part of that convoy had passed through our region. Everyone was talking about what was happening, and some thought naïvely that the Russians had come to help us. One hajji, they said, had even showered the tanks with flour to bless them. It turned out later that they had shot thirteen people that day—a drunken captain was amusing himself that way. (Khava I.)

. . .

> In the early days of the war, they sent incompetent young conscripts here. Silly pups, unable to defend themselves, let alone attack. They flocked together like chicks round a hen. I was sorry for them—why did they send such kids? Perhaps to stage a real disaster, to rouse people's anger and incite a real war, of the vicious kind. Otherwise no real hostilities could occur—just a bit of sporadic shooting, and then things would be quiet again. Most people in the beginning didn't think there would be a war; some Russian tanks would arrive, shoot a little, disperse the *boyeviki,* and we'd return to peaceful life. We didn't understand then that the war had been planned in earnest. Why else would the Soviet army have left so many arms in Chechnya after withdrawing? There's no use talking of it now. The war was needed by politicians and those who feed them. (Visit M.)

The initial artillery bombardment and aerial bombing stunned and horrified the people of Chechnya. Air raids were suffered not only by Groznyy but by other population centers as well. Apartment-block cellars were the only available shelters in the cities, and villages lacked even that. On January 3, 1995, cassette bombs were dropped on the market and hospital in Shali, killing 55 and wounding 186. An investigation by the "Memorial" Human Rights Center concluded that the indiscriminate bombing of civilian targets was deliberately carried out to intimidate areas loyal to Dudayev (Orlov and Cherkasov 1998: 196). I have testimony from the Shali residents:

> On January 3, in Shali, I was cooking a chicken in my aunt's kitchen when I heard a noise in the street. I ran out to see what was happening, and saw my brother pointing to the sky—the shadows of two fighter planes and a heavy bomber covered us with their deadly wings. I could barely drag my brother home. They bombed the market, the filling station, the hospital. Nobody had time to get down to a bomb shelter; adults just ran home, and children who were caught in the streets far from home gaped at "the wonders of modern technology." My mother had just enough time to run in and close the door. To this day I can't forgive myself for hiding behind her and screaming. I was frightened. My mouth was full of broken plaster and bits of glass. They bombed our little town of Shali for five hours. Mother tried to bring us to our senses and make us laugh. She scolded me for the burnt chicken and made us eat it. The following day we buried about two hundred civilians. They had even bombed the cemetery. We spent many nights in the cellar. A bomber would come every morning at the same time, like a bus running on a schedule. I couldn't relax, I ached all over with tension and had no thought of food. A phrase I'd heard somewhere kept running through my mind: "and the living shall envy the dead." I envied the dead, but I didn't want to die. Every morning I repeated a verse I'd learned at school: "All the kids get up at dawn, the sky's lit up and there's no war." What sweet words, I wished it were just like that. (Zareta)

. . .

> One day my friend and I took our goods to the Shali market to sell. It was Sunday, there were crowds of people, and trade was booming. No one thought they would bomb villages, that was only in Groznyy, but we were mistaken. Suddenly two fighter planes emerged from nowhere, flying low, and began strafing people with their machine guns. Screams, moans, blood, the wounded were everywhere. Some people tried to run for shelter, but the planes returned again and again and cut them down—men, women, the elderly, children. The place was smoking with blood. Everything inside me turned upside down. It wasn't that I was wounded, though I was, slightly. I just understood that my life as I had once known it was over. I felt pain for my people, for my land. I didn't want to join the *boyeviki,* but I couldn't stand aside any longer. I decided to help transport the wounded and the dead. Many people were looking for missing loved ones, and the dead had to be buried, according to our Muslim custom. The Russian commanders charged a price for returning bodies of the dead because they knew that a Muslim would give anything in order to bury the fallen according to the custom of our ancestors. The alcoholics among them would do it for a bottle of vodka, and I was grateful for the store of vodka I'd kept since prewar days. I found my place in the war, and I saw a lot in those terrible months. (Said M.)

. . .

> I went to Shali, and I fell under the bombing on market day. Next to me there was a young woman with her daughter. There was fire, smoke, terrible screams and moans. Helicopters came in waves, one after the other. The market square was a bloody mess of smoke and fire. Another missile blew up near us, and I saw that the girl's leg had been torn off. The mother kept dragging her away, failing to understand what had happened. I seized them both and pulled them to a pickup parked at the curb. I turned on the ignition mechanically, giving no thought to whose vehicle it was—I just wanted to get away from that horror as soon as possible. I drove a ways and turned to look at them: the woman's eyes were bulging, she was beside herself, unable to cry or even breathe, as if paralyzed. I slapped her face but she didn't feel it. I crushed a cigarette and stuffed tobacco up her nose. She sneezed, tears poured from her eyes, and she came around. The girl lay on the back seat dead, quite white, maybe from the loss of blood. I advised the woman to go home. She got out, but left the girl behind. I said, "Take your girl," but she answered, "It's not my girl." I said, "Not yours?! She called you 'Mama.'" She said, "No, my daughter is at home." I realized she was out of her mind. And I was near it myself. We went our separate ways, and the dead girl was left in the vehicle. That's the kind of strange war it was. (Ismail K.)

From these statements and much other testimony, it seems clear that many people in Chechnya thought at first that all these tanks and soldiers were part of one big demonstration, similar to the many they had watched when the Soviet army showed off its might—from annual Red Square parades to the invasion of Czechoslovakia in 1968. I have a feeling that even the high command and the military planners launched the Chechen operation based on the cliché of historical shows of force by Soviet tanks in Budapest and Prague. When this miscalculated strategy failed, something unfathomable from the point of view of a legal, modern state happened: the military unleashed indiscriminate violence against its own civilian population. Abandoned by their top commanders, the president and the minister of defense, who simply disappeared from the scene, Russian generals and soldiers found themselves unconstrained by formal rules of engagement and started to rely on the same tactics as the rebels. In this way, the state subverted its own claim to legality. The moral asymmetry of legal order versus guerrilla uprising was lost when the bombing and torture began.

THE CRUELTY OF BOTH SIDES

The fighting in Chechnya during 1994–96 was marked by extreme cruelty. Many Chechens who had grown up in a time of peace following World War II had never witnessed such hostility or experienced such violence against civilians on the part of their own army. Naturally, they reacted with shock and disbelief, initially seeing the events as a bad dream or a terrible mistake. This was followed by despair, a sense of helplessness, and mounting fear for their lives, families, and property.

Ample evidence of the federal forces' brutality has been compiled, much of it by the Russian human rights organizations Glasnost and "Memorial." Most of the casualties among combatants and civilians occurred in this initial period. In Groznyy and elsewhere, the dead and the wounded were often left on the battlefield. The theme of abandoned bodies runs through many war stories, frequently amplified by rumors.

> I saw many terrible things. The value of human life in wartime is next to nothing. Bodies were stacked in piles in the streets, and the Russians didn't let us bury them. At the outset of the war, the Russians didn't count their own dead, or if they did count them, they kept no record of identities. Eventually, however, if a unit of one hundred lost half its men, the commander had to produce fifty dead bodies or be demoted. If he didn't have the right number, his men picked up any corpses, including Chechens, or dug them up and smashed the heads to make identification impossible. Then he could hand them over and sign his papers, resulting in mix-ups in which people in Russia buried people they didn't know. (Visit M.)

Another popular story was that of Russian soldiers killing each other, sometimes for money. Some Chechens think that more soldiers were killed in that type of mutual battering than in actually fighting the Chechens.

You will hardly believe me if I tell you that more Russians were killed by Russians than by Chechens. I couldn't believe it either till I saw it with my own eyes. Say a unit of mercenaries ["contract soldiers"] is offered a large reward to overrun a settlement or road. They do their best, Chechen *boyeviki* surrender the place to them, and they occupy it. Next an air raid follows—bombers or helicopters—and the outfit that initially contracted to do the job is wiped out, somebody else pockets the money that was due to the first unit. Can you ask the dead if they'd been paid or not? Fewer zinc coffins to send back to Russia, less talk about them, less trouble or transport expenses.

Maybe that's why they dropped the Russian dead on burning oil derricks or into inaccessible mountain gorges. It was only later that they began balancing numbers to produce as many bodies as losses. Then they started picking up bodies to make up the number or getting them from the Chechens by exchange or even by extortion. They would take some Chechens hostage and demand that by morning they be exchanged for so many bodies or be killed. Or it could happen this way: two Russian army units face each other on opposite hilltops. "Fire!" the command rings out, and they pound each other into the ground to the last soldier. I think there were many quarrels like these among the contract troops—they were desperate fellows, ruthless, often recruited in prisons. Some of them seemed off their rockers. People said they were drug fiends, but I know that kind and can tell the difference—these were downright maniacs. Drug fiends are milksops compared to them.

Of course, there were some decent men among the hundreds of scoundrels. Not all pilots agreed to bomb peaceful civilians. Some of them would drop their bombs into the river or the wasteland. My neighbor found an unexploded bomb in a ravine behind the village with the words "I help as I can" written on it. (Musa P.)

The federal troops' treatment of civilians gave rise to stories of cruelty toward Chechen men, most of who were suspected of participating in the rebellion. Not even old men who had fought for Russia in World War II were exempt. Many felt they were being persecuted by the very generation whose future they had defended against Hitler's Germany.

I always kept a cow, and I raised four grandchildren on the milk, thanks to living in a suburb. The milk they sell in government shops—what good is it? Before the war there were enough cattle kept around here to make up a whole herd. We even had to hire a herdsman, and when I was in better health, I held that job. When the war began, I hid my cow in a dugout I'd made in a former warehouse that had been ransacked, and I covered the entrance with old crates. My younger son helped me to feed and water it, and it was such a clever animal! It never mooed after the war started, not a sound. It just looked at you with its clever sad eyes. But once we were caught by drunken soldiers. They hit my son on the head with a gun butt and dragged him into the house. I told them I was a war veteran, showed them my certificate, my war awards, and the sergeant just smashed my last remaining teeth, saying, "I know you, you all shoot at us from behind." They beat us up. Never mind me, it was my son, only

> seventeen, whom I was worried for. They put us against a wall and prepared to shoot us down. I could hardly stand, because they'd hurt my one good kidney, and my son was supporting me. Young as he was, he never even moaned. At that moment a captain walked up and asked what was going on. They answered, "Doing away with enemies." "What enemies—this old man and his boy?" Then the sergeant ran up to my son and shoved something in his pocket. I looked and saw a handful of cartridge cases. I was flabbergasted. But the captain was an experienced man and didn't believe the sergeant. He looked at my son's hands and saw no traces of weapons on them. He went to report to the battalion commander and told the soldiers to do nothing till his return. We waited, and I fell down again. The young guard who'd been left with us was sorry for me. His name was Ravil. My son had revived a little and asked the guard to let him go feed the cow. "I'll come back, I can't leave my father alone." Ravil went to ask the sergeant for permission. The sergeant came back with two drunken soldiers and let us off to feed the cow. "You have half an hour, don't come back before that." At first I didn't see why, but when we returned they were gone and the house had been robbed. They'd cleared out everything—all the valuables, even my son's tape recorder hidden in the larder under old rags, and all the warm clothes too. What they couldn't carry, they'd ruined. But never mind our possessions. My son changed after that; he became sad and silent—not bitter, but withdrawn. (Vadud)

Equally unlucky were those Chechens who had served in the local militia and thought of themselves as loyal Russian citizens. They were automatically lumped together with the enemy by the federal forces, even though many had welcomed the troops' arrival in hope that they would restore order in the republic.

> I'm convinced now that war is always senseless. It's dark, insane. I had a neighbor, a lieutenant colonel of militia, young for his rank. When the federal troops came, they began house-to-house searches for weapons. I was away on a trip then, but my wife saw that man hand over his regulation gun to the patrol and show his documents. She heard him address them as comrades and colleagues. "Well, lads, we'll soon put things here in order," he said. The commander of the patrol accepted his gun and then roared, "Up against the wall, black face!" and discharged his magazine into him. Later we found out that those were contract soldiers recruited in prisons. People were seized in the streets, in cellars. Some were former officials with papers and protection from high institutions or from Groznyy's commandant. Such citizens were allowed, as a legal formality, to pass through the nearest military checkpoint. But when they relaxed, believing Russia's lawful authorities had taken over, they were rounded up and shot dead—the whole crowd, young and old, women too—and buried in common graves. I dug up the bodies of people I knew and took them away from those pits. Enough, I can't tell you any more. (Said M.)

Investigations by human-rights organizations failed to find such mass burials, and some of these stories may have been exaggerated. Nevertheless, the following account by Mudar K., a 60-year-old Ingush lawyer from Groznyy, is compelling:

> At the end of January 1995, when the whole city was on fire, and war had become a bitter reality, I decided to try to escape to Ingushetiya with my son, a college student. We loaded our car with our most valuable belongings, lined it with cushions against bullets, and departed. Military checkpoints had been set up, and that evening soldiers were firing on anything that moved above ground, just for fun. I could swear that the whole Russian army was drunk, including the commanders.
>
> We were stopped with other people at the Zavodskoi district's blockhouse—to check documents, they said. As we approached the blockhouse, bombs were exploding, shells were whining, automatic guns rattled. Our escort soldier was so drunk, he fell into the snow twice and we had to help him up. Near the post, we saw a huge pile of dead bodies by adjacent houses. They shot people with no mercy even for women or children, then hauled the bodies here from all over the district. The cars that were being stopped ahead of us stood with their engines running. Their owners were being shot in front of us and died calling for help. It felt like a dream. Then I saw a man I knew and we were taken into the command post where there was the captain, also drunk, talking unsteadily. "Why do you bring them here, idiot, you have orders to shoot all of them!" The escort winked at him. "Look at their sheepskin coats and fur caps." They told us to take them off, and we obeyed. Then they took us to a room that looked like a canteen or a bathhouse, for it had baths and tables too. We saw heaps of undressed bodies in some of them.
>
> We were placed against a wall. It still looked like a bad dream, even more because the room was full of steam and smoke. I felt a sting in my shoulder and arm and realized that we were being executed, but then I remembered that this was a former laundromat, and that next to it was a warehouse for the City Food Supply Department. I'd been their lawyer and knew that before the holidays, they'd received a large consignment of sausage and vodka. My son lay unconscious near me. I bent down to him. A bullet ricocheted from the wall above my head; the drunken soldier had missed me. He came closer and asked, "Want a drink before you die? You're not a mullah, are you?" I said no, and in turn offered to take him to the warehouse where there was lots of vodka. He asked me the way and went alone, saying, "You won't run away, will you?"
>
> Before he left I had managed to lift the safety catch of his automatic. I wonder now how I was able to do it, but it must have been a subconscious move from my army service. I felt blood running down my arm and onto my leg. My son came to himself and looked at me with wild eyes. We had nowhere to go, but we had to save our lives. I grabbed his hand and we ran into the street. Around the corner we met our soldier, carrying an armful of vodka bottles. He didn't recognize us immediately, and only as we reached the park did we hear him swearing because his gun didn't shoot. We were saved by the dark and the bitter cold: it was 20 degrees below freezing. I don't know how we managed to run to Kirov Street and into the apartment of an elderly Russian woman, where I passed out from the loss of blood. I can't say how long I remained unconscious. When I came to, it was morning. A fire was humming in the stove. My

son lay at the foot of the bed. My wounds were bandaged. Maria Vladimirovna, our hostess, smiled at us with understanding. How she managed to nurse us back to health in that embattled city, where executions went on day and night, is another story. From what she told me, I understood that Russians in Groznyy weren't spared either—the military shot everybody. I would testify on the Qur'an to any international court that hundreds of civilians were shot dead in the Zavodskoi district of Groznyy in January 1995. (Mudar K.)

Alcohol was a constant companion in the federal army, and was often the cause of violence in Chechnya. During the war, vodka was sent to Chechnya in enormous quantities, from high-level headquarters to soldier's knapsacks. Intoxication, of course, relieved soldiers from moral constraints. A drunken commander could organize his men and order violence with greater ease, even if with less competence. Russia's civil and military leaders, including the former Defense Minister Pavel Grachov, regularly consumed large quantities of alcohol while in Chechnya. He was drunk when he made his fatal decision to send a tank column to Groznyy during a storm on New Year's night in 1995, and even during meetings with journalists on camera, the minister was rarely sober. As one journalist remarked upon arriving in Vladikavkaz from Ingushetiya with his camera smashed and his car pockmarked with bullet holes, "They are nearly all drunk out there, 'no limits' appears to be the order of the day."[4]

Mirroring the above stories, an extensive mythology about Chechen cruelty emerged within the Russian military and within Russian society at large, and some evidence collected by human-rights organizations confirms it. Torturing the wounded and desecration of the dead were widespread. Captured contract soldiers and air force pilots were nearly always executed. Rank-and-file conscripts were held hostage and used as slave labor for various works, from building fortifications to handling domestic chores.

After Groznyy was taken by the Russians, we didn't let them relax for a day. The war was cruel, of course. The fighters in our battalion never took Russian prisoners, they killed even the wounded. There were some sadists among us who enjoyed cutting up Russian prisoners, letting out their entrails, but I never did that, I find it revolting. I wouldn't do that to a pig. Most of our men disliked and condemned it. Once, our commander saw a sullen, middle-aged man named Shakhri cutting up a Russian prisoner who had beem shot dead. Later, it turned out that Shakhri had been in a lunatic asylum. We had all sorts of men, and we were all brutalized by the war. I, for one, have never liked Russians, because I heard so many stories of what they did to Chechens in 1944 and after our return from exile. (Khizir I.)

. . .

I never thought such a war was possible at the end of the twentieth century. It was the first time such things had happened to us. It was like a nightmare.

> Houses turned to skeletons, trees were burnt to charcoal. In May, we returned to the city and renewed our trade, but had few customers. Lawlessness ruled the city. Soldiers drove around the streets in tanks at high speed, crushing cars. We were always afraid. We witnessed an incident in our market where two Russian officers and a girl were walking around looking at expensive audio and video equipment. They stopped to buy some tapes and found the price too high, so they just took the tapes and were about to leave without paying. When the seller asked them to pay, the girl snapped at him, "You can do without it, black face." In the next instant, a young man grabbed the girl by the hair and fired a shot down her throat. Then he shot the officer who was next to her, ran into the market pavilion, and was lost in the crowd. The guards held everyone at gunpoint, demanding who had fired. We were terribly frightened. I thought it was the end, and I hardly hoped to make it home. The market was surrounded by troops and a search began, but that man was never found. It was perfect work—he made them pay dearly for their words. Russians were often killed in public places, in large crowds. They behaved like masters, provoking people with their vulgarity and insults. (Khava)

Chechen cruelty took perhaps its best-known forms in massive terrorist attacks on civilians, ambushes of military convoys, assaults on bases, and the rise of hostage-taking for ransom, which began as early as 1994 and had escalated to a much higher level by 1999.

POSTWAR PERCEPTIONS OF THE VIOLENCE

Most of our interviews were recorded after August 1996. Interpretations of the war among most of our interviewees, even those devoted to Dudayev, did not follow the lines of official slogans like "a just war for independence" or "a national revolution." Instead, they simplified the conflict as a basic obligation to protect their homes and families, or as a *ghazavat* (holy war). Often included in the explanations was the idea of being forced to fight under moral obligations and/or out of despair. This was the most widespread sentiment we encountered, and it gained more ground among Chechens in the zones occupied by federal troops in the new round of war that started in autumn 1999.

> Most of the Chechen people didn't want that war. They were pulled in, immersed in it against their will, and this can be seen in people's understanding of *ghazavat*. One of the most respected theologists in Chechnya, who had twice held the post of mufti, said at the beginning of the war that according to the Islamic canon, it wasn't *ghazavat*. He was removed from office and replaced by a more accommodating man, one who changed his principles like gloves, but the people didn't trust him. Then our leaders appealed to some foreign Islamic authorities, who equated our war with those in Yugoslavia, Afghanistan, and India, declaring that Chechens were among the highest ranks of fighters for the faith. But after the horrible genocide of 1944, many

Chechens were unwilling to accept the dubious honor of dying in the name of the global *ghazavat.* They weren't ready to be wiped out for that idea. I'm no good at theology, but I think that the war could only be considered *ghazavat* toward its end. By that time our entire economic and cultural life had already been ruined. Most Chechen families had lost members, and many families had perished altogether. The barbarous mass bombing and shelling of civilians called the very existence of our people into question. Then those who had refrained from fighting took up arms because they had no choice. It was a matter of life or death for our nation. (Said M.)

Another motive for fighting was "to prevent the disgrace of our women" and to defend the native land. A 40-year-old bus driver from the village of Dachu-Barzoi said in October 1997:

You ask me if I took part in the war. I did, but not with the *boyeviki.* I had nothing to do with them. When the troops approached our village, we already knew about the massacres in Groznyy and Samashki. Everyone who could handle arms swore on the Qur'an to die before permitting the disgrace of our women. None of our village people were with the *boyeviki* except my brother, who fought in Groznyy. Even though he's younger than me, he had been a desperate rascal since boyhood and served two prison terms. He isn't popular in our village. Once he came to us with his pals, saying they would defend us because they had arms and ammunition, but all our men were against that. Our elders told him to get out or take orders from me. Since I'd been a major in the Soviet army, I was elected head of our local defense. The elders were right—my brother was associating with lawless cutthroats. I heard that later they all joined the marauders. But we fought honestly. The Russians thought they'd get us with their artillery and made noise around the clock, but as a reserve officer, I knew it was more frightening than effective: we had dug in so deep, they could only get us with a depth charge, and our village is too small a target for air strikes. We had taken our women and children to the mountains, where we have deep caves. Though they leveled our village to the ground, they killed only 8 of our 120 men. And even that was mostly through the silliness of our younger lads, who would attack without command or start stupid hand-to-hand fighting. The federals could never cut off our road to the mountain gorge. We destroyed lots and lots of their machinery, killing over two hundred of their men. We hadn't counted them, but when we captured an army captain, he told us. (Khizir B.)

And that is how many recruits for fighting often emerged, moved by anger, not by political calculation:

Right after the war began, my brother-in-law was killed. Then my niece was taken away by Russian troops, and we haven't found her to this day. Then Russian troops began to extort money for the bodies of Chechens they had killed. My hands reached for arms involuntarily. I sold my Moskvich car and bought an automatic gun. I can tell you that our army wasn't really provided with arms. Dudayev and his pack had sold all the weapons left by the Soviet army before the war. Actually, Dudayev had no proper army—no call-up, no strategic reserves. The rumors that Dudayev had secret weapons, that he would fight on the enemy's territory, that he would blow up the atomic power plants there, were nothing but shameless barefaced lies. He had no fronts, no army. What sort of army could it be, tell me, if at the peak of the war, he had little more than one thousand men moving from place to place in the mountains? Two brigade generals for every ten men, it was a joke, like kids playing war. And with that baloney he hoodwinked the whole nation—I could howl with anger! The real war began when the people took up arms to defend their homes and their families. Look at me—I hadn't wanted to fight, they made me! I knew about the contract soldiers, with their atrocities and other outrages. When I thought that my daughter might fall into their hands, I reached for the gun. I had to take part in the war. (Kyura)

A CONSPIRACY AGAINST THE PEOPLE

A common interpretation of the war among Chechens suggested that it was a conspiracy against the people. Political leaders and other self-interested parties deceived the public with slogans and promises, intentionally turning the populace into killers against their own will. In contrast to the predominant public discourse during the war (revolution, liberation, defense of motherland), this version attempted to explain the violence by framing it as an unwanted imposition upon ordinary people who had taken no part in instigating it. Alik A., a 35-year-old schoolteacher from Groznyy, shared his thoughts in the autumn of 1997:

> It was the dirtiest war, the most criminal and disgusting of all those I have ever read about. In other wars, the ruling elite would betray their people and gain fabulous profits from their country's bloodshed, but here it was a man [i.e., Dudayev] who was alien to our nation in his origin, faith, upbringing, language, and way of life who succeeded in deceiving it, tempting and mesmerizing it. He led the nation astray like the Pied Piper of Hamelin and drowned it in its own blood. He buried our people under the debris of their own homes. Many noted that while Dudayev traveled around in his comfortable wagon, equipped with all the conveniences and means of communication, the federal air force would raid only the places where he'd stopped, about seven to ten minutes after his departure. Where in history could you find another nation that applauded its idol, made verses in his honor, and extolled him above the prophets while being led to the slaughter?

The 60-year-old Ingush lawyer Mudar K. observed in Groznyy in November 1997:

> I think that the leaders on both sides set people of different nationalities—Russians and Chechens—at each others' throats like wild beasts. I'm con-

vinced that the war was needed by politicians in order to divert attention to Russia's outskirts. In the long run, the war benefited those businessmen who had unleashed it in order to shed the blood of both peoples, to rob Russia and break its back so that it could never rise again. Those men of Jewish and Chechen origin who made great fortunes on the war, I'd bring them to justice. They now possess villas and yachts from Switzerland to the Canary Islands, and from America to Israel.

Kyura A., a 50-year-old former dancer in a folk ensemble, who had previously lived in the rural Shatoiskii *raion* but was now (autumn 1997) working as a guide in Groznyy, said:

> I've racked my brains over the question: was it worth it to destroy the Chechen republic, killing tens of thousands of people, in order to bring a bunch of nobodies, dirty rascals, and profiteers to power? What kind of sovereignty or national freedom must we pay such a price for? I polled people about it, and I swear that 99 percent of our population don't even understand the word "sovereignty" and never thought of the USSR as an empire. Chechen men had actually made good livings by traveling all over the country as seasonal labor. I know from my own experience that ordinary people of all nations never think of sovereignty as long as they aren't driven to war. Isn't that the paradox of history? The people had no wish or intention to fight, but politicians made them kill each other.

Khozhahmed Sh., a 35-year-old small businessman from the village of Belgatoi, shared his own vision of war (Groznyy, November 1997):

> The war stunned me, I was just lost. I'd had a good business, I'd been doing well. Maybe for that reason I thought the war would end sooner. They would shoot a little, I thought, then write off some machinery, property, and ammunition, and that would be the end of it. But no, the war went on and on, month after month. At first the federals threw young boys, untrained conscripts, into it. Later, I realized they had done it deliberately to anger the [Russian] people and stir up mutual hatred. Then both sides used contract soldiers, mercenaries. The instigators wanted a mass murder of the civilian population or they would never provoke the full-scale war they needed. They doomed the people in order to pursue their own far-reaching goals. When I recognized that my whole nation was at stake, that huge fortunes were being made out of its blood, that villas were being built in the West and palaces raised on people's bones in Chechnya, I couldn't stand aside. Groznyy was destroyed, villages were smoking in ruins, there was no family that hadn't lost one of its members. I came under fire many times, and my house had been blown up. I went to live with my parents, but I still refrained from taking up arms. Something held me back, though I'm far from a timid man; I'd never hesitate to fight for the right cause.
>
> While I was taking care of my parents, I saw that a unit of Chechen forces was deployed in a gully behind our settlement, where Oil Field No. 12 was. They kept up a barrage of fire with antiaircraft guns. Strangely enough, the

> federal air forces never dropped any bombs into that gully, but methodically bashed our settlement instead. It was a common procedure: first the gully boomed with weapons, followed by a raid on our township, then on Alkhazurovo and Goyskoye, those closest by. They didn't touch a hair of the *boyeviki*'s heads in all the three or four months I spent in the cellar of our bombed house. At the end of March, there came a lull in the raids, and the *boyeviki* were bored by inaction. So they rolled out two tanks on the hill in front of their gully and started firing on Groznyy. The nearest and easiest targets for them were the oil derricks, but I saw them take aim at the apartment blocks and schools in the Savodskoy district instead. I watched through binoculars I'd swiped from a Russian officer, as the blocks caught fire and they hit city hospital No. 4. I saw the people in the hospital, the staff and the wounded, running around in panic. But on my word, not a shot came in answer from the federals, though I knew that the district had been provided with well-armed blockhouses, a commandant's post, and a lot of artillery. That's how things were! Soon after that the gully was abandoned by the *boyeviki.* They left on a moonlit night, clear as day. The next morning the empty gully was hit with heavy air raids, which had never happened in all the preceding months.

A common refrain evokes an "honest and decent people" eventually broken down by empty slogans and promises. Said M., a 41-year-old employee of the state cooperative system, expressed this in Groznyy in September 1997:

> Our people were led into temptation by slogans. I'm convinced that the people didn't want war, or *ghazavat,* but they were forced to fight. For a long time, the majority of honest and decent citizens preferred to stand aside and watch. They hoped things would settle down, that the unrest would subside and life would resume its normal course. It wasn't indifference that held them back, but hope that their restraint would help bring about peace and calm. They were only playing into the hands of those who immersed people in the slaughter.

Here is probably the most important testimony from an active participant in the fighting. Taus A., a 30-year-old "general" under Dudayev, said in August 1997:

> I didn't want to have anything to do with that man Dudayev, but he turned out to be our commander-in-chief. I can tell you it was only because of his words, not for a single example of his command. When we were in the mountains, suffering from cold in our dugouts, the high command never sent us a word of encouragement, or even first aid materials, although so many of our wounded died for lack of proper medication and bandages. The war wasn't won by Dudayev, but by the people. When they saw what the Russian soldiers were doing, they understood what was in store for them, and their blood boiled. The people's militias were the main force behind our victory, and Dudayev had little to do with it, except by sending some commanders to the front. I saw them: our guys would prevail in an operation by their own wits, then a commander would pop up from nowhere.

WAR AS INFERNO

Philosophical and even semi-religious perspectives on the war were also aired, illustrating how its brutal defiance of rational explanation contributed to an existential confusion and search for deeper causes. Interpretations were articulated by those men who were rather like sherpas of war and did not take an active part in the fighting. One of them offered a version that bordered on the mystical:

> I took bodies in my truck to Urus-Martan, to the Terek, to be identified by their relatives. I happened to find the remains of people I'd known, sometimes for years, or all my life. We'd gone to school together or met while raising our children. I began to understand that war isn't always brought to us from outside. War, death, ruin—those horrors are right under our feet, so close to us that a man can sink into the abyss at any time. The very foundation of human life is insecure. We all tread on a thin crust, as it were, and might at any moment plunge through into the depths. The bodies I hauled had quite recently been live people who had loved, hoped, trusted. Then the crust cracked under their feet, and they fell into the pit. I can't forget the body of one young man—fair, handsome, casually clad in jeans. He looked so pure, tranquil, and beautiful, as if asleep. There was a bunch of wilted roses still clutched in his hand. It's not often you'd see a Chechen boy carrying flowers; he must have been going to meet a girl, maybe for her birthday, and then was suddenly strafed in an unexpected air raid. His body was piled up with the others, the roses still in his hand. (Said M.)

The dissolution of the old order was not necessarily seen as progress. Nearly every village, for example, had an armed war veteran who assumed political authority. In Kheda's village, his own judgment settled disputes that had stumped local authorities. "He just sat there with his automatic and ordered people about, though he was incompetent in most matters and hadn't enjoyed any public respect before the war." Thus, a new social hierarchy and norms of behavior emerged in the postwar years. Although many Chechens disapproved of it, they were forced to adopt the new system under the armed supervision of newly risen war veterans.

> My son lost his hearing. I too suffered from shell shock, and my memory is weak now. But what did we fight for, I ask you? After the war everyone rushed to seek official posts, to occupy the seats of the *khalims* [heads of village administration], but most of them are ignorant or ill-qualified for the jobs. They've never worked in government, have no proper notion of official service, and confuse a state institution with their own houses. All their relatives form long lines at their doors, seeking government posts. African chiefs may behave that way, but that just isn't a modern state, it's tribal life. If we aren't developed enough for a proper state, what did we fight for then? Though my sons have obtained official posts, I still doubt that we can build a legitimate state. . . .
>
> To dodge the question of why so many had died, people answered simply,

"For freedom." But what kind of freedom is it if the commanders have built themselves mansions for hundreds of thousands of dollars while ordinary people suffer desperately from poverty, starvation, and hopelessness? How can those commanders sleep peacefully in their mansions and feast in company with their many wives? It's the vogue now to compete with each other for the greatest number of wives. Of course, an Islamic state permits them to have at least four wives. There are many ambitious young men who will certainly try to win themselves a place of power, moving up or ousting the present leaders, which means we won't have either freedom *or* stability in the near future. In general, I think that people lacking an education will never be able to build a proper state. We must value educated, knowledgeable people, collect them, invite them to take part in the government, but the present rulers are afraid of intelligent and competent specialists. They are busy providing posts for all the *boyeviki* and do nothing to consolidate society. They think that a state can survive with the coexistence of several private armies, but that was never successful in the past. If I—a man who has worked a lifetime in cooperative trade—can see it, why isn't it clear to those who claim the supreme power of the state? No, things won't work this way. Afraid to say what so many people died for, we say for the revolution, for freedom. (Visit M.)

DEFINING THE VIOLENCE

The war in Chechnya is a civil war, with citizens of a single state fighting one another—on one side, in the form of a regular government army; on the other, as paramilitary fighters, aided by foreign mercenaries and with both internal and external support. As in Sri Lanka, Kashmir, Tibet, East Timor, Northern Ireland, the Basque country, and other places where there has been civil and secessionist warfare, civilians suffer most. They are victims of the regular army, of the rebels, of local paramilitaries, and of armed criminals, of routine killing without any reason, and, finally, of "collateral damage."

Stathis Kalyvas, who has studied civil wars in Greece and other countries, raises a question with important normative implications: "Whose decision was it to use violence?" There are usually two answers to this question, which define two distinct research agendas: the leaders or elite (in political science and especially international relations), or individual perpetrators (in history and especially psychology). Kalyvas suggests that "both answers fail to take into account the complex dynamics of civil war," and he introduces "an alternative conceptualization based on a more realistic understanding . . . derived from testable hypotheses about the spatial distribution of violence within civil war" (Kalyvas 2001: 2). The Chechen war, at least from the aspect of "whose decision it was," was spatially distributed. The direct violence (terror, fighting, and bombing, etc.) did not cover the whole territory, and there were villages and areas that did not suffer destruction—a great surprise for those watching from the moonscape to which central Groznyy had been reduced.

Another important issue is the role of those who commit violence and the status of intermediaries. As Kalyvas observes:

> [C]ivil war violence does not always resemble the Hobbesian world of random and generalized mayhem of all against all, one typically depicted by the media. A significant number of people and communities escape the violence that engulfs neighboring places; many people are victims of selective rather than indiscriminate violence; although few individuals perform the actual killings, far more people make what are violent choices by providing information leading to the violence—often for reasons unrelated to the conflict's political agenda. Violence in civil wars does not necessarily presuppose the processes of "dehumanization of the other" that one usually expects (at least not initially): informing on one's neighbor is often motivated by the kind of petty and trivial conflicts and feuds which constitute the stuff of everyday life and under normal conditions do not lead to homicidal violence. Processes of dehumanization take time to develop and tend to emerge only after a number of iterations. Violence is not a haphazard process, but a highly regulated one, taking place in a sequential fashion. New informal and formal institutions emerge to regulate violence: denunciations and the violence that follows are often shaped by these institutions.
>
> . . . Violence in civil war contexts is often the result of choice under varying degrees of certainty; but these choices entail a joint logic, one that requires the convergence of two distinct choices: of political actors *and* civilians. (Kalyvas 2001: 29)

My immediate purpose is to offer an overview of theoretical approaches to the phenomenon of violence to illustrate their applicability or limitations in explaining post–Soviet era conflicts. Charles Tilly, in his introduction to a special issue of *Social Research* on violence, writes that "observers of human violence divide into three camps: idea people, behavior people, and relation people. *Idea people* stress consciousness as the basis of human action. . . . *Behavior people* stress the autonomy of motives, impulses, and opportunities. . . . *Relation people* make transactions among persons and groups far more central than do idea and behavior people" (Tilly 2000: iii–iv). I am trying to introduce a complex view of this research theme, where no holistic theory is able to explain the phenomenon in its entirety, possibly because too many different societal events have been erroneously put in the general category of violence. Our primary interest is in collective violence, especially in its militant manifestations. One of the reasons for this interest lies in the fact that the twentieth century was marked by an unprecedented increase in killings motivated by race, class, ethnicity, and religion. Perhaps no sociopolitical movement has ever escaped from what the French philosopher Michel Foucault called the "paradox of the hegemonic consequences of liberation movements." In fact, among modern political movements, "freedom fighters" are the most likely to use violent struggle to achieve their goals. During the waging of the struggle, it not only develops its own set of subjects, but mitigating arguments as well. As David Apter writes, "in search of moral justification, violence turns death into ritualistic sacrifice, transforming suffering into proof. With death becoming a measure of one's commitment to a noble cause, victims themselves become accomplices, as long as they view it as some historic necessity. This is one way political violence tries to gain legitimacy" (Apter 1997: 1–2).

Violence is a phenomenon of human culture. The anthropology of modern violence includes a number of issues as complex and difficult to understand as the most complex murder rituals of the past. Compared to an individual act of violence, collective violence cannot exist outside of some form of collective discourse. In order to plan and commit violent acts, people have to verbalize these actions first. Violent messages in political platforms or religious preaching become inflammatory in nature. It manifests itself in brochures, works of literature, even in academic lectures. In other words, such violence involves people who put their intellectual abilities to work for the cause. "Therefore, political violence doesn't have a purely interpretive nature. It employs intellects reaching beyond the scope of the ordinary. Violence makes people forget who they are" (Apter 1997: 2). Involving large numbers of people, both perpetrators and victims, violence gains its own momentum, and the various arguments made by its participants and co-participants (including the scientists) acquire a different perspective from that of the victims or those on whose behalf the actions were committed. It is this cultural dynamic that appears to be the most important.

Among other findings, I would like to mention the idea of the nature of violence being primarily collectivist rather than individualist; that violence is a social, rather than an antisocial, phenomenon; and that it is constructed and interpreted within a given culture. This statement is illustrated by a number of authors who conducted field research among Northern Ireland extremists, victims of religious conflicts in India, and war victims in Sri Lanka, the former Yugoslavia, and many other places (Brass 1997; Das 1990; Feldman 1991; Petersen 2001).

Modern theories combined with thick ethnography can provide an opportunity to launch a comprehensive approach to this complex topic and break it down into several important components. *First,* the cultural input into the definition of violence—different societies under different sets of circumstances will define this phenomenon differently. *Second,* violence manifests itself in two different spheres: one dealing with bodily harm and even death, the other defined as symbolic violence. Overall, theoretical models of violence are underdeveloped, and as Simon Harrison points out, "an adequate theory of war has to await the emergence of a theoretical understanding of the more global problem of violence, which is so far not well developed in anthropological science" (Harrison 1996: 562).

I believe that the study of violence is better conducted when the subject is viewed, not as a cognitive category, which can be taken out of its social and semantic context, but as a phenomenon, which can be studied empirically. In other words, violence can be better understood if viewed as a function of the values and norms existing in a given society. We don't need a metatheory in order to understand and explain violence; ethnographic studies of different cultural (social) environments producing behavior currently classified as violent will contribute more toward doing so. This approach will enable us to answer the question regarding the reasons for some regions of the former Soviet Union suffering from large-scale conflicts, even full-blown wars as in Chechnya; while others in a similar situation (having great numbers of refugees and displaced persons, suffering from economic crises, and populated by a number of ethnic groups) enjoy relative peace.

Otherwise, we shall have to employ simplistic approaches to explaining violence in Chechnya, as well as violence against Chechnya, which are plentiful both in academic work and in the media. In other words, the key to understanding violence and conflict is recognition of the primary role of the specific social situation in the interpretation of the human behavior and institutions. The key point is an examination of human responses to common existential problems under different social conditions. Only by accepting the diverse spectrum of human abilities and restrictions in a given social situation shall we be able to concentrate our efforts on studying specific manifestations of violence in different societies.

What is especially interesting is how seemingly "set in stone" and non-negotiable principles become subject to negotiations and compromise; how former enemies become partners, all the way to sharing a Nobel Peace Prize. This happened during the Chechen war after the signing in August 1996 of the Khasavyurt agreements. Dealing with the conflicts in the former Soviet Union and in many other parts of the world, I have witnessed the way peaceful negotiations revealed the total absurdity of the recent violence and its total inexplicability. Interaction relatively quickly erased all former lines of division (whether ethnic, religious, or ideological). The question "Why did we need this war?" has become increasingly widely asked. Many Chechens, even the most militant of them, posed it after the cessation of hostilities in 1996, as many of the testimonies cited show

What prolongs violence? What makes it renewable (or cyclical)? There are several answers to this question, proving once again the discretionary nature of this phenomenon, and therefore the need for discretionary analysis. Certainly, there are several factors attributable to the "hard reality" rather than discourse. Conflict itself can generate not only front lines but also other physical divisions capable of ending violence. Among those are the borders of newly established political entities separating hostile parties (as happened in Yugoslavia). Externally imposed "green lines" can also serve this purpose, as is the case in Cyprus. A concrete wall with barbed wire was erected in Belfast to separate militant factions. A mud wall with barbed wire was installed at the border between Chechnya and the neighboring Stavropol *krai*. My observations of these physical dividers led me to the conclusion that violence cannot be stopped this way. Violence can be suppressed, but it is never completely removed from discourse, and it therefore remains ready to resurface. I concluded that peace and violence, as well as the transition from one stage to another, are first of all parts of a certain discourse, and without it none of these three elements can exist, let alone interact. Without talking about conflict or trying to explain it, as well as without the first violent speeches of the conflict itself, physical violence is simply impossible. The speech act precedes, produces, and puts an end to violence. However, sporadic violence and separate violent acts can still take place even during peace talks and after pacification.

The next stage in analyzing collective violence is to determine whether stopping verbal violence can eliminate or reduce political violence and prevent direct physical violence. Also, does the cessation of direct violence mean de-escalation of political violence? Or are there no laws governing the transformation of violence from one form into another? The latter appears to be important in light of the reopening of hostilities in Chechnya in 1999.

Words can be a very important component of violence. Armed conflict in Chechnya started with its legitimization through verbal expressions and introduction of such slogans as "national revolution" and "national self-determination," as well as charges of "nation-killing" and Russian "imperial domination." Writings by Chechen authors, numerous publications by local and Moscow historians, nationalist brochures from other parts of the USSR portraying a heroic Chechen history and calling for the correction of past injustices all contributed to the outbreak of violence. Scientific conferences devoted to the prominent leaders of the "liberation movement" aired not only mythical versions of the past (replacing the heavily censored version of the Soviet era) but direct appeals "to complete the mission of liberation."

I can suggest the point at which all these words are transformed into bullets, that is, direct violence, although the link between verbal and direct violence is rather peculiar. As a rule, those who put forward these appeals or develop moral or ideological justification rarely fight themselves. Fighters are recruited from different groups. Most often they are recruited among young males in rural areas or on urban margins. That is the situation with numerous "jihads," "liberation movements," "revolutions," and other collectively violent movements. Different players, often changing the very nature of these appeals, will relay academic and other appeals. With the escalation of violence, the original slogans are not only transformed beyond recognition, they quite often are simply forgotten.

TEN

The Impact on Family Life

It was a kingdom of elders where the youngsters lived lavishly.

RUSTAM KALIYEV

That is what this war has brought for me. It took from me the most sacred thing every person possesses—my parents. I must live with it all my life now. I do not know how long I shall last.

MALIKA SALGRIYEVA

THE SOCIOLOGY OF THE CHECHEN FAMILY

As it is in all contemporary societies, the family is the primary social institution in Chechnya, and before the conflict, nuclear family structures and marriage customs there were essentially similar to those in the Russian Federation as a whole. There was some cultural specificity in the child socialization and family rituals observed by Russian ethnographers and sociologists doing fieldwork in Checheno-Ingushetiya in the 1980s (Pchelintseva and Solovieva 1996). Chechen social scientists conducted a number of serious research projects proving rapid modernization changes and a high degree of sociocultural commonalities in local life compared with other parts of the North Caucasus and the country as a whole (Khasbulatova 1985, 1986; Madayeva 1985, 1986; Zaurbekova 1986). There were some significant differences, such as a higher birthrate, and in 1989, according to the last Soviet population census, the average family in Checheno-Ingushetiya (which also includes the non-Chechen population) had 5.3 members, compared with the average of 3.8 in greater Russia. In this republic, 46 percent of all families had five or more children, while only 3 percent did in Russia. Dzhabrail Gakayev notes,

> We all thought, particularly after the deportation, that we must have as many children as possible in order to restore our nation, which had suffered so much in exile under Stalin. We had lost more than half of our people, and many of them were scattered all over the Soviet Union. Even living in the city, as vice president of Groznyy University [and hence among the elite of Chechen intellectuals], I shared that view. So my wife, Yakha, and I had our six children [one of the boys died quite young]. People were proud when they had more boys. We all tried our best to give them a college education, and by so doing we re-created our nation. All of us thought then that having many children could in itself solve our national problem.

In its final decades, the USSR had one of the highest percentages of interethnic marriages in the world: according to the 1989 census, every seventh Soviet family was ethnically mixed, and in large cities, particularly the capitals of the Union's republics, that level was even higher (in the Latvian capital city of Riga, for example, it was every fourth family). Ethnic homogeneity in marriages was often due to the ethnic composition of a given population and its degree of urbanization, rather than to discrimination or endogamous traditions.

Aside from an undeniable cultural trend toward endogamy, the Chechens' rural lifestyle was a powerful factor in determining marriage patterns. Chechens were among the Russian Federation's least urbanized peoples, with an urban population of 39 percent in Chechno-Ingushetiya, compared to an average of 73 percent in the Federation overall. Moreover, only 24 percent of ethnic Chechens lived in cities; Russians and Ingush, who made up the majority of Groznyy's population, were more highly urbanized. "[O]ne of the reasons for the insignificant proportion of interethnic marriages was the negative attitude of parents," says Zulai Khasbulatova, a leading Chechen sociologist who studied mixed marriages in Chechnya. "The survival of religious and other prejudices in a mentality of rural population also played a part" (Khasbulatova 1985: 45). In the 1989 census, 93.7 percent of the families in Checheno-Ingushetiya were monoethnic, and the figure was still 88.5 percent when all Chechen families in the Russian Federation were included. Among rural, more ethnically homogeneous communities, finding a spouse of another nationality was difficult. The divorce rate, too, was very low, although Chechen men often engaged in extramarital relations.

Traditionally, the two most important Chechen family values are respect for elders and honoring your parents. A father's authority dominates, but mothers and grandmothers are also highly respected. Respect for elders finds expression in many small but significant points of etiquette. When Dzhabrail brought me to his Moscow apartment, one of his sons hastened to meet us, helped us off with our coats, and bent down to untie his father's boots. (In Russian families, such consideration is usually only accorded the infirm elderly.) Khazhbikar Bokov described his elderly parents to me with warm humor:

> My father spoke Russian well. He had served in Poland and in Finland and had fought in the Civil War on the side of the Reds. Then for some reason he was arrested in 1933 and served several years in prison. It was only in 1978 that I got him officially exonerated. He had no money to help me get an education, but he was never in my way when I tried, with great difficulty, to get one on my own. I even had to leave school for two years to earn enough money to get on with my plans. I began to write early, in my school years, and I had my

> first publications in the *Pavlodar pravda*. In 1955, I met my Valentina. She had come to Pavlodar from Oryol to work as an engineer. When I decided to marry her, most of my relatives tried to talk me out of bringing "an alien" into the family. But my father said, "Miserable folk, they think Allah created only them and no one else." He liked asking his daughter-in-law occasionally to cook borscht for him.

According to the traditional ethnography, Chechen marriages are "by mutual agreement, by running away, or by abducting brides" (*Narody Rossii* 1994: 402), although in recent years abducting brides has been a rare occurrence, mostly acted out as a traditional make-believe show. According to Kheda Abdullayeva, "We never had cases when the parents decided the marriage against the wishes of the young couple. I remember only once that a young girl, Nastya, was abducted by a young man she had gone out with, but her family took her back and then she married another. Such things do happen, but the girl is never violated. The groom may carry her off, but then what follows all has to be arranged with the parents' participation."

Relations between spouses varied, but the tendency was for men to dominate overtly, while women quietly made many key decisions. Women took important roles in the working life of the family and in public production. Neither young girls nor married women covered their faces or hid in the presence of men, who, in turn, were brought up to be respectful in their conduct with women. Yan Chesnov points out that Chechen women dominate in the home, are socially and politically active, and are presented in folklore as bearers of high moral standards (Chesnov 1999: 72).

My ethnographic materials do not fit this generalized conclusion. There was family violence against women in Chechen families. There has been more involvement of women in collective violence since the time of the "national revolution." Women were active participants in and journalistic observers of the public meetings that brought Dudayev to power, playing a part similar to that of the so-called black pantyhose supporters of the late President Zviad Gamsakhurdia in Georgia. Women were used as human shields in seizing the Russian army arsenal in Chechnya. Something that has only rarely been observed among Chechens, however, is the raping of women. The probability of retaliation by male relatives (especially brothers) is a major restraining factor, and it was only in this connection that Kheda expressed her regret at not having brothers: "Brothers are the most formidable protection for sisters in Chechnya. I did not enjoy this privilege." Kheda mentioned one case from her village stories. "Rape was an extremely rare crime where I lived. I remember only one case. When I was in the sixth form at school, a ten-year-old girl was raped by a forty-year-old man. It was such an earth-shaking event that it was the talk of our settlement for a long time. Never again. He got a 15-year prison term for it, and then I don't know what became of him—he never returned. Nor is rape widespread even now during the war."

Few cases of rape by armed groups were reported, even at the height of the violence, and federal soldiers, too, rarely violated this taboo. In this respect, the first Chechen war differed from many other violent conflicts, in which rape is common. During the second campaign, the situation has changed for the worse, probably because of more massive and permanent presence of the military in the Chechen settlements, as well as a prevailing climate of "finishing with all bandits." There were notorious cases of collective and brutal raping of local women: one of the cases is linked to Colonel Budanov, who took a young girl from her home to his barracks, where he raped and killed her.

To get back to the prewar Chechen family, some of our interviews offer moving examples of united and enduring families in the prewar period. Chechen women usually speak of their mothers with complete devotion, as do Chechen men of their fathers. Kheda gave the following account of her family before the war:

> We never had much money in our family, but I never felt any shortage of it. We all knew where it was kept, and I took as much as I needed for shopping, which I began doing when I was in the fifth form at school. I would shop for food, linen, crockery, and I never accounted for how much I had spent. My parents both went out to work. When he was young, my father was a lecturer with the popular education society Znanie ["Knowledge"]. The second day after my mother began working as a milkmaid on a dairy farm, he came to give them a lecture. They each tell the story in their own way: he says she never took her eyes off him, and she says she never raised her eyes to look at him. My mother is a unique person. She comes from a great and strong family. My father was an orphan, brought up by his cousin, and among us the cousins are as close as brothers and sisters. My father distinguished himself by being one of the first who succeeded in gaining a higher education. He was an active member of the Young Communist League, but that never made him rich. My grandmother was dead against their marriage, but he abducted his bride—with her agreement, of course. Granny mustered about a hundred armed relatives to get her back, but neither my mother nor my father would submit, so my parents remained married.
>
> Later my mother graduated from the agricultural college, in vine-growing. She is noble by nature and would not be at a loss even at a reception for the British queen, I think. She has a kind of intuitive tact, an aristocratic dignity in her blood. She never asked me to do anything for her. She would rather do it herself. When I was little, I was a weak child, and everyone expected me to die, but my parents nursed me to good health. My mother told me Chechen fairy tales at night. I knew them all by heart. They also read me Russian tales from a book. We also had a three-volume collection of Chechen folklore, published about 1966, and my mother read to me from it. I could already read myself, but

I liked to listen to her intonation. She never read anything for her own pleasure but was always busy about the house and the yard. She kept everything meticulously clean, down to every speck of dust. We had the toilet in the yard, and she always kept a jug of warm water there. She went out to work all her life.

PARENTS AND WAR

The war had its greatest impact on Chechens in their family life. They took up arms to defend their homes and families, and many fought only near their own settlements, both before and after the introduction of federal troops. No propaganda was as likely to turn an ordinary Chechen into a *boyevik* as the destruction of his home or the loss of his family. Joining the *boyeviki,* however, was not always seen as a positive solution, and many tried to prevent members of their families, particularly young men and teenagers, from participating in the war in this way. The oldest of our informants, a citizen of Groznyy, told the following story in October 1997:

I am seventy-seven. I live by the road leading to the city from the airport. All the Russian troops passed before my windows. I have three sons. The two younger ones took part in the war, though to tell you the truth, I did not want to let the youngest one go. At first it was only the second son who joined the fighting. He came to visit us here when we were hiding in the cellar. I kept the youngest boy with me, but following his brother's example, he left without my permission. I had not objected to the oldest one leaving—I knew people would shame him if he held back while others fought—but I wanted to keep the younger one as a last resort in my old age. I felt a sense of foreboding, and he was eventually killed. Look at me, I have lived through every trouble: first the war with Finland, then World War II, which left me a lame invalid. And this time I could not understand who we were fighting against—we are all one country. When I was called up during World War II, our column marched off right here along Pervomaisky Road, and now the Russian troops marched in down the same road against us. It is as if the world had turned upside down. (Vadud)

Many did their best to leave the combat zones, to send their children away, or, if possible, to leave Chechnya altogether. Ismail Munayev told me how he risked his life to take his teenage children out of Groznyy, struggling to arrange their schooling first in Nalchik, then in Moscow. Dzhabrail Gakayev took shelter in a cellar with his five children, two of them grown-up, from the bombing during his second flight from Groznyy in August 1996. The following statements describe parents' attempts to protect their children and to deal with their own feelings of helplessness:

I felt such bitterness, despair, and shame before my children, who saw that I, their father, was lying in that cellar with them, unable to do anything about the situation. I was ready to rush at the culprits and fight, but with whom and against whom? And what would happen to the children? (Dzhabrail Gakayev)

. . .

> All through the war my thoughts were about the children. I suffered terribly for their sake. I wanted to protect all children. During the August storm [the storming of Groznyy by the Chechen *boyeviki* in August 1996 after the federal troops had been withdrawn], we stayed in the cellar for three days. Shells exploded in the street next to our house. The children were crying. They wanted to get out of that cellar. If that had lasted two more days. I would have gone crazy, I can never forget it. (Malika I.)

. . .

> Many teenagers ran away from home to join the war without their parents' permission. They would collect weapons in the city and help the grown-up fighters. All the parents tried to take their smaller children to a safer place—Dagestan, Ingushetiya, Kabardino-Balkariya—to worry less about their dearest. (Ramzan D.)

. . .

> Everyone tried to take their children out, but not all were able to do so. Many children suffered in the war, many were crippled, and it was impossible to keep boys aged 12–15 at home. (Elina S.)

There were also opposite reactions from some parents, mostly fathers, who wanted their children to participate in the war. Their motives varied; some believed that the *ghazavat* and the struggle for independence were their duty; others felt they had to stand in solidarity with the fighters or face shame. They repeated the well-circulated stories from World War II of parents who heroically sacrificed their sons in the struggle against the Nazis. Here is why one parent urged his sons to go to war:

> I was sixty when the war began, and I'm no longer fit to fight. I never parted with my automatic, but I rarely fired it, and I did not rise to attack the enemy in action. I mostly stayed in cellars with women and old men—they, too, needed someone to guard them. But all three of my sons were active fighters. You ask me why? I sent them myself. How would we have faced the people after the war? What, everyone else took up arms and we hid away? No, the M.'s are not that kind, we stand with our people. Nobody will point a finger at us after the war. (Visit M.)

Conduct of this sort was glorified after the war by Chechen leaders in public speeches, as well as in the political writings of Zelimkhan Yandarbiyev (1996) and Lema Usmanov (1997). There were also other motives for urging one's sons to join in the fighting, including simple profit. The following remarkable story, recorded in the village of Goity in summer 1998, describes one family's exchange of human loss for such gain:

Our father gave us his blessings when it was time to go to war. My older brothers were then in Moscow preparing for an international wrestling competition, and they were all invited to stay in Moscow. Father, though, called them back here and said that it had been predicted in an old legend that the country [the Russian Federation] would fall apart. The Communists would not be able to hold it together. The winners would be those who were first to lay their hands on the wealth. Father always wanted to be rich. That's why we went in for wrestling—the pay was good. Then we set up a cooperative. We bribed the school's headmaster to turn the school's plot of land into a paid parking lot. Father felt we had to hurry. We were also first in the fighting. At the outset of the war, we—the four brothers—hit nine tanks between us. Dudayev gave us a special reception and held us up as an example. When the Russians mounted their big offensive, we were the last to leave. Adlan was angry that we had to retreat. He was fearless, always standing completely upright during an attack. He intimidated the enemy, not only because he was a master of oriental wrestling, but because he never thought of being killed.

They say the first hand-to-hand fighting occurred in Bamut, but that's not true. We began it ourselves, when the federal troops first marched on Groznyy from Pervomaisky and when we retreated, Adlan was furious. I loved Adlan very much, and it was he who taught me to wrestle. I was only fifteen then, and Mother wanted me to stay with her, but Adlan said real men were made in the war. When bullets struck him, he refused to fall down, he walked onto another street under fire before passing out. More of our fighters came by and we hid him in a cellar. Later we took him out to our village and buried him in his camouflage uniform.

After that we fought even more bitterly to avenge Adlan. Our sister Leila also joined us. Then some informers tipped the federals off about where our house was in Groznyy, and they torched it. Our father was nearby at the time, and they say he laughed as he watched the house burn; people thought he had lost his mind. After that all of us—the surviving brothers and Father—met with Dudayev. He shook our hands and asked Father what reward he would like for what we had done. He answered that the best reward was land. Dudayev asked him how much land, right in the field where they were standing. "Up to that post," Father indicated, and Dudayev began to write an order for it. Then Father corrected himself, "Up to that high-voltage pylon," farther off. Everyone laughed hearing that, including Father. When he was given a copy of the revised order, he crawled and rolled over that land, and I feared he had gone off his rocker. To this day that village has refused to cede that field to us, but we count it as ours because we have Dudayev's order.

Later, my third brother, Aslan, was killed. He had won the international judo competition and the Russians wanted him to join the Olympic sports school, but Father wanted him to make war. We all wanted to make war. After the war, Yandarbiyev gave me a job at the Department of Agriculture. While there, I was able to select good plots of land for Father and our relatives. They say land will always rise in value, and we had been fully compensated for our losses in Groznyy; we became as rich as Father wanted to be. We now run two auto service stations, in town and in the village, and we also have several oil wells. All the dirty work is done by hired men. So it was not for nothing that we went to war. We knew what we were fighting for, and we got what we counted on. Now Father has joined the Wahhabite faith after talking with their chief mullah, Mahomed Vakhitov. We must keep what we had acquired—our power and our riches. (T-ov)

In spite of stories like T-ov's, there is much evidence that many young men and teenagers joined the fighting without their parents' permission. Most *boyeviki* made their decision as a conscious response to external challenges and the emotional tide of war propaganda, often following the examples of older brothers or friends. Some young men simply wanted adventure, but others fought because they felt they had no other choice. Elina S., a 22-year-old teacher of Russian language and literature from Groznyy, said: "My cousin Muslim disappeared. He was only twenty-two. He had defended the presidential palace to the end, but after that we knew nothing about his whereabouts. Then in January, he came to my father and said he had taken on the *ghazavat* vows and would fight to the end for victory." And Khava I. remembered: "Many young lads ran away from home. They argued constantly about it with the old ones. The old people refused to believe that the Russians had come to kill us all. They said that nothing we had done was so bad as to provoke them to massacres, and besides, it was different from 1944, when the Chechens were deported. They persisted in that conviction till the bodies of our first fallen fighters were brought home."

THE CHILDREN OF WAR

The conflict in Chechnya thus made "child soldiers" out of teenagers who were given arms and trained to use them. For their fighting, they received blessings from grown combatants and even special decorations. Here is one moving story from the early 1990s, told by a 15-year-old fighter:

That year there was no heating in our *medrese* [Islamic school], and we had few lessons. So we all ran off to see the rallies in the central square. It was jolly business—they cooked meat in large cauldrons there, and we ate as much as we pleased. They brought truckloads of melons, all free of charge. People were in high spirits and wanted to make speeches, and here and there circles were formed to dance the *zikr.* At sunset the mood usually changed, and threats were made against Zavgayev's government.

But the local Russians never came to the rallies. Chechens began to oust them from their apartments, and many people from our village moved to town. Next to our school in Groznyy was a house where Russians had lived. Our teacher occupied all the apartments on one of its floors. My three school friends and I took over an apartment in the next block and moved in there. We had no more classes, because the mullah was always at the rally. Those who attended the rallies regularly were given free soap and detergent. My friends and I got several of these handouts and then sold them in the market. Soon they started paying us money for attending the rallies, but we—the minors—

got little at first. Then our teacher arranged that we should be paid as grown-ups, but he put most of that money in his own pocket.

It was Dudayev who brought that good life to us. He held great authority with the people, and I liked him. The Chechens are fond of the military uniform, and my friends and I decided to become generals. We felt like real military men when we obtained arms from the local Russian garrison. We knew that its commander lived in mortal fear of Dudayev. He had abandoned the arms stores and fled with all his soldiers. When people started grabbing the arms, it turned out that the stores had been mined and there were some explosions, but nobody paid much attention to them. Everyone, both men and women, tried to gather as many weapons as possible. Our group was led by Hassan. What we got in our first go, he hid in an abandoned garage, in case the authorities tried to confiscate the goods. He kept watch, and we made six more raids on the stores before Dudayev's guards came and surrounded them. Everyone carted off weapons, including old men, women, and even little kids. Towering over the show was Soslambekov in his tall fur cap. He pretended to guard the stores, but I saw him load a truck with weapons and drive away. But we did not mind that. We took our arms to Hassan's relatives at night. They sold them, and we got a lot of money. For ourselves we kept two automatics and a pistol each. Only then did I feel like a real man. I bought a camouflage uniform, and our teacher's wife shortened it for me. The teacher gave us a certificate as his guards, and we gave him an automatic for it.

When the war began, we were not admitted into the army at first. Then Dudayev mobilized all men over the age of fourteen. I was fourteen by that time, so I became a real soldier. The way we made war is another whole story. We were elated, as if we had roles in a movie. You shoot and throw grenades and you have a feeling it is not you but someone else who is doing it. And you enjoy it just the same. When we met the tanks rolling toward Groznyy from Pervomaisky, we were the first to engage them. Near the cannery, a dozen tanks were already hit. Other tanks passed them, and one got about as far as School No. 7. The driver knew how to dodge. He threw his tank about—back and forth, from side to side—and we could not hit him. Then Hassan, carrying grenades in his hands, caught up with it—he always had grenades strapped to his belt. I did not understand at first how it happened, but Hassan was running after the tank from behind, the tank backed up, and there was a great blast—the flame leapt higher than the roofs. People said Hassan had thrown himself under the tank and detonated his grenades.

In the fighting for the tram depot, Pasha and Sultan were killed. Sultan was a year younger than me. When he ran out of ammunition, he too blew himself up. They talked about us on the radio, called us heroes. I was the only one left alive. But we had not shamed our general, who said that one Chechen could cope with ten or twenty of the enemies. When Dudayev was killed, I cried—for the first and the last time in my life. (Said G.)

In Chechnya, Dudayev mobilized all males between fourteen and seventy. Journalists on TV showed children toting automatic weapons as proof of "everyone's solidarity in the war." No one stopped to think about the protection of minors' rights, and the only adequate study of human rights violations in the war, carried out by Russia's "Memorial" organization (Orlov and Cherkasov 1998), never mentions the problem. Neither has it been mentioned by Chechen politicians and intellectuals.

Yandarbiyev describes the initial period of the war in glowing terms:

> Everyone competed in heroism. The commanders showed the world a new epoch of the glory of the Chechen arms. . . . The ranks of the Fatherland's defenders were not weakened, but in fact replenished. . . . Not only men, but also women, took up arms. Teenagers of thirteen to fifteen performed acts of fantastic bravery. It becomes clearer every day that the Chechens will never give up their independence. But when will Russia and the world community recognize that? (Yandarbiyev 1996: 354)

Chechen leaders did not hesitate to treat children as potential combatants. Even before the hostilities began, many children trickled way from villages and Groznyy suburbs to the central square. Almost immediately, they were involved in actions organized by political radicals, such as creating a "living shield" when seizing government property and army arsenals. In my discussions with Yusup Soslambekov, I was unable to get him to acknowledge this tactic as a problem, but in his brochure about the Chechen independence movement, he implicitly recognized the fact that youngsters were receiving token payment to do some of the most provocative and dangerous work (Soslambekov n.d.: 17).

What influenced these minors' behavior during the conflict? Parents were the most important factor, of course, but not all of them were able or willing to prevent their children from participating in the violence. Simplistic proclamations by professional agitators like Yandarbiyev that every Chechen should fight and die for freedom and independence influenced many young people. Other people also had a strong impact, and in Said G.'s story, we see the decisive influence of the mullah of the Islamic school, who cancelled his classes and encouraged his pupils to participate in the events.[1] But in general, it was the logic of collective behavior, to be precise, mob psychology, at a time when young people were escaping routine life, stimulated by exciting appeals and unclear expectations.

THE LOSS OF FAMILY MEMBERS

The loss of loved ones was naturally the effect of the war most deeply felt by all our interviewees. And yet neither side in the war established, or cared to research, the exact number of deaths in the conflict on either side. Owing to the indiscriminate use of heavy weapons, deliberate attacks on the civilian population, and extrajudicial executions, civilian losses in the war exceeded those of the Russian federal military or Chechen combatants. Air raids, artillery bombardments, attacks on towns, and mass detentions all made the numbers of civilian casualties unpredictable and hard to assess after the fact. In the chaos of armed conflict, relatives were often lost without a trace. This happened with Malika Salgiriyeva.

> I have been unable to find my mother since 1994. She went out in the early days of the war, November 1994, and just disappeared. I have been looking for her ever since then, always carrying her documents with me, along with mine. In mid January, the fighting was going on in other places, but a commandant's office had been established in our district. I applied for permission to inquire about my mother at all the blockhouses. I explained the situation to the commandant and told him I was the wife of an Interior Ministry officer, a lieutenant colonel. He issued me a month's permit, though the official limit was two weeks. I walked all over the city, and it is a wonder I was not killed by a stray bullet. The streets were empty, no women were out. I went to my parents' house, of course. It is a good brick house, fenced off, with a gate. All the windows were smashed. It took me two or three hours to board them up with pieces of plywood. I got to talking with some Russian army soldiers, and they said, "We are Muslims too, we are Tatars. We see you had a rich life here, such good houses, what more did you want?" I asked them, "Why do you burn our houses? This one belongs to our family, I used to live here." They answered, "We obey orders—they tell us to burn down this or that quarter."
>
> I looked for Mother everywhere. Last spring they exhumed bodies from mass graves, and I looked at all of them. Such horror, it was like Hitler's Germany. The smell was unbearable, my eyes were bloodshot, my hair turned gray, my feet were swollen, I could no longer wear my shoes. I developed heart trouble from all that. And before 1994 I had never been to a doctor.
>
> In November 1995, they dug up the mass grave in Samashki, and I went there with my husband. All the women wailed and lamented over it, myself included. The old mullah, to whom I showed her photo, said he had performed rites over all the dead and had not seen such a woman. After four o'clock, it was getting dark, and we could not return to Groznyy because of the curfew. We stayed the night with our relatives in Sernovodsky.
>
> In addition to the mass graves, I searched a lot of cellars but found no trace of her. She was born in 1918, in Vedeno, of the Gordoloy *teip.* I also went to special [spiritualist] séances [and] showed the people [i.e., the mediums] a map of Chechnya in the hope they might locate her [on it]. (Malika Salgiriyeva)

Here is another story of a difficult search, by 25-year-old Malika Idrisova, a resident of Groznyy and the mother of two children:

> On August 11, 1996, my father went out and was seen no more. Mother had been sent to Staraya Sunzha with other sick people, but after a week, she was brought back. When she learned that Father had disappeared, it was the last blow for her. She felt it was her fault. Even before that she had been terribly distressed by everything that was happening. She could not understand it and believed that those in Moscow did not realize how barbarous the Chechen war was. She kept telling us that the Russian people were not guilty, that they were suffering as much as we did.

My mother, as you can see, was a true internationalist and had a lot of friends of other nationalities. We had long lived in Manghyshlak [a peninsula on the Kazakh coast of the Caspian Sea]. Father worked on the oil fields there. We left because of anti-Chechen riots, and Mother was upset over them. Generally, though, she was a sunny person, always cheering others up with her vitality and optimism. Even when mortally ill, she made jokes and laughed. She was bedridden for nearly a year and died May 6, 1997. I miss her very much.

All that time. our family and other relatives went in search of Father. I did not lose hope that he might be alive. Maybe he had been kept in a Russian prison somewhere. My uncle applied to the Russian secret services, went to Pyatigorsk, and Rostov, and searched among the dead. After the war, more and more communal graves were discovered, many in the most unlikely places. Each time that happened, our men went to see them, but Father was not there. My aunt and I went to all sorts of clairvoyants and fortune-tellers and they all said he was alive. We believed them because we wanted to believe. Our hope sustained us even after Mother's death. Finally, in August 1997, we heard that some other people looking for their relatives had found his body. It turned out that some old man had found him dead in a transformer booth near his house. He had bullet wounds and his hands were tied. The old man had buried him in his garden, but before doing that, he had cut bits off his clothes and that is how his body was identified—he had left home wearing those things. I knew it was Father, but I refused to believe it. That was the most horrible day in my life.

Thus, within three months my brother and I lost both our parents. We had been such a tightly knit family! I'm sorry for my brother, who is only twenty. I'm married now, with children, and he is single. We support each other as best we can, but still it is very hard on him. That is what the war has done to us. I live only for my children, and my husband is very good to me. I would not know what to do without him. (Malika Idrisova)

"PURE ISLAM"

Some say that the war in Chechnya brought with it a revival of the Islamic way of life. Islam, experts maintained, is more than a religion; it is an entire way of life, one that persisted in Chechen society despite its official suppression. After gaining control of Chechnya in August 1996, separatist leaders introduced Shari'a law, which includes rigid norms for women's behavior, and legalized polygamy. There was universal shock over a TV report that showed the public execution of two young men sentenced to death by a Shari'a court for adultery.

How did the introduction of Shari'a law affect the Chechen family? Before the war, family life in Chechnya had never been determined by Shari'a law, and many in the modern generation did not even know its name. This is what Kheda knew of Shari'a law:

> We had a sort of traditional law that was used in rare cases, as in case of manslaughter, for instance. We did not call it a Shari'a court, and I had never known such courts existed. It was just that some respected old men came to settle such a case. The same was done if a bride was abducted without her consent. They would come and try to settle the matter, and if they failed to do so, the girl was returned. But serious crimes would go to the usual official court. As for blood vengeance, I cannot remember any in our settlement. I only once heard an old woman say that a family had moved to our village because they were trying to escape blood vengeance.

Because of the war, Kheda says, she knows of people in the village of Benoi who are introducing a new order called "pure Islam." They reproach people for inviting too many relatives and friends to funerals or weddings and point out that it is wasteful to slaughter so many head of cattle. "They may be right in that, but in Chechen tradition it is a shame even to listen to such stingy constraints," Kheda asserts. "Nor would Chechen women ever behave in the way they prescribe: stay at home, cover their faces. Actually, it is women alone who work in Chechnya now, while all the men hang about with automatic guns or sit at home jobless."

This observation of Kheda's pinpoints the conflict of values provoked by the war. Radical Islamic conversion is a way of coping with such a breakup. Certain aspects of "pure Islam" are also a response to the current demographic situation, although Chechen society will probably not change enough to adopt the Shari'a norms completely. Polygamy became viable because so many marriageable men had been killed in the war or had fled the region. Loved ones were geographically scattered as far as Moscow, and many fathers, husbands, and sons died in the armed resistance. The war destroyed many families, but in the wake of its losses, people are struggling to reestablish meaning and purpose in their lives.

What does the future hold for Chechen families, which were a pillar of survival in hard times? I doubt that old norms will come back. The human losses, geographic dislocations, and political cleavages have been too serious. There will clearly be changes. But in many respects, these changes will occur within the parameters of a distinct Chechen society, with family and kin playing a crucial role in seeking to recover from the present traumas.

ELEVEN

Religion and the Chechen Conflict

Our scholars do not want to translate the Qur'an into the Chechen language because there is nothing about Chechens in it.

KHAMZAT IBRAGIMOV, PRESIDENT OF THE CHECHEN ACADEMY OF SCIENCES

Well, our women will put on veils and cover their faces, but who will be standing in the marketplace in the cold? As for men, they do not have a place to work.

FROM A CHECHEN DIALOGUE, GROZNYY, AUGUST 1999

The spread of Islam into the land of the Chechens and Ingush has a long history. Archaeological data and various written documents link it to the period of the Arab-Khazar wars of the eighth to eleventh centuries, the dominance of the Cumans in the eleventh and twelfth centuries, and the invasions by the Golden Horde and Khan Timur (Tamerlane) in the thirteenth and fourteenth centuries (Muzhukhoyev 1979). Many old beliefs and cults of the mountaineers have been transformed or adopted wholesale into Islam. For a long time, Islam was present in social life alongside the *'adat*—a broad term for the system of secular customs, customary law, local norms, and traditions. Veneration of shaikhs (*ustaz,* a distinguished elderly person), imams (leaders of the official prayer rituals), the *khoja* (a prominent figure in the Naqshbandiyya Sufi order), and sacred places linked to these, typified the region.

Historically, Islam tended to take moderate forms in Chechnya. People primarily practiced Sunni Islam and adhered to the Sufi *turuq* (sing., *tariqah:* the path, or method of instruction; a religious brotherhood that forms the organized expression of religious life in Islam). The Naqshbandiyya and the Qadiriyyah Sufi fraternities have existed since ancient times, each with its own followers, or *murids* ("aspirants"). At the end of the nineteenth century, several separate branches (*wirds*) emerged from these two brotherhoods. The differences among them lay in the way the rites of collective prayer (*dhikr*) and other religious hymns and prayers were performed (i.e., between so-called loud and silent dhikrists) (Umarov 1985; Akayev 1999a).

Leading experts on Islam in the North Caucasus recognize that before the formation of Shamil's imamate in the middle of the nineteenth century (on Imam Shamil, see Pokrovskii 2000), the *'adat* system of social norms based on local customs, mainly of non-Islamic origin, reigned in Dagestan and Chechnya. The life of the relatively autonomous mountain communities was often regulated by their own *'adats*, systems of norms that were not the same throughout the North Caucasus. How strong those customs were is seen in the fact that even after Islam had become established there, the *'adats* were not replaced by Islamic Shari'a law. A probable reason why Islam in the North Caucasus was tied to Sufism and inalienably connected, before Shamil's reforms, with the practice of the *tariqah* is that such a selective perception of Islam did not require the mountaineers to give up their way of life. Leonid Sykiainen writes:

> Before Shamil, the *Shari'ah* functioned in the Northern Caucasus on a very modest scale: it only regulated the performance of strictly religious duties and to some extent marriage, family and inheritance relationships which were strongly influenced by *'adat*. Having become a religious and political leader and taking charge of the state—the *imamate*—Shamil was obliged to solve the problem of *'adat* and take resolute measures to eradicate many of them. As an Islamic ruler, he came out first and foremost against those customs that not only violated *Shari'ah* precepts outright but also hindered reforms aimed at uniting the mountaineers and opposing the colonial policy of tsarist Russia. (Sykiainen 1999: 89)

At the beginning of the twentieth century, all the local populations of Checheno-Ingushetiya were Muslims, and there was a numerous and influential Islamic clergy without a rigid internal hierarchy. Islam played a mobilizing and ideological role in times of armed uprisings of the local people against tsarist Russia and against Bolshevik rule in the early Soviet period (Yandarov 1975; Bennigsen and Wimbush 1985; Gammer 1994; Avtorkhanov 1992).

The establishment of Soviet power in Chechnya was accompanied by a bitter civil war, which took on an almost religious character. In August 1917, prior to the Bolshevik seizure of power in Russia, the Islamic Congress of local clergy elected Shaikh Nadjimuddin (Gotsinsky) as imam of Dagestan and Chechnya. With Shaikh Uzun Hadji, he attempted to unite the two regions into a theocratic state. Shaikh Hadji proclaimed Chechnya and the northwestern part of Dagestan "the North Caucasian Emirate," and the following words are ascribed to him: "I am making a rope to hang engineers, students, and all those [others] who write from left to right." After his death in May 1920, several Chechen leaders turned to the Bolsheviks, and by 1922 the Islamic movement had collapsed (Akayev 1994).

The new communist rulers saw Islam as a harmful "rudiment of the past," and it was driven to the periphery of Chechen life. The mosques and the Muslim clergy were placed under state control, and their religious and political activities were much reduced. After functioning until the mid 1920s,

Shari'a courts were abolished, and legal persecution and open repression of Islamic clergy followed. Many mosques were destroyed or converted to other purposes. Nevertheless, Islam persisted in Chechnya, probably more than in many other parts of the country (North Caucasus and Volga region). In 1929, there were 700 village mosques and 2,000 small ("quarter") mosques in Chechnya. In 1931, there were about 2,000 students at 180 *medrese* (religious schools) (*Islam na territorii* 1998, 1: 108).

With the coming of the Stalinist regime, Islam as a doctrine and institution fell under brutal suppression, and it was pushed out of the mainstream into the domain mainly of the older generation, which continued to follow its tenets. The young and middle-aged elements of the population became atheists; they no longer read the Qur'an (since it could not be reprinted or sold), said daily prayers, or observed regular religious rites. By the beginning of perestroika, in all of Chechnya, only thirteen mosques and one Muslim school remained active.

PROPAGANDA AGAINST RELIGION

In the Soviet period, Chechnya was subjected to a considerable amount of anti-religious propaganda. Khazhbikar Bokov, the chairman of the presidium of the supreme soviet of the Checheno-Ingush Autonomous Republic and one of the leading figures opposed to "reactionary religious manifestations," published numerous articles on the subject in well-known journals.[1] The following extract from one of these reflects the attitude of many Chechen leaders at the time:

> Let us look, for instance, at the religious festivals. . . . In defense of them, the clergy all use the same formula: "Unless you observe Uraza (Kurban-Bairam, Mavlud, etc.), you are not a Chechen, an Ingush, etc." Our atheists have written enough to demonstrate the anti-people and anti-national essence of the Muslim festivals. Here I would like to point out this peculiarity: while celebrating [these festivals] a person is always humiliated, stripped of his own will, and reduced to the role of a supplicant. By observing the ritual, he tries to please God (or the saint) so as to deserve mercy, clemency. I am convinced that this feature of Muslim festivals runs counter to the true national character of highlanders—their pride, independence, and ability to cope with difficult situations while retaining their honor and dignity. There is also the fact that different religious festivals tear people of different nationalities apart.[2]

The Soviet bureaucracy spent much time dismantling "old customs" that it believed hampered social and economic progress. Shari'a law and the unwritten code of conduct of the *'adat* were portrayed as reactionary. Shari'a law was viewed as sanctifying private property and inequality, as well as the enslavement of women. The *'adat,* it was asserted, sanctioned the buying and abducting of brides and permitted crimes to be covered up by the relatives of the perpetrators. Here is another quotation from Bokov:

> The religious funeral ceremony uses an intensely emotional moment to represent earthly life as futile, to assert the idea that only Islam can show the way to salvation and immortality. The parents and other relatives of a dying person often call the mullah to bless him according to Muslim custom and "to give him the symbol of the faith." The rite consists of the mullah chanting the same lines at the sufferer's bedside, irrespective of whether he was a believer or an atheist. Friends and relatives play a great role in all this. They feel obliged to slaughter one or two head of cattle and to hand out the meat to neighbors in the street or around the whole village. This is the funeral sacrifice, the cost of which is seen as a measure of the family's mourning for the deceased; the practice provokes a sick rivalry, leads to unnecessary butchery of cattle, and lays an excessive burden of expenses on the bereaved.[3]

Thus, before the mid 1980s, Checheno-Ingushetiya had little choice but to share in the general atheistic character of Soviet society. That is why postfactual representation of Chechnya as an "Islamic Republic" and of Chechens as ardent followers of Islam is a romantic simplification. The facts in Chechnya before and during the war were a good deal more complicated.

THE RETREAT OF ISLAM

Although religious worship declined under Soviet rule, many families maintained their adherence to certain ritual aspects of Islam. A sociological survey in the mid 1980s recorded only 12 percent in the Checheno-Ingush Autonomous Republic as "believers," without specifying denominations (some of these people surely belonged to the Russian Orthodox religion). The word "believer," in any case, was hardly appropriate to the Chechen religious context. As Rustam Kaliyev told me, "At least among our family's friends and acquaintances, I knew no real believers. But all of us have always thought of ourselves as Muslims," and in this sense, there were probably more Muslims than the census numbers would lead one to believe.

In Rustam's family, only his mother said the regular Muslim prayers and observed the annual fast. She was born in 1941, joined the Communist Party in 1970, and was employed in the party apparatus. She also served as a member of soviets (elected councils) at various levels, including district, city, and republic. Despite all this, she taught all of her seven children—the two oldest were born in exile in Kazakhstan—some of the Qur'an. She knew some *ayats* (individual verses of the Qur'an) by heart, although she could not read the Arabic text, and the family had no copy of the Qur'an at home. Even at the height of anti-religious propaganda, during the 1960s and 1970s, she kept her faith and said her prayers, but she never tried to impose them on other members of the family. "They will come to it as they grow older," she said. Nonetheless, Rustam said that certain Chechen *'adats* were often strictly observed:

> A certain amount of respect for Islam was always palpable. Profanity was forbidden by the Qur'anic *ayats*. Nearly all weddings, funerals, circumcisions, and even farewell parties for Soviet army conscripts were held in keeping with traditional religious rites. It was common in the villages, even in the cities, with the possible exception of central Groznyy, to give alms and treats to the neighbors on Thursdays. Those who failed to do so lost people's respect. In our Groznyy suburb, Yermolovka, for instance, all neighbors, of any nationality–even Russians, Ukrainians, Jews, and Germans—observed this [Muslim] custom.

The modern generation of Chechens, those who were brought up under the Soviet system, tend toward atheism or at least become nonbelievers. None of our interviewees mentioned a concern for religion or the clergy in their general discussions. Muslim festivals, such as Uraza and Kurban-Bairam, tended to be celebrated at home as merrymaking holidays rather than for their religious content. When asked about God, Rustam responded, "I cannot recall the question ever being discussed among our relatives, friends, or acquaintances."

The retreat of Islam from Chechen life upset many mullahs and provoked intergenerational friction. Dzhabrail Gakayev remembers that one of the few times his father was displeased with him was when he learned that Dzhabrail would be teaching so-called "scientific communism" courses at the university: "It was the only really serious quarrel with my father I ever remember. He even refused to talk to me for a while."

THE "NEW MUSLIMS"

Liberalization under Gorbachev after the mid 1980s altered these religious contexts. There was now greater freedom for clerical activities, making *hajj* (pilgrimages to Mecca), openly preaching Islam, and the publishing of religious texts. The Qur'an was reprinted throughout Russia, and a new translation into Russian, supplemented by scholarly commentaries by Moscow orientalists, became one of the state publishing business's best-selling titles. The main initiators of organized hajj trips to Saudi Arabia were leaders of the new Russian democracy, including the head of the Russian parliament, Ruslan Khasbulatov. The so-called "religious revival" was particularly striking among the Chechen youth.

At first, however, the resurgence of religion developed in isolation from the movement toward independence. The declaration of sovereignty and Dudayev's constitution were purely secular documents, without reference to Islam, but during the president's inauguration ceremony (on November 9,

1991) "the chairman of the Mekh-Khel [council of elders], Said-Akhmad Azimov, carried the Qur'an onto the stage. Dzhokhar Dudayev took the microphone and read the oath of office. A storm of applause broke out, cries of 'Allah akbar!' filled the air; many eyes were filled with tears of joy: the people's age-old dream of [establishing] their own state had come true" (Dudayev 1992: 10).

Attitudes toward Islam among Dudayev's close followers and himself were cautious and uncertain, and they essentially remained nonbelievers. Dudayev was never seen praying; there were no Islamic symbols in his home or offices; and he never went to a mosque. On the other hand, he never missed a premiere at the Groznyy drama theater. "His office looked like a picture gallery, in which prominence was given to works by local painters on historic and patriotic subjects" (Abubakarov 1998: 34). Taimaz Abubakarov asserts that the futility of pursuing ordinary means of coping with the situation in post-Soviet society was evident not only to Dudayev's enemies but also to his friends. Most of them saw a way out through the Islamicization of the state. There were more and more calls to substitute the Qur'an for the republic's constitution and proclaim Dudayev imam. For some time, Dudayev ignored these trends, but finally, at the last prewar convention of the Chechen elders in 1993, he expressed his opinion. He was not in favor of the impatient Islamists. Abubakarov quotes Dudayev's speech on that occasion:

> The Qur'an and the imamate are holy causes, and we should not use those words in vain. There is a time for everything. There are many Muslim countries in the world, but few of them live in strict observance of Shari'a law. Besides, as we know only too well, not every Chechen is a Muslim. The roots of Islam have been badly damaged here by the communists, and we cannot restore them in an hour or even a year. I respect your insistence, but I find it premature. If we declare the rule of the Shari'a law today, tomorrow you will demand that the heads and hands of offenders be cut off, giving little thought to the fact that the day after tomorrow, it will be a rare man, even in this assembly, who keeps his head and hands. You are not ready for that, nor am I. So let us put our souls in order according to the Qur'an, and our lives according to the constitution. (Abubakarov 1998: 34)

Zelimkhan Yandarbiyev, the leading ideologue of the Chechen revolution, has rarely discussed religious aspects of the events in Chechnya, and only in the preface to his 1996 book *Chechnya—Bitva za svobodu* (Chechnya—The Struggle for Freedom), published in Lvov, Ukraine, does he make explicit reference to Islam:

> The heroic deeds of the Chechen people as a whole and of their individual members, their courage and unrestrained devotion to their country, to the idea of independence, their self-sacrifice in the holy *ghazavat* waged in the

> name of Allah, will all, I hope, be the subject of many future books, not only by the author of this one, but also by many other participants in the 1991–95 events. (Yandarbiyev 1996: 79)

The Ukrainian editor of the book, the journalist and radical Ukrainian nationalist Maria Bazeluk, even more firmly places the Chechen leader in an Islamic context:

> The members of the small Chechen elite to which Zelimkhan Yandarbiyev belongs have to a remarkable degree remained brave warriors, distinguished by civil courage, resolute action, and deep faith, as well as by high intellectual achievements and refined taste in the fine arts. The Qur'an delivers a man from fear of death in a struggle for the right cause. . . . The Islamic philosophy of life and death has always made of that religion an active national political force in the liberation of enslaved peoples. (Yandarbiyev 1996: 7)

But contrary to the widespread belief that all Chechens were turning back to religion during liberalization, many had actually begun to lose interest in it by 1992. This came about owing to "the behavior of the rotten old mullahs," as Rustam put it, who "profaned the mystery, the conviction, the dedication of religion. Islam lost its charm." Rustam noted a negative metamorphosis of the "Islamic revival":

> Closer to 1990, it was fashionable to be able to read Arabic, to know the main *ayat*s of the Qur'an by heart, to wear the skullcap, to say the prayers, to observe the fast, and so on. Teaching Islamic knowledge was booming with us by then, more than lessons in English in Moscow! But it became clear rather soon that reading the Qur'an or showing off Islamic rites, and the activities pursued by the "new Muslims," had little in common with spiritual purity. The period 1992–94 was marked by the most radical Islamic slogans and most ostentatious piety, in stark contrast to what was happening in everyday life. And the people sensed it quite soon. . . . So sullied was the reputation of the "new Muslims" in Chechnya that they earned the nickname *mehka-khella,* literally "national trash."

These "new Muslims," who had little to do with the spiritual practice of Islam, joined the political movement and became a force that encouraged its corruption. The use of Islam served pragmatic purposes for both the civil authorities and the clergy. The latter, mostly of the senior generation, sought greater power and material gain through Islam and the political changes taking place. In Yandarbiyev's description of the first stages of Dudayev's accession to power, chaos reigned supreme:

> Everyone rushed to offer advice, proposals, demands, and dictates to the president and parliament. Some elements of the Mehk-Khel [which in the Chechen language means "national court" or "high court"] even produced direct claims to supreme power, and a delegation of Mehk-Khel arrived at the

> parliamentary session with an ultimatum. Our attempts to explain the difference between the body of state power and a public organization, the role and place of parliament in the state hierarchy, were taken by them as an insult. . . . Similar attempts were made more than once by the mufti of Chechnya, S.-A. Adizov, and his followers. . . . The Mekh-Khel organization basically supported the idea of independence, although because of its anarchic predisposition, it negated both the state as such and the essential institutions safeguarding independence. (Yandarbiyev 1996: 85)

For a wider public opinion on corruption in religion and politics, here is the July 1997 testimony of a 40-year-old architect from Groznyy, a former communist, later a sympathizer of the radical Islamic Wahhabite movement:

> In this war, religion is used as an ideological weapon by unscrupulous people, who are known as such to the entire republic. One cannot be a true believer and have no morals. Unfortunately, there were many such people among our clergy. Dudayev intimidated those who under the Soviets had cooperated with the secret services, ordering them about as he pleased. He contemptuously called them "the rank-and-file of the revolution." Out of their number, he formed a kind of public council—the Mehk-Khel—which became notorious for ransacking all the government stores and lining their pockets with bribes. In the end, the head of that council got a bullet in his mouth. But the corruption among that part of the clergy grew worse.
>
> To be fair, we must add that in protest against the corrupt clergy there emerged a religious association called Jamaat [Accord] which proclaimed the principle of moral purity, *ghazavat* [holy war], and a return to the original pure Islam. Similar to them were the Wahhabites, who rejected the people's religion—Sufi Islam. That movement is still in the making, and I do not know where it will lead us. The interesting thing is, you might expect the clergy's corruption to make the people turn away from religion, but instead they were still reaching for Islam, all over the country. (Timur Kh.)

The first to raise the alarm over religious corruption were the imams of the mosques, those keepers of Sufi Islam who for the most part led a quiet life and shunned politics. They had remained in their rural communities and confined themselves to calling for stronger civil powers in the republic. Their demands were moderate and aimed mostly at creating favorable conditions for those wishing to say regular prayers, and until 1996 they had succeeded in curbing religious extremism.

The mass revival of Islam in the period of conflict might be seen as a search for God in circumstances so extraordinary as to place one's life beyond one's own control. Many of our talks with Chechens ended with them calling on God for "salvation," "justice," "visitation," or "vengeance." Elina Salazhieva, a citizen of Groznyy, remarked that "the role of religion had grown markedly, and faith was the only thing that supported people. What was happening surpassed the limits of logic. So they turned to God. I will never forget that five-year-old child in Shatoi who was praying to the Almighty to have mercy on us all."

Ramzan Dzh. felt that "religion was the only consolidating force. The fast was strictly observed; even those who had never done it before fasted now. It was not always possible to bury the dead within one day, or in the old family cemeteries because the route there was too dangerous, so they had to be laid to rest in other villages. But that dhikr dance in the square was nothing but eyewash. The word *dhikr* in Arabic means invoking Allah, and I don't think that had to be turned into a show."

THE ADVENT OF THE WAHHABITES

Competing with traditional Sufi Islam was Wahhabism, the new "pure Islam." No one had known about the Wahhabites before the war or even heard of them, and to the people in the Chechen towns and villages, they initially resembled a circus, with their beards, long hair, and strange clothes. The spread of Wahhabism in Chechnya was initiated by itinerant missionaries arriving from Arab countries, who had first brought it to Dagestan, as well as by the first Islamic university graduates who started to return to Chechnya from abroad in the mid 1990s. The movement was led by Omar ibn al Khattab, who had fought in Afghanistan before coming to Chechnya in 1995 with a group of Arab guerrillas, with money supplied through Osama bin Laden. Khattab found support in the community of Karamakhi, Dagestan, where he married a Darghin woman.

Islam in this radical form arrived in Chechnya precisely when more powerful means of mobilization were needed. The ordeals of war—fear, losses, and the horrors of fighting—were weighing heavily on people, and the Chechen combatants needed symbols to distinguish themselves from the enemy, as well as to build solidarity. They began to wear green headbands and to cry "Allah akbar!" perform the *zikr,* and say Muslim prayers in front of video cameras before going into battle. The references to religion helped justify the sacrifices being made for the "holy war in the name of Allah." Islamic names were given to squads of Chechen fighters: "the Wolves of Islam," "the Warriors of Islam," "Jihad," and "Jamaat."

Wahhabist fundamentalist proselytizing, aimed at the younger generation and often funded by Saudi sources, proved appealing to many of the Chechen combatants. The doctrinal content of Chechen (or wider North Caucasian) Wahhabism is difficult to pinpoint, and none of our informants were able to explain it very clearly. One of them gave me an issue of the newspaper *Nasha nedelya* (Our Week) published in 1995 (the paper shows no exact date and no place of publication) by the Wahhabites in Dagestan. This is how it sets forth the principal Wahhabite objections against Sufi Islam:

> The Sufis say that their shaikhs, or *ustaz*es, know the sacred mysteries, but this claim stands in contradiction with the Qur'an. Many Qur'anic *ayat*s can be pointed out in which Allah tells us that the holy secrets are known only to Him, and that they belong to Him. We say that the mysteries are known to none but Allah, and that even the prophets can know only what He tells them.
>
> The Sufis say that a shaikh is needed as a mediator between Allah and His slaves. This is one of their main ideas. We say that this notion is outside the framework of Islam. The Sufis picture a shaikh (*ustaz*) as a kind of secretary or doorman through whom prayer can reach Allah faster, a view similar to the practices of Christianity, which practices mediation, indulgences, absolution of sins, and so on.
>
> The Sufis claim that their *ustaz*es are without sins or error, that they are directed in all they do by Allah. This, too, is contrary to Islamic belief. We, the Jamaat [the Wahhabites call themselves Salafiyun, i.e., those who follow the predecessors, and their community is a Jamaat], say that only the Prophet was made proof against error by Allah. We call on all people to avoid the pitfall of worshiping many gods. We understand the wish of the *ustaz*es to trap as many people as possible into their care, for their own material gain. For if people turn away from them, the *ustaz*es will lose their positions and authority. . . . Fearing that, they treat Jamaat as enemies and fight against us, calling us "Wahhabites."
>
> Some civil authorities cooperate with the Sufis, barring Jamaat from appealing to the people through the press and other mass media. They defend this tactic by pointing to our deviations from the understanding of Islam. In reality, it is the *turuq* Sufis themselves who act outside the Qur'an and the hadith [the body of traditions relating to Muhammed and his companions].

One would think that the Wahhabites could not have achieved much success with the Chechens, with their offering of antiquated views and norms of behavior, which include compulsory prayers, Arab clothes, a ban on shaving, banishment of the *ustaz*es, repeal of the highland *'adat*s, and wholesale revision of women's role and rights in society. In 1996, women suddenly began covering their faces—a surprising development, especially since most Chechen women are educated and earn wages outside the home. The two men quoted below tell us why they found Wahhabism appealing:

> By the end of the war, I had made friends with some of the Arabs. I liked those people. They said they had come to us to correct our religion. I was glad that they simplified the prayers: shorter *rakyat*s, less time spent on washing, no need to mention anyone after the prayer asking for help and intercession. The Arabs say that God is one, and nobody but He can help any of the living or the dead. And the Chechens honor many saints; they also revere their elders, living and dead, and always stand up when any of the elders come near them. The Arabs said none of that follows from our religion. I liked what they said. I found it all convenient, because I am a busy man. And time is money, as they say on television. I am always on the road, trading, doing business. For

my acceptance of the new purified faith, the Arabs gave me money as a gift and told me that if I brought round two more followers, they would give me $5,000 for each of them. So I brought two of my relatives from Dagu-Barzoi. They gave them $1,000 each, and I earned $10,000. (Ramzan B.)

. . .

My sister became a proper Muslim: she began to wear Islamic dress, and then joined the women's battalion. Then Arabs began to arrive in Chechnya. They opened our eyes to the fact that our religion had been distorted by the mullahs. The Arabs said that all Muslims are one people, no matter what nation they come from. We should not distinguish between nations at all. A Muslim should behave in any country as if it was his motherland. The Arabs told us that we should not worship our ancestors, that it is useless. That the dead ancestors, even the Prophet himself, cannot help people in this or the other world. We used to have divisions in our religion: most Chechens followed Tob Kunta Haji. Others preferred Naqshbandiyya. The Arabs said it was all wrong, and I agreed with them. They carried on their propaganda, and they gave money to those who joined them. From their example, we all grew beards, and we really all became equal.

I liked it that the Arabs want to go on making war until they liberate the whole world from the *giaours* [infidels]. Some of our people disagreed with that. But the Arabs said that the *ghazavat* [holy war] should go on until all the Christians are converted to Islam. That is the great *ghazavat*. The small *ghazavat* is to defeat all infidels. The great *ghazavat* will be completed when all Muslim minds turn toward the teaching of [the fundamentalist preacher Muhammed ibn] 'Abd al-Wahhab [1691–1787]. Then all the Islamic countries will become one common motherland for all Muslims.

Our great *byatchi* [leader, meaning Dudayev], sent to us from heaven, died in combat. We cried for him. My mother fell ill over it and soon died. But our cause will win all the same, because we have been taught the true faith. At first they called us Wahhabites, then we were told that it is more correct to be called Jamaat. But I do not think the change of words is important. We are going to make war on all infidels, as Dzhokhar Dudayev told us. (Shamil A.)

AFTER THE FIRST CHECHEN WAR

The Islamicization of society and state remained a popular idea after the first Chechen war. All enterprises and educational establishments reserved special rooms for prayer and put up placards with religious slogans. Shari'a courts began to function and meted out Shari'a punishments. The Muftiyat (clerical council) was loyal to the civil authorities, which in turn relied on the clergy for support. A rivalry eventually arose between the adherents of traditional Islam and those of Wahhabism regarding influence on state institutions, education, and the norms of daily life.

In the period between the wars in Chechnya, Islam became the official religion of the new power structure. Although the government had professed a negative attitude to Wahhabism, it was unable to do anything about its appeal to the people. Aslan Maskhadov's election as president was followed by Shari'a public executions of two people in January 1998. Religious symbols were made visible in all public places, including government offices. Qur'anic studies were introduced in school curricula. Certain Islamic norms regarding clothes, family relations, and the legal system became more widely accepted. Maskhadov, a former Soviet military officer, proclaimed Shari'a to be the basis of the existing order in Chechnya, and missionaries from Saudi Arabia and other Islamic countries contributed large amounts of money to the spreading of fundamentalist Islamic beliefs throughout the republic.

In a certain sense, the imposition of radical Islamism differed little from the atheism promulgated under the Soviet Union, aside from the fact that the former was introduced by militant outsiders and the latter by official propagandists. One particularly striking story, told by a young Wahhabite convert, contains a curious mixture of conviction and ambiguity:

> Our teachers tell us that our religion is the best in the world, and that all people will adopt it sooner or later. (I converted two Russian lads to it, by the way. Now they live in Russia.) When I saw prisoners of war, I asked the commander, for a certain [payment], to let me convert to Islam those of them willing to do so. I got a decent sum of money for the two. Now they are spreading our faith where they live. That is how it is.
>
> I hear that [the interviewers] are learned people. You can see for yourselves that all your learning is of no use. Here you are, wandering about, asking us questions, and we may answer or may tell you to go to hell. They say you are a well-known man. Well, we need people like you. Why don't you join us? I will talk about it with my teachers.
>
> My father was a Murjite, a follower of Kunta Haji, so we held the *zikr* ceremony once or twice a year in our house. Crowds of people came to it. We had to slaughter some cattle to treat all those brother Murjites, because after dancing the *zikr,* people sweat heavily and then eat a lot of meat. With our poverty, we could hardly afford it. When I told my father that I was not going to spend my money on such gatherings, he protested at first, but then agreed. For that, my new friends gave him a new car and they gave me a jeep. The Arabs thought that many others would follow our example after seeing that, and they were right. More people gave up the *zikr* meetings and got some money for it. No cars, though, but you can't expect that many cars. But they were promised a hajj next year with all expenses paid.
>
> Not everyone approved of us, of course, and even now some people hate us. But they see that our time has come, and we are on top, we give the orders. They could not always have it their way, for "not even a wolf can eat well every day," as the saying goes. The mullah is also displeased with us. He is thought to be an *'alim,* a learned man. The whole village is still for him, otherwise we would have driven him out long ago. But what of it, that he is learned? Our teachers tell us that much learning is good for nothing, it can only confuse

> you, and everything is clear to me anyway. We must act as our teachers tell us, and then we will get the upper hand. The people in Urus-Martan were always against Dudayev, but now they have made one of our men their prefect, and he gave us a building to use. We occupied that large village without firing a shot. True, they keep shooting at our men from under cover, but we pay them back in kind. Every third Wahhabite there now has a new car, a Volga 6 or a foreign model. People can see what good the new religion can bring them. With time, we shall all be rich—that is what our teachers tell us. Our family now lives by the new law, the women wear Arab dress, and the men also follow the forms required by our pure religion. A Muslim's face should never be touched with a razor. Look at my brother: he has a thin beard, just a few hairs, but he never shaves. We wear our shirts over the trousers to cover the shame. We turn up the trousers' cuffs or push them into our socks, because a Muslim's clothes should never reach below the ankle, so as not to get dirty. Otherwise, we will not be clean for prayers.
>
> You call us Wahhabites. I too nearly used that expression, but our teachers tell us that the right word is Jamaat. First, we preach the purest form of religion. Second, we are brothers united not only against infidels but also against those Muslims who are led astray. Most of the commanders support us, and [Movladi] Udugov is also with us, even though he was not a commander. We will conquer the entire Caucasus, beginning with Dagestan, and then the whole world.
>
> We shall not find it easy, of course. Some of our men's parents are against their taking the true Muslim's path. When my friend Beibulat told his father not to go to the *zikr* meeting, he ignored him. When his father came home, Beibulat did not rise to his feet, and they had a huge row. Beibulat told him he could not stay under the same roof with a heretic and left home that night. And we, his brothers in faith, bought a house for him in Groznyy; when he marries, we shall buy him furniture and a car. Though Beibulat has some money of his own, we have a rule about helping each other when we are rejected by other people. (Ramzan B.)

Although this sense of exclusive Islamic solidarity appealed strongly to young people striving to make their way in life amid the chaos that followed the collapse of the USSR and the outbreak of war, intragroup cleavages have nevertheless survived in war-torn Chechnya

A NEW SPLIT IN A TORN SOCIETY

After the first war, it was unclear what lay ahead for the Chechen Wahhabites. Rustam Kaliyev sees Wahhabism as a foreign religion. "Those who sympathize with the Wahhabites or join them are 80 percent young men from disadvantaged families in which devotion to the Chechen *'adat*s is weak or even completely absent. . . . They study Islam from Russian translations . . . and their most powerful religious incentive is the foreign currency they get regularly from their new patrons. The fact is so well known that they make no attempt to conceal it." My other Chechen partners in research, Akhmadov, Gakayev, Yandarov, Akayev, and Munayev, strongly share the idea of the destructive foreign nature of the fundamentalist Islam (on this, see further Tibi 1998) introduced into Chechnya during the bloody conflict.

The Chechen population's religious faith and institutions, which had barely been restored in the period of post-Soviet liberalization, were effectively fragmented by the war and, as we shall see, by foreign influences. This split created deep intergenerational conflicts and provided justification for increased terror and violence. Religious differences simmered at an innocuous level before the war, though there was atheistic propaganda in the local clubs and college lecture halls, and fathers mutely resented their sons' lack of faith. After the war, these differences became violent. The leader of traditional *tariqah* Islam, Said-Akhmad Adizov, was shot dead in his home without any reaction by the official authorities. Some families banished those of their sons who were "infected with Wahhabism," after all admonition had proved futile. In the village of Aldykh, a father shot his son after the young man had not only joined the Wahhabites and refused to disassociated himself from them, but had begun to terrorize his mother with his "pure religion." The villagers supported the father, who said, "My son died for me when he joined that scum. He became then an alien man, cruel and dangerous to others."

The conflict left ordinary Chechens confused and despairing, blocking the way toward rational choice and creative action. At one time, the majority of the population was fatalistically ready to accept any scenario put forward by armed groups or by a more emotionally mobilized faction of society. I have discovered that the prevailing mood is to accept everything "so as not to make things any worse" and a disinclination to discuss possible ways out of the desperate situation. That is why until the fall of 1999, a radical Wahhabite analogue to the Taliban in Afghanistan was a possible outcome in Chechnya. The alternative was the rejection of any religion at all. Listen carefully to two direct voices:

> Wahhabism is just another game, a political show. During the war, I heard talk that we had been handed over to England, and we were glad that that would bring some order, but nothing so far. From Moscow, we can expect no good. Maskhadov goes now to America, now to Turkey, but no relief for the people comes from all that. Maskhadov has played his role. The people trusted him at first, but he's disappointed us. Now we need a new man, someone unstained. They are all in cahoots—Maskhadov, Basayev—no difference. The Wahhabites have some good qualities—unity, respect for each other, also money. People have started saying already, let even them come, maybe life will get back to normal and children will go to school. We would like to have at least $100 a month for the family to get the necessities. This is our dream, we

> cannot dream of any luxury. There's no chance to think of oneself, or of any self-education—we are all in a kind of stupor. This is regression, our people have fallen back fifty years. I cannot say how it will all end. (Khava)

Isa M. had this to say:

> Speaking of religion, I have always respected it, and, as a man not without sin, I felt I was not yet worthy of truly serving God. But now that I see what these religious bastards are doing, I think—no, I am not going to join those Satanist ranks. For lots of people they have provoked a revulsion against religion. They are snatching from the people the last holy and pure things that remained to them.

These statements reflect the typical state of anomie that follows conflict caused by demodernization, a time when the mass of people feel unable to influence the ruling powers and religion becomes a weapon and an incitement to violence. In 1998, many people, no longer able to tolerate the aggressive program of the Wahhabites, wanted to banish them from the republic. Maskhadov's government made such an attempt, and a government force led by S. Yamadayev attacked the Wahhabite armed formations in Gudermes, routing some of their groups, but the Wahhabites were saved from complete annihilation by the "peacemaking" of Vakha Arsanov—Maskhadov's vice president.

But when Shamil Basayev turned in opposition to Maskhadov, the Wahhabites raised their heads once again. Basayev in fact joined them in order to carry out new armed actions directed toward spreading separatism in the North Caucasus. To the stronghold of Wahhabism in the Urus-Martan region, he added the mountainous Vedeno region, where he began ideological and military training of radical youth from both Chechnya and Dagestan. Religious radicals constituted a basis of political opposition to Maskhadov and those who supported his government. On October 26, 1998, there were failed attempts on the lives of Mufti Akhmad Kadyrov and the field commander Sulim Yamadayev. When Kadyrov later became a head of the provisional administration in Chechnya, he announced publicly that as the mufti of Chechnya, he had no enemies except the Wahhabites.

As Vakhid Akaev writes, "In early 1999, the tension between the authorities and the opposition increased. Maskhadov faced fresh accusations of having deviated from Dudayev's path, including numerous violations of the constitution of Chechnya, failure to observe Shari'a law, lack of interest in creating an Islamic state, and concessions to the hated Russia. To investigate the accusations against Maskhadov, a commission was set up, one comprising members of the opposition, the parliament, and the presidential staff" (Akayev 1999b: 54). It was in this context that Maskhadov was forced to proclaim Chechnya a Shari'a state in early 1999. Although this was approved by Moscow-based retired Chechen politicians and even various experts, several of whom were interviewed on Russia's Independent Television channel (NTV), none of the Chechens I knew welcomed the outcome personally. Not long after proclamation of the Shari'a state, the joke went around, "How do you tell a Chechen? He's missing one hand!" (i.e., if the Shari'a punishment of amputation for stealing were to be applied, hardly anyone in Chechnya would be left with two hands).

Yet with all this, many of my Chechen informants argued that there was still a possibility that the Sufi brotherhoods that follow certain saints or teachers— Kunta Haji, Kaidy-Verdi, Avdiy-Virdi, Deniy-Virdi, or Baha al-Din al-Naqshbandi—might play a powerful role again in post-Soviet Chechnya. They had to build on *'adats*, Chechen traditions, and family ties if they were to be effective. In the absence of a strong state and with the institutions of civil society severely damaged, these types of social coalitions might be able to curb armed religious extremism. Later events in 1999–2001 disclosed the superficiality of foreign-born Islamism for Chechnya. Dzhabrail Gakayev was right in commenting to me, upon the announcement of the Shari'a state in Chechnya, "Chechens will prefer Russification of their society to Wahhabist Arabization, which is absolutely alien to their culture."

As it seems to me now, when Wahhabism has left Chechnya and the Taliban has been defeated in Afghanistan, postwar Chechnya will return to the kind of symbiosis of traditional secularity and more open humanistic Islam that is preached in some of Russia's other republics, like Tatarstan and Bashkiria. Doors are not closed even for the Russian Orthodox Church in Chechnya, which suffered most as a result of the war.

In spite of these ambiguous times, some people seem to be clear about what they believe in. Let me come back to one of my earliest talks with Chechens. When I asked Akhyad, "What do you think of religion?" his answer surprised me:

> My religion is simple. You must wash your hands five times a day, your feet too—you must always be clean. They say that a Russian general once asked [Imam] Shamil [1797?–1871] what he was fighting for. Shamil called one of his men and told him to take off his boots. The Chechen had clean feet and neatly clipped toenails. Now let us call one of yours, he said, and the Russian soldier was found to have dirty nails and smelly feet. See now what we are fighting for? Shamil asked. Even now, Russian soldiers sometimes leave their hands unwashed for three days running.

TWELVE

The Myth and Reality of the "Great Victory"

The Chechen elders convene yet again for another Mekh-Khel. Sitting in state on their stone seats under the great dome of dark-blue sky, they try to define the most difficult thing in the world. After three days' deliberation they answer that the hardest lot is being a Chechen. One of them still voices his doubt: isn't there anything harder than that? The chairman then corrects the verdict, saying the hardest thing is to go through life remaining a Chechen to the end.

"PRESENT-DAY CHECHEN FOLKLORE," *Mekh-Khel*, NO. 1 (JULY 1999)

We need now to analyze postwar Chechen society during the three years between August 1996 and the onset of the new war in 1999. Certain aspects of this period are self-evident, including the devastated infrastructure, a thorough economic collapse, a mass exodus from the republic, and the disintegration of civil institutions, leading to the proliferation of high-level criminal activities such as hostage-taking. Thomas Graham, an academic-turned-politician under the Bush administration, one of the thoughtful observers of Russia, described the situation as follows:

> After the victory in 1996, Chechnya once again fell quickly into a state of near anarchy. The Chechen elite shared most of the blame for that, even if the brutalization and destruction of the first Chechen war undoubtedly complicated the task of building a reasonably functioning, coherent state. Field commanders quickly seized control over small bits of territory and undermined the influence of the popularly elected Chechen president, Aslan Maskhadov. By the time of the Russian invasion in September 1999, Maskhadov no longer controlled the situation in his country. Kidnapping of Chechens, Russians, and others for ransom had become a growth industry. Between the two wars, over a thousand persons were kidnapped. Many were sold into slavery; others were tortured and mutilated; some were simply murdered. Little, if anything, was in fact done to rebuild the economy or consolidate Chechnya's de facto independence. At the same time, forces emerged in Chechnya that were interested not simply in creating an independent state, but in attacking and destabilizing neighboring regions of Russia, especially Dagestan. The most important alliance was between Chechen field commander Basayev and the followers of Khattab, whose goals included the formation of an Islamic state uniting Chechnya and Dagestan. In addition, there were numerous terrorist

> attacks launched from Chechnya into neighboring Russian regions. (Graham 2001: 24; see also Lieven 2000)

I had come across similar evaluations earlier in my interviews and while reading local Chechen publications. Soon before the new war started, for example, I read an article by Khamzat Gakayev that asserted: "We are witnessing a rapid destruction of the economic, cultural, legal, and spiritual foundations of the young Chechen state and of its civilian life. We see a discrediting of the Muslim and national moral values, customs, and traditions, all of which the Chechens were proud of, and which they cherished in the hardest periods of their lives."[1]

Why did a new cycle of violence erupt? How does Chechnya differ from other societies that have gone through such deeply violent conflicts?

THE DIFFICULTY OF GETTING BACK TO NORMAL

Essentially, the war did not truly end for Chechnya in August 1996. It lived on in the minds and actions of armed veterans, politicians, and various intellectuals. It was revived daily in the propaganda about the "great victory" that had asserted Chechen superiority over the rest of the world. Chechens had cultivated the image of an enemy (Russia and the Russians), and the resumption of fighting was encouraged by outsiders who supported complete secession from the Russian Federation. The circles supporting Chechnya's continued fighting after 1996 were in fact wider and more influential than those that had been dominant during the war. In the aftermath of the Khasavyurt agreements and the treaty signed by Yeltsin and Maskhadov in May 1997, the idea of Russia's disintegration, the federation having lost first Chechnya and then other Muslim regions, seemed increasingly plausible. The outside world assumed that Chechnya's independence was already decided: From the academic community to journalists and the general public, Chechnya was addressed as an independent state. The French photojournalist Brice Fleutiaux, who was released from Chechen captivity in the summer of 2000, said he actually "did not know Chechnya was [still] a part of Russia" when he crossed its border from Georgia. In an interview with Ichkeria's state television, the well-known Moscow radical activist Valeria Novodvorskaya counseled: "A peace treaty is a good thing, of course. But knowing how unpredictable Russia is, I would advise the Chechens to trust to Allah. As long as Chechens have arms, peace will be observed. Therefore they should not lay these arms down."[2]

D. E. Furman observed in the preface to *Rossia i Chechnia: Obschestva i gosudarstva* (Russia and Chechnya: Societies and States), a book he edited:

> The Chechens' resistance and victory were a kind of miracle, which was made possible by the same reasons that had led to the war. Such a war and such a vic-

tory required a complete unwillingness and inability to "bow to reality"—the only attitude that can reverse and overcome this same reality. Chechen resistance was led by two factors: the desperate resolve by a people once subjected to genocide to never let that happen again . . . and a revolutionary popular upsurge, similar to [those of] the victorious French revolutionary wars or the Bolshevik army. (Furman 1999b: 14)

This Western and domestic support for Chechnya and its imagined independence changed partly when the Chechen leadership transferred its allegiances from the West to the Islamic world. This change derived both from changes in the political positions of leading Western countries that had limited their attention to and moral support for Chechnya and from Chechnya's growing reliance on the ideological and military resources of Arab allies. Chechen ideas about the external world also began to shift: The West began to be perceived as treacherous, Israel and Russia as archenemies, and the Muslim world became the republic's main friend, aside from the Baltic countries. In February 1998, after attending a World Muslim Congress in Pakistan, Chechnya's minister of defense, Khamzat Gelayev, reported:

In Pakistan there lives an elderly emir, head of the Muslim society, and I had a long talk with him. I asked him to say a prayer to alleviate the suffering in Chechnya. Later, he said that he and his followers had recited 125,000 prayers for peace in Chechnya—more than they had ever said in his seventy years of preaching Islam. They said Allah had blessed the Chechens who, though small in numbers, have chosen the way of *ghazavat* [holy war]. [That is why] the Almighty sent them victory and all the Muslim world loves them.

Our delegation was given a top-level reception. For the opening of the Muslim Congress they had built a shrine modeled on the Ka'ba [in Mecca]. After a long deliberation, the holy *(shura)* council decided that the new shrine *(ziayrat)* should be consecrated by the Chechen clergy. That surprised the Arab guests, descendants of the Prophet Muhammed (may Allah bless and greet him), in whose language the Qur'an was written. Pakistan also has famous *'alims* who work hard for the good of Islam. They have twenty million followers who know the Qur'an by heart, and they were also surprised by the preference that was given to the Chechen delegation.[3]

Similar blessings and encouragement came from all over the world, with the intention not so much of supporting Chechnya as of punishing Russia. In reality, too, Chechnya got not only sympathy but cash and ammunition to go on fighting.

At the same time, there was little acknowledgment of the steps that had been taken by Russia to maintain basic social and economic functions in Chechnya during and after the war. Reports of international and humanitarian efforts often omit the fact that from 1995 to 1996, two successive governments in Groznyy—under Salambek Khadzhiyev and Doku Zavgayev—

worked with the federal authorities to provide basic necessities and carry out large-scale restoration of public services. When I visited Groznyy in October 1995, all of its schools and hospitals were functioning, and this was also true of regions less affected by the war than the capital. Yet international humanitarian organizations refused to cooperate with the governments of Khadzhiyev and Zavgayev, labeling them pro-Moscow "puppet regimes." Instead, they tried to channel humanitarian and other aid to Chechen militants. (This position, which actually perpetuated the violence, is never admitted by Western analysts.)

The illusion of a "great victory" limited efforts at restoring public order after the war. Chechen politicians found ways to represent Russian policy in Chechnya in the most negative ways, identifying its federal aid as reparations due from a foreign state for its aggression. For three years, Chechnya received federally supplied electricity and gas at no cost, the financing of social relief (including old-age and disability pensions and child benefits), and salaries for state employees such as doctors, teachers, and civil servants. Under agreements between Moscow and Groznyy, grain was also supplied, including 10,000 tons of wheat in 1999. Considerable aid was also offered by other Russian regions, particularly the neighboring North Caucasian republics and Dagestan. "In the past six months, we have sent five truckloads of medicine to Chechnya, but our Chelyabinsk servicemen sent on a mission there had to buy medical supplies on the local market," Governor Sulmin of the Ural Chelyabinsk region reported at the funeral of twenty militiamen who were killed in a terrorist act staged in Argun in July 2000.

Although the people of Chechnya could not fail to have seen that their republic would face a humanitarian disaster without help from the Russian authorities and the rest of the federation, few voiced that observation. Notions of "state" and "country" had by then been enshrined by the separatist cause. The opinion that the independent country of Ichkeria (or Chechnya) should nonetheless be restored and compensated by those who had ruined it was universally proclaimed in local propaganda, and it was common to blame the general postwar crisis on Russia's alleged economic and political blockade of Chechnya.

Alexander Lebed had signed the Khasavyurt agreements with Aslan Maskhadov in full hopes that they would be followed by a period of restoration in Chechnya, including the resumption of peaceful relations with the federation and the identification of an acceptable definition of its political status. What actually followed—Chechnya's further militarization, the aggression of armed groups toward adjacent regions, massive levels of hostage-taking, the republic's failure to comply with the agreements, and its refusal to cooperate with federal authorities in financial and other matters—all produced charges of betrayal against Lebed on the part of Russian hardliners. Later, with Vladimir Putin's rise to power, the Khasavyurt agreements were publicly condemned as a mistake. "We will never let this happen again," the new president said. Alexander Lebed expressed the problem as follows:

> We had succeeded in reaching an agreement to terminate the war in Chechnya through hard talks and compromises, so as to end the slaughter of our soldiers and the civilian population. But the terms on which we agreed to end the war were not observed. They were breached first by forces in Chechnya that had turned war and violence into a lucrative business. . . . Then those forces, with external support, contrived to unleash a new armed adventure in August 1999, this time in Dagestan—another senseless war, more senseless losses. (Tishkov 1999b: 5)

It cannot be denied that Chechnya had been devastated by the 1994–96 war. The economic collapse of state resources that had begun under Dudayev was exacerbated by the destruction of a large part of Groznyy and more than twenty large villages, the damage caused to roads and bridges, the destruction of forests, the spoiling of nearly a third of the republic's arable fields by military vehicles and land mines, and the contamination of water sources. Most production facilities were destroyed, with the exception of some of the large petrochemical industries, and most of their property was pilfered. State and public institutions had withered. Yet in spite of the republic's losses, the general approach to postwar life of most Chechens and other residents of Chechnya (including ethnic Russians and other non-Chechens) was one of innovative enterprise and amazing endurance. The devastating experience of war and violence did not mean that the entire population had been swept up in the fighting. Peaceful everyday activities still formed the ongoing basis of life in many local communities.

The world's idea of the war never included images of a functioning Chechnya. Journalists and press photographers did not produce pictures of schools in operation or of farmers working in the fields, although these tasks had occupied many people, particularly in the rural areas. The armed minority continued its campaign of violence. But most Chechens were preoccupied with the hard work of restoring their disrupted lives. Upon his return to his home city of Ivanovo, the Russian officer Grigory Stitzberg, deputy commander of a riot police unit sent to Chechnya, published the following observations in a local newspaper:

> In Chechnya we always observed local life as if from the outside. The Chechens get up early and start working at five in the morning, riding out on horseback or bikes to cut the hay. Many have six or eight cows, about a hundred geese, and other animals. They are a very industrious folk. For what is Chechnya, come to think of it? They have one big city—Groznyy, which has been nearly wiped out, Gudermes—a medium-size town, and Argun—just a little town. All the rest is countryside. It is a predominantly peasant land, and most people farm, for they have nothing else to do unless they are fighting. All they think about is how to get spare parts for farm machinery. They come to

the federals asking for fuel oil, lubricants, ball bearings, and other things. They are good with their hands, they know how to handle machines, and you can generally get on with such people just fine. Although their children may have thrown stones at the federals with cries of "Allah akbar" during the war, their parents also taught them to wave their hands at us and smile. If you stop to ask for a drink of water, they will often offer some bread as well, though they may be short of it themselves.

Riding from Groznyy to Mozdok, we passed about a dozen villages. We saw children going to school, the girls turned out in ribbons and white aprons, with school bags on their backs. On May 25, for the ceremony of the last school bell, there were crowds of children carrying flowers. Though the schools had been forgotten during the last war, they have resumed once more. In the morning, people gather at the offices of the collective farms, then go out to the fields to work; these are the scenes that now meet the eye.

It's important to distinguish between the flatland known as minor Chechnya on the left bank of the Terek and the greater Chechnya of the mountains, where people think of themselves as "the real Chechens." The relations between these two parts of Chechnya are very uneasy. While television reports focus on Chechens abducting Russians, Jews, and foreigners, it's less known that hundreds, perhaps thousands, of Chechen highlanders abduct their lowland countrymen. Nationality means little, since the main objective in these cases is a ransom. I once spoke with a Chechen whose 80-year-old father and 16-year-old son had been abducted. He knew who had taken them by name and address, and could even visit them, but he couldn't free them without paying the ransom.[4]

It is important to bear in mind that these activities were observed following the war, and that many Chechens were more preoccupied with the mundane questions of survival and reconstruction than with the political dramas that local propaganda and the foreign media portrayed. Below is some material from interviews with people in Groznyy conducted by Vakhit Akayev at my request in the summer of 1999. Several of the conversations were with local university teachers of rural origin, and they reveal the doubt and anxieties that plagued many struggling to reconstruct their lives and careers in the war's aftermath.

Akayev began by asking, "Tell me, what is your life like now, how do you support your family, what sources contribute to your budget, and what are your monthly expenses?"

Apti Tepsayev, an associate professor of history at the Chechen State University, said:

My brother in Moscow, when he visits, helps me with money. My wife's relatives from Shalazhi village help with wheat meal, meat, and sour cream. Relatives give $50 to $100 to my children. At current prices, we need about 1,000–1,200 rubles [around $35–$40] a month for food for the family, allowing for meat once a week. It is possible to live on tea and bread, and one can eat pota-

> toes for weeks, but it is hard. A lot depends on one's ability to manage household affairs. If someone gets sick, that's the end, only God can help you. We are lucky to be supported by relatives.

Aslambek Labazanov, a teacher in the department of physics, Chechen University, said:

> I repair radios and TV sets and do some home tutoring for illiterate children who were brought from the mountains to our city quarter. When I have from five to seven pupils, I collect 150 to 200 rubles a month from each of them. That is how we live. Parents are eager to educate their children, and the children want to study. Many of them in the third or fourth grade still do not know what five plus seven equals, which is a reflection of our state of misery. The neighbors say there is no way out but to raise a national rebellion, but these armed men in power steal everything at hand and sell it outside. If there is no work what are people to do? Are we destined to die?

Akayev then asked, "Can rebellion improve your conditions?"

> Tepsayev: Any rebellion makes the government think about its policy if it is destroying ordinary people. Any ruler must understand it. Take, for example, basic facts. When Ayatollah Khomeini raised a rebellion against the shah [of Iran], who was such a mighty power, his house had only two rooms. All ministers came to his place by public bus, for it was forbidden them to go by car. If our rulers consider themselves real Muslims, let them follow the Ayatollah Khomeini's example and give up all these Mitsubishi jeeps to pay people pensions instead.

Akayev continued, "You teach at the university. How do students live?"

> Tepsayev: They want to study but they cannot afford to pay 2, 4, or even 8 rubles for public transportation to get to the place. There is no dormitory and many live in villages. Their lives are hard. Those who became students recently are poorly prepared. They do not know even simple fractions and mathematical equations, what pupils should know in the fifth grade. The situation deteriorates each year. There are no textbooks and other instruction materials. Teachers are not paid. The whole situation is discouraging and sad. It will be very hard to return to normal.

THE POSTWAR ECONOMY

The rebuilding of Chechnya's economy was hampered by a lack of civil order and the destruction of much infrastructure. It was asserted that "the better part of Ichkeria's population are busy trading in the large and small markets,"[5] but this seems to have been an exaggeration. Although there were many traders, since anyone who could produce or acquire something promptly offered it for sale, wherever there might be any demand—from private shops and cafes to market stalls and sidewalks—the principal center of commerce remained Groznyy's central market. Petty trading is a sign of postwar recovery, but trade in Chechnya had to follow force: one could not trade without armed support—in other words, it was necessary to pay off those with arms. A municipal tax agent responsible for collecting fees from market vendors explained:

> We have a hard job, since most people can't make ends meet. Frankly, it's a shame to collect taxes from traders who sell next to nothing in a long summer day. But what can we do, that's our service. On the other hand, the bane of our life is the market sharks, the wholesale traders. They break all the official rules and threaten us with physical violence. The result is that most taxes are collected from the poorest traders, while nothing is done about big business. We get no protection from the armed services. How can a few policemen patrolling the market control the insolent "moneybags"? So we collect taxes with sweat and blood. Legally, we are entitled to 10 percent of the collected sum, but in reality we never see that. We are set upon by the bullies who pinch our share, yet accuse us of penny-pinching. We face "inspectors" who produce dubious papers or don't even bother to give their names, and who probably specialize in racketeering and blackmail.[6]

Though agriculture met the basic food needs of postwar Chechnya, farm production was severely curtailed by the war. In some areas, private gardens around farmhouses, small rented farms, and a few large state farms had survived. Eight state farms remained in operation, but many suffered from shortages of fuel and equipment, despite the republic's oil wealth. All the livestock raised in postwar Chechnya was equivalent to what one big farm would have produced before the war. Private farms were now producing just enough for their own families, often sharing what they had with city relatives.

Under Maskhadov, the question of land sales was never raised, and Musa Yusupov and other experts assured me that private ownership of land would not be supported by the population. Nevertheless, in villages and particularly in the mountains, former collective farmlands were being divided among private owners, and disputes often arose in this process. "Highlanders Return to Their Lands in Hay-Mowing Time" was the headline of a report on the advent of the mowing season in the Cheberloy *raion* in 1999:

> Isolated farmsteads in the mountains have lost most of their inhabitants since all have gone to the flatlands or left Chechnya altogether. But life prompts many of them to return to their old homes for the hay-mowing time—not to work, but to share out their hereditary lands between sharecroppers from Dagestan who cut the hay, take their share of the crop, and pay the landowners. The trouble is that the animal-feed producers living on the flatlands and traveling in their chic foreign-made cars have no intention of working, and, what's more, none of them quite know the boundaries of their former lands. So many disputes arise. Some of the villagers . . . propose convening everyone in their family *aul*s to redistribute the plots of land.[7]

In the highland and foothill districts the main problem of the *raion* administrations was less in developing the local economy and infrastructure than in preventing deforestation and controlling the poppy crops grown to produce narcotics. These areas were controlled by local warlords whose main sources of livelihood were either hay crops and beehive honey or ransoms from hostage-taking.

In the lowlands, various former industrial enterprises moved into the production of household goods. The Electropribor plant, which had previously produced electrographic equipment, turned to casting bread-baking forms and making plastic lids for jars. The Krasny Molot plant began producing iron gates and other domestic appliances instead of petroleum-industry equipment. A prefab construction plant was restored in Groznyy, and a mill and sugar refinery had been repaired in Argun, but neither resumed operations for lack of raw materials and qualified personnel. Of the light industries, only the Druzhba cardboard factory continued operating. Of forty-four former industrial enterprises, only seventeen were functioning in 1999, representing about 5–8 percent of prewar industrial production.

The Chechen Republic has not developed a state budget since 1992, and therefore has not controlled its income or expenditure. Because the collection of taxes ceased, the state treasury received none of the revenue it might have expected in 1999 from the sale of oil and oil products. Beginning in 1998, the illegal pillaging of oil resources reached unprecedented proportions. Clashes between economic interests erupted between the government and the armed opposition, particularly in the oil business. Most oil wells were seized by armed groups, and the state's industrial oil production dropped to 400 tons daily in 1999, compared to 4,200 tons in 1998.

Small-scale, private oil production burdened Chechnya's environment. In one settlement, there were over 200 clandestine oil refineries. Chechen acquaintances told me that as they descended from the mountain heights to the lowlands, smog from the villages on the plain made it difficult to breathe. One report noted:

> Thousands of privatized and stolen vehicles, many of them oil tankers, without license plates, run up and down crumbling dusty roads, throwing clouds of dust and exhaust fumes on the villages they pass. All that smoke and soot descends, like flour from a sieve, onto the Kurchaloy hospital, the trees, and people's houses. Black clouds gather over the villages, owing to that pernicious private oil production. If we fail to see what harm this does to our own and our children's health, if we just wait for the authorities to put things to order, we may be forced to swallow this poison for a long time to come. It's no secret to the local people who is doing it. But we haven't yet seen the villagers set a precedent by going to the road and blocking the passage of those oil tankers through their settlements and their lands.[8]

SOCIAL LIFE

The period of conflict also saw dramatic changes in Chechnya's demography, its social cohesion, and its standard of living. There are no precise data on the postwar emigration from Chechnya, but general evidence suggests that about half of its prewar population remains, roughly 700,000 people. (Perhaps another 100,000 left Chechnya after the outbreak of the new war in 1999 but returned after 2001.) The staffs of many industries and organizations have dwindled dramatically, and most trained personnel have emigrated. Only some 15,000 people are still employed in the state industries, and there are about 150,000 elderly pensioners in the republic. Both receive their wages and pensions only after long delays, when federal transfers from Moscow arrive and are not stolen.

Standards of living have dropped sharply for the majority of the population. Tens of thousands of people have lost their homes, cars, valuables, livestock, and savings. With no sources of income, they are reduced to poverty and sometimes starvation or malnutrition. Health problems are widespread, but few doctors remain in the republic, some of the hospitals have closed, and there is a shortage of both medical equipment and medicines. Child mortality has reached a level unprecedented in the post-Soviet era (more than 100 babies out of 1,000 under one year old die). Prenatal mortality rates are also high, especially in the Kurchaloy *raion,* which has become an important area of oil production, with some 1,500 clandestine oil refineries.

The transportation system's collapse has disrupted links both within and beyond the republic. Separatist leaders and politicians have access to modern communication, including the Internet, but ordinary people struggle with the postal service. For three months of 1999, with 241 post offices still open in small towns and rural areas, only 11,000 letters were received and 2,000 sent out of a population of about 600,000.

Theft in postwar Chechnya reached pandemic proportions, and although this was partly because of the economic devastation, violence, and collapse of legal norms, the reasons are more complex. War gave carte blanche to robbery, which many perceived as the acquisition of legitimate war booty or a compensation for losses. Both Chechen combatants and Russian federals indulged in it. Large-scale embezzlement continued into the first period of restoration work under the governments of Khadzhiyev and Zavgayev. The disappearance of federal financing was so scandalous that it was acknowledged by President Yeltsin, and the Chechen government that came to power in 1997 under Maskhadov instituted criminal investigations against former officials who had left the republic. No one was convicted in Chechnya, and in Moscow only the former mayor of Groznyy, Beslan Gantemirov, was imprisoned (though he was later released to lead the Chechen militia supporting federal forces in the new war of 1999).

What is perplexing is why all this corruption and thievery, instead of diminishing, became even more rampant in the era of Chechen statehood. Economic deprivation may be far from being the chief cause, since the new leaders of Chechnya—its military and civil administration—were in the forefront of large-scale embezzlement. Dudayev's "underground economy" acquired a sophisticated character and even its own philosophy. A local newspaper wrote:

> Billions embezzled in Chechnya's agriculture, construction industry, and oil production show that corruption has entered the war. It's no longer an exception when bribe-takers, extortionists, and swindlers in public offices trample the law underfoot. They use their posts and influence in various power structures to grab millions before withdrawing into the shadows and the commercial sector. The new era has opened many opportunities for state officials. The old proverb "Would you sit near a spring and not drink?" has acquired a new, sinister meaning. Not having satisfied their thirst for gain, they suck our state's and our own lifeblood, believing that some should rise to the heights of wealth while others are left in misery. Neither the new—and mostly impotent—laws nor undermined moral precepts can protect us from the rampant corruption. . . .
>
> Many channels drain off "social money" [federal funds transferred for pensions and social benefits]. Large-scale embezzlement persists, particularly under contracts for the purchase of computers, copiers, and medical equipment. Against the background of economic ruin and devastated industry and agriculture, a special niche is reserved for the shadow economy. Profits from informal activities constitute a large part of the population's total income. Examples of the shadow economy are private oil refineries, condensate production [leaked gasoline extracted from the ground], and the plunder of our forest resources.[9]

On a smaller scale, a great deal of theft was also pursued by those lacking recourse to sophisticated organizations or financial operations. The stealing of steel frames, industrial equipment, and nonferrous metals was common. One of Groznyy's largest and most modern industries, the Anisimov oil refinery (with an annual output of 450,000 tons of petrol and 1.8 million tons of diesel fuel) was totally ransacked after August 1996. Damaged buildings of architectural value were taken apart for building materials. The journalist Dmitri Balburov told me that he spent his first week in Chechen imprisonment separating bricks from dried cement that had been brought in from a dismantled building in order to build someone a new private home.

In the summer of 1999, the Vedeno *raion* in the mountains was left without electricity because its generator and power lines had been stolen. "The copper electric lines have been stolen from the Gudermes-Ishcherskaya railway, which means that the electric suburban trains will not run," a report noted. "In Nadterechny *raion* and other settlements, they have stolen telephone cables. There is no sense in restoring them, for [the thieves] just seize the opportunity to steal again. As a result, a large part of Znamensky village was left without telephone communications." Petty theft began to occur even in the mountain villages, which had once taken pride in personal honesty as a fundamental virtue: the old custom of putting a pitcher of cool drinking water by the road near one's house so that a tired traveler could assuage his thirst had come to an end, because the copper pitchers were stolen and sold to illegal traders in nonferrous metals. Meanwhile, Groznyy endured a chronic water shortage owing chiefly to the fact that much of the Starosunzhensk water-supply system's equipment had been pillaged.[10] Chechnya's social climate was diagnosed by the journalist Aset Vazayeva:

> The entire territory of the postwar republic is a war zone. The gutted houses, the dirty markets at every turn (since there are no other sources of income), heaps of garbage, and the crowds of armed men in camouflage fatigues present a picture of unrelenting gloom. There is total unemployment, most people live well below the poverty line, and the young have no prospects. It is an environment devoid of any aesthetic motivation—depressing, alienating, and embittering. It is no wonder that we have so many destructive people in today's Chechnya, and so few creative ones. Journalists find it hard to work in such situations. Not only do they face constant threats to their own lives, now that gangs of armed combatants recognize only the law of the Kalashnikov, but the populace is interspersed everywhere by unbalanced people whose psychic problems have been aggravated by the war. We journalists also have our own problems, expressed in these poetic lines:
>
> When your soul is in discord,
> Your words can't come out right
> They must bear the stamp,
> The ring of that discord.
>
> It's hard to cope with discord in your soul when you see no better prospects ahead, when "the fathers of the nation" drive it into an abyss with their feuds. . . . I have come to hate politics and the politicians. They have deprived me not only of my home and property, but much more—my native city, my republic, and my countrymen. And I don't mean only those who were killed, but also those who were unable to stand the trials of war and turned from human beings into beasts. (*Chechnya: Pravo na kulturu* 1999: 36–37)

GROUP RIVALRIES AND THE COLLAPSE OF GOVERNANCE

The "national revolution" also shattered the foundations of the civic system and its former political frameworks. Many new political parties and assorted public organizations emerged, few with real influence and few with outstanding leaders. During the three years following the war, Chechnya had few civil institutions. Many of their enterprises and organizations had disintegrated, leaving the military and religious-political groupings as the dominant actors. Various internal Chechen conflicts, including clan tensions and clashes between mafia groups, emerged or were revived. The new society, so thoroughly dominated by the armed segment of the population, amazed even many Chechen observers. Malik Saidullayev, a leading Chechen businessman in Moscow who headed the Chechen Republic's Moscow-appointed State Council, visited Chechnya and Ingushetiya late in 1999. Upon his return, he remarked, "I can't believe I'm back in Moscow. I feel as if I've returned to normal society from another planet, one that is run by force of arms and the right of might."[11]

War veterans, carrying the formal stamp of the PRM (Participants of the Resistance Movement) and claiming the rights of *shahids* (warriors of jihad) who gave their lives in the "centuries-long war for independence," took higher posts, enjoyed better living conditions, and demanded privileges denied to the rest of society. A state commission with regional branches was set up to manage PRM affairs, registering 1,347 people, divided into four categories: close relatives of fallen soldiers; organizers of and participants in rallies; those who had actually fought in the war; and those who had given them material and moral support. The first three categories were given special identity cards; the fourth received only certificates. The PRM were entitled to free use of public transport, and preferential admission to educational institutions. Material aid to the *shahids* (many of whom have no jobs or wages, or whose pensions are paid after delays) was provided regularly.

The government enacted measures for the social rehabilitation of war veterans and for aid to the children of those who had fallen in battle. Maskhadov issued a decree giving them preferential admission to establishments of secondary and higher education; 10 percent of the state educational quota was to be reserved for war veterans and resistance activists, and 5 percent for orphans. Yet the number of claimants far exceeded the available posts, and state resources were often used by people who had never engaged directly in battle, causing bitter squabbles.

After the peace agreements that ended the war were signed, many field commanders favored exporting their "liberation revolution" to other autonomous republics of the North Caucasus and gaining access to both the Caspian and Black Sea coasts. Another segment of the military and political elite preferred a path of peaceful development, supporting Maskhadov's efforts to open talks with Russia and to ensure the republic's participation in the transshipment of Caspian oil.

In 1997, five Chechens were arrested in North Ossetia, most likely as a countermeasure by the Ossetian administration, which was seeking the release of several Ossetian citizens, including a high official, who had been abducted and held hostage in Chechnya. On July 20, a "Council of Chechen warriors" was convened at the Dynamo stadium by the vice president of Ichkeria, Vakha Arsanov, who announced: "Since you have elected Aslan and myself as the top leaders of Ichkeria, we are guarantors of the rights and safety of Chechen citizens. I appeal to you with the following question: what shall we do with Vladikavkaz [the North Ossetian capital], liberate it or annihilate it?"[12]

His words were met with loud cries of "Allah akbar!" and all present agreed they should liberate the arrested Chechens by force. Salman Raduyev called for "wiping out those infidels," the majority of Ossetians being Orthodox Christians. "Real Caucasians," he continued, "particularly Muslims, never forgive treachery. If the Ossetians were true people of the Caucasus, they wouldn't have shot us in the back when we were fighting the Russian armada. They are low cowards and should be treated as such." The federal authorities, however, weren't prepared to launch a new military campaign against Chechnya, especially outside the republic's own borders. Nor could North Ossetia afford such aggression, and its president, Akhsarbek Galazov, quickly ordered the arrested Chechens' release.

Maskhadov's government did take measures to cope with the armed organizations of former combatants, but it was difficult to deal with their leaders, among whom were many prominent field commanders who had set themselves up in opposition to him: radical Islamists like Khattab, Basayev, and Raduyev, later joined by Gelayev, Udugov, and others. Maskhadov began a campaign against them under a slogan of combating "the hostage-takers," and in early autumn of 1998, he issued a decree to disband illegal armed groups, while forces loyal to him launched operations to liberate hostages. This was essentially a declaration of war against the former field commanders, since hostage-takers and the political opposition were often the same people. The year 1998 witnessed clashes in Gudermes, where Barayev's band had attempted to gain control, resulting in losses among both the radical Wahhabites and the pro-Maskhadov forces.

On July 3, 1999, a Congress of War and Resistance Veterans passed a resolution addressing eight items on Chechnya's list of internal problems, particularly the tension between its traditional *tariqah* Islam and the growing appeal of Wahhabism, and the potential establishment of Shari'a law. First, the Congress proclaimed "a universal agreement among all the war veterans and the patriotic forces for the cause of strengthening the Islamic state." Second, it resolved to settle internal conflicts peacefully, in keeping with Shari'a law. Third, it banned religious persecution, particularly that directed at the Wahhabites. Fourth, it declared abductions to be "the worst crime against the Chechen state under Shari'a law." The Congress also decreed the establishment of a national security council, or *shura,* which was to include the leaders of the resistance movement and other prominent people. It recommended that Maskhadov create a legal basis for independent Shari'a courts, as well as the suspension of all political rallies, marches, and demonstrations in the republic.

Maskhadov's government was nonetheless unable to control the situation. The leadership divide was so deep that he launched an appeal to the nation,

> Chechens, citizens of Ichkeria, brothers and sisters! Having passed long years on the road of war with confidence and dignity, we have suddenly become unrecognizable. Yesterday's comrades in arms look askance at each other with suspicion, and the source of discord between us is the hunger for power. There is no other explanation but lust for power, owing to the fact that erstwhile leaders of the liberation movement, once united by one idea and one aim, have failed today to stand the test of time and are immersed in petty feuds, rumors, and gossip. . . . Leaders of jihad! Be worthy of the love and respect of the Chechen people, shake off your arrogance in the name of this great people. You are flesh of its flesh, so rally your ranks against our common enemy! Our fight is not over; it has taken on other low and treacherous forms, aimed at all costs at draining the blood of the Chechen people, at alienating you from your people, at discrediting the warriors of jihad. Stop basking in the rays of past glory! There is but one step between the people's esteem to their hatred. Better to take a step toward each other, toward unity and accord. We still have a chance—a great chance at the final victory of the Chechen people—a nation of toil, of war, and of triumph in its centuries-long hard struggle for independence and sovereignty.[13]

SHARI'A LAW FOR CHECHNYA?

Making Shari'a law the basis for a new political order had been a long-cherished dream of some Chechen leaders. When Zelimkhan Yandarbiyev became president of the republic after Dudayev's death, he issued a decree on the criminal code with the purpose "of consolidating the basis of the state's independence and legal system on the principles of the Shari'a law as given by the great Allah, gracious and merciful, the Lord of the worlds." As Vakhit Akayev points out, the new Chechen criminal code was copied from that of the Sudan.[14]

In August 1996, a military Shari'a tribunal was established as a branch of the Supreme Shari'a Court of Ichkeria. The tribunal tried all cases involving members of the armed services and activists of the resistance movement and handed down sentences, including the death penalty. In September 1998, Maskhadov founded a special regiment of the Shari'a courts and police, commanded by Colonel Rizvan Daudov, whose functions included guarding the Shari'a courts, escorting the accused, enforcing court summons, and observing compliance with the Shari'a norms among officials and ordinary citizens. In an interview, Daudov said that "we should gradually oust the European style of dress from our republic, introduce uniforms at schools conforming to the Islamic traditions, and indoctrinate the children in Islam at younger ages." In collaboration with the Shari'a guard, his regiment made raids through rural settlements and in Groznyy neighborhoods to see if there were any breaches of Shari'a rules, particularly in the use of and trade in alcohol and narcotics. In just one day, July 27, 1999, they confiscated 600 bottles of vodka and detained seven drunken men, who were punished with forty strokes of the rod.[15]

Maskhadov officially introduced Shari'a law in February 1999, with the aim of undercutting his opponents in the struggle for power, but this move marked his surrender to the radical Islamists. His power in Chechnya increasingly became nominal, and his opponents from the Yandarbiyev-Basayev faction demanded the abolition of the office of president and the election of a religious head of state, or imam.

The public execution in 1996 of two Chechens who had no family to defend them shocked not only the external world, but also many in Chechnya. Also shocking was the death of the well-known singer Apti Dalkhanov after he was punished for drinking alcohol with eighty strokes of the rod. A similar execution was meted out to M. Kh. Alsabekov, the former mufti during Dudayev's time, who had at first declared the war against Russia to be *ghazavat,* then repudiated that stance and left Chechnya.

The majority of Chechens had lived the greater part of their lives under the rule of civil law, as well as under the influence of their traditional religious leaders. The question of introducing Shari'a law caused an ideological and political split in Chechnya, further paralyzing the government of the republic. A weakened Chechen society was unable to oppose the dictates of the extremists, but nevertheless disapproved of them. This tense situation did not last long, and open conflict inevitably erupted.

THIRTEEN

An Ideology of Extremes

European anthropologists called the white race "Caucasian" because the Chechen, Ingush, and to some extent other groups in the Caucasus were classic examples of that race. Russia's name itself is not of Germanic but rather of Chechen origin.
ALBERT MACHIGOV

The future of Chechnya is its distant past.
KHOZH-AHMED NUKHAYEV

In the months following August 1996, striking changes occurred in Chechnya. While the air around the Palace of Culture was being rent by automatic gunfire in honor of President Maskhadov's inauguration, influential media in the republic erupted with calls for vengeance. There was a sudden outburst of cultural and political theorizing; newspapers were filled with historical articles, poems, and pseudo-philosophical rhetoric by local authors. Verses about the glorious new Chechen heroes began appearing in great abundance (mostly in Russian). Texts and photos celebrating Chechen history and its achievements served as a means of propaganda and political mobilization, all the while distracting people from the woes of dealing with the terrible consequences of the war. Traditional institutions of scholarly research and academic integrity were discredited by the new intellectual elite, which consisted primarily of political and cultural ideologues of the militant new leadership. Numerous war memoirs describing the exploits of Chechen fighters were popular. Each issue of the newspaper *Zashchitnik otechestva,* published by the Chechen Defense Ministry, carried detailed commentaries about, or interviews with, the heroes of the Russian-Chechen war, accompanied with photographs of them in full military gear.

At the same time, there was nostalgia for the prewar era, reflected in photographs of Groznyy's past published in *Groznenski rabochiy.* For many of the capital's residents, those images recalled the modern city that had been devastated by the Russian army. Many had regarded Groznyy as the center of power, wealth, learning, prestigious government posts, and modern apartments. Though dozens of photographs were published in the newspapers, few, if any articles actually discussed steps toward restoration and rehabilitation of the city.

A NEW CHECHEN ANTHROPOLOGY

During and after the war, Chechen intellectual life became dominated by ideologies that focused on territorial expansionism and cultural mythmaking. What happened to the local academic community, in particular its social scientists? Before the war, Groznyy had housed a large school of social research based in the Checheno-Ingush Institute of History, Sociology, and Philology, as well as analogous departments at Groznyy University. The first heavy blow to the humanities occurred under Dudayev's regime, when the Institute was closed down. Its director, Vakhit Akayev, described to me what happened in these words:

> Dudayev summoned me and told me that we were working in the wrong direction. We should show, he said, that the Chechens were the most ancient people in the world, and that he had seen ancient Chechen monuments in many countries with his own eyes. We should expose Russian colonial oppression. Generally, he saw little use for the social sciences, now that it was time to fight for our independence. After that conversation, no more money was allocated to the Institute, though no official decision had been made to close it. I still keep the Institute's seal with me.[1]

Dudayev issued a decree on June 18, 1992, founding the Chechen Academy of Sciences. He personally instructed its nineteen elected members on the research they should be conducting, before summarily cutting off their financing. Through this sort of inconsistency and disorganization, the war completely disrupted the scholarly community in Chechnya. The fine art nouveau building housing Akayev's Institute of History, Sociology, and Philology was destroyed, along with its library and an archive containing photographic materials, over 4,000 pages of collected folklore texts, and dozens of books prepared for print. Fearing for themselves and their work, many scientists and scholars fled Chechnya.

Before the war, Groznyy had also had a Center for the Development of Ethnic Culture, headed by Said-Magomed Khasiyev, an ethnographer educated under Professors Vladimir Gardanov and Boris Kaloyev at the USSR Academy of Sciences' Institute of Ethnography. The Center had collected over 500 audio- and videocassettes of Chechen folk music, dances, customs, and rituals. Khasiyev relates,

> Shortly before the war, I moved my card index to the Center because I feared for its safety. I had more than 70,000 thousand cards carrying notes collected throughout thirty years of work. There aren't, for instance, many known myths about the creation of the world that differ from those of the Holy Scriptures, and I had eight such myths that had been handed down by generations of Chechens, pointing to links with regions remote from Chechnya. All those materials perished. How can I restore all that? How long will it take me? Who knows? We seem to have reached an impasse, with no material base for

> research, no financing, and, worst of all, no young people who wish to devote themselves to scholarship. As the elders of our profession die out, no new cadres come along to replace them.

The newly sanctioned currents of thought now lay in asserting a culturally and politically independent state. They were intrinsically opposed to the rationalism, secularism, and pan-Russian values shared by the older generation of Chechen intellectuals. The Chechen historian Lema Vakhayev, who stayed in Groznyy until the second Chechen war broke out, described the situation thus:

> The old generation of Soviet intellectuals, too Russified and divorced from their people, too tame in the Soviet style, failed to take the lead in the turbulent process of cultivating a national consciousness and a search for "the national idea." That generation lost out in the events of 1991, and all subsequent developments only pushed it farther from the center of public discussion. During the war, they were needed by no one, and for the most part they left Chechnya. Immediately after the war, the Chechen parliament passed the law "On the Lustration" [purification], which was a means of getting rid of those who had failed to leave of their own accord.
>
> New people came to power in Chechnya—brave and devoted (in their way) to their people, but also ignorant: field commanders risen from the lower social strata, some of them with criminal or semi-criminal pasts and [questionable] connections, others with just a little education, and the nouveaux riches whose wealth wouldn't bear investigation. Those people were the winners of the 1991 revolution and the war of 1994–96, and it was they who set the spiritual climate of the society and worked out their variants of "the national idea," elevating their own poor mentality to the status of national ideology. (Vakhayev 1999: 325)

Emerging in Chechen discourse were myths not only of the new nation's birth but of a people chosen by God. These themes were emphasized by President Maskhadov. They endowed Chechens with a sense of superiority over other peoples in the Caucasus, particularly the Orthodox Christian Ossetians, and with a glorious new history that had supposedly been concealed from them by Russian colonizers for centuries. Earlier nationalist myths locating the origin of the Chechens in ancient civilizations like those of Sumeria, Aratta, and the Hurrians were no longer ancient enough. In fact, their direct descent from Cro-Magnon man was suggested in Movladi Udugov's newspaper *Islamskaya natsia,* which wrote that Cro-Magnon men were Caucasians and ancestors of the Vainakhs. Also popular among the Chechen ruling elite were theories espoused by Nazi anthropologists who had traced the Aryan race to the Caucasus. "Hitler on the Chechens," a 1997 article by R. Varayev, asserted:

> The Europeoid white race was named Caucasian because anthropologists found the Caucasian type normative for that race—the pure standard of

> which was seen in the Chechens. Works by modern anthropologists note that the farther to the northwest the Germanic tribes lived, the more stable were their traditions, pointing to their origin from the Caucasus. The medieval annalist Saxon [i.e., the thirteenth-century Danish historian Saxo Grammaticus] relates the legend of the Caucasian origin of the Vikings. We don't claim to be more Aryan than scholars define us as being. But it is all the more offensive to hear the Chechens called "blacks" in Russia, when in reality they are taken to be the standard of the white race.[2]

Before the war, diverse opinions had been expressed on the origin of the term "Nokhchi," the Chechens' name for themselves, but no one traced it to the biblical patriarch Noah. After the war, Khasan Baksayev, of "the research center of the Nokhchi Latt Islam movement," argued that "the theory of domination by the Jewish dialects is now a fossilized dogma of linguistics" and that the Chechen language had been spoken by the patriarchs from Adam to Noah. That name, or its variant "Nukh" in Islam, forms the first part of Nokhchi, meaning "Noah's people."

Chechnya was even asserted to be the world's most ancient state, with a history of several thousand years. The former state secretary of the Chechen republic, A. Akbulatov, assured his compatriots that "the Chechens kept their statehood in the period of Scythians, Sarmatians, and Alans." The Chechens, he said, were the creators of the most ancient state on earth, as well as the earliest democracy. "The unwritten Chechen traditions show that neither ancient Greeks, Romans, nor the modern civilized states could invent more perfect laws. This is therefore the only country in the world with a genuine working democracy, bowing to no one, not amenable to a modern world community dominated by the dictates of the imperialist state."[3]

OFFICIAL AND ETERNAL ENEMIES

Who were the principal enemies of Chechnya-Ichkeria? "The official, eternal, and permanent enemy of the Chechen people" was, of course, Russia. Characteristically, the Chechen mass media referred to the Khasavyurt agreement of August 1996 simply as "the truce," and great pains were taken to maintain Russia's hostile image. Some authors insisted that Russia was headed for collapse, its sprawling state being an unnatural formation "needed by no one, least of all by the Russians." In a 1997 article entitled "The Chechens Are the Founders of Russia," Albert Machigov, of the Chechen Academy of Sciences, forged linguistic, geographic, and historical evidence to support his contention: linking the name of Kiev with that of a similar village name in Chechnya, insisting that the Dnieper River had been named by the Chechens, and that "Rus" was not a Germanic but a Chechen name. Proceeding to more recent history, the author pointed to the great contribution Chechens had made at crucial moments in the Polish intervention of the seventeenth century, which had been rebuffed not only by the leadership of Minin and Pozharsky, but also by that of Chechnya's Count Cherkessky. Still later, in World War I, the German "iron regiment" had been routed by the Checheno-Ingush Savage Cavalry Regiment, to which Tsar Nicholas II gave special thanks in 1916. And when Germany attacked the USSR in June 1941, "the greatest concentration of Chechen conscripts in the Red Army were in Brest-Litovsk [where the first strong resistance to the Germans took place], though none of the 200 Chechens who served there was decorated with the Hero Star in his lifetime." Machigov also proclaimed:

> In Jordan, Turkey, and Iran, the greater and better half of army generals are Chechens. In court, a Chechen's word is taken as sworn testimony, as they are the mainstay of the law and of the army. And in Russia, Chechens are held to be "born bandits" because the state rests on the wrong ideas—what ideas precisely, they have not decided to this day. . . . Chechen-Slavonic unity is much more tangible than Turkic-Slavonic unity, or cosmopolitan unity with the West. In the military sense, a union of Russia with Ichkeria would be more formidable to the West than any NATO enlargement to us.[4]

A peculiar theme in Chechen discourse was concerned with the problem of their language. For as illustrated above, Chechens had largely assimilated the Russian language, and all the texts produced during the Chechen revolution, including the declaration of sovereignty and the constitution, were originally written in Russian. Even more ironic, the military orders of Chechen fighters were in Russian, and the ballots for the elections of Presidents Dudayev and Maskhadov were printed in Russian. Few Chechens could read Chechen.

After the war, the Russian language was seen as a vestige of imperial domination, an imposition to be done away with. Attempts were made to restore the Chechen language to the status due to it in the newly independent state. But this effort was problematic, given that the society had lost all of its educated linguists, including experts in the Chechen language. In the words of the local ethnographer Said-Magomed Khasiyev, "We have lapsed today into the opposite extreme—anyone who can speak a couple of phrases in Chechen claims to be a linguist or an ethnographer."

In 1997, the newspaper *Chechenets* offered a prize of $5,000 to anyone who proved that the words *club, service, freund, pravda,* and *rodina* (the latter two are Russian words meaning "truth" and "motherland") were of Chechen origin. The challenge was taken up by Kharon Vastigov, who wrote:

> The Chechen language *[mat]* is the source of all other languages. But the question was formulated incorrectly. It should be, "Do the said words belong to the ancient Chechen (Aryan) civilization?" Yes, undoubtedly. Our language is the clue to the linguistic civilization of all other nations. . . . The prize of $5,000 is what I am after, why pretend? I need it to be able to publish a

> newspaper . . . in which I intend to prove that the Chechen stock is that of the first man, and that the Chechen language is the tongue of tongues *[mati-mat]*.[5]

No prize has been awarded.

LIBERATING THE CAUCASUS

Motifs of Chechen greatness and Islamic messianism coexisted with the expansionist idea of liberating the Caucasus, both North and South, from Russia's imperial domination and creating a single "Caucasian Home," or "Caucasian Confederation." The chief ideologues of these projects were Zelimkhan Yandarbiyev, Movladi Udugov, and Khozh-Ahmed Nukhayev. They explained their projects before many audiences, and their ideology found influential sponsors abroad. As for those in the South Caucasus (Azerbaijan, Armenia, Georgia), few took the Chechen liberation projects seriously, though some made encouraging gestures toward Chechnya.

Throughout the postwar years, Chechen leaders cultivated the idea of liberating and uniting the entire Caucasus. Books and brochures on the subject appeared, and Udugov's newspaper *Kavkazsky vestnik* reprinted chapters from a book on the peoples of the Caucasus by German philologist Friedrich Bodenstedt (1819–92). Yandarbiyev explained the goals of his political movement, known as "The Caucasian Confederation":

> The Caucasus has been oppressed for centuries by the Russian empire. It is not free yet. We have no right to pretend we see nothing around us now that we have our freedom at last. We can't truly be free if the rest of the Caucasus is not. All its people—the Dagestanis, Azeris, Ingushi, Georgians, Circassians, Cossacks—of whatever faith, are our brethren, we are all a single Caucasian nation. . . . We are opening a new era in building a Common Caucasian Home free of slavery. Ichkeria plays the main role in that process, since we have shown ourselves as the most intrepid and dedicated fighters in five years of jihad.[6]

Radical Chechen leaders used the idea of Caucasian unity and liberation to form a broader anti-Russian coalition and "liberation front," as Yandarbiyev called it. The confederation held two congresses, on August 7, 1997, and May 24, 1998. The latter, in Urus-Martan, was dedicated to the eightieth anniversary of the forming of the North-Caucasian, or Gorskaya, Republic, which existed for a year in the early Soviet period. On that occasion, Yandarbiyev wrote an "Address to the Peoples and Political Organizations of the Caucasus," saying:

> Brothers and sisters! Caucasians! The national liberation struggle of our peoples has reached the decisive stage on its centuries-long path. Life itself raises the question before us: to be or not to be—not only free, but to be nations at all. . . . This worry is profoundly felt by all our people in the face of a looming ethnic catastrophe accelerated and aggravated by the advent of the so-called

market economy. . . . Not only economic relations, but also our culture and ideology, our spiritual life, are thrown onto a ruthless market with no other rules except the ruble and the dollar. . . . Caucasians! If we wish to develop for our own and the world's good and to restore what we have lost, . . . we can do so only by liberating ourselves from Russia and from the game that is being forced upon us—it is called international law, but in reality it is the right of might. We must make our own rules for an honest life. . . . And we shall do it with God's help![7]

At that congress, Yandarbiyev also declared that, in reality, the Caucasus had only two independent states, Ichkeria and Azerbaijan, but that their efforts at strengthening statehood were being undermined by "the ideological policy, subversion, and sabotage of the Russian secret services and the Russian state in general." Russia's role in the Caucasus, he said, was that of an aggressor. The irreconcilable contradictions between the Caucasus and Russia could only be resolved "on condition of a full liberation of the Caucasus! Any other option would be contrary to the interests of each of the Caucasian peoples and of the Caucasus as a whole."[8]

The history of the short-lived Gorskaya Republic, which lasted only until 1921 before being reorganized into several new territorial autonomies by the Soviet Union, was seen as a kind of "unlearned lesson" among North Caucasian "anti-imperialists." The principal speaker at the congress, Said-Khasan Abumuslimov, formulated their new goals:

Ten years have passed since a situation favorable for liberating and uniting the Caucasus emerged, but next to nothing has been done to reach that goal. To avoid missing yet another chance, we must make it a priority, without turning the struggle against Russian colonial oppression into a fight with our neighbors and making ourselves a laughingstock around the world. To that end, we must first declare a moratorium on all territorial disputes. . . . We must actively, with all available means, spread the ideology of liberation and unity and the common destiny of all Caucasian peoples, the priority of their common interests, and we must rule out conflicts between them. We must publish mass editions of books promoting that ideology . . . including memoirs and analytical articles by the participants of the struggle for independence in the Caucasus between 1917 and 1921. In order to educate the younger generation in the spirit of liberation and unity of the Caucasus we must bring out a single textbook for all the Caucasian peoples—"Studies of the Caucasus"—and make it a compulsory subject to be studied at schools and other educational establishments throughout the Caucasus.[9]

The final declaration of the congress ran as follows:

Russia's treacherous, inhuman policy in the Caucasus takes the most monstrous forms. While declaring its readiness to resolve its relations with Ichkeria on the principles and norms of international law, Russia, in collaboration with the world community, including some Muslim states, continues its heinous

> policy of genocide against the Caucasian peoples, in particular, the Chechen Republic of Ichkeria. . . . Because the Chechen Republic of Ichkeria is now the lawful successor of Shamil's *imamat* and of the North Caucasian Republic, and because Ichkeria's Independence Day of September 6 marks the restoration of independence for the entire North Caucasus, we resolve to celebrate that day throughout the Caucasus as the Day of the Beginning of the Restoration of Independence in the North Caucasus.

This was a reference to extending the struggle against Russia "by all means available." The most aggressive militant groups in Chechnya began preparations to "liberate" the Caucasus.

MODELING STATE AND NATION ON ISLAM

In addition to these themes of war and of Russia as enemy number one, Chechnya's public discourse focused on Islam as a grounding for political and cultural resistance. After the long period of Soviet atheism, followed by the pro-Western liberalization that characterized Gorbachev's period, Chechen periodicals sought to promote an Islamicization of the republic, publishing countless theoretical articles on the theme of Islam. As illustrated in chapter 11, religion had been an important factor in mobilizing Chechnya and distancing it from Russia in the period leading up to, and during, the first Chechen war. After the war, radical Islamic groups began using religion as a basis for political reforms in the republic. They promoted the idea that the "desecrated and aggressive constitutionalism" of Russia and the West should be replaced by a constitutional theocracy, often quoting Dudayev's phrase, "The power of Shari'a law should be absolute and unlimited."

The framework for a traditional Chechen form of *tariqah* Islam was actually being established during the 1990s. Initially, the dhikrists (followers of Kunta Haji, founder of the Qadiriyyah tariqah in the North Caucasus) strengthened their positions through one of the Sufi *turuq,* or fraternities. Vakhit Akayev believes that in placing dhikrists in high Islamic clerical posts, Dudayev and his inner circle openly revealed their motivation to share power first among "their own" (Akayev 1999b). This view was echoed by the rector of the Islamic Institute, M. Hasukhanov, "Earlier the power in Chechnya belonged to the followers of Naqshbandi; now it is in the hands of the dhikrists."

Shortly before the war, when Ruslan Khasbulatov set up his peacekeeping mission, some prominent Naqshbandiyya members joined him, publicly declaring that Chechen resistance to Russian authorities could not accurately be called *ghazavat,* or holy war. Field commanders tried to conceal this position of the Chechen muftiate from their troops. Many journalists sympathetic to the militants kept silent about it. Things changed sharply after the war, when armed groups influenced by the radical Islamism known as Wahhabism rose to power. Encountering few obstacles, these parties sought to promote Wahhabism and install Shari'a. Udugov, the leading ideologist of the Chechen "national revolution," favored this politicized doctrine. It seems crucial—certainly to me—that this man's charisma influenced the spiritual climate in Chechnya and encouraged the adoption of radical forms of Islam. Here are some excepts from Udugov's periodical *Put Dzhorhara:*

> The Islamic peoples in Russia live in the same conditions as Russians, but they are not degenerating by turning to vodka and licentiousness because they possess the true faith. Their numbers are growing, while the Russian population decreases annually. . . . The twenty-first century will be the age of Islam in Russia. Islam proves in practice its true and divine nature by making Muslim families strong and united, even in the face of Western advertising and other values. Islam encourages enterprise . . . and respect for market relations, but still prioritizes giving alms to the needy.
>
> Under Shari'a law, the tax on honest businessmen does not exceed 2.5 percent, which aids a rapid growth of the middle class while allowing the burden of state expenditure to fall on the basic commodity and energy industries. Islam puts natural resources at the service of the entire nation, which is why the Arabs, who have nothing but oil, enjoy higher living standards than Russians who have much more. The 30-million-strong Islamic community in Russia and the principle of Islamic legislation will permit us to form one of the largest factions in the State Duma. The 2.5 percent tax is the best of advertisements, and a union with the Arabs and Chechnya would be Russia's best answer to NATO's enlargement. . . . A search for the truth must lead Russia to Islam, or it will sink into degeneracy. There are about 3 million Muslims in Moscow alone, and many of them are Russians.[10]

Vakhit Akayev's analysis of the situation after August 1996 concludes,

> Dudayev's men returned to power. The dhikrists once again became very active in trying to regain their lost positions in public life, with the support of Ichkeria's government. Then dhikrists and Wahhabites began earnestly competing for the greater influence on the population of the republic. The two groups were not ready to compromise, though both of them called for the "full sovereignty of Chechnya" and for a struggle against "Russian colonialism." (Akayev 1999b: 50)

The Islamic theme underlay most political projects during that period, with references to the Qur'an, the nation, and the state featuring prominently in both religious and political debates. One proposal for an anti-state structure in postwar Chechnya was proposed by Khozh-Akhmed Nukhayev, a man who had served prison terms for criminal activity before 1991, grown rich through illegal financial dealings under Dudayev, fought in the war in 1994–95, left for the West, and then risen to prominence with the help of a Pole named Mansur Jakimczyk (reportedly a British secret agent), who became his intellectual guru. Jakimczyk adopted the Islamic faith and became an active supporter of Chechen independence, setting up a Chechen information center in Kraków and establishing various links between Chechnya and Western countries. Nukhayev and Jakimczyk promoted the Caucasian Common Home project after the war and managed to meet a number of world leaders, including Margaret Thatcher, to discuss the issue.

The gist of that plan was explained first in a newspaper published by Nukhayev's Nokhchi-Latt-Islam movement and then in a book he authored (Nukhayev 2001). Whereas Yandarbiyev's notion of "the people" included "any plowman or shepherd," Nukhayev promoted an elite version of Chechen identity as a sort of select heroic lodge, "a category of people committed for a lifetime to a moral code of honor." Here is an extract from an editorial piece in his newspaper:

> The elders of Mehk-Khel were right in their verdict that to be and remain a Chechen is the most difficult thing in the world. This demands a preordained consciousness, the code of our blood. Though we use different words to express it, we nevertheless understand it. To be false to it would destroy us and scatter us throughout the world, for we can find no peace elsewhere and we keep returning—in body or in spirit—on bitter waves of nostalgia. The compass in our hearts displays only one direction—the land of our fathers, our Chechen land. This force is irresistible, it is above our petty differences and bigger than ourselves. It's the inevitable, which we accept and follow.
>
> . . . Chechen wisdom nurtured heroes, not the mob. The mob may disgorge torrents of words, but the hero, or *kyonakh,* disdains the mob and stands aloof from the crowd. So we address our paper not to the mob, but to the Chechen *kyonakh*s, who are the pillars of this ancient land. . . . We know they will finally speak their word, and the Chechen code will again be the basis of our life like the stone tablets of commandments that our creator gave us.

Lema Vakhayev justifiably links Nukhayev's views with those in Chechnya who identify themselves as "progressive fascists,"[11] who find the present situation in Chechnya ripe for a transition to an aristocratic political system. Such a system rejects democratic elections as an insult to men of authority, to the *kyonakh*s (i.e., heads of families, men of learning, models of good conduct, honor, and etiquette), by equating their votes and participation in public life with those of "the mob." Instead, they favor a system of trust and best selection, akin to the corporate fascism of Benito Mussolini.

Nukhayev offers an unusual explanation for the postwar crisis in Chechnya. He locates its causes neither in "the Russian factor" nor in material and financial hardships but in the attempts by some leaders to impose an alien model of state governance on Chechnya. The time has come, he says, to build a national order on the principles of Islam alone, without any state interference. He goes on:

> A state order inevitably leads society to a loss of the national spirit and/or religion. Since the religion of Allah is the basis of our national spirit, I am sure the Chechens will never accept a system that does not agree with our national understanding of freedom. . . . Let me repeat, I am against the state because I am all for order, but an order arranged by free people. Such an order is based on laws strongly rooted in ancient customs. . . . Custom *[ʿadat]* absorbs the experience, wisdom, and morality of a national history dating back millennia. Such laws cannot be changed by the whims of a few enthusiastic reformers. To change them, you would have to change the entire nation, along with its world outlook and values.[12]

In Nukhayev's view, postwar Chechen nationalism remained ethnic in essence, but if earlier it was based on an ideology of the downtrodden who had suffered historical injustice and the collective trauma of deportation and discrimination, it now thrived on ideas of exclusivity and superiority. That new nationalism retained all of its anti-imperial force but acquired the additional feature of religious dedication:

> The Chechen nation is the last stronghold of an Islamic world order that is deeply alien to the idea of the state, just as the Islamic religion is deeply alien to the satanic innovations that dim its clear and logical system. Islam and the nations abiding in it have a common enemy—the state that turns people away from both religious and national ideas. The law and social structure for the life of the nation—the multiethnic *umma*—was laid down clearly in our Prophet's Medical Constitution *[sic]*; Nukhayev presumably meant the Medina constitution]. Any Chechen can see in it a striking similarity to the public order in which the Chechen nation had always lived, by tradition. Ours is probably the last society in the world that still preserves the principles of our Prophet. When we understand that fact, we shall realize what a great mission was entrusted to us by the Almighty. We have no right to ignore that mission; we must rouse the Islamic peoples like a detonator; we have a duty to set an example for the whole world and to bring our nation into full compliance with its traditional worldview, and with the principles of our Prophet's constitution. For that we should understand the simple truth that the nation is the abode of Islam, the state is the abode of Satan.[13]

Nukhayev's ideas were for the heroes, or *kyonakh*s, and not for the mob. They were absorbed by a contingent of Chechen society who opposed President Maskhadov's government and favored an unlimited rule of Shariʿa law in the republic. The newspaper *Mehk-Khel* was the primary vehicle for this propaganda: "Over the past ten years Allah has given us a chance to test all variants of state power except the best. We have emerged from those experiments with a ruined land—vast spaces filled with graves, poverty, injustice, and monstrous crimes. Can't we see, isn't it clear, that there is only one way out, and it is on every tongue—Shariʿa?"[14]

The fact that Islam historically entered Chechnya comparatively late was also addressed by these Chechen ideologists. The government's newspaper *Ichkeria* explained, "Since time immemorial every true Nokhcho [i.e., Chechen] has been Muslim, for we are the descendants of Noah. . . . Therefore, our customs and traditions are in full keeping with the Qur'an."

ANTI-SEMITISM AND WITCH HUNTS

Chechens shared forms of anti-Semitism that were common throughout the former USSR, both in everyday life and in the official attitudes of both party and state, though it was probably less prominent among ethnic minorities in the Caucasus than among the Russian, Ukrainian, and Baltic peoples. The Jew Yefim Guelman reflected, "I lived in Checheno-Ingushetiya a very long time and held various posts in the field of education, but frankly, before the 1990s, I had never felt that any anti-Semitic slurs were aimed at me." Earlier in the decade, there was speculation concerning the Jewish origin of certain Chechen *teips*, in particular Tati-Nikyi, from which Dzhokhar Dudayev hailed. But these speculations were usually followed by public denials and arguments for the "purity" of his descent. In Lema Vakhayev's words:

> The Chechen mentality includes a sense of being unlike any other people, but until recently it exhibited little xenophobia in general or anti-Semitism in particular. The Jews were regarded as any of our neighbors, neither better nor worse than others, and today there are still no objective grounds for anti-Semitic moods. It's ridiculous, after all, to talk of mass anti-Semitism in a land where no Jews are left. Anti-Semitism is now cultivated by the ruling elite under the influence of Islamic fundamentalists. That's why the TV channel Kavkaz, controlled by the Wahhabite movement, has as its motto "We have no equals, we're on the march, we'll show Russia what we are!" combined with the slogan "Jerusalem will be ours!" (Vakhayev 1999: 328)

A new brand of post-Soviet anti-Semitism appeared in Chechnya under the influence of radical Islamism and a pro-Arab orientation. The trend flourished over the next few years as Chechnya became immersed in "ideological wars," some of which served as a distraction from the republic's internal problems. The most striking example of this is the reprinting in Udugov's paper *Veliki jihad* of "The Catechism of the Jew in the USSR."[15] Udugov, president of the Center for Strategic Research and Political Technologies, said in an interview with the Armenian news agency Mediamax,

> We are not inclined to maintain the political games that mask the true state of affairs. The truth is that by the end of the twentieth century, we see distinct outlines of a Christian-pagan union centered round and based on Zionism. That alliance has declared war on the Islamic world. In fact, it proceeds with

> blatant occupation of Islamic lands. . . . Islamic armed forces will not wait for a resumption of war in Nagorno-Karabakh. We have information that in the year 2000, they are planning to begin a campaign for restoring the Muslim territories of Transcaucasia.[16]

Chechen anti-Semitism manifested itself in versions of "the world Zionist conspiracy" and crude anti-Jewish material borrowed from the arsenal of Russian nationalism. Udugov's "international independent newspaper" *Kavkazsky vestnik* published many chapters from a treatise by an anonymous author entitled *Zloveschii iudaism* (Sinister Judaism). Here are some excerpts from it, first from "Chapter 5. Jewish Domination of the Modern World":

> Thanks to their special talents in various financial operations and utter lack of scruples in business relations, the Jews have gradually taken control of the major banks and exchanges in the capitalist world. With capital in their hands, they have had no difficulty taking over the world press, television, news agencies, theater, cinema, and radio. Having at their disposal the banks and the means of manipulating public opinion, they gradually acquired full equality in the countries where they live. Then they actually subjugated political life in the liberal-democratic states. It would be a mistake to think that this crusade for power by the world Jewry met no stubborn resistance on the part of "stupid goys." In the first portion of these essays, we gave many examples illustrating how the best minds of Aryan humanity consistently warned us against the danger of Jewish domination. The scope of these essays does not permit us to go into all the historical details of the global seizure of power by the Jews. We can point out only that the so-called "emancipation" (i.e., liberation from all legal limitations) of the Jews is a comparatively recent phenomenon.

This is followed by various "historical" facts and quotations from Benjamin Franklin and the nineteenth-century French historian Jules Michelet, concluding with the following passage:

> The astounding success of that crusade for power, which became obvious after the Great War of 1914–18 and the Russian Revolution, would have been impossible if the Jewish Diaspora had not been led by a conscious will and a strong tribal instinct that preserved them from mixing with other nations and dissolving in their midst. The racial problem, the preservation of their tribe, had always been present in Jewish minds. . . . That conscious racial policy could not have yielded such obvious fruits if the Jews had not created a powerful network of Jewish organizations encompassing the whole world. Studies of the Jewish question too often ignore that important fact. We will therefore undertake to acquaint the reader in more detail with the organizations of the world Jewry—that gigantic apparatus of militant Judaism.[17]

The next issue carried a page listing Jewish organizations in the United States, Great Britain, and France, though the data were taken from outdated reference books and accounts from between the two world wars. The page concludes with information on the World Jewish Congress in Geneva in

August 1936, the results of which are interpreted in such a way as to blame the Jews for unleashing World War II. Anti-Semitic ranting filled many Chechen papers and peppered daily conversations with aphorisms like, "To have a Jewish mode of thinking, one doesn't have to be a born Jew or to marry a daughter of Zion—it's enough to be a hypocrite, a coward, and a miser," and "We don't have to wait long before they call Chechnya 'another Judea.'" The militant hostage-taker Arbi Barayev declared in the summer of 2000 that he and his people would kill all Jews who fell into their hands.

It would be inaccurate to think that Chechen anti-Semitism was characteristic only of radical Islamists or Wahhabites. The more moderate Chechen leadership believed that Wahhabism "had been introduced and spread by our enemies and the Jews." President Maskhadov made such pronouncements whenever it was necessary to name the culprits of the atrocious crimes committed in the republic. In instances such as the brutal murder of the three Britons and one New Zealander, Chechen leaders usually pointed to the special services of Russia and Israel.

Traumatized by the war, many Chechens turned to crude ideological simplifications, and Chechen society became increasingly susceptible to a collective paranoia. There were incidents occurred that resembled the medieval witch hunts, such as this one, reported by *Groznenski rabochiy:*

> In the evening of July 25, the Sixth Department of Ichkeria's State Security Ministry was besieged by an angry crowd of men and women armed with stones, metal pipes, and spades, bent on an immediate lynching of a well-known woman pop singer who, they alleged, was involved in kidnapping with the aim of selling children's organs for transplants abroad. The mob had no doubts that the bloodcurdling crimes had been committed, and that the culprit was being held in the office before them. At first the policemen tried to placate the mob, even letting two women search the cellars of the building. No one was found, but this only exacerbated emotions, as the seekers of justice insisted on finding the pop star, attributing sadistic crimes to her, while, in fact, the singer was far away on tour of the Tyumen region with her Dzhovkhar ensemble. Finally, policemen lost their patience and resorted to releasing a round of machine-gun fire into the air. The crowd dispersed.[18]

The paper's interpretation of the incident noted, "If slander is planted artificially, with no grounds at all, to incite the masses into violence, then someone had a purpose for it," hinting darkly at subversive activities by "foreign special services."

Chechnya's violence had become a hunger internalized not only by those toting Kalashnikovs, but also by ordinary civilians. Public executions and the mass production of amateur videocassettes showing murder and other acts of cruelty would not allow the war to end. This chaotic atmosphere and the discourse spawned by it generated more and more violence, and more and more paranoia, in a vicious circle.

FOURTEEN

Chechnya as a Stage and a Role

A strange kind of war. It was definitely real—so many people killed, such devastation. But beyond that, it also seemed like a kind of theater: pretense, make-believe, as if children were playing a war game.

ISMAIL K.

I have a dream that a new stage director will come to Groznyy—a brave man who won't be put off by fear of abduction or of all our other difficulties, who will breathe new life into our company. We are thirsting for work, for new productions, for new roles.

ZURA RADUYEVA, A CHECHEN ACTRESS

I began writing this concluding chapter late on August 8, 2000, upon returning from the building that houses Russia's Federation Council, where, in the office of Krasnoyarski *krai*'s Governor Alexander Lebed, I had been working on the documents of his peacemaking mission in the North Caucasus, especially those having to do with the release of hostages in Chechnya. As I was driving back home, I passed Pushkin Square, and, turning into Tverskaya Street, I heard the muffled sound of an explosion in the underpass behind me. At home that evening, I saw on the television news the horrific scenes of that terrorist attack and the first comments on it. Among them, there were two episodes that particularly caught my eye: first, Moscow's Mayor Yuri Luzhkov putting the blame squarely on "Chechen terrorism"; second, a group of activists from Vladimir Zhirinovsky's so-called Liberal Democratic Party carrying—in the midst of the chaos at the site of the disaster—a sign bearing the words "A good Chichik is a dead Chichik" (a recently coined and decidedly derogatory nickname for a Chechen).

But neither of these was replayed later; in just a couple of days, the tone had changed. There were some new comments and official statements, including an address by President Putin condemning attempts to spread the stain of terrorism on the entire Chechen people and warning against unlawful attacks on citizens of Chechen origin. Even more remarkable was the admission by the Moscow administration that "we live in the capital of a state at war," calling for a high degree of "responsibility and vigilance from both the police and the population." Thus, the Chechen war had arrived in Moscow once again, in the form of a tragic explosion and in the awareness that the war is not confined to remote fringes of the country. Not only

Chechnya and its population but the whole of Russia can be seen as a war-torn society today. I felt this a year before the events of September 11, 2001, in the United States. It became a horrific reality when, in October 2002, Chechen terrorists took some 700 hostages at a Moscow performance of the musical *Nord-Ost,* of whom 120 died as a result of gas used in the rescue operation (in which all 40 of the guerrillas were also killed).

THE TRUTH AND THE MORAL OF THE CONFLICT

Let me, then, offer some concluding observations about the Chechen conflict. I have deliberately avoided excessive theorizing and have concentrated on presenting "direct voices" as the method of my anthropological narration. I realize that my frequent long excerpts from personal accounts, interviews, and documents may seem tiresome reading to some—not quite fit for a scholarly text. But so much has been written about the war in Chechnya, such torrents of words—clever, silly, and mostly secondhand—that it is hard to hear and still harder to understand what has really been happening there in the lives of the people actually involved in the conflict. Who better to consult than those who were on the ground? One other fundamental question, both theoretical and practical, has also to be faced: What is the truth in such a conflict? Is there a reliable, unquestioned version of the conditions, intentions, and events that can be accepted by all of the parties involved?

I am finishing this chapter after August 20, 2000, the day of a by-election in Chechnya to the Russian Federation's State Duma. The one seat to be filled is being contested by thirteen candidates—most pledging "to put an end to the war," "to organize paying wages," "to consolidate the people," and so on. The platform of the foremost contender, the retired Chechen general Aslambek Aslakhanov, includes a pledge "to mobilize intellectuals to clarify the real causes of the war in Chechnya." This promise is an expression of pain, as well as of hope that underlying the war, there is some dark secret, and that bringing it to light will lead to reconciliation.

Aslakhanov won the election, but he has not been able to fulfill that promise. Not only because there is no single construction of the "real causes," but also because he did not realize (and would probably never admit) that he, too, contributed to them. Having been a deputy to the Supreme Soviet of the Russian Federation under Ruslan Khasbulatov, he was active in the "decommunization" of Chechnya, which toppled the then leader Zavgayev, and dismantled the Checheno-Ingush Autonomous Republic's state structure. Aslakhanov went to Chechnya on Khasbulatov's instructions immediately after the August 1991 putsch, which ended in Yeltsin's triumph. Through August and September, he stayed in Chechnya, whereas other leaders of the anti-Gorbachev revolution (Gennadi Burbulis,

Mikhail Poltoranin, Galina Starovoitova) paid only brief visits. It was Aslakhanov and Dudayev who organized a continuous rally in Groznyy and led the crowd to attack the republic's Supreme Soviet Building. After the old Communist Party functionary Zavgayev was ousted from power, it was he—Aslambek Aslakhanov, a former Chechen police general, chairman of the Parliamentary Committee on Security and Organized Crime—who said to Dudayev, "I've fulfilled all your conditions, now get that rally off the square." But Dudayev replied, "I have told them to disperse, but they won't listen to me."

Thus, Dudayev got the better of the federal politicians, who had been planning to install Salambek Khadzhiyev as head of the republic following the election scheduled for November 26, 1991. That would not have been a bad scenario for the change of power in Chechnya: Khadzhiyev was an intelligent, liberal-minded leader, a member of the Russian Academy of Sciences, and a prominent specialist in the field of petrochemistry making his first successful forays into business. Dudayev and his supporters got around Aslakhanov and Khasbulatov by moving the election up a month and thus getting Dudayev elected (see further Gakayev 1997: 148–62). That turn of events was later taken by many analysts to be "a genuine national uprising against foreign occupation" (Ignatieff 1999: 125).

Even with all my efforts to maintain a proper distance from the events while seeking to gather reliable information, I cannot claim to have succeeded on all fronts. One must realize that when the madness of a localized nationalism is raging and the global propaganda machines are grinding, there is little chance that even an earnest observer, in the midst of events, can come up with a universally accepted version of what happened. Just as it is hard to expect that in the foreseeable future, the people of Chechnya and Russia will by and large agree on any kind of common history of the conflict. My own version can hardly coincide even with those of my Russian colleagues Dmitri Furman and Yan Chesnov, or my Western colleagues Gail Lapidus (1998), Frédérique Longuet Marx (2003), and Tamara Dragadze (1995). Success in such an enterprise does not depend on how well informed we all may be, or how deeply involved emotionally and politically we were, or even on our professional integrity and competence. If a common view of what happened existed, we might now be able, collectively, to move beyond that tragedy.

Questions about truth come up in the aftermath of every great social upheaval or destructive war. Such questions must be faced by the scholars observing the drama as well as by its participants. Truth-finding commissions are often set up to discover "the facts," as witness Chile, Argentina, and South Africa. After World War II, and more recently, after the wars in the former Yugoslavia, international tribunals were established to search for culprits and war criminals in these regions. To some extent, that helps to bring about peace—in the sense not only of ending hostilities but of fostering reconciliation.

If no external arbitration or internal judgment is undertaken to establish the truth, the unmet need for an accounting may yield an idée fixe, as was true of Turkey's genocide of Armenians in 1915. Generations of Armenians have been seeking a formal recognition of Turkey's role in the slaughter. Why such enduring persistence? It is not only about uncovering the facts or the true role of historical actors. It is also a ritual that seeks to legitimize the victim's status as victim and to brand the guilty party as villain before the whole world. Members of the victimized group then use confirmation of their status as an important element of identity and solidarity—as an advantage in professional careers, as a point of argument in debates.

The German ethnologist Ina-Maria Greverus chided Croatian anthropologists for their politically motivated efforts to construct a victimization complex among the Croats in the period of Yugoslavia's disintegration. In her words, "The step from being a victim of the enemy to becoming a 'professional victim' . . . can be a small and brief one" (Greverus 1995: 92). We read in the works of Maja Povrzanovic (2000) that a group of female ethnographers at the Institute of Ethnology and Folklore Research in Zagreb saw as their mission discovering "small-world/real-life insights as a corrective to the dominant media-promoted national narrative" and went on to produce a number of cultural studies of the war in Croatia. They collected children's stories about the war, stories about Croats ("defenders") and Serbs ("attackers"). These stories served what a new country needed—ethnic nation-state-building, which is why there was no place for stories about Croats attacking Serbs living in Croatia.

Similarly, the Chechens made a major effort to create a memorial saga of suffering and sacrifice so as to build up group images that would call forth sympathy from outsiders. Such images were needed not so much for establishing the truth (for the crime of their deportation under Stalin is a recognized fact) as for justifying their rejection of the laws of Russia and the resort to armed force by those who had not personally experienced the trauma of deportation. The image of victim was thus used for shedding moral and civil obligations and replacing them with arguments of historical revenge.

I am not going to discuss to what extent the history of the past two centuries may release the Chechens or anybody else from their obligations to the law, the state, and their own people. First, I see little difference between their experience and that of other peoples of the North Caucasus and other regions of the former Soviet Union, or for that matter the experience of the French Canadians, Northern Irish, Kurds, New Zealand Maoris, American Indians, Hawaiians, or hundreds of other peoples who went through, to put it gently, asymmetric power relations within a single state framework.

Second, I see nothing confirming Anatol Lieven's belief that the Chechens have traditionally been free of civic responsibilities, that "they owe no moral obligation to any other people, state or set of laws," and that they have "a long score of their own to settle" with the Russians (Lieven 1998: 353), which is a slur on the many Chechen families who have Russian distant relatives or close friends. The "anti-Russianism" in pronouncements by Dudayev, Yandarbiyev, and Udugov was not universally shared by Chechens even during the war years.

That does not mean that the Chechens had no basis for constructing the image of victims for themselves—certainly their mass deportation by Stalin and Beria (both of them ethnic Georgians) was criminal and amoral. But equally amoral was the violence leveled against the non-Chechen part of the republic's population in the early 1990s. This ethnic cleansing went unacknowledged by most human rights activists. Nor have these activists paid much attention to the banishment of Azeris from Armenia before the pogrom of Armenians in Sumgait (Azerbaijan). In each of these cases about 200,000 people were forced to leave their permanent residences and homeland. Neither the authorities nor society in general offered any adequate response. Nor did the world community offer to protect the rights of these Azeris and Russians. Such a spiral of violence leads to a tangle of charges and countercharges and to mutually exclusive arguments.

A debate over the truths of who did what during the Chechen war is a thus a tactic I would like to avoid here. In the words of Michael Ignatieff, "The truth that matters to people is not factual or narrative truth but moral or interpretive truth. And this will always be an object of dispute in the Balkans." That is precisely what will emerge from the conflict in Chechnya: there will always be several moral and interpretive truths. So it is all the more important to hear the versions of those people who have no Internet sites, TV cameras, or newspaper columns. These media resources (and a measure of perspective) are at the disposal of the opposed elite and various external actors, not of the common people who are up to their ears in the conflict as fighters or victims.

Just as Michael Ignatieff suggests regarding the Balkan war, I think it is an illusion to expect an outsider to produce an impartial and objective version of the conflict in Chechnya. A stranger cannot conjure up an interpretation that would be accepted by both sides. The very fact of being an outsider undermines, rather than supports, an objective view. I cannot believe that my version will be accepted on both sides of the divide, even if I receive positive comments from both participants in the events and fellow outsiders. "For there is always a truth that can be known only by those on the inside. Or if not a truth—since facts are facts—then a moral significance of these facts that only an insider can fully appreciate. The truth, if it is to be believed, must be authored by those who have suffered its consequences.

But the truth of war is so painful that those who have fought each other rarely if ever sit down to author it together" (Ignatieff 1999: 175).

The stance I take here is not an apology for the boundless relativity of truth vis-à-vis absolute knowledge. It is, rather, recognition of the fact that no truth lies between the opponents in a violent conflict, because it is impossible for the two to reach a compromise between the opposing versions—on the one hand, that Russia's federal authorities attacked, or invaded, Chechnya (the version of many Chechens, many in the Western public, and the resolution on Chechnya passed by the European Parliament) or, on the other hand, that there was an armed coup d'état in Chechnya resulting in the rise of an aggressive paramilitary regime that challenged both the Russian state and its armed forces (the version of the Russian authorities, the Russian military, a majority of the Russian public, and some Chechens). That the two versions will at some point be molded into agreement is scarcely to be anticipated. Nor can we ever expect to see a single narrative history of this war, since, in the first place, there was never one concerning the incorporation of Chechnya into the Russian state, or the nineteenth-century Caucasian war, or of the role played by Imam Shamil. Over the course of time, one or another version of the facts of a case usually gets the upper hand, depending on the political landscape or on the perspective chosen by this or that author. And I do see potential agreement in recognizing the suffering and the damage wrought and borne by *both* sides in the Chechen war.

But there is another problem here: the greater the responsibility of those who planned and perpetrated the violence, the less inclined they are to admit it. Only once did I hear Boris Yeltsin say—from a truck platform in Yekaterinburg during the election campaign of 1996—that the war in Chechnya had been his worst mistake. An indirect admission was also made by his daughter, Tatyana Dyachenko, who said that her father felt himself responsible for that war. But then nothing was heard of it again, and nothing like that was ever admitted by Dudayev or Yandarbiyev or Maskhadov. As Michael Ignatieff writes, "Peoples who believe themselves to be victims of aggression have an understandable incapacity to believe that they too have committed atrocities. Myths of innocence and victimhood are powerful obstacles in the way of confronting responsibilities" (Ignatieff 1999: 176).

I therefore see my mission to lie in *empowering through expression* those individuals whose voices, whose visions, are least of all heard in the course of a conflict, who are least of all responsible for it, but who suffer the most from it. Both the leaders and the experts usually speak in their name. Here my position corresponds to that of a Croatian "war ethnographer": "It falls to us, narrative ethnographers, to record witnessing, trauma testimonies, and personal accounts of everyday life in prewar days and wartime and to interpret them or evaluate them as a contribution to . . . understanding multifaceted social realities" (Jambresic Kirin 1995: 26).

My long, though still unavoidably selective, quotations from the testimonies we have gathered here have enabled me, I believe, to understand important aspects of the war, even if I am unable to hear, and explain, all that stands behind these stories. I believe these recorded interviews are of interest, not only as material additional to the main text here, but as ethnographic sources for future research.

"LIBERAL INTERVENTIONISM"

In the period between the first and second Chechen wars, another factor, derived perhaps from the earlier Cold War, surfaced in the West. The first Chechen war ended, it seemed to many external actors, with the complete triumph of Chechnya (the title of Anatol Lieven's book is *Chechnya: The Tombstone of Russian Power*). This made it hard to accept Russia's subsequent retaliation in the second Chechen war. Because of a firm (though false) conviction that Chechnya's independence was an accomplished fact, the "international community" assumed an overly harsh tone and stance toward Russia. Who would not join the condemnation of violence and destruction? Who would not lament the losses and deprivations suffered by the people of Chechnya? But the undoubtedly sincere concern of various writers was tainted by an inability to see the other side of the coin. They fancied themselves as the ultimate arbiters of the situation.

They dehumanize the state, failing to see the people who constitute it, treating it as an impersonal power wielded by invented "Russians," although over half of the ruling circle in Moscow are non-Russians, including ethnic Chechens. On the other hand, they ascribe human values to the Chechen "ethnos," or "primordial nation," failing to see any bandits or extremist leaders in its midst. I agree with Michael Ignatieff when he writes, "However paradoxical it may sound, the police and armies of the nation-states remain the only available institutions we have ever developed with the capacity to control and channel large-scale violence" (Ignatieff 1999: 160).

In that light, we may ask to what extent people who remain in zones of relative security can help those who find themselves in a zone of violence to re-create viable and effective institutions of the state, and to what extent external interference further exacerbates the situation. One of the prudent answers is the following: "Sometimes, hard as it is, the best thing to do is to do nothing, to let a victor emerge, and then to assist him to establish and sustain the monopoly on violence upon which order depends. In the other case, where the adversaries are too evenly balanced to allow a decisive outcome, we may have to intervene on the side that appears to be most in the right and assist it to consolidate power. This means, of course, accepting [the view] that war may be an unavoidable solution to ethnic conflict. It means accepting a moral pact with the devil of war, seeking to use its flames to burn a path to peace" (Ignatieff 1999: 160).

This explicit statement is not meant for social scientists but for policymakers. But in some cases, it is relevant to the issue of restraint and nonintervention. With certain reservations, it can be applied to the practice of intellectuals, often seen as interfering in local societies and conflicts only in a partial way—by conducting their research or staging public and political actions. During the years of my involvement with the Chechen problem, I have observed noncombatant Chechens taking part in conferences and roundtables in Moscow, in the North Caucasus, and abroad. Facing total condemnation of Russia and enthusiastic support for the Chechen militants, such as was expressed in the resolution of the Pen Club, or by the international conference organized by *Moscow News* in December 1999, these Chechens avoided softer words or positions more moderate than those of the plenary speakers. Though most of them rejected the regime of Maskhadov, they could not bring themselves to say so before audiences bent the other way. None of them ever said, "Stop speaking in our name, or at least let us be the first speakers on your agenda, not at the end, when it is difficult to express disagreement."

I found an expression of their contrasting position only twice—in the publications of the Sakharov Foundation that I have mentioned above (*Chechnya: Pravo na kulturu* 1999; Furman 1999a). Among the chapters on events in Chechnya, those written by local Chechen authors expressed more tolerance than those by others. The Chechen authors wrote about Russia as their own country and conveyed a sense of being its citizens, even though the volume editors presented these collections as discussions of two different states and societies. The Chechens condemned the war and demonstrated their strong Chechen identity and local patriotism without mentally exiting the common state. But their tentative and seemingly ambivalent message to the rest of society was either ignored or, in some cases, censored by the Moscow editors or compilers, who stifled such dissonance—emphasizing instead texts by foreign and Russian authors pushing their own versions of the Chechen war.

One of the principles of the anthropologist's professional code—not to disturb the integrity and balance of the society you are studying—was sorely violated in Chechnya. I blame those who, having never before heard the name "Chechnya," and having made no apparent effort to learn much about its society, nonetheless assumed the right of interference and incitement. I do not observe a similar level of sympathies or incitement on behalf of the armed separatism of the Turkish Kurds (though there are some in favor of the Iraqi Kurds) or the armed separatists in the Basque country or in Northern Ireland. The label "democratic country," or "NATO member," or "EU member" evidently justifies the use of force by the states that intervene in those cases. But as early as 1950, the same "liberal interventionist" (Ignatieff's expression) club caused destabilization in Tibet by supporting the actions of the local Buddhist monks against the Chinese state. The latest victims of that "international concern" were the Kosovo Albanians, who were given arms, training, and political support from outside in order to complete the process of destruction ("self-determination") of the new Yugoslavia. Talking of double standards is not just empty rhetoric. This is the sad reality where external forces manipulate the local scenes chosen as targets for geopolitical rivalries. Chechnya has become one of such scenes, a stage on which external actors deliver their performances.

But when and why is this or that spot on the globe chosen as the scene for yet another violent conflict or destructive war? It would be both wrong and naïve to think that such intervention can be undertaken without indicative internal conditions and enthusiastic participation from the local activists. But the world abounds in situations that can be summarily described by the formula "minorities at risk." The risk factors may consist in the parent state's being unable to maintain tolerable living standards for its people; or being unwilling to permit some part of the population to preserve its cultural and group identity; or failing to provide security for local communities and individuals. All such factors may indeed breed fear and concern, even a desire to withdraw from the common political space.

To what extent radicals—bent on militant opposition to the state as a result of certain injustices—express the "will of the people" is an important question, one that shapes opinions on how "just/unjust" a struggle is. That "just/unjust" dichotomy has become the curse of our modern world. True, it was the USSR that adhered to the moral principle of distinguishing between "just and unjust wars" as one of the basic principles of the Marxist ideology for world revolution. In fact, the conception of just and unjust wars has far deeper roots than the USSR or Marxist theory. This notion has a long history and is still being invoked, both in social anthropology and in real politics. Even such a thorough thinker as Michael Ignatieff gave a bow to that dubious dichotomy in writing, "In Afghanistan and Chechnya, wars that began as genuine national uprisings against foreign occupation have degenerated into vicious fights for territory, resources, drugs, and arms among militias who are often no different from criminal gangs" (Ignatieff 1999: 125).

Why is Chechnya listed alongside Afghanistan and not with Sri Lanka's Tamils or the Turkish Kurds? Aren't the slogans and the "inside narrative" quite similar in all these cases?

In many cases, national states cope adequately with their ethnopolitical problems through bettering their own governance, or through talks, affirmative action, concessions, or the use of law, but where necessary, by the use of armed force. Ethnic radicalism and ethnic wars arise where the state encourages ethnic divisions as a basis of its system of governance (as was the case in the USSR and still is in the post-Soviet states) and/or where the state loses its grip on law and order, or its control over arms arsenals, and permits the rise of irregular armed groups led by ethnic entrepreneurs. That becomes the opportune moment for external forces to foster the image of an "enslaved people" struggling for freedom and independence.

FORGING CHECHENS FROM ETHNOGRAPHIC REFERENCES

Paradoxical as it may seem, it was not so much the Chechen people who generated a deep conflict in the country (surely with the participation of the Russian state and its army) as the war that generated that image. Just as Serbs and Croats, before the war in Yugoslavia, had identified themselves less by their ethnic characteristics and more by belonging to certain civic networks or local communities, so Chechens, before 1991, had defined themselves as Soviet citizens, some as members of the Communist Party and/or state bureaucracies, as Muslims or atheists, and as members of various professions, age groups, and family circles. The Russian language had become the language they spoke and read. Even the label "formerly deported" was not exclusive to Chechens, for there were millions of other people of other nationalities who had been deported, exiled, dispossessed, and limited in their rights. That was the legacy of the Stalin years.

The evidence my research partners and I collected shows that for the prewar (1990s) generation of Chechens, neither their ethnic identity nor the fact of deportation constituted a central element of their identity. As for tribal *(teip)* affiliation, very few of them made reference to it. They were concerned with their earnings and living, their chances of getting a good education, professional careers, service in the army or various state agencies—just like the rest of the population of the Soviet Union.

The reification of Chechenness arose under conditions of conflict and the social transformations of the Gorbachev-Yeltsin period. It arose in a dramatic, mythologized form constructed from historic and ethnographic materials, and from literary and pseudoscientific writings, as well as from deliberate political prescriptions. These materials and prescriptions imposed on Chechens a kind of heroic primordial and premodern identity involving a changing mixture of nationalistic narcissism, victimization, and messianic ideas about being the "grave-diggers of the empire," the "liberators of the Caucasus," and a force in "the vanguard of Islam."

The mythopoeic Chechen past is used to forge an image for living Chechens and to prescribe their present-day roles. Such a forging procedure tends to destroy the relevancy that surrounds it, including the everyday regularities and concerns that fail to correspond to the constructed image. I put the blame here on those who through superficial historical analyses and cultural essentialism reduce a whole group to the level of a "premodern nation" with a unique fighting morale. It is interesting how arguments travel from one text to another. Much of what look like manifestations of a society in crisis and wracked by demodernization can be found first as postulates in academic texts. Such references are borrowed by journalists and policymakers. They then become part of everyday conversation and take on a reality of their own. Articles published by a member of my institute, Yan Chesnov, are often a source of references for Chechen ethnography. Some authors regard his research as "irreplaceable work on the structures of Chechen traditional society" (Lieven 1998: 335). On the contrary, I think my colleague contributed to the forging of myths of a unique Chechen civilization and a 400-year fight between Chechens and Russians—a source of nationalistic narcissism later parroted by Yeltsin and Maskhadov. The following is one of his superficial but "politically correct" observations:

> Russian totalitarianism always attempts to suppress the mountain democracy of the nationalities of the Caucasus—first and foremost that of the Vainakhs—in the most barbaric fashion. It has been 400 years since Vainakh civilization liquidated the institutions of a feudal aristocracy and of a natural, inherited inequality among people. The individual's natural freedom is the essence of Vainakh democracy. This freedom found powerful support in the institutions of the Islamic religion. For totalitarian imperial regimes, a free nationality within Russia is not simply a thorn in the side, but by its example provokes dangerous thinking among the enslaved fellow-citizens of the entire country. . . . We should recognize that the ancestors of these peoples once lived on the banks of the Tigris and the Euphrates, where the great beginnings of the spiritual life of humanity were born. These nationalities are the creators of the unique Vainakh civilization, which we know maintains the freedom of the individual as the most important value. Among the Chechens, this concept is so highly developed that I once had the opportunity to record the assertion, "One cannot be a slave—even to circumstances." (Chesnov 1995–96: 32)

Sergei Arutiunov, a well-known Russian anthropologist, also tends to focus on the traditional Vainakh brand of democracy and the long historical memory of its people in explaining the high degree of mobilization of the Chechens in the conflict.

> Chechnya was and is a society of military democracy. Chechnya never had any kings, emirs, princes, or barons. Unlike other Caucasian nations, there was never feudalism in Chechnya. Traditionally, it was governed by a council of elders on the basis of consensus, but like all military democracies, such as the Iroquois in America or the Zulu in southern Africa, Chechens retain the institution of military chiefs. In peacetime, they recognize no sovereign authority and may be fragmented into a hundred rival clans, but in time of danger, when faced with aggression, the rival clans unite and elect a military leader. This leader may be known to everyone as an unpleasant personality, but can be elected nonetheless for being a good general. For so long as the war continues, this leader is obeyed. (Arutiunov 1995: 17)

These two Russian authorities on Chechnya constitute a basis for other texts that repeat or superficially elaborate on these postulates. The same kind of misuse of scholarly texts for the sake of politicized or nationalistic mythmaking can be observed in abundance all over conflict areas (on Transcaucasia, see Shnirelman 2001). Journalists and political scientists love to strengthen their power of representation with deep ethnographic references. The following is one of many examples:

> They are a nationality having no identification with the state and the society in which they live, and no motivation whatsoever to conform with its laws; equipped with ancient traditions which are in contradiction to those of "enlightened," "pluralist" and "progressive" liberalism; with social forms which make them opaque to outside investigation; internally cohesive, and remarkably efficient and ruthless in pursuit of their aims; and in a country in which a mixture of poorly institutionalized "democracy," social disintegration, state weakness and state corruption have opened up the most enormous opportunities and spaces for organised criminal activity. One might almost say, to adapt a phrase of Robert Musil's, that if the modern Western bourgeoisie could dream, it would dream Chechens. (Lieven 1998: 353–54)

Anatol Lieven calls "the Russian intervention" "an error of colonial ethnography," implying that there were fundamental misconceptions among the Russian KGB and military experts regarding the nature of Chechen society as "traditional, irrational, divided, static, and inflexible." We confront here a serious phenomenon of anthropological reductionism, a culturally distinct but modern people characterized as an "ancient tribal ethnos" or "premodern nation." The logic of such paternalistic (unintentionally neocolonial) reductionism suggests a group that deserves sympathy, support, and protection. By citing poorly proved or even fictitious data on the ways in which their culture differs fundamentally from those of others, and by rejecting commonalities, this kind of anthropology creates myths of its own.

Putting modern Chechens into iron ethnographic cages and allowing them carte blanche to oppose established laws harms them in more general ways. At one time, I did field research among the Iroquois, and I remember well Grand Chief Joseph Norton of the Mohawk Territory of Kahnawake in Québec telling me that his main concern was to get his people to obey the law with respect to smuggling across the U.S.-Canadian border and casino gambling on the reserve. Why does this principle not extend to other peoples? Why is a "military chief" like Leonard Peletier serving two life prison terms for challenging the state by organizing armed "resistance" to FBI agents at the Pine Ridge Reservation? I have a dream, a dream that the Chechens will be able to escape the Western bourgeoisie's dreams of Chechens. The imposed role is not easy to avoid, and one should note that the same kind of ethnography that praises Chechen freedom-fighting efficiency is now being used to explain their failure as well:

> Blood is everything in Chechnya. . . . In 1994, all Chechens were united as a *k'am* [an entire people] in their common struggle with Russia, but in the course of the war and during subsequent years, Chechen military and social structures gradually reverted to their tribal foundations. A member of one *teip* [clan] is loath to place himself under a commander from another teip, and conversely all Chechen field commanders became aldermen of their own teips. After the war this peculiarity became the major obstacle to the formation of the national political institutions and state discipline. . . . Except in the most acute crisis, Chechens will never submit to leadership from any teip other than their own, and each teip will remain a rival of the others. Chechens lack a tradition of a suprafamilial political organization, and in this respect may be regarded, however unpalatably, as a premodern society. The result has been a catastrophic social implosion that has engulfed all of Chechnya, and within which the current war is merely the latest phase. (Kisriev and Ware 2000: 6–7)

Some now find the Chechen independence project to be unrealizable. Among them, Robert Ware has noted the dynamics of Russian politics, the impact of Chechen lawlessness upon neighbors, and the failure of Chechnya's economic, social, and political development. "Chechnya lacks capital, infrastructure, nonmilitary investment, and viable trade routes through non-Russian territory. It has essentially no civil society and the hardships imposed by its lawlessness are even greater for ordinary Chechens than for citizens in the neighboring territories. It has developed no authoritative political order. . . . Some of these problems can be traced to traditional Chechen social structure" (Kisriev and Ware 2000: 6). Exactly the same factors of Chechen failed state-building are uncritically repeated by Thomas Graham (2001: 23).

As we see from my data, during the war the Chechens were not united in their struggle with Moscow, and Russian society, too, was deeply divided in its views of the disastrous war. In the three years following the first war, Chechen society disintegrated even further, with in-group rivalries, political/military factions, and outlaw gangs sprouting like weeds. Power was divided between the Maskhadov group, which was relatively conciliatory in its approach to Moscow, and an opposition that turned toward a militant expansionism and Islam in an effort to acquire legitimacy. Many people opposed both factions, but lacking Kalashnikovs, they could not raise their voices without inviting immediate punishment. These people became hostages to a political ideology.

It was not because of its ancient cultural traditions that Chechen society failed to build its own nation-state; more "contemporary" factors were involved. First, many Chechens found comfort in their nationalist mythology and in seeing it enriched by the postwar discourse of a "great victory." Heroic mythology served well as an inspiration for fighting, but it proved far less useful in a time of reconstruction and in negotiations with the warring party. It proved itself first self-perpetuating and then self-destructive.

Second, a newborn Chechen identity that arose during the conflict looked to Islam for ways to address the deficiencies of the postwar political situation. Traditional Sufi brotherhoods emerged among a populace with strong, secular Soviet legacies—and thus a populace with a poor background in religious education. Traditional Islam did not play the pacifying role expected of it, overtaken as it was by a warrior mythology, ethnic and regional cleavages, and the widespread persistence into the post-Soviet era of an atheism that excluded a unified Islamic *umma.* Islam's return to Chechen society was further complicated by the introduction of Wahhabi Islamic fundamentalism, which spread among the more militant factions of the society in opposition to a disunited *muftiat,* as well as to Maskhadov's weak government. Moreover, the Wahhabi brand of fundamentalism came with material and financial support from groups in the Persian Gulf, Pakistan, and Afghanistan.

Third, it is not simply the case that Wahhabism and other outside influences interfered with Chechnya's fragile intragroup balances. Rather, they reinvented so-called *teip* cleavages, and political rivalries emerged around kin/family and fragile local coalitions striving for power and resources. It was such cleavages that prevented the Maskhadov regime from establishing civic foundations for political legitimacy, law and order, economic sustainability, and public services.

Finally, no less important but often ignored, the Chechen revolution both destroyed the former Soviet system of rule and simultaneously indulged in an unrealized project of restoring an imagined order (based on clan structure and religion) that had never previously existed or, at the very least, had not existed since Chechnya's incorporation into the Russian state. The most realistic option for forming an independent state—restoration of some semblance of prewar autonomy—was delegitimized by both internal and outside actors. This egregiously war-torn society sought a future based on invented images of the past, applying answers that were, ultimately, alien to Chechen society itself.

Conclusion

In mid June 2001, an all-Russian television station announced that a group of Russian scholars was conducting "the first scholarly study of the Chechen war." The very fact of such a study, leaving aside its results, is now newsworthy. How do we explain this? Does it reflect hope of some miraculous insight, of a formula for resolving the problem, or is it just part of the usual lobbying efforts of the academic community for financial support and publicity? Is it naïve to hope that scholarship holds the key to solving the challenge presented by the Chechen war? It would be imprudent of those "who are doing real things" in Chechnya (implementing anti-terrorist measures, rebuilding amid the ruins, helping refugees, keeping the wheels of commerce and industry turning, treating and educating children) to ignore the work of academic researchers.

My thirty-five years as a scholar and brief experience as a Russian federal minister have led me to the conclusion that there is nothing more practical than a good theory and adequate diagnosis of a problem. The work of scholarship involves taking good aim, and not, as the well-known saying goes, "shooting among the sparrows." During the course of the Chechen war, there were more than enough stray shots. For example, at one point in 1996, a discussion of the Chechen situation in the State Duma was based on expert information that determined "the index of sociocultural development" of the Chechens and Russians in Chechnya and the "civilizational" differences between these two groups. According to this, the Chechens are "somewhere at the end of the ideological phase of modernization," while the Russians "have gone farther, they are in the political phase of modernization"; the Russians are "close to contemporary values," whereas the Chechens and others "still tend toward traditional values, characterized by conservatism, hierarchical political structures, and "communal" property"

(Skakunov 1996: 112–14). With such assessments, it is not surprising that the growing alienation of the Chechens and treatment of them as barbarians belonging to "a different civilization" found approval in Russia's political circles and society at large.

Perceptions of this nature also produced projects seeking to establish order in Chechnya on the basis of mythical structures and so-called traditional social institutions (the *teip* system, the Mekh-Khel, blood feud, etc.). The use of pseudoscientific arguments to degrade groups is not new. For example, in the nineteenth century, the mostly illiterate European colonists deemed the Florida Indians, whom they expelled to the wilds of Oklahoma, to be "uncivilized," even though they possessed a written language and had their own newspapers and enlightened leaders, such as the Seminole chief Osceola. And yet it was the Indians who needed to be "civilized" and not the Europeans.

In the conclusion to my book *Ethnicity, Nationalism, and Conflict in and after the Soviet Union,* I discuss the difficulty of analyzing conflict situations that are complex in both an absurd and surreal way, and when reality might be destroyed (not constructed or deconstructed!) through theory (Tishkov 1997a: 294–98). The difficulty has not been overcome in this study. Much remains outside the purview of this book, in particular an analysis of the actions of the so-called federal side and the interactions between the Chechens and "the federals" (I would prefer to say "the rest of the Russia" or "the larger society") and a closer examination of the realm of emotions and psychological factors, a critical aspect of human conflict that is underestimated by scholarship. One is reminded of the observations of Galina Zaurbekova, who conducted many interviews for this book in Chechnya, focusing on the "paradoxical tendencies" of the Chechen war:

> For those who had been wrecked by the war, everyone was an enemy, whether they were mercenaries, federals, Wahabbis, or *boyeviki.* People rushed from place to place, finding themselves in the deadlock. Many in such a situation often lost their reason. Many went mad during this war. They lost the ability to react appropriately to those around them and could not even understand orders, such as "Stand up! Hands up!" . . . These are all visible, tragically tangible displays of the absurd, which permeated all of society, penetrating the public and personal lives of people. Irrationality inevitably accompanies separatism in all of its forms. (Zaurbekova and Yandarov 2001: 170)

Meanwhile, certain general conclusions can be drawn. *The postwar reconstruction can only be achieved through the renewal of empowering self-analysis, which is the primary condition for reconstruction in the postwar era.* In the past two to three years, Chechen scholars, politicians, and activists have significantly improved their understanding of what took place in Chechnya, and the prospects of arresting violence and of reaching accord are much better than they were previously, all of which offers hope for the future. Thus, I was struck by the accuracy of the analysis provided by Ruslan Khasbulatov in a series of articles published in *Nezavisimaia gazeta* in 2000–2002, in particular his views on the character of Chechen society, the nature of Chechen separatism and of the war itself, and on the strategies necessary for peaceful reconstruction (Khasbulatov 2000a, 200b, 2001). His extravagant statement that "Chechnya has been lost for Russia for ever" (*Novaya gazeta,* January 28–30, 2002) was to some extent a personal message to those at the top who can call upon this man to manage the crisis. Dzhabrail Gakayev has also offered interesting analyses, which he has presented to the federal government, international gatherings, and the republic's population via the radio program *Free Chechnya* (see Gakayev 2001: 73–90). In another example of this positive trend, the Chechen professor Khasan Turkayev joined the Institute of Ethnology and Anthropology of the Russian Academy of Sciences in organizing a conference in April 2001 on the issue of preserving and developing Chechen culture. The conference included insightful presentations, including some on historical-archeological topics, which were very different from the irrational gibberish characteristic of the period dominated by radical ideas and politicians. In addition, a collection of scholarly papers on the problems of reconstruction in Chechnya in the postwar era, mostly by Chechen authors, was published in the summer of 2001 (Gakayev and Yandarov 2001), followed by another publication based on the April 2001 conference (Turkayev 2002).

Intellectual advances on the topic have also been made among outside observers, albeit not without great difficulty. Foreign scholarship continues to be hampered by an antipathy to "neo-imperial" or "mini-imperial" Russia and a justification of armed separatism in Chechnya. For example, in April 2000, the Swedish Institute of International Affairs held a conference in Stockholm on "Chechnya: The International Community and Strategies for Peace and Stability." The Russian and foreign scholars who participated in the conference were worlds apart in their assessments of the situation. Gail Lapidus of Stanford University holds a rigid position. She believes that positive prospects for Chechnya existed only after the August 1996 Khasavyurt agreement and under the leadership of the Maskhadov government. At that time, there was the possibility of reestablishing normalcy in Chechen society, restoring the urban infrastructure, attracting investments in the local economy, increasing employment, and developing the public health and educational sectors. In addition, "This was also a period that offered an opportunity for working with the international community to implement a serious program of regional development, a kind of Caucasus stability pact." According to Lapidus, the new war destroyed these opportunities. She criticizes all of the initial premises of the new Kremlin policy in the North Caucasus and concludes that Russia now faces a more serious challenge than the one that led to the war, and possesses fewer options and resources for ending the conflict (Lapidus 2000: 30–42).

Another participant at the conference, Marta-Lisa Magnusson, is a Danish scholar studying the Chechen problem who (with the U.S. scholar Paul Henze) undertook a mission to Chechnya in the fall of 1992 for the nongovernmental organization International Alert, and co-authored an apologetic paper on the "national revolution." She continues to view events in Chechnya as part of a "decolonization conflict." She believes that

> ordinary Chechens . . . consistently refuse to cooperate with the federal authorities and various marionette structures established by the Russians in Groznyy. Again and again the Chechen population has demonstrated that when confronted with external threats it rallies around its own political leaders—even unpopular ones [i.e., Aslan Maskhadov]. Why is that? Because these figures are not only political leaders. They are symbols of national liberation, national pride, national self-determination and even national security. Even weak Chechen leaders become strong symbols as soon as the Russians come too close. (Magnusson 2000: 46)

What is the source of such superficial views, and how long will all these "national" metaphors (liberation, pride, self-determination, "even security") continue to be used as analytical categories? Another vexing issue has to do with the fact that, as in the old days of the "war with falsificators," the divergence of views on Chechnya is influenced by ideology and personal feelings, which poses a challenge to professional relations between colleagues. This time, though, the ideological watchdogs are more the Western scholars than the Russians. In other words, while the current armed conflict is weakening on the battlefield, it remains an all-encompassing issue over which virtual and academic battles are waged on the basis of increasingly hardening positions.

The conflict lives on as each side seeks to prevent the other from gaining the upper hand. I have the impression that, having transferred to Turkey for more effective presentation, Movladi Udugov, through his Internet site and mass-media empire, including a new Chechen-language broadcast on Radio Svoboda, seeks to convince, not only the Chechens, but the rest of the world that a restoration of peace (or peace enforcement) in Chechnya based on the consolidation of federal and local power is nothing but a reinstatement of the colonial order, a continuation of the genocide of the Chechen people, a violation of international law, and a crime by Russia before the world. According to this view, those ethnographers who were "pro-government" and "anti-minority," who did not sufficiently protect the "small nation" from the big bad enemy, are also guilty.

My friend Tamara Dragadze, a British anthropologist, e-mailed me on November 8, 1999:

> I heard from the Chechens that you are very pro-government and that Sergo Arutiunov was less hawkish than you. I have been travelling very much lately and I did not always have access to CNN, and even less to BBC. . . . What can I say about this? If Russia sends its eighteen-year old boys to death, it will suffer because of it. And if its government is incapable of conducting a criminal investigation into the blowing up of buildings, then all people in Russia will suffer because there is no legal evidence that the Chechens planted the bombs, and a war should not be started on the basis of this lie. All of this is on Russia's conscience—the countries, people, and culture that are dear to me. As for the Chechens, it seemed to me that we already had enough genocide for one century, and that they should not be destroyed, as the military is trying to do. . . . I do not know how much is shown on your television of what is happening in Chechnya right now. But, Valerii, please do something to stop this war. And if you think that I can help somehow, then please let me know. As ethnographers, we must save as many small nations as possible from extinction, whether we like them or not.

I heeded Dragadze's advice. The Fund for Humanitarian Assistance to the Republic of Chechnya, established by the Institute of Ethnology and Anthropology, has led numerous philanthropic efforts, including the collection of 45,000 books for the restoration of Chechnya's libraries. But the question remains: Who should be saved, by whom, and where? I saw a kind of "small Chechen nation" of my own on June 19, 2001, when the Fund, along with the Chechen businessman Malik Saidullayev, organized a charity concert to help the children of Chechnya, which brought 3,500 people to the Rossiya State Concert Hall, the overwhelming majority of whom were Chechens living in Moscow. To me, these people represent the Chechen nation, as do the heads of the local administrations and the social activists from Chechnya who attended a roundtable in Stockholm on issues related to the peaceful reconstruction of the republic two weeks before the concert. For certain foreign participants and observers, these latter Chechens are not the "nation" or "people." They are "Quislings" (according to Gail Lapidus) or "puppets" (according to Marta-Lisa Magnusson). Even the title of the Stockholm roundtable was delicately changed by the Western co-organizers from "Post-Conflict Reconstruction" to "Peaceful Reconstruction."

For them, the conflict is not yet over and, apparently, should not be over unless scripted by CNN, or when they say so, which amounts to the same thing. For them, the "Chechen nation" is somewhere in the mountains and the ravines, continuing the armed resistance, which includes terrorizing Chechens themselves. The fact that the Russian courts have established that terrorists from Chechnya participated in blowing up residential buildings in Moscow and other cities is already old news that "experts on Chechnya" do not consider worthy of analysis, because it does not correspond to the widely shared consensus, constructed and imposed by academics and the media, as to what constitutes a Chechen nation.

At an international conference on ethnic conflicts held in Bonn in December 2000, Tim Guldimann, the former head of the OSCE mission to Chechnya and the current Swiss ambassador to Iran, told me, "I would gladly offer some help to Chechnya and to the work being done by your Fund, but I would not want to offend the Chechens with whom I closely worked in Chechnya." I encountered similar references to "the public," "our own radicals," "anti-Russians," and so on, more than once when discussing peace initiatives and humanitarian assistance for Chechnya. A kind of reluctance and deliberate negation of positive changes in the dynamics of the conflict have been and are still present behind the scenes. This led me to the next conclusion: There are not only two sides in an armed conflict, but many, and while some of the participants are visible, others are concealed.

Similar observations were made about the Balkans by the well-known columnist William Pfaff with reference to Allen Kassof, the head of the Project on Ethnic Relations (like William Pfaff, I too am a member of this project's council).[1] *Those who plant explosives, man blockades, and even just sit at headquarters or military offices are merely the frontline in the current conflict. The real battalions are formed in a more complex and capricious manner, as are the dividing lines in the conflict.* When we talk about the Chechen war and the fighting forces or sides involved, it should be realized that in this conflict, there is no social or even ethnographic reality that can be called the "Chechen people" or "Chechen nation," and likewise no sociopolitical monolith to be identified as "Russia" (Rossiya) or, even less so, "the Russians." Among those directly involved in the conflict, there are those who want to fight and those who do not, no matter under what banner or command the war is waged. The war pits Chechens against Chechens and Russians against Russians. Typically stronger in this scenario, the hawks attack the doves and, more often than not, gain the upper hand. Initially, Dudayev, Yandarbiev, and Maskhadov broke up a meeting and even killed some of their own who did not want to fight. Then Yeltsin, Grachev, and Yegorov trampled on the opponents of war in Chechnya and drove them from office. Subsequently, the moderate General Anatoly Romanov, commander of the Russian forces in Chechnya, was seriously wounded by bombs planted in central Groznyy, and the Nazran agreements signed by the Russian minister for nationalities, Vyacheslav Mikhailov, and Maskhadov in June 1996 were shredded. This was followed by Maskhadov's ouster at the hands of Basayev, Khattab, and Raduyev, who launched an Islamic jihad and began to kill the Dagestanis, while the Russian "strongmen" embarked on a course aimed at "total destruction," often confusing bandits with peaceful citizens.

During all these years, "peaceful voices" were heard on both sides, but as often happens in conflict situations, they came too late. In September 1996, Vladimir Zorin, who spent a year in Chechnya as one of the heads of the federal territorial administration, expressed the following thought: "It is time for us to understand once and for all that, in this kind of conflict, there are neither winners nor losers. We repeated this view a year ago at the peace negotiations in Groznyy, and in Nazran, and it was heard again in the recent negotiations" (1999: 301). It seems that the war will come to an end only when the doves overpower the hawks, hard as that is to imagine, and not when either the "Russian side" or the "Chechen side" overpowers the other.

Another conclusion that can be drawn from this war and from Pfaff's observations with respect to the Balkan wars is that *in an armed conflict, not only are goals of both a practical and ideological nature pursued, and military prowess displayed, but both direct and indirect participants also engage in what is commonly called "good" and "bad" behavior.* Extreme cruelty and the reckless squandering of the lives of conscripted soldiers and peaceful inhabitants constitute bad behavior, as do the murders and bombings committed by Chechen *boyeviki.* But it is precisely this kind of behavior that prevails. Good deeds are not rewarded and thus are rarely displayed. From the outset of the new war, federal soldiers and officers assumed the exemplary role of protectors of the peaceful Chechens, and then, with the greeting "Merry Christmas," Colonel Yuri Budanov's guns blew apart houses and villages inhabited by his fellow citizens. The country did not shudder at this, thus countenancing behavior that led subsequently to the rape and murder of an eighteen-year-old Chechen girl, Elza Kungayeva. *The Chechen war was the price paid for the low value placed on human life. We inherited this "value" from the past, and it persists to this day in Russian society.*

The atrocities of the Chechen war and the difficulty in settling the conflict were rooted in the coarseness and drunkenness of the officers of the Russian army, the brutal treatment of recruits *(dedovshchina)* by old-timers, and the poor education and immaturity of village boys recently conscripted from the countryside and the fighters of the Chechen mountain villages. Hatred, fundamentalist preaching, and hard currency payments, on the one hand, and the desire to avenge the victims and protect the country from bandits and outside forces, on the other—these are all of secondary importance in explaining the spiral of violence and human behavior in general in conditions of war. The war will not end if it is so easy to kill other humans and squander soldiers' lives with impunity.

For all the circumstances and explanations, the issue of what the Chechen war represents and how to end it is situated in the realm of human interactions, and, in my view, is of a global historical nature. The boundary between violence and nonviolence, between peace and war, is very unstable, and it is all too easy to cross it, even unwittingly. As my Chechen informant Said M. said, "We all tread on a thin crust, as it were, and might at any moment plunge through into the depths." No society is immune to open conflict, including conflict between peoples of similar cultures. Even the slightest of differences can be used to justify violence. The real rupture takes place during war itself, however, which is why restoring peace is more complicated than starting a war. But it is possible to refrain from war if the danger is understood and the boundary is perceived. It is precisely this awareness that was lacking among those directly involved at the outset of the Chechen war. In my archives, in my handwriting, there is the draft of an agreement, reached during the course of negotiations in Vladikavkaz, in the North Caucasian Republic of North Ossetia–Alania, between representatives of the Russian Federation and the Republic of Chechnya, dated December 12, 1994 (the second day of the war). It reads in part:

> During the course of negotiations on regulating the situation in the Chechen Republic, an understanding was reached on the necessity of an immediate halt to the bloodshed on its territory, and on an agreement in principle to begin the disarmament of the armed contingents in Chechnya, and to devise a concrete mechanism for implementing the disarmament in conjunction with the withdrawal of Russian military forces.[2]

The Chechen delegation, headed by Taimaz Abubakarov, accepted this draft agreement and submitted the document to Dudayev in Groznyy for approval. Some of the delegates, led by Vyacheslav Mikhailov, stayed behind in Vladikavkaz in anticipation of an answer, but none came. Dudayev disavowed the efforts of his envoys, and Moscow did not insist on keeping the talks going. The first Russian tanks were already burning in Groznyy, and the first victims had fallen. The hawks wanted war.

NOTES

PREFACE

1. In 2001, Nauka, the publishing house of the Russian Academy of Sciences, brought out the Russian text (which is twice as long as the translated version) under the title *Obschestvo v vooruzhennom konflikte: Etnografia chechenskoi voiny* (A Society in Armed Conflict: The Ethnography of the Chechen War).

2. See Aukai Collins, *My Jihad: One American's Journey through the World of Usama Laden—as a Covert Operative for the American Government* (New York: Pocket Star Books, 2002).

3. Russia was able to provide reliable information that Osama bin Laden donated at least $25 million and dispatched numerous fighters to Chechnya, including Ibn Khattab, a Saudi who led one of the best-trained contingents from 1995 until his death in 2000. The United States agreed that Ibn Khattab had al-Qaeda ties and cited those links when it added three Chechen rebel units to its list of terrorist organizations in 2003, after more energetic measures on the part of the international anti-terrorist coalition. Interpol announced a number of Chechen field commanders as wanted criminals, including the most famous, Shamil Basayev.

2. INDIGENIZATION, DEPORTATION, AND RETURN

1. Interview with Professor Rauf Munchayev, March 13, 2001, Moscow.—Author's files.

2. On Soviet policy of indigenization, see further Chugayev 1968; Mikhailov 1997; Lieber 1992.

3. The standardization of Soviet bureaucrats with rigidly prescribed functions made it possible to execute mass social experiments with easy rotation of actors. See Scott 1998.

4. Conversation with Ruslan Aushev, Nazran, February 23, 1995.—Author's files.

5. *Groznenskii rabochii,* no. 28 (July 28–August 3, 1999).

3. CONTRADICTORY MODERNIZATION

1. Conversation with Isa Buzurtanov, Nazran, Ingushetiya, February 22, 1995.
2. Author's files.
3. Author's files.
4. Author's files.

4. CHECHEN IMAGES

1. Dzhabrail Gakaev disagreed with this observation by Rustam: "Melkhistins pretended to be different, but that was with Dudayev, who was not Melkhistin himself. (It was his sister who married a Melkhistin.) This group did not strengthen its position, and they received nothing. It was the Yalhoroy group, like Adam Albakov, that profited. In any case, Melkhistins were considered Dudayev's most devoted supporters." Yan Chesnov describes them as the most noble and militant Chechen group (Chesnov 1999: 99). I checked this assertion with the outstanding Russian archaeologist Professor Rauf Munchayev, who worked for two decades in Chechnya, precisely in the Bamut village area, where there is a homogeneous Melkhistin population. He could not recall any exceptional militancy or talk of noble roots on the part of the local inhabitants, including young people employed in the archaeological excavations. However, a major Soviet anti-missile launch site was constructed near Bamut in the 1970s, which may have served to incite local young males, who later turned this concrete colossus into a fortress. Quite possibly, the story of exceptional Melkhistin valor and militancy was a late Soviet and specifically wartime product, especially after successful retaliation by federal troops around Bamut.

2. To be sure, Dudayev had not yet learned that a kin group living in the Akhmetovskii region of Georgia is known as Kisty or Kistintsy. (It does not have any special relationship to the Melkhistins.) He subsequently corrected his nomenclature descriptive of the Chechen "ethnos."

5. THE ROAD TO WAR

1. The well-known Russian politician and former professional ethnographer Galina Starovoitova, who was a close associate of Andrei Sakharov's, considered herself the main author of this draft constitution, as she indicated in personal conversations with me during our joint work in the Yeltsin government. Starovoitova, who was assassinated in Saint Petersburg in 1998, also wrote a paper on national self-determination (Starovoitova 1997).

2. Resolution of the National Congress of the Chechen People, November 25, 1990.— Author's files.

3. V. B. Vinogradov was a graduate of the Moscow State University in archaeology; he took my history class while at the university. Since that time he had been politically quite active. In Groznyy, he became a major authority on the official version of this republic's history and a kind of a self-appointed watchdog over local heresies.

4. Notes from Rutskoi's statement in the State Duma, February 20, 1995.— Author's files. I suspect strongly that this was one of Yeltsin's alcoholic binges.

5. Author's notes.

6. Notes from Rutskoi's statement in the State Duma, February 20, 1995.—Author's files.

7. Conversation with Gakayev, October 8, 1995, Groznyy.

8. Interview with Ballaudi Movsayev, February 23, 1995, between Nazran and Samashki, Ingushetiya.

9. Testimony of Yegor Gaidar at the State Duma Commission on the Investigation of Events in the Chechen Republic, February 20, 1995.—Author's files.

10. Dzhokhar Dudayev to Yegor Gaidar, May 10, 1992, Groznyy.—Author's files.

11. Testimony of Yegor Gaidar, State Duma Commission on the Investigation of Events in the Chechen Republic, February 20, 1995, vol. 3, pt. 3, p. 16.

12. Ibid., p. 9.

13. Dzhokhar Dudayev to Boris Yeltsin, March 30, 1993, Groznyy.—Author's files.

14. Dzhokhar Dudayev to Boris Yeltsin, April 11, 1993, Groznyy.—Author's files.

15. Ibid.

16. *Argumenty i fakty,* March 9, 1995, 3.

17. *Izvestiia,* February 9, 1995, 2.

18. Ibid.

6. DZHOKHAR: HERO AND DEVIL

1. Dudayev, interview with Gagik Karapetyan, *Stolitsa,* no. 15 (1992): 1–3.

2. Ibid., 3.

3. Ibid.

4. G. Esenbayeva in *Put' Dzhokhara,* no. 9 (July 28–August 3, 1997): 1.

5. *Put' Dzhokhara,* no. 11 (August 11–18, 1997).

6. Ibid.

7. THE SONS OF WAR

1. I. V. Kochubei, statement to the Russian Federation security council's committee investigating the situation in Chechnya, March 31, 1995, Moscow.—Author's files.

2. My cross-reviewer Rustam Kaliyev noted, however, that it was not always like this: "There are people from different *teip*s living in every village. It is true that armed groups were formed along territorial lines, but *teip* membership also played a part. For example, the Galaizhoiskaya brigade in Yermolovka were practically all from one Galai *teip.* In Zakan-Urt, the Chaberloy special regiment, headed by Kurdi Bazhiyev, consisted mainly of Chaberloy *teip* members."

3. Rustam Kaliyev observed, however: "The military genius of the Chechen leaders, including Maskhadov, and the dauntless valor of the fighters are silly romantic clichés that beg the question: even if Maskhadov was a brilliant commander, how could he ever have put his military talents to work during the war without a functional army, or at least a large, well-equipped force?"

8. THE CULTURE OF HOSTAGE-TAKING

1. Interview with Alexander F. Mukomolov, July 18, 2000, Moscow.—Author's files.

2. Ibid.

3. Zakharovich 1999: 302, citing Tom Masland and Andrew Nagorski, "Doing Dirty Work," *Newsweek,* June 26, 1995, 28–29.

4. Conversation with Dmitri Balburov, July 20, 2000, Moscow.—Author's files.

5. Ibid.

6. Interview with Alexander F. Mukomolov, July 18, 2000, Moscow.—Author's files.

7. Ibid.

8. Ibid.

9. Ibid.

10. *Argumenty i fakty,* no. 23 (June 2000): 20.

11. Ibid.

12. Interview with Alexander F. Mukomolov.

13. *Argumenty i facty,* no. 10 (2000).

14. *Komsomolskaya pravda,* March 10, 2000, 4.

15. *Groznensky rabochiy,* no. 26 (July 14–20, 1999): 1.

9. VIOLENCE IN SECESSIONIST WARFARE

1. Institute for Socioeconomic Reform in the Transition Period, minutes of roundtable session on Chechnya, Moscow, June 5, 1995, 32.

2. Conversation with Andrei Kamenshikov, June 15, 1995, Golityno, Moscow region.

3. While minister in 1992, I received several collective petitions from non-Chechens in Chechnya listing crimes and atrocities committed against them. I took this up with Minister of Internal Affairs Viktor Yerin, who responded: "What could I do?" The state practically abandoned this category of its citizens, thus opening the road to more violence.

4. Author's notes, Vladikavkaz, North Ossetia, December 12, 1995.

10. THE IMPACT ON FAMILY LIFE

1. Cross-reviewer Rustam Kaliyev commented: "The cult of the elder has always been there in Chechnya. It has been exploited cynically by the so-called Chechen elite, with the support of those especially active old people who imagined themselves to be Hercules and Aristotle rolled into one. It was something extraordinary for our society: the younger generation—in opposition to Dudayev and Co.; heads of families and *teip*s, grandfathers—they not only supported Dudayev but they participated in all these meetings and rallies. The 'revolutionary masses' included people over sixty. Young people, who were critical of Dudayev, participated in politics in their spare time, and they were not so politicized. People of the older generation were more aggressive. There were many conflicts over political views. An interesting situation arose during elections: fathers voted for Dudayev and their children against him. It

had never been like this in Chechnya. Before the conflict, even issues of life, death, and honor had been resolved in 99 cases out of 100 the way the elders decided. And it was not regarded as suppression of personality. After 1991, the older generation, represented by the elders, stopped being an effective regulator of social processes in Chechen society."

11. RELIGION AND THE CHECHEN CONFLICT

1. See, e.g., Khazhbikar Bokov in *Nauka i religiia* (Science and Religion), no. 8 (1976); no. 11 (1983); no. 5 (1987).

2. Khazhbikar Bokov in *Nauka i religiia*, no. 8 (1976): 5.

3. Khazhbikar Bokov in *Communist*, no. 16 (1979): 29.

12. THE MYTH AND REALITY OF THE "GREAT VICTORY"

1. Khamzat Gakayev, "Nobody Can Ruin Us but Ourselves," *Groznensky rabochiy*, no. 29 (August 5–10, 1999): 3.

2. Valeria Novodvorskaya quoted in *Put' Dzhokhara*, no. 9 (July 28–August 3, 1997): 4.

3. *Zashchitnik otechestva* (Chechen Military Newspaper), no. 1 (February 1998): 1.

4. Grigory Stitzberg in *MK-Ivanovo*, June 14–21, 2000, 2–3.

5. *Groznensky rabochiy*, no. 25 (July 7–13, 1999): 2.

6. Ibid.

7. *Groznensky rabochiy*, no. 29 (August 5–11, 1999): 1.

8. *Groznensky rabochiy*, no. 28 (July 28–August 3, 1999): 3.

9. *Zashchitnik otechestva*, no. 1 (February 1998): 4.

10. *Groznensky rabochiy*, no. 25 (July 7–13, 1999); no. 28 (July 28–August 3, 1999): 1; no. 29 (August 5–11, 1999): 1–2.

11. *Versia*, no. 1 (January 11–17, 2000): 8.

12. *Put' Dzhokhara*, no. 9 (July 28–August 3, 1997): 1.

13. *Groznensky rabochiy*, no. 27 (July 21–27, 1999): 1.

14. *Ichkeria*, no. 25 (1996): 2. The full Russian text of the Criminal Code can be found in ibid., nos. 24–26 (1996).

15. *Groznensky rabochiy*, no. 28 (July 28–August 3, 1999): 2.

13. AN IDEOLOGY OF EXTREMES

1. In 1999, after completing my study, I initiated inviting to the IEA RAS a group of Chechen social scientists, former members of the Groznyy institute, now living in Moscow or other cities. This group of about ten researchers is still working in its "internal exile" status.

2. R. Varayev, "Hitler on the Chechens," *Put' Dzhokhara*, no. 11 (August 17–23, 1997).

3. A. Akbulatov in *Ichkeria*, no. 8 (1999): 2.

4. Albert Machigov, "The Chechens Are the Founders of Russia," *Put' Dzhokhara*, no. 11 (August 17–23, 1997).

5. *Chechenets,* no. 11 (1997): 16; Kharon Vastigov, "In the Beginning Was the Word," *Put' Dzhokhara,* no. 9 (July 28–August 3, 1997): 4.

6. Zelimkhan Yandarbiyev, "The Caucasus Is Our Common Home; the Caucasus Is One; the Caucasus Is Free," *Put' Dzhokhara,* no. 9 (August 17–23, 1997): 1.

7. Zelimkhan Yandarbiyev, "Address to the Peoples and Political Organizations of the Caucasus," *Kavkazskaya konfederatsiya,* no. 6 (June 1998): 1.

8. Ibid.: 1–2.

9. Said-Khasan Abumuslimov in ibid.: 3.

10. *Put' Dzhokhara,* no. 11 (August 17–23, 1997): 4.

11. See their declaration "On the Basic Organization of State Power in the Chechen Republic of Ichkeria," *Groznensky rabochiy,* no. 4 (1999): 3.

12. Ibid.

13. Ibid.: 1–2.

14. Ibid.: 4. The main idea is that "the future of Chechnya is in her distant past," and that only by returning to the historic stage of evolution called "barbarism" will Chechnya and Russia be able to find harmony and peace: "It is good that Groznyy has been destroyed. It should be destroyed as an embodiment of all the sins of contemporary civilization." See also Kh.-A. Nukhayev in *Nezavisimaya gazeta,* December 10, 2000 (the same issue in which my article on "words and images in the Chechen war" was published).

15. "The Catechism of the Jew in the USSR," *Veliki jihad,* no. 5 (1998): 17.

16. Movladi Udugov quoted in *Kavkazsky vestnik,* no. 11 (August 1999): 3, 6.

17. *Kavkazsky vestnik,* no. 10 (July 1999): 7.

18. *Groznensky rabochiy,* no. 28 (July 28–August 3, 1999): 2.

CONCLUSION

1. *International Herald Tribune,* July 5, 2001.

2. "O khode peregovorov ob uregulirovanii obstanovki v Chechenskoi respublike" [On Negotiations to Regulate the Situation in the Chechen Republic], Vladikavkaz, December 12, 1994.—Author's archives.

MAIN CHARACTERS

Abdulatipov, Ramazan (1946–), prominent Russian politician of Dagestani origin; chair of the House of Nationalities in Boris Yeltsin's first Supreme Soviet of the Russian Federation, 1990–93; minister of nationalities, 1998–99; member of the Council of the Federation (the upper chamber of the Russian parliament), 2001–.

Abubakarov, Taimaz (1948–), minister of industry and finance in the Dudayev government; leader of the Chechen delegation in negotiations with the federal delegation in Vladikavkaz (North Ossetia), December 11–13, 1994; lives in exile.

Adizov, Said-Magomed (1930–95), former leader of traditional *tariqah* Islam in Chechnya and of the Mekh-Khel (council of elders) during the Dudayev "national revolution." Murdered by radical Islamists for his refusal to announce a war against the Russian government as a *hazavat* war.

Akbulatov, Aslambek (1942–), philologist and journalist; chief of Dudayev's presidential staff.

Akhmadov brothers, a family of eight brothers from the Ahchoi-Martan region of Chechnya; notorious kidnappers involved in hostage-taking for profit and other criminal activities under Dudayev and Maskhadov.

Akhmadov, Khali (1940–), lawyer; chairman of the Chechen parliament, 1991–93; now head of the Law Department at Groznyy State University.

Alimsultanov, Imam (1960–96), Chechen pop singer.

Alsabekov, Mukhamman-Khussein-Khadzhi (1958–), mufti in Chechnya in Dudayev's time.

Arsanov, Vakha, former highway policeman; member of a special squad for taking hostages; vice president under Maskhadov.

Arutiunov, Sergei (1931–), prominent Russian ethnologist; member of the Institute of Ethnology and Anthropology; corresponding member of the Russian Academy of Sciences.

Aslakhanov, Aslambek (1942–), a former Chechen police general; chairman of the Parliamentary Committee on Security and Organized Crime in the first Supreme Soviet of the Russian Federation; member of the State Duma from Chechnya.

Atgiriyev, Turpal (1969–2002), field commander during the first Chechen war in 1994–96; deputy prime minister in Basayev's government; prosecuted in Russia and died in prison.

Aushev, Ruslan (1954–), retired general; Afghan veteran; president of Ingushetiya, 1993–2001; member of the Council of Federation of the Federal Assembly of Russia.

Avtorkhanov, Abdurakhman (1908–97), Chechen political scientist and historian; emigrated from the USSR in the 1930s and lived in Germany; author of numerous books.

Barayev, Arbi (1978–2001), field commander from Urus-Martan; head of special Islamic regiment under Maskhadov; organized several major terrorist acts; killed in a special forces operation.

Barsukov, Mikhail (1947–), former Russian minister of internal affairs.

Basayev, Shamil (1965–), leading military figure of the Chechen war; led the terrorist attack on Budennovsk in June 1995; prime minister under Maskhadov; leader of military raid on Dagestan.

Berezovsky, Boris (1946–), Russian businessman involved in Chechen war and peacemaking; secretary of the Russian Security Council, 1996; lives in exile.

Beria, Lavrenty (1899–1953), henchman of Stalin; as a head of the KGB implemented the deportation of the North Caucasus peoples; arrested and shot under Nikita Khrushchev.

Bersanova, Zalpa, Chechen sociologist from Groznyy.

Betelgiriyev, Khusein (1953–), Chechen pop musician and singer; teacher at Groznyy State University.

Bisultanov, Antu (1959–), Chechen poet and public figure.

Brezhnev, Leonid (1906–82), first secretary of the Communist Party of the USSR, 1964–82.

Burbulis, Gennadii (1945–), state secretary under Yeltsin, 1991–92; member of the State Duma and president of the Strategy Foundation.

Chernenko, Konstantin (1911–85), first secretary of the Communist Party of the USSR, 1984–85.

Chernomyrdin, Viktor (1938–), Russian prime minister, 1992–98.

Chesnov, Yan (1935–), senior researcher at the Institute of Ethnology and Anthropology, Russian Academy of Sciences.

Dadayeva, Raisa, Chechen journalist; editor of pro-Dudayev newpaper *Put' Dzhokhara* in Groznyy.

Dalkhanov, Apti (1957–96), Chechen pop singer who bore the title of Distinguished Artist of the Checheno-Ingush Republic; died after Shari'a punishment.

Daudov, Rizvan, field commander; head of special Shari'a police regiment under Maskhadov.

Derluguian, Georgi M. (1960–), Russian writer and analyst on Caucasus affairs; lives in the United States; senior fellow of the U.S. Institute of Peace; teaches at Northwestern University.

De Waal, Thomas, British journalist working in Chechnya, co-author with Carlotta Gall of books on the Chechen war.

Dudayev, Dzhokhar (1944–96), former general in the Soviet army who commanded a strategic bomber wing in Estonia in the late 1980s; leader of the Chechen "national revolution"; president of the Chechen Republic, 1991–96; died in a Russian rocket attack on the village of Gekhi-chu.

Dzhavtayev, Umar, Akkin Chechen from the Khasav-Urt region; activist of General Lebed's Peace-Making Mission in the North Caucasus.

Esambayev, Makhmud (1924–2000), famous Chechen dancer; bore the title of Hero of Socialist Labor in the USSR.

Filatov, Sergei (1936–), deputy chairman of Supreme Soviet of the Russian Federation, 1990–93; head of the presidential administration under Yeltsin.

Fleutiaux, Brice (1968–2001), French photojournalist taken hostage in Chechnya from October 1999 to June 2000; committed suicide.

Foteyev, Vladimir, Communist Party leader in Checheno-Ingushetiya in the 1980s.

Furman, Dmitri (1945–), senior researcher at the Institute of Europe, Russian Academy of Sciences; wrote on Chechnya.

Gaidar, Yegor (1956–), leader of the Democratic Choice of Russia Party; member of the State Duma; prime minister, 1991–94.

Gakayev, Dzhabrail (1942–), Chechen historian; former vice-rector of Groznyy State University; chairman of the Chechen Cultural Center in Moscow; leading researcher at the IEA RAS.

Gakayev, Dzhokala (1888–1985), Dzhabrail's father.

Galazov, Akhsarbek (1929–), president of the Republic of North Ossetia, 1990–97.

Gantamirov, Beslan (1963–), leader of anti-Dudayev opposition; mayor of Groznyy in 1995.

Gelayev, Ruslan (1954–), militant Chechen leader; commander of presidential special regiment in 1995; defense minister and Shari'a guard under Maskhadov.

Geshayev, Musa (1940–), Chechen poet and writer; director of Filarmony in Groznyy, 1979–92, then moved to Moscow; member of the Russian Union of Writers.

Gorbachev, Mikhail S. (1931–), first secretary of the Communist Party of the USSR, 1985–91; president of the USSR, 1990–91.

[Gotsinskii], Sheik Nadjimuddin (1859–1925), well-known religious and public figure who became imam of Dagestan and Chechnya in 1917; killed by the Bolsheviks.

Grachev, Pavel (1948–), Russian defense minister, 1992–96.

Gusinskii, Vladimir (1952–), Russian businessman; head of Media-MOST; lives in exile.

Henze, Paul, fellow of the RAND Corporation; expert on the Caucasus; leader of the International Alert fact-finding mission to Chechnya in 1992.

Ibragimov, Khamzat (1936–), president of the Chechen Academy of Sciences under Dudayev; director of the Research Institute in Groznyy since 2000.

Kadyrov, Akhmad (1951–), pro-Maskhadov religious leader prior to 1998; head of the Provisional Chechen Administration since 2000; elected president of the Chechen Republic in October 2003.

Khadzhiev, Salambek (1941–), Chechen scholar and businessman; corresponding member of the Russian Academy of Sciences; head of Chechen government in 1995.

Khamidova, Zulai (1940–), Chechen philologist and sociolinguist; professor at Groznyy State University.

Khasbulatov, Ruslan (1942–), chairman of the Supreme Soviet of the Russian Federation, 1990–93; corresponding member of the Russian Academy of Sciences; professor of economics.

Khasieyv, Said-Magomed (1942–), Chechen ethnographer; professor at Groznyy State University.

Kotenkov, Alexander (1952–), deputy head of the Provisional Chechen Administration, 1995; presidential representative in the State Duma.

Kovalev, Sergei (1930–), member of the State Duma; leading Russian human rights activist.

Kunta Haji (1830–67), founder of the Qadiriyyah *tariqah* in the North Caucasus.

Kutsenko, Vitalii (19??–91), chair of Groznyy City Council; killed by Dudayev's people.

Labazanov, Ruslan (1967–95), Chechen paramilitary leader; killed in blood revenge.

Lapidus, Gail (1933–), professor of political science at Stanford University; a specialist in Soviet and Russian affairs.

Lebed, Alexander (1950–2002), Russian general; secretary of the Security Council of Russia; governor of Krasnoyarsky krai; founder of the Peace-Making Mission in the North Caucasus.

Lieven, Anatol (1950–), British writer; describes himself as "an amateur anthropologist; a historian by training, a journalist by profession"; covered the Chechen War of 1994–96 as a correspondent for the *Times* (London); published a scholarly monograph on the Chechen War (1998); senior associate at the Carnegie Endowment for International Peace.

Lobov, Oleg (1937–), secretary of the Russian Security Council, September 1993–June 1996; Boris Yeltsin's chief representative in Chechnya, where an attempt was made to assassinate him in 1995.

Magamadov, Lecha (1938–), head of the Supreme Soviet of the Checheno-Ingush ASSR; anti-Dudayev opposition figure; leader of the Edinstvo Party in Chechnya.

Mamakayev, Magomed (1910–73), outstanding Chechen writer; published historical novels in Chechen; member of the Soviet Union of Writers.

Mamodayev, Yaragi (1953–), Chechen prime minister ousted by Dudayev in 1993.

Mansur, Shaikh Ushurma (1760–94), famous Naqshbandi leader of the *ghazavat* against tsarist forces in Chechnya; said to have commanded as many as 25,000 men; said to have been a Jesuit priest named Elisha Mansour who converted to Islam; died in Russian captivity.

Maskhadov, Aslan (1951–), former Soviet military officer; commander of Dudayev's army; president of Chechnya, 1996–1999; leader of military resistance to the Russian army.

Mikhailov, Vyacheslav (1935–), Russian minister of nationalities, 1995–98, 1999–2000; headed two sets of Russian-Chechen negotiations in 1994 and 1995.

Movsayev, Abu (1959–), Chechen field commander; head of the security service under Maskhadov.

Nukhayev, Khozh-Akhmed (1954–), Chechen businessman and publicist; founder of the Caucasus House public organization.

Poltoranin, Mikhail (1939–), minister of information in Yeltsin's government.

Putin, Vladimir (1952–), president of the Russian Federation.

Raduyev, Salman (1967–2002), Chechen field commander; radical Islamist; died in prison.

Rutskoi, Alexander (1947–), vice president of the Russian Federation under Yeltsin; governor of Kaluga oblast.

Saidullayev, Malik (1964–), Chechen businessman and public figure.

Shakhrai, Sergei (1956–), born in Ingushetiya; deputy prime minister in the Yeltsin-Gaidar government; minister of nationalities, 1992–93; member of the State Duma, 1995–96.

Shamil, Imam (1799–1871), famous religious and military leader of Dagestani origin; led resistance to tsarist forces in the Caucasus, 1817–64.

Shpigun, Gennadi (19??–1999), born in Dagestan; general of the Russian Interior Ministry; special presidential envoy for Chechnya; taken hostage on his mission to Groznyy and killed.

Shternberg, Leo (1861–1927), prominent Russian anthropologist and linguist.

Soslambekov, Yusup (1956–99), leading activist of the Chechen secessionist movement; chairman of the Chechen National Council, 1990–91; assassinated in Moscow.

Starovoitova, Galina (1947–98), Russian politician and ethnographer; Yeltsin's aide on nationalities issues, 1991–92; member of the State Duma, 1994–98; assassinated in Saint Petersburg.

Turpalov, Lema (1954–), Chechen historian, journalist, and writer.

Udugov, Movladi (1962–), radical Islamist and leading ideologue of the Chechen secession; minister of information under Dudayev; lives in exile.

Usmanov, Lema, Chechen political writer; lives in exile; author of numerous pro-Dudayev publications.

Vinogradov, Vitalii (1939–), historian and archaeologist; lived in Groznyy prior to Dudayev's rule.

Vlasov, Valentin (1945–), Yeltsin's envoy in Chechnya and Russian co-chairman of the Russian-Chechen Joint Commission for a Chechen settlement; taken hostage and released for $2 million ransom.

Yamadayev, Sulim, field commander in Gudermes; head of special forces under Maskhadov.

Yandarbiyev, Zelimkhan (1952–), leader of the Chechen secessionist movement; founder of the Vainakh Democratic Party; served as vice president under Dudayev and as acting president after the latter's death in April 1996; lives in exile.

Yeltsin, Boris (1930–), president of the Russian Federation, 1991–99.

Yushenkov, Sergei (1950–2003), member of the Russian State Duma; leader of the Liberal Russia Party; assassinated in Moscow.

Zavgayev, Doku (1940–), first secretary of the Communist Party of Checheno-Ingushetiya, 1988–91; head of the Chechen provisional government, 1995–96.

Zorin, Vladimir (1948–), Russian minister in charge of nationalities affairs, 2001–; head of the State Duma Committee on Nationalities Affairs, 1996–99; deputy-head of Provisional Chechen Administration, 1995.

INFORMANTS AND INTERVIEWERS

INTERVIEWS DONE BY VALERY TISHKOV IN MOSCOW AND CHECHNYA

Abdullaeva, Kheda (1969–), Chechen philologist, born in Benoy-Yurt; a graduate of the Groznyy Pedagogical Institute; Ph.D. from the Institute of World Literature, Russian Academy of Sciences. Informant and collaborator. Interviews in Moscow, 1998–2000.

Akayev, Vakhit (1951–), historian, born in Shatoi; director of the Checheno-Ingush Institute of History, Sociology, and Philology in Groznyy. Informant. Interviews in Groznyy, 1995, Moscow, 1998–2000.

Akhmadov, Yavus (1947–), professor of history; minister of information in Khadzhiyev's government and Kadyrov's administration. Interviews in Groznyy, 1995, Moscow 1998–99.

Balburov, Dmitrii (1967–), *Moscow News* journalist who spent three months in Chechen captivity in 1995. Interview in Moscow, 2000.

Bokov, Khazhbikar (1935–), writer, born in Nazran; former chairman of the Supreme Soviet of the Checheno-Ingush Republic, 1974–90; Russian deputy minister of nationalities, 1991–97; editor of *Zhizn natsionalnostei.* Interviews in Moscow, 1992–2000.

Dadayev, Akhyad (1968–), member of Dudayev's guard regiment, born in Urus-Martan. Interviews in Moscow, 1997–98.

Gakayev, Dzhabrail (1942–), Chechen public figure; professor of history; leading researcher, IEA RAS. Interviews in Groznyy, 1995, Moscow, 1998–2000.

Gelman, Efim (1933–), former minister of education of the Checheno-Ingush Republic; spent several months in Chechen captivity in 1992; consultant for the Russian Ministry of Education. Interview in Moscow, 1999.

Kaliyev, Rustam (1974–), born in Pervomayskoye (Galashki); student at the Moscow High School of Management. Interviews in Moscow, 1998–2000.

Movsayev, Bagaudi (1961–), field commander; chief of staff of the "Afghan battalion." Interview in Nazran, February 1995.

Mukomolov, Alexander (1948–), historian; retired FSB officer; adviser to Alexander Lebed; after Lebed's death, deputy head of the peacemaking mission in the North Caucasus. Interviews in Moscow, 1998–2000.

Munchayev, Rauf (1928–), former director of the Institute of Archaeology, Russian Academy of Sciences; led archaeological excavation in Chechnya; published several books on ancient history of the North Caucasus; corresponding member of the Russian Academy of Sciences. Interview in Moscow, 2001.

Salgiriyeva, Malika (1953–), social and local government worker, Groznyy. Interviews in Moscow, 1997–99.

Zainalabdiyeva, Zhovzan (1950–), assistant to Doku Zavgayev; civil servant in the Russian Ministry of Nationalities. Interviews in Geneva and Moscow, 1998–99.

INTERVIEWS DONE BY GALINA ZAURBEKOVA AND ANDARBEK YANDAROV IN CHECHNYA

Aindi Yu., 20, Dachu-Borzoy village. Interview, spring 1998

Akhyad Kh., 47. Interview in Groznyy, November 1997

Ali Ismailov, 18, student, Groznyy. Interview, spring 1998

Alik A., 35, schoolteacher, Groznyy. Interview, November 1997

Chingiz Z., 36, Duba-Yurt village. Interview in Groznyy, October 1997

Isa M., 37, utility technician, Groznyy. Interview, August 1997

Isa M., 65, Kolaus settlement, fifteenth state milk farm. Interview, October 1997

Ismail K., 32, truck driver, Novyy Atagi village. Interview, fall 1997

Ismail M., 18, Khal-Kiloy village. Interview, spring 1998

Khalid U., 32, Duba-Yurt village. Interview, August 1997

Khizir B., 40, bus driver, Dachu-Borzoy village. Interview, November 1997

Khizir I., 21, Tashkala settlement. Interview in Groznyy, summer 1998

Khoz-Akhmed Sh., 35, small businessman, Belgatoy village. Interview, November 1997

Kyura A., 50, town of Shatoy. Interview in Groznyy, October 1997

Lecha S., 17, wounded fighter, Roshni-Chu village. Interview, spring 1998

Makhdi B., 18, Davydenko village. Interview in Groznyy, winter 1997

Masud B., 19, Sharoy mountain. Interview in Groznyy, spring 1998

Mudar K., 60, lawer, Groznyy. Interview, November 1997

Musa Kh., 46, Novyy Atagi village. Interview, September 1997

Musa P., 40, Duba-Yurt village, lives in Groznyy. Interview, winter 1997

Ramzan B., 20, Duba-Yurt village. Interview, summer 1998

Said M., 41, Groznyy. Interview, September 1997

Said Y., 45, physician from Goyty village. Interview in Groznyy, 1997

Said-Khusein Z., 41, Groznyy. Interview, September 1997

Said-Selim G., 18, Makhkety village. Interview in Groznyy, summer 1998

Shamil A., 20, Gerzel-aul village. Interview in Groznyy, summer 1998

Taus A., 30, fifteenth state milk farm, second division. Interview, July–August 1997

Timur Kh., 40, architect, Staryy Atagi village. Interview, July–August 1997

T-ov's brothers, Goyty village. Interview, summer 1998

Vadud, 77, "Rodina" state farm. Interview in Groznyy, October 1997

Vakha G., 63. Interview in Groznyy, winter 1997

Vazayeva, Asya, 54, philologist and journalist from Chishki village, Groznensky *raion,* lives in Groznyy. Interview, July 1997

Visit M., 70, former worker of the state cooperative service, Urgehk village, Shatoysky *raion.* Interview, 1996

Zura M., 63, housewife, Urus-Martan village. Interview, December 1997

INTERVIEWS DONE BY KHEDA ABDULLAYEVA IN CHECHNYA

Abdullayeva, Malika

Idrisova, Malika

Ismailova, Khava

Mazdayeva, Khava

Saidullayeva, Malika

Salazhiyeva, Elina

SELECT BIBLIOGRAPHY

Abubakarov, Taimaz. 1998. *Rezhim Dzhokhara Dudayeva: Pravda i vymysel. Zapiski dudayevskogo ministra ekonomiki i finansov* [Dzhokhar Dudayev's Regime: Truth and Falsehood. Essays from Dudayev's Ministry of Economics]. Moscow: INSAN.

Abumuslimov, S. 1995. *Genotsid prodolzhaetsya* [The Genocide Is Continued]. Kiev: n.p.

Akayev, Vakhid Kh. 1994. *Shaikh Kunta-Khadzhi: Zhizn' i uchenie* [Shaikh Kunta Maji: Life and Teaching]. Groznyy: Checheno-Ingush Izdat.

———. 1999a. *Sufism i vakhabism na Severnom Kavkaze.* Issledovaniia po prikladnoi i neotlozhnoi etnologii [Sufism and Wahhabism in the North Caucasus. Working Papers in Urgent and Applied Ethnology], no. 127. Moscow: IEA RAS.

———. 1999b "Religious-Political Conflict in the Chechen Republic of Ichkeria." In Lena Jonson and Murad Esenov, eds., *Political Islam and Conflicts in Russia and Central Asia,* 47–58. Stockholm: Swedish Institute of International Affairs.

———. 2001. "Islam i politika na primere Chechni" [Islam and Politics: The Case of Chechnya]. In Dzhabrail D. Gakayev and Andarbek D. Yandarov, eds., *Chechnya: Ot konflikta k stabilnosti (problemy rekonstruktsii)* [Chechnya: From Conflict to Stability (Problems of Reconstruction)], 126–47. Moscow: IEA RAS.

Akhmadov, Sharputdin V., and Vakhid Kh. Akaev. 1992. *Shaikh Mansur i osvoboditel'naya bor'ba narodov Severnogo Kavkaza v poslednei treti XVIII veka. Tezisy dokladov i soobchenii mezhdunarodnoi nauchnoi konferentsii* [Shaikh Mansur and the Liberation Struggle of the Peoples of the North Caucasus in the Last Third of the Eighteenth Century. Summaries of Papers and Reports of the International Conference]. Groznyy: Chechen NII.

Akhmadov, Yavus Z. 2001. *Istoria Chechni s drevneishikh vremen do konza XVIII veka* [History of Chechnya from Ancient Times to the End of the Eighteenth Century]. Moscow: Mir Domu Tvoemu.

Akhriyev, Chakh. 1875. *Ingushi: (Predaniya i verovaniya). Sbornik svedenii o kavkazshih gortzah* [Ingush People (Folk Legends and Beliefs): Collection of Evidence about the Caucasus's Mountaineers]. Vol. III. Tiflis.

Alexeev, Valery P. 1974. *Proiskhozhdenie narodov Kavkaza* [The Origins of the Peoples of Caucasus]. Moscow: Nauka.

Ali, Rabia, and Lawrence Lifschultz, eds. 1993. *Why Bosnia? Writings on the Balkan War.* Stony Creek, Conn.: Pamphleteer's Press.

Aliroyev, Ibragim. 1978. *Nakhskie yazyki i kultura* [Nakhs Languages and Culture]. Groznyy: Checheno-Ingush Izdat.

Aliyeva, Svetlana, ed. 1993. *Tak eto bylo: Natsionalnye repressii v SSSR. 1919–1952* [It Was Like That: Repression of Nationalities in the USSR, 1919–1952]. 3 vols. Moscow: Insan.

Alker, Hayward R., Ted Robert Gurr, and Kumar Rupesinghe, eds. 2001. *Journeys through Conflict: Narratives and Lessons.* Boston: Rowman & Littlefield.

Allen, Tim. 1999. "Perceiving Contemporary Wars." In Tim Allen and Jean Seaton, eds., *The Media of Conflict: War Reporting and Representations of Ethnic Violence,* 11–42. London: Zed Books.

Andresen, T., B. Bull, and K. Duvold, eds. 1997. *Separatism—Culture Counts, Resources Decide.* Bergen, Norway,

Apter, David E., ed. 1997. *The Legitimization of Violence.* London: Macmillan.

Armstrong, Patrick. 2002. "How to Turn a Local War into Part of the International Jihad." Johnson's Russia List, #6191, Research and Analytical Supplement no. 7 (April), Special Issue on the Situation in Chechnya, 14–17, http://www.cdi.org/russia/johnson/6191-3.cfm.

Arutiunov, Sergei A. 1995. "Ethnicity and Conflict in the Caucasus." In Fred Wehling, ed., *Ethnic Conflict and Russian Intervention in the Caucasus.* Institute for the Study of Global Conflict and Cooperation, University of California, San Diego, Policy Paper no. 16.

———. 1999. "Zakony gor vne zakonov ravnin" [The Law of the Mountains Overrides the Law of the Plains]. *Itogy,* January 19, 14–16.

Avtorkhanov, Abdurahman. [1988] 1991a. *Imperiia Kremlia: Sovetskaia tip kolonializma.* Garmisch-Partenkirchen: Prometheus Verlag. Reprint. Moscow: Polifakt.

———. 1991b. *Ubiistvo checheno-ingushskogo naroda: Narodoubiistvo v SSSR* [The Killing of the Checheno-Ingush People: People-Killing in the USSR]. Moscow: Vsya Moskva.

———. 1992. *The North Caucasus Barrier: The Russian Advance towards the Muslim World.* Edited by Marie Bennigsen Broxup. London: Hurst.

Balburov, Dmitrii. 2000. "Zapiski chechenskogo plennika" [The Diary of a Chechen Captive]. *Novaya Yunost* 41, no. 2: 93–114.

Beissinger, Mark R. 2002. *Nationalist Mobilization and the Collapse of the Soviet State.* Cambridge: Cambridge University Press.

Beissinger, Mark, and Lubomyr Hajda, eds. 1990. *The Nationalities Factor in Soviet Politics and Society.* Boulder, Colo.: Westview Press.

Belayev, S. [1848] 1991. *Devyat' mesyatsev v plenu u chechentsev* [Nine Months in Chechen Captivity]. Groznyy: Groznenskii rabochii.

Bennigsen, Alexandre, and Samuel Enders Wimbush. 1985. *Mystics and Commissars: Sufism in the Soviet Union.* Berkeley: University of California Press.

Bersanova, Zalpa. 1999. "Sistema zennostei sovremennykh chechentsev" [The Value System of Contemporary Chechens]. In Dmitri Furman, ed., *Rossia i Chechnia:*

Obschestva i gosudarstva [Russia and Chechnya: Societies and States], 223–49. Moscow: Andrei Sakharov Foundation, Politinfo.

Berzhe, Adolf P. 1859. *Chechnya i chechentsy* [Chechnya and the Chechens]. Tbilisi.

Bliushov, A., A. Guryanov, O. Orlov, and A. Sokolov, comps. 1995. *Vsemi imeiuchimisya sredstvami* [By All Available Means]. Moscow: Memorial.

Bocharov, Viktor M., and Valery A. Tishkov, eds. 2001. *Antropologia nasiliya* [The Anthropology of Violence]. Saint Petersburg: Nauka.

Bokov, F. P., and R. Chabiev. 1994. *Yad kriminala* [The Poison of Criminality]. Moscow: Insan.

Bokov, Khazhbikar 2000. *My—vainakhi* [We Are Vainakhs]. Moscow: Slavyanski dialog.

Bookman, Milica Zarkovic. 1992. *The Economics of Secession.* New York: St. Martin's Press.

Brass, Paul R. 1997. *The Theft of an Idol: Text and Context in the Representation of Collective Violence.* Princeton: Princeton University Press.

Bremmer, Ian, and Ray Taras, eds. 1993. *Nations and Politics in the Soviet Successor States.* Cambridge: Cambridge University Press.

Bromley, Yulian V., ed. 1977. *Sovremennye etnicheskie protsessy v SSSR* [Contemporary Ethnic Processes in the USSR]. Moscow: Nauka.

———. 1983. *Ocherki teorii etnosa* [Essays on the Theory of Ethnos]. Moscow: Nauka.

Brubaker, Rogers. 1996. *Nationalism Reframed: Nationhood and the National Question in the New Europe.* Cambridge: Cambridge University Press.

Brubaker, Rogers, and David D. Laitin. 1998. "Ethnic and Nationalist Violence." *Annual Review of Sociology* 24: 243–52.

Brzezinski, Zbigniew. 1994. "The Premature Partnership." *Foreign Affairs* 73, no. 2 (March–April): 67–82.

Bugai, Nikolai F., ed. 1994. *Repressirovannie narody Rossii: Chechentsy i Ingushy. Dokumenty, fakty, komentarii* [Repressed Peoples of Russia: Chechens and Ingush. Documents, Facts, Commentary]. Moscow: TOO Kap.

Bugai, Nikolai F., and A. M. Gonov. 1998. *Kavkaz: Narody v eshelonakh* [The Caucasus: The Peoples Railroaded into Exile]. Moscow: Insan.

Burton, John W. 1987. *Resolving Deep-Rooted Conflict: A Handbook.* Lanham, Md: University Press of America.

———. 1990. *Conflict Resolution: Resolution and Prevention.* New York: St. Martin's Press.

Carbonnier, Gilles. 1998. *Conflict, Postwar Rebuilding and the Economy: A Critical Review of the Literature.* War-Torn Societies Project Occasional Paper no. 2. Geneva: UN Research Institute for Social Development.

Carley, Patricia. 1996. *Self-Determination, Sovereignty, Territorial Integrity, and the Right to Secession.* Report from a Roundtable Held in Conjunction with the U.S. Department of State's Policy Planning Staff. Washington, D.C.: U.S. Institute of Peace.

Carment, David, and Patrick James. 1997. "The International Politics of Ethnic Conflict: New Perspectives on Theory and Policy." *Global Society* 11, no. 2: 205–32.

Chechnya Report. 1992. *Chechnia: Report of an International Alert Fact-finding Mission, September 24–October 3, 1992.* London: International Alert.

Chechnya: Pravo na kulturu [Chechnya: The Right to Culture]. 1999. Moscow: Andrei Sakharov Foundation.

Chervonnaya, Svetlana. 1994. *Conflict in the Caucasus: Georgia, Abkhazia and the Russian Shadow.* London: Gothic Image Publications.

Chesnov, Yan V. 1994a. "Chechentsem byt trudno: Teipy, ikh proshloe i rol v nastoiyaschem" [Hard to Be a Chechen: *Teips*, Their Past and Contemporary Role]. *Nezavisimaya gazeta,* September 22.

———. 1994b. "Zhenschina i etika zhizni v mentalitete chechentsa" [Woman and the Ethnic of Life in Chechen Mentality]. *Etnograficheskoe obozrenie,* no. 5, 34–44.

———. 1995–96. "Civilization and the Chechen." *Anthropology and Archeology of Eurasia* 34, no. 3 (Winter): 28–40.

———. 1996a. "Etnokulturnyi potentsial chechenskoi natsii" [Ethnocultural Potential of the Chechen Nation]. In V. A. Tishkov and S. V. Cheshko, eds., *Severnyi Kavkaz: Etnopolitical and Etnocultural Protsessy v XX veke* [The North Caucasus: Ethnopolitical and Ethnocultural Processes in the Twentieth Century], 33–51. Moscow: IEA RAS.

———. 1996b. "Chechenskaya kultura detstva" [The Chechen Youth Culture]. In V. A. Tishkov and S. V. Cheshko, eds., *Severnyi Kavkaz: Etnopolitical and Etnocultural Protsessy v XX veke* [The North Caucasus: Ethnopolitical and Ethnocultural Processes in the Twentieth Century], 143–74. Moscow: IEA RAS.

———. 1999. "Byt chechentsem: Lichnost i etnicheskie identifikatsii naroda" [To Be a Chechen: Personality and Ethnic Identification of the People]. In Dmitri Furman, ed., *Rossia i Chechnia: Obschestva i gosudarstva* [Russia and Chechnya: Societies and States], 63–101. Moscow: Andrei Sakharov Foundation, Politinfo.

Chugayev, Dmitri A., ed. 1968. *Istoria natsionalno-gosudarstvennogo stroitelstva v SSSR, 1917–1936* [History of National State-Building in the USSR, 1917–1936]. 2 vols. Moscow: Mysl.

Coakley, John. 1992. "The Resolution of Ethnic Conflict: Towards a Typology." *International Political Science Review* 13, no. 4: 343–58.

Cohen, Stephen. 2001. *The Failed Crusade: America and the Tragedy of Post-Communist Russia.* New York: Norton.

Collier, Paul, and Anke Hoeffler. 2000. "Greed and Grievance in Civil War." Paper presented at the World Bank–Center for International Studies Workshop on "The Economics of Civil War," Princeton University, March 18–19.

Conquest, Robert. 1960. *The Nation Killers: The Soviet Deportations of Nationalities.* London: Macmillan.

Cordier, Bruno de. 1996. "The Islamic Influence on Ethnic Nationalism in the North Caucasus: The Cases of Chechenia and Dagestan." *Eurasian Studies* 3, no. 1 (Spring): 27–43.

Critchlov, James. 1991. *Punished Peoples of the Soviet Union: The Continuing Legacy of Stalin's Deportation.* New York: Helsinki Watch.

Dalgat, U. B. 1972. *Geroicheskii epos chechentsev i ingushei* [Chechen and Ingush Heroic Mythology]. Moscow: Nauka.

Daniel, E. Valentine. 1996. *Charred Lullabies: Chapters in an Anthropology of Violence.* Princeton: Princeton University Press.

Das, Veena, ed. 1990. *Mirrors of Violence: Communities, Riots and Survivors in South Asia.* Delhi: Oxford University Press.

Dauyev, Salamu. 1999. *Chechnia: Kovarnye tainstva istorii* [Chechnya: Treacherous Secrets of History]. Moscow: n.p.

David, Steven R. 1997. "Internal War: Causes and Cures." *World Politics* 49, no. 4: 552–76.

Derluguian, Georgi M. 1997. *Chechnya and Tataria.* Washington, D.C.: U.S. Institute of Peace.

———. 1999. "Chechenskaya revolutsiia i chechenskaya istoriia" [The Chechen Revolution and Chechen History]. In Dmitri Furman, ed., *Rossia i Chechnia: Obschestva i gosudarstva* [Russia and Chechnya: Societies and States], 197–222. Moscow: Andrei Sakharov Foundation, Politinfo.

Desheriev, Yunus D. 1960. *Fonetika sovremennogo chechenskogo literaturnogo yazyka* [The Phonetics of the Contemporary Chechen Language]. Groznyy: Checheno-Ingush Izdat.

———. 1963. *Sravnitelno-istoricheskaya grammatika nakhskih yazykov i problemy proiskhozhdenia i istoricheskogo razvitia gorskikh kavkazskikh narodov* [Comparative-Historical Grammar of the Nakh Languages and Problems of the Origin and Historical Evolution of the Mountain Peoples of the North Caucasus]. Groznyy: Checheno-Ingush Izdat.

Diamond, Larry, and Marc F. Plattner, eds. 1994. *Nationalism, Ethnic Conflict, and Democracy.* Baltimore: Johns Hopkins University Press.

Dragadze, Tamara. 1995. "Report on Chechnya." *Central Asian Survey* 14, no. 3: 463–71.

Dudayev, Dzhokhar M. 1992. *Ternistyi put' k svobode* [The Thorny Way to Freedom]. Groznyy: Kniga.

Dunlop, John B. 1998. *Russia Confronts Chechnya: Roots of a Separatist Conflict.* Cambridge: Cambridge University Press.

Eller, Jack David, and Reed M. Coughlan. 1993. "The Poverty of Primordialism: The Demystification of Ethnic Attachments." *Ethnic and Racial Studies* 16, no. 2 (April): 183–202.

Elster, Jon. 1999. *Alchemies of the Mind: Rationality and the Emotions.* Cambridge: Cambridge University Press.

Enloe, Cynthia H. 1980. *Ethnic Soldiers: State Security in Divided Societies.* New York: Penguin Books.

Feldman, A. 1991. *Formation of Violence: The Narrative of the Body and Political Terror in Northern Ireland.* Chicago: University of Chicago Press.

Feldman, Lada C., Ines Prica, and Reana Senjkovic, eds. 1993. *Fear, Death and Resistance: An Ethnography of War, Croatia, 1991–1992.* Translated by Renée Prica et al. Zagreb: Institute of Ethnology and Folklore Research, Matrix Croatica, X-Press.

Furman, Dmitri E., ed. 1999a. *Rossia i Chechnia: Obschestva i gosudarstva* [Russia and Chechnya: Societies and States]. Moscow: Andrei Sakharov Foundation, Politinfo.

———. 1999b. "Samyi trudnyi narod dlya Rossii" [A Most Difficult People for Russia]. In Dmitri Furman, ed., *Rossia i Chechnia: Obschestva i gosudarstva* [Russia and Chechnya: Societies and States], 5–15. Moscow: Andrei Sakharov Foundation, Politinfo.

Gakayev, Dzhabrail D. 1997. *Ocherki politicheskoi istorii Chechni (XX vek)* [Essays on the Political History of Chechnya (Twentieth Century)]. Moscow: Chechen Cultural Center.

———. 1999. *Chechenskii krisis: Istoki, itogi, perspektivy (Politicheskii aspekt)* [The

Chechen Crisis: Roots, Results, and Perspectives (Political Aspect)]. Moscow: Chechen Cultural Center.

———. 2001. "Postkonfliktnaia Chechnya: Analiz situatsii, problemy rekonstruktsii (Politicheskii aspekt)" [Post-Conflict Chechnya: Analysis of the Situation, Reconstruction Issues (Political Aspect)]." In Dzhabrail D. Gakayev and Andarbek D. Yandarov, eds., *Chechnya: Ot konflikta k stabilnosti (problemy rekonstruktsii)* [Chechnya: From Conflict to Stability (Problems of Reconstruction)], 73–90. Moscow: IEA RAS.

Gakayev, Dzhabrail D., and Andarbek D. Yandarov, eds. 2001. *Chechnya: Ot konflikta k stabilnosti (problemy rekonstruktsii)* [Chechnya: From Conflict to Stability (Problems of Reconstruction)]. Moscow: IEA RAS.

Gall, Carlotta, and Thomas de Waal. 1998. *Chechnya: Calamity in the Caucasus.* New York: New York University Press.

Galtung, Johan. 1996. *Peace by Peaceful Means: Peace and Conflict, Development and Civilization.* Thousand Oaks, Calif.: Sage Publications.

Gammer, Moshe. 1994. *Muslim Resistance to the Tsar: Shamil and the Conquest of Chechnia and Daghestan.* London: Frank Cass.

Gantskaya, Olga A. 1977. "Obschie tententsii etnosotcialnogo razvitiya brachnosemeinykh otnoshenii." In Yulian V. Bromley, ed., *Sovremennye etnicheskie protsessy v SSSR* [Contemporary Ethnic Processes in the USSR], 433–59. Moscow: Nauka.

Geshayev, Musa. 1999. *Znamenitye chechentsy* [Famous Chechens]. Brussels: Cartier.

Gorlov, A. G., ed. 1995. *Kriminalnyi rezhim: Chechnya, 1991–1995* [The Criminal Regime: Chechnya, 1991–1995]. Moscow: Ministry of Internal Affairs.

Grafova, Lidia. 2000. *Bezhentsam iz Chechni bezhat' nekuda* [No Place to Go for Chechen Refugees]. Moscow: Coordinating Council for Forced Migrants.

Graham, Thomas E. 2001. "Can Russia Win in Chechnya?" *Brown Journal of World Affairs* 8, no. 1 (Winter/Spring): 21–29.

Greverus, Ina-Maria. 1995. "Speak Up or Be Silent? On an Ethno-Anthropological Approach to War." *Anthropological Journal on European Cultures* (Frankfurt a/M) 4, no. 2: 87–94.

Gritzenko, Nikolai P., and Abdul-Khakim A. Salamov, eds. 1971. *Checheno-Ingushetiya v trudakh sovetskih issledovatelei* [Chechen-Ingushetiya in Soviet Research]. Vol. 1. Groznyy: Checheno-Ingush Izdat.

Gritzenko, Nikolai P., and Andrei G. Popov, eds. 1985. *Checheno- Ingushetiya v trudakh sovetskih issledovatelei. Gumanitarnye nauki: Bibliograficheskii ukazatel, 1970–1982* [Checheno-Ingushetiya in Soviet Social Science and Humanities Research: Bibliographic Guide, 1970–1982]. Groznyy: Checheno-Ingush Izdat.

Grossman, Dave. 1995. *On Killing: The Psychological Cost of Learning to Kill in War and Society.* Boston: Little, Brown.

Gudkov, Lev D. 2000. "Chechenskaya voina i 'my'" [The Chechen War and the "We"]. *Neprikosnovennyi zapas,* no. 5: 32.

Gumilev, Lev N. 1989. *Etnogenez i biosfera Zemli* [Ethnogenesis and Biosphere of the Earth]. Leningrad: Leningrad State University Press.

Gupta, Akhil, and James Ferguson, eds. 1997. *Anthropological Locations: Boundaries and Grounds of a Field Science.* Berkeley: University of California Press.

Gurr, Ted Robert. 1993. *Minorities at Risk: A Global View of Ethnopolitical Conflicts.* Washington, D.C.: U.S. Institute of Peace.

Gurr, Ted Robert, and Barbara Harff. 1994. *Ethnic Conflict in World Politics.* Boulder, Colo.: Westview Press.

Haas, J., ed. 1990. *The Anthropology of War.* Cambridge: Cambridge University Press.

Hall, John A. 1995. "Nationalism Classified and Explained." In Sukumar Perival, ed., *Notions of Nationalism,* 8–33. Budapest, London, and New York: Central European University Press.

Hansen, Greg, and Robert Seely. 1996. *War and Humanitarian Action in Chechnya.* Thomas J. Watson Jr. Institute for International Studies Occasional Paper no. 26. Providence, R.I.: Brown University.

Hardin, Russell. 1995. *One for All: The Logic of Group Conflict.* Princeton: Princeton University Press.

Harrison, Simon. 1993. *The Mask of War: Violence, Ritual, and the Self in Melanesia.* Manchester: Manchester University Press.

———. 1996. "War, Warfare." In Alan Barnard and Jonathan Spencer, eds., *Encyclopedia of Social and Cultural Anthropology,* 561–62. New York: Routledge.

Hechter, Michael. 1987. *Principles of Group Solidarity.* Berkeley: University of California Press.

———. 2000. *Containing Nationalism.* Oxford: Oxford University Press.

Hill, Fiona. 1995. "*Russia's Tinderbox*": *Conflict in the North Caucasus and Its Implications for the Future of the Russian Federation.* Report of the Strengthening Democratic Institutions Project, Harvard University. Cambridge, Mass.

Horowitz, Donald. 2001. *The Deadly Ethnic Riot.* Berkeley: University of California Press.

Howell, S., and R. Willis, eds. 1989. *Societies at Peace: Anthropological Perspective.* London: Routledge.

Huttenbach, Henry, and Francesco Privitera, eds. 1999. *Self-Determination from Versailles to Dayton: Its Historical Legacy.* Ravenna: Longo.

Ignatieff, Michael. 1998. *The Warrior's Honor: Ethnic War and the Modern Conscience.* New York: Holt.

Iskandaryan, Alexander. 1995. *Chechenskii krisis: Proval rossiiskoi politiki na Kavkaze* [The Chechen Crisis: The Failure of Russian Policy in the Caucasus]. Moscow: Moscow Carnegie Center.

Islam na territorii byvshei Rossiiskoi imperii: Entsiklopedicheskii slovar' [Islam in the Territory of the Former Russian Empire: Encyclopedic Dictionary]. 1998–2001. 3 vols. Moscow: Vostochnaya Literatura.

Ivekovic, Ivan. 2000. *Ethnic and Regional Conflicts in Yugoslavia and Transcaucasus: A Political Economy of Contemporary Ethnonational Mobilization.* Ravenna: Longo.

Jambresic Kirin, Renata. 1995. "Testimonial Discourse between National Narrative and Ethnography as Social-Cultural Analysis." *Collegium Anthropologicum* (journal of the Croatian Anthropological Society, Zagreb) 19, no. 1: 17–27.

Jambresic Kirin, Renata, and Maja Povrzanovic, eds. 1996. *War, Exile, Everyday Life: Cultural Perspectives.* Zagreb: Institute of Ethnology and Folklore Research.

Jonson, Lena, and Murad Esenov, eds. 1999. *Political Islam and Conflicts in Russia and Central Asia.* Stockholm: Swedish Institute of International Affairs.

———. 2000. *Chechnya: The International Community and Strategies for Peace and Stability.* Stockholm: Swedish Institute of International Affairs.

Kaldor, Mary. 1999. *New and Old Wars: Organized Violence in the Global Era*. Stanford, Calif.: Stanford University Press.

Kaloyev, Boris A. 1960. "Chechentsy" [The Chechens]. In Mark O. Kosven et al., eds., *Narody Kavkaza* [The Peoples of the Caucasus], 1: 345–74. Moscow: Nauka.

Kalyvas, Stathis N. 2001. "Violent Choices in Civil War Contexts." Paper prepared for presentation at conference on "Preferences, Choice and Uncertainty: Analyzing Choice in Political and Social Settings," University of California, Davis, May 18–19.

Kaufmann, Chaim. 1996. "Possible and Impossible Solutions to Ethnic Civil Wars." *International Security* 20, no. 4:136–75.

Khamidova, Zulai. 1999. "Bor'ba za yazyk: Problema stanovleniya i razvitiya chechinskogo yazyka" [Struggle for Language: The Problem of Formation and Development of the Chechen Language]. In Dmitri E. Furman, ed., *Rossia i Chechnia: Obschestva i gosudarstva* [Russia and Chechnya: Societies and States], 128–49. Moscow: Andrei Sakharov Foundation, Politinfo.

Kharuzin, Nikolai. 1888. "Zametki o yuridicheskom byte chechentsev i ingushei." In *Sbornik materialov po etnogtafii* [Notes on Customary Law of the Chechens and the Ingush: Ethnographic Materials], 2: 65–92. Moscow: n.p.

Khasbulatov, Ruslan. 1995. *Chechnya: Mne ne dali ostanovit' voinu* [Chechnya: I Was Not Allowed to Stop a War]. Moscow: Palea.

———. 2000a. "Gosudarstvo, politika i separatism" [State, Politics, and Separatism]. *Nezavisimaya gazeta*, December 14.

———. 2000b. "Situatsia v Chechenskoi respublike" [The Situation in the Chechen Republic]. *Nezavisimaya gazeta*, December 29.

———. 2001. "Ot nesvobody k tiranii" [From Dependence to Tyranny]. *Nezavisimaya gazeta*, June 21.

Khasbulatova, Zulai I. 1985. "Mezhnatsionalnye braki v Checheno-Ingushetii." In Zura A. Madayeva, ed., *Novoe i traditsionnoe v kulture i bytu narodov Checheno-Ingushetii* [Innovation and Tradition in Culture and Everyday Life of the Peoples of Checheno-Ingushetiya], 34–51. Groznyy: Checheno-Ingush Izdat.

———. 1986. "Otrazhenie sotsialno-kulturnykh izmenenii v sovremennoi semie chechentsev i ingushei (50–80-e gody)" [Sociocultural Changes as Reflected in Contemporary Chechen and Ingush Families (1950–1980s)]. In Zura A. Madayeva, ed., *Etnosotsialnye i kulturno-bytovye protsessy v Checheno-Ingushetii* [Ethno-Social and Cultural Processes in Checheno-Ingushetiya], 40–57. Groznyy: Checheno-Ingush Izdat.

Khazanov, Anatoly. 1995. *After the USSR: Ethnicity, Nationalism and Politics in the Commonwealth of Independent States*. Madison: University of Wisconsin Press.

Kisriev, Enver, and Robert Ware. 2000. *Social Tradition and Political Stability in Dagestan and Chechnya: Developments since September 1999* (manuscript).

Klaproth, Julius von. 1812–14. *Reise in den Kaukasus und nach Georgien: Unternommen in den Jahren 1807 und 1808, auf Veranstaltund der Kaiserlichen Adademie der Wissenschaten zu St. Petersburg. Enthaltend eine vollstandige Beschreibung der kaukasischen Länder und ihrer Bewohne.* 2 vols. Halle: Buchhandlungen des Hallischen Waisenhauses.

Koch, K.-F. 1974. *The Anthropology of Warfare*. Reading, Mass.: Addison-Wesley.

Koehler, Jan, and Christoph Zürcher, eds. 2003. *Potentials of Disorder.* Manchester and New York: Manchester University Press.

Kogan-Yasnyi, Viktor V. 1995. *Chechenskie perekrestki: Stat' i, ocherki, dokumenty* [Chechen Crossroads: Articles, Essays, Documents]. Moscow: Erebus.

Kozlov, Viktor I. 1995. *Russkii vopros: Istoriia tragedii velikogo naroda* [The Russian Question: A History of the Tragedy of a Great People]. n.p.

Krupnov, Eugenii I. 1960. *Drevnaya istoria Severnogo Kavkaza* [The Ancient History of the North Caucasus]. Moscow: Nauka.

———. 1971. *Srednevekovaya Ingushetiya* [Medieval Ingushetiya]. Moscow: Nauka.

Kulikov, Anatoly S., and S. A. Lembik. 2000. *Chechenski uzel: Khronika vooruzhennogo konflikta 1994–1996 gg.* [The Chechen Knot: The Chronicle of Armed Conflict, 1994–1996]. Moscow: Dom pedagogiki.

Kulturnoe stroitelstvo v Checheno-Ingushetii (1920–iyun 1941): Sbornik dokumentov i materialov [Cultural Construction in Checheno-Ingushetiya (1920—June 1941): Collection of Documents and Materials]. 1979. Groznyy: Checheno-Ingush Izdat.

Kusheva, Yelena N., ed. 1997. *Russko-chechenskie otnoshenia. Vtoraya polovina XVI–XVII vv.: Sbornik dokumentov* [Russian-Chechen Relations, Second Half of the Sixteenth Century–Seventeenth Century: A Collection of Documents]. Moscow: Vostochnaya literatura.

Kuzio, T. 1995. "International Reaction to the Chechen Crisis." *Central Asian Survey* 15, no. 1: 97–109.

Lan, David. 1985. *Guns and Rain: Guerrillas and Spirit Mediums in Zimbabwe.* Berkeley: University of California Press.

Lapidus, Gail W. 1998. "Contested Sovereignty: The Tragedy of Chechnya." *International Security* 23, no. 1: 5–49.

———. 2000. "Russia's Second Chechen War: Ten Assumptions in Search of a Policy." In Lena Jonson and Murad Esenov, eds., *Political Islam and Conflicts in Russia and Central Asia,* 30–42. Stockholm: Swedish Institute of International Affairs.

Larsen, Knud, ed. 1993. *Conflict and Social Psychology.* Thousand Oaks, Calif.: Sage Publications.

Laudayev, Umalat. 1872. *Chechenskoe plemya: Sbornik svedenii o kavkazskih gortsah* [The Chechen Tribe: A Collection of Evidence on Caucasian Mountaineers]. Vol. 6. Tbilisi.

Lieber, G. 1992. *Soviet Nationality Policy, Urban Growth, and Identity Change in the Ukrainian SSR, 1923–1934.* Cambridge, Mass.: Cambridge University Press.

Lieven, Anatol. 1998. *Chechnya: Tombstone of Russian Power.* New Haven, Conn.: Yale University Press.

———. 1999. "Voina v Chechne i upadok possiiskogo moguschestva" [War in Chechnya and the Decline of Russian Power]. In Dmitri Furman, ed., *Rossia i Chechnia: Obschestva i gosudarstva* [Russia and Chechnya: Societies and States], 250–89. Moscow: Andrei Sakharov Foundation, Politinfo.

Liono, A. 1999. *The Chechen Problem: Sources, Developments and Future Prospects.* Danish Institute of International Affairs Working Paper no. 12.

Little, David. 1994. *Sri Lanka: The Invention of Enmity.* Washington, D.C.: U.S. Institute of Peace.

Longuet Marx, Frédérique, et al. 2003. *Tchétchénie: La Guerre jusqu'au Dernier?* Paris: Mille st une Nuits.

Madayeva, Zura A. 1985. "Novoie i traditsionnoe v trudovykh prazdnikah vainakhov" [Innovation and Tradition in Labor Holidays of the Vainakh People]. In Z. A. Madayeva, ed., *Novoie i Traditsionnoe v kulture i bytu narodov Checheno-Ingushetii* (Innovation and Tradition in Culture and Everyday Life of the Peoples of Checheno-Ingushetiya], 6–18. Groznyy: Checheno-Ingush Izdat.

———. 1986. "Sotsialno-kulturnye izmeneniya v selskikh raionakh Checheno-Ingushetii (na primere sovkhoza 'Shalinskii')" [Sociocultural Changes in Rural Areas of Checheno-Ingushetiya: The Case of the Shalinskii State Farm]. In Z. A. Madayeva, ed., *Etnosotsialnye i kulturno-bytovye protsessy v Checheno-Ingushetii* [Ethno-Social and Cultural Processes in Checheno-Ingushetiya], 32–39. Groznyy: Checheno-Ingush Izdat.

Magnusson, Marta-Lisa. 2000. "Comments." In Lena Jonson and Murad Esenov, eds., *Political Islam and Conflicts in Russia and Central Asia,* 44–46. Stockholm: Swedish Institute of International Affairs.

Mamakayev, Magomed. 1962. *Chechenskii teip (rod) i protsess ego razhlozhenia* [The Chechen *Teip* (Clan) and the Process of Its Disintegration]. Groznyy: Checheno-Ingush Izdat.

Markakis, John. 1990. *National and Class Conflict in the Horn of Africa.* London: Zed Books.

Markovin, Vladimir I. 1969. *V strane vainakhov* [In the Vainakh Country]. Moscow: Iskusstvo.

Marsh, Peter E., Elisabeth Rosser, and Romano Harré. 1978. *The Rules of Disorder.* London: Routledge & Kegan Paul.

Maskhadov, Aslan A. 1997. *Chest dorozhe zhizni* [|Honor Is More Than Life]. Groznyy: n.p.

Mekenkamp, M., P. van Tongeren, and H. van de Veen, eds. 1999. *Searching for Peace in Africa: An Overview of Conflict Prevention and Management Activities.* Utrecht: European Platform for Conflict Prevention and Transformation.

Mikhailov, Vyacheslav, ed. 1997. *Natsionalnaya politika v Rossii: Istoria i sovremennost* [Nationality Policy in Russia: History and the Present]. Moscow: Russkii Mir.

Miller, Vsevolod F. 1888. *Terskaya oblast: Arkeologicheskie ekskursii. Materialy po arkeologii Kavkaza* [Tersk Oblast: Archaeological Excursions. Materials on Archaeology of the Caucasus]. Vol. 1. Moscow.

Milova, Olga L., comp. 1992. *Deportazii Narodov SSSR, 1930–1950* [Deportations of the Peoples of the USSR, 1930–1950]. Part 1. Moscow: IEA RAS.

Montville, Joseph V., ed. 1990. *Conflict and Peacemaking in Multiethnic Societies.* Lexington, Mass.: Lexington Books.

Munchayev, Rauf M. 1975. *Kavkaz na zare bronzovogo veka: Neolit, eneolit, ranniaya bronza* [The Caucasus on the Eve of the Bronze Age]. Moscow: Nauka.

Musgrave, Thomas D. 1997. *Self-Determination and National Minorities.* Oxford: Oxford University Press.

Muzayev, Timur. 1999. *Etnicheski separatism v Rossii* [Ethnic Separatism in Russia]. Moscow: Panorama.

Muzhukhoyev, Maksharip B. 1979. "Proniknovenie islama k chechentsam i ingusham" [The Spread of Islam among Chechens and Ingush]. In V. B. Vinogradov, ed., *Arkeologicheskie pamaytniki Checheno-Ingushetii* [Archaeological Sites in Checheno-Ingushetiya], 125–50. Groznyy: Checheno-Ingush Izdat.

Narody Rossii: Entsiklopedia [Peoples of Russia: Encyclopedia]. 1994. Edited by Valery Tishkov. Moscow: Rossiiskaya entsiklopedia.

Nekrich, Aleksandr M. 1978. *The Punished Peoples: The Deportation and Tragic Fate of Soviet Minorities at the End of the Second World War.* New York: Norton.

Nordstrom, C., and A. Robben, eds. 1995. *Fieldwork under Fire. Contemporary Studies of Violence and Survival.* Berkeley: University of California Press.

Nukhayev, Khozh-Akhmed. 2001. *Vedeno ili Vashington* [Vedeno or Washington]. Moscow: Arktogeya-Zentr.

Nunuyev, Said-Khamsat. 1998. *Nakhi i svyaschennaya istoriia* [The Nahks and Sacred History]. Moscow: Yaroslavl-Ichkeria Collection.

Orlov, Oleg P., and A. V. Cherkasov, comps. 1998. *Rossiya—Chechnya: Tzep' oshibok i prestuplenii* [Russia and Chechnya: A Circle of Mistakes and Crimes]. Moscow: Zvenia.

Oshayev, Khalid D. 1928. *V serdse Chechni* [In the Heart of Chechnya]. Groznyy.

Ovkhadov, Musa P. 1983. *Checheno-Russkoe dvuyazychie* [Chechen-Russian Bilingualism]. Groznyy: Checheno-Ingush Izdat.

Pain, Emil, and Arkadii Popov. 1995. "Chechenskaya tragediia" [The Chechen Tragedy]. *Izvestiia,* February 7, 8, 9, 10.

Pallas, Peter Simon. 1799–1801. *Bemerkungen auf einer Reise in die südlichen Statthalterschaften des Russischen Reichs in den Jahren 1793 und 1794.* 2 vols. Leipzig: G. Martini.

Panfilov, Oleg, comp. 1995. *Zhurnalisty na chechenskoi voine: Fakty, dokumenty, svidetelstva* [Journalists in the Chechen War: Facts. Documents. Testimonies]. Moscow: Prava cheloveka.

———. 1997. *Informatsionnaya voina v Chechne. Fakty, dokumenty, svidetelstva. Noyabr 1994–sentyabr 1996* [Information War in Chechnya. Facts, Documents, Testimonies. November 1994–September 1996]. Moscow: Prava cheloveka.

Paskachev, A. B. 1993. *Ekonomocheskie i metodologicheskie problemy vkhozhdeniya v rynok v Chechne i Ingushetii* [Economic and Methodological Problems of Transition to Market in Chechnya and Ingushetiya]. Moscow: Delo.

Pchelintseva, Natalia D., and Lubov T. Solovieva. 1996. "Traditsii sotsializatsii detei i podrostkov u narodov Severnogo Kavkaza" [Traditions of Youth Socialization among the Peoples of the North Caucasus]. In V. A. Tishkov and S. V. Cheshko, eds., *Severnyi Kavkaz: Etnopolitical and Etnocultural Protsessy v XX veke* [The North Caucasus: Ethnopolitical and Ethnocultural Processes in the Twentieth Century], 91–132. Moscow: IEA RAS.

Peluso, Nancy Lee, and Michael Watts, eds. 2001. *Violent Environments.* Ithaca, N.Y.: Cornell University Press.

Perepelkin, Lev S. 1994. "Chechenskaya respublika: sovremennaya social'no-politicheskaya situatsiia" [The Chechen Republic: The Contemporary Sociopolitical Situation]. *Etnograficheskoe obozrenie,* no. 1 (January–February): 3–15.

Petersen, Roger D. 2001. *Resistance and Rebellion: Lessons from Eastern Europe.* Cambridge: Cambridge University Press.

Petrov, Nikolai V., et al. 1995. *Chechenski konflikt v etno- i politiko-geograficheskom izmerenii* [Ethno- and Politico-Geographical Dimensions of the Chechen Conflict]. 2d ed., rev. *Bulletin, Politicheskii Landshaft Rossii* [Political Landscape of Russia] (January).

Pfaff, William. 1993. *The Wrath of Nations: Civilization and the Furies of Nationalism.* New York: Simon & Schuster.

Pohl, Michaela. 2002. "'Neuzheli eti zemli nashei mogiloi stanut?' Chechentsy i ingushi v Kazakhstane (1944–1957 gg.)" ["It Cannot Be That Our Graves Will Be Here!" Chechen and Ingush Deportees in Kazakhstan, 1944–1957]. *Diasporas,* no. 2: 158–204.

Pokrovskii, Nikolai N. 2000. *Kavkazskie voiny i imamat Shamilya* [The Caucasian Wars and Shamil's Imamate]. Moscow: ROSSPEN.

Polyan, Pavel M. 2001. *Ne po svoiei vole . . . Istoria i geografia prinuditelnyh migratsii v SSSR* [Not of One's Own Free Will . . . The History and Geography of Forced Migrations in the USSR]. Moscow: O.G.I.–Memorial.

Povrzanovich, Maja. 2000. "The Imposed and the Imagined as Encountered by Croatian War Ethnographers." *Current Anthropology* 41, no. 2: 151–62.

Pravovye aspekty chechenskogo krizisa [Legal Aspects of the Chechen Crisis]. 1995. Moscow: Memorial.

Premdas, Ralph R. 1995a. *Ethnic Conflict and Development: The Case of Guyana.* Aldershot, UK: Avebury.

———. 1995b. *Ethnic Conflict and Development: The Case of Fiji.* Aldershot, UK: Avebury.

Prince, R. 1985. *The Legacy of the Holocaust. Psychohistorical Themes in the Second Generation.* Ann Arbor: University of Michigan Press.

Report of the Edinburg Missionary Society for 1817, with an appendix, containing a geographical and historical account of the society missionary stations in Asian Russia. 1817. Edinburgh.

Rich, Paul B., and Richard Stubbs. 1997. *The Counter-Insurgent State: Guerrilla Warfare and State-Building in the Twentieth Century.* New York: St. Martin's Press.

Riches, David, ed. 1986. *The Anthropology of Violence.* Oxford: Basil Blackwell.

Robakidzhe, A., ed. 1986. *Kavkazskii etnograficheskii sbornik: Ocherki etnogafii gornoi Chechni* [Caucasian Ethnographic Studies: Essays on the Ethnography of Mountain Chechnya]. Vol. 6. Moscow: Nauka.

Rotar, Igor. 2001. *Pod zelenym znamenem islama: Islamistkie radikaly v Rossii i CNG* [Under the Green Banner of Islam: Islamist Radicals in Russia and the CIS]. Moscow: n.p.

Rubinstein, R. A. 1994. "Collective Violence and Common Security." In Tim Ingold, ed., *Companion Encyclopedia of Anthropology,* 983–1009. New York: Routledge.

Rule, James B. 1988. *Theories of Civil Violence.* Berkeley: University of California Press.

Rywkin, Michael. 1982. *Moscow's Muslim Challenge: Soviet Central Asia.* Armonk, N.Y.: M. E. Sharpe.

Sabli raya: Gorskoe oruzhie v Kavkazskoi voine [The Sabres of Paradise: The Mountaineers' Weaponry in the Caucasus War]. 1992. Groznyy: Groznensky rabochy.

Sandole, Dennis. 1992. *Conflict Resolution in the Post-Cold War Era: Dealing with Ethnic Violence in the New Europe.* Institute for Conflict Analysis and Resolution, George Mason University, Working Paper no. 6. Fairfax, Va.

Scheper-Hughes, Nancy. 1992. *Death without Weeping: The Violence of Everyday Life in Brazil.* Berkeley: University of California Press.

Scott, James C. 1998. *Seeing Like a State: How Certain Schemes to Improve the Human Condition Have Failed.* New Haven, Conn.: Yale University Press.

Searle, John R. 1969. *Speech Acts, An Essay in the Philosophy of Language.* New York: Cambridge University Press.

———. 1995. *The Construction of Social Reality.* Boston: Free Press.

Semenov, Yuri I. 1999. *Filosofia istorii: Ot istokov do nashikh dnei* [The Philosophy of History: From the Origins to the Present]. Moscow: Staryi sad.

Service, Robert. 1998. *A History of Twentieth-Century Russia.* London: Penguin Books.

Shenfield, Stephen. 2002. "Chechnya at a Turning Point." Johnson's Russia List, #6191, Research and Analytical Supplement no. 7 (April), Special Issue on the Situation in Chechnya, 3–10, http://www.cdi.org/russia/johnson/6191-1.cfm.

Shermatova, Sanobar, and Leonid Nikitinskii. 2000. "Generaly rabotorgovli" [Generals of the Slave Trade]. *Moskovskie novosti,* no. 12 (March 28).

Shnirelman, Viktor A. 2001. *The Value of the Past: Myths, Identity and Politics in Transcaucasia.* Senri Ethnological Studies 57. Osaka, Japan: National Museum of Ethnology.

Shternberg, Leo. 1903. "Chechentsy." In *Entsiklopedicheskii slovar'* [Encyclopedic Dictionary], 76: 785–86. Saint Petersburg: F. A. Brockhaus and I. A. Efron.

Sigauri, Ibragim M. 1997. *Ocherki istorii gosudarstvennogo ustroistva chechentsev s drevneishikh vremen* [Essays on the History of Chechen Statehood since Ancient Times]. Moscow: Russkaya zhizn.

Simon, Gerhard. 1991. *Nationalism and Policy toward the Nationalities in the Soviet Union: From Totalitarian Dictatorship to Post-Stalinist Society.* Boulder, Colo.: Westview Press.

Sivertsev, Mikhail A. 1997. *Charismaticheskaya kultura: Lider v posttotalitarnom prostranstve* [Charismatic Culture: The Leader in Post-Totalitarian Spacc]. Moscow: Moscow Scientific Fund.

Skakunov, Eduard I. 1996. *Chechenskii konflikt: Mezhdunarodnye issledovania* [The Chechen Conflict: International Studies]. No. 10. Moscow: RATMMO.

Smirnova, Yaroslava S. 1983. *Semia i semeinyi byt u narodov Severnogo Kavkaza: Vtoraya polovina XIX–XX veka* [Family and Family Life among the Peoples of the North Caucasus: Second Half of the Nineteenth Century–Twentieth Century]. Moscow: Nauka.

Sorensen, B. 1998. *Women and Post-Conflict Reconstructions: Issues and Sources.* War-Torn Societies Project Occasional Paper no. 3. Geneva: UN Research Institute for Social Development.

Soslambekov, Yusup. 1996. *Odinokii volk na trope nezavisimosti* [The Lone Wolf on the Road to Independence]. Moscow: n.p.

———. N.d. *Chechnya (Nohchio)—vzglyad iznutri* [Chechnya (Nohkchi)—A View from Inside]. N.p.: n.p.

Starovoitova, Galina. 1992. "Nationality Policies in the Period of Perestroika: Some Comments from a Political Actor." In Gail Lapidus and Victor Zaslavsky, eds., *From Union to Commonwealth: Nationalism and Separatism in the Soviet Republics,* 114–21. Cambridge: Cambridge University Press.

———. 1997. *National Self-Determination: Approaches and Case Studies.* Thomas J. Watson Jr. Institute for International Studies Occasional Paper no. 27. Providence, R.I.: Brown University.

Starovoitova, Galina V., and Konstantin Kedrov. 1992. "Deklaratsia prav cheloveka dolzhna poluchit' garantii ot vsekh stran'" [Declaration on Human Rights Must Get Guarantees from All Countries]. *Izvestia*, August 10.

Stavenhagen, Rodolfo. 1996. *Ethnic Conflicts and the Nation-State*. New York: St. Martin's Press.

Stepanov, Eugenii I., ed. 1999. *Konflikty v sovremennoi Rossii: Problemy analiza i regulirovania* [Conflicts in Contemporary Russia: Problems of Analysis and Regulations]. Moscow: ROSSPEN.

Stern, Paul. 1995. "Why Do People Sacrifice for Their Nations?" *Political Psychology* 16, no. 2: 217–36.

Stiefel, Mattias. 1998. *Rebuilding after War: A Summary Report of the War-Torn Societies Project*. Geneva: UN Research Institute for Social Development.

Sultygov, Abdul-Khakim. 2001. *Chechenskaya Respublika: Poisk ideologii politicheskogo uregulirovania* [The Chechen Republic: In Search of a Political Solution]. Moscow: Pomatur.

Suny, Ronald G. 1993. *The Revenge of the Past: Nationalism, Revolution, and the Collapse of the Soviet Union*. Stanford, Calif.: Stanford University Press.

———. 1998. *The Soviet Experiment: Russia, the USSR, and the Successor States*. New York: Oxford University Press.

Sykiainen, Leonid. 1999. "*Shari'ah* and Muslim-Law Culture." In Lena Jonson and Murad Esenov, eds., *Political Islam and Conflicts in Russia and Central Asia*, 82–100. Stockholm: Swedish Institute of International Affairs.

Tambiah, Stanley J. 1996. *Leveling Crowds: Ethnonationalist Conflicts and Collective Violence in South Asia*. Berkeley: University of California Press.

Tibi, Bassam. 1998. *The Challenge of Fundamentalism: Political Islam and the New World Disorder*. Berkeley: University of California Press.

Tilly, Charles. 1978. *From Mobilization to Revolution*. Reading, Mass.: Addison-Wesley.

———. 2000. "Violence Viewed and Reviewed." *Social Research* 67, no. 3: iii–vii.

———. 2002. "Violence, Terror, and Politics as Usual." MS. Columbia University, March 31.

Tishkov, Valery A. 1997a. *Ethnicity, Nationalism, and Conflict in and after the Soviet Union: The Mind Aflame*. Thousand Oaks, Calif.: Sage Publications.

———. 1997b. *Ocherki teorii i politiki etnichnosti v Rossii* [Essays on the Theory and Politics of Ethnicity in Russia]. Moscow: Russkii mir.

———. 1997c. "The Political Anthropology of the Chechen War." *Security Dialogue* 28, no. 4 (December): 425–37.

———. 1999a. "Ethnic Conflicts in the Former USSR: The Use and Misuse of Typologies and Data." *Journal of Peace Research* 36, no. 5: 1–21.

———, ed. 1999b. *Puti mira na Severnom Kavkaze* [The Ways to Peace in the North Caucasus]. Moscow: Aviaizdat.

———. 2000. "Forget the 'Nation': Post-Nationalist Understanding of Nationalism." *Ethnic and Racial Studies* 23, no. 4 (July): 625–50.

———. 2001a. *Etnologia i politika* [Ethnology and Politics]. Moscow: Nauka.

———. 2001b. "The Culture of Hostage Taking in Chechnya." In Alex P. Schmid, ed., *Countering Terrorism through International Cooperation*. Milan: International Scientific and Professional Advisory Council of the United Nations Crime Prevention and Criminal Justice Programme.

Tishkov, Valery A., Yelena Belyaeva, and Georgi Marchenko. 1995. *Chechenskii krizis* [The Chechen Crisis]. Moscow: Business Roundtable of Russia's Research Center.

Tishkov, Valery A., and S. V. Cheshko, eds. 1996. *Severnyi Kavkaz: Bytovye traditsii v XX veke* [The North Caucasus: Everyday Life Traditions in the Twentieth Century]. Moscow: IEA RAS.

Tokarev, Sergei A. 1958. *Etnografiia narodov SSSR: Istoricheskie osnovy byta i kultury.* Moscow: Moscow State University Press.

Trenin, Dmitri, and Ekaterina Stepanova. 2000. *Kosovskii krizis: Mezhdunarodnyi aspekt* [The Kosovo Crisis: International Aspect]. Moscow: Moscow Carnegie Center.

Troshev, Gennadi. 2001. *Moya chechenskaya voina. Chechenskii dnevnik okopnogo generala* [My War: Chechen Diary of a Field General]. Moscow: Vagrius.

Turkayev, Khasan V., ed. 2002. *Kultura Chechni* [The Culture of Chechnya]. Moscow: Nauka.

Turpalov, Lema. 1999. "Sredstva massovoi informatsii Chechenskoi respubliki v usloviaykh rossiisko-chechenskogo protivostoiyania" [Means of Mass Communication of the Chechen Republic under Conditions of Russian-Chechen Conflict]. In Dmitri Furman, ed., *Rossia i Chechnia: Obschestva i gosudarstva* [Russia and Chechnya: Societies and States], 335–42. Moscow: Andrei Sakharov Foundation, Politinfo.

Umarov, Sirazhudin Z. 1985. *Evoluitsia osnovnykh techenii islama v Checheno-Ingushetii* [Evolution of the Main Trends of Islam in Checheno-Ingushetiya]. Groznyy: Checheno-Ingush Izdat.

Uslar, Petr K. 1869. *Etnografiia Kavkaza: Chechenskii yazyk* [The Ethnography of the Caucasus: The Chechen Language]. Tbilisi.

Usmanov, Lema. 1997. *Nepokorennaya Chechnya* [Invisible Chechnya]. Moscow: Parus.

Vakhayev, Lema. 1999. "Politicheskie fantazii v Chechenskoi respublike" [Political Fantasies in the Chechen Republic]. In Dmitri Furman, ed., *Rossia i Chechnia: Obschestva i gosudarstva* [Russia and Chechnya: Societies and States], 324–34. Moscow: Andrei Sakharov Foundation, Politinfo.

Väyrynen, Raimo. 1994. *Towards a Theory of Ethnic Conflicts and Their Resolution.* Notre Dame, Ind.: Joan B. Kroc Institute for International Peace Studies, University of Notre Dame.

Vinogradov, Vitalii B. 1966. *Tainy minuvshikh vremen* [The Secrets of the Past]. Moscow: Nauka.

Vinogradov, Vitalii B., ed. 1982. *Semeino-bytovaya obryadnost vainakhov. Sbornik nauchnykh trudov Checheno-Ingushskogo instituta istorii, sotsiologii i filosofii* [Family Rituals of Vainakhs. Studies of the Scientific Checheno-Ingush Institute of History, Sociology, and Philosophy]. Groznyy: Checheno-Ingush Izdat.

Voina v Chechne: Mezhdunarodnyi tribunal: Materialy oprosa svidetelei, pervaya sessia, Moskva, 21–25 fevralya 1996 [War in Chechnya International Tribunal: Testimony Materials, First Session, Moscow, February 21–25, 1996]. 1996. Moscow: Glasnost Foundation.

Volkova, Natalia G. 1974. *Etnicheskii sostav naseleniia Severnogo Kavkaza v XYIII–nachale XX veka* [The Ethnic Composition of the Population of the North Caucasus, 1800–Early Twentieth Century]. Moscow: Nauka.

Volkova, Natalia G., ed. 1992. *Stranitsy otechestvennogo kavkazovedenia* [The Chronicle of Russian Caucasian Studies]. Moscow: Nauka.

Voslenski, Michail. 1991. *Nomenklatura: Gospodstvuischii klas Sovetskogo Soiuza* [The *Nomenklatura:* The Ruling Class of the Soviet Union]. Moscow: Sovetskaya Rossiya.

Whitmer, Barbara. 1997. *The Violence Mythos.* Albany: State University of New York Press.

Woodward, Susan L. 1996. *Balkan Tragedy: Chaos and Dissolution after the Cold War.* Washington, D.C.: Brookings Institution.

Yakovlev, Nikolai F. 1927. *Voprosy izuchenia chechentsev i ingushei* [The Problems of Studying the Chechen and Ingush Peoples]. Groznyy.

———. 1939. *Morfologia chechenkogo yazyka* [The Morphology of the Chechen Language]. Moscow: Nauka.

———. 1940. *Sintaksis chechenskogo literaturnogo yazyka* [The Syntax of the Chechen Language]. Moscow: Nauka.

Yandarbiyev, Zelimkhan. 1996. *Chechnya—Bitva za svobodu* [Chechnya—The Struggle for Freedom]. Lvov, Ukraine: n.p.

Yandarov, Andarbek D. 1975. *Sufism i ideologiia natsional' no-osvoboditel' nogo dvizheniia: Iz istorii razvitiia obschestvennykh idei v Checheno-Ingushetii v 20–70 gody XIX v.* [Sufism and the Ideology of the National-Liberation Movement: From the History of Public Thought in Checheno-Ingushetiya, 1820–1870]. Alma-Ata: Nauka.

Yusupov, Musa M. 1999. "Orsthoitsy: Kto oni?" [Orstoitsy: Who Are They?]. *Bulletin of the Network of Ethnological Monitoring* 26: 60–61.

———. 2000. "Struktura i dvizhuschie cily chechenskogo konflikta" [Structure and Moving Forces of the Chechen Conflict]. *Ethnopanorama* 1, no. 13: 35–43.

"Zachistka": Doklad pravozaschitnogo zentra ["Zachistka": Report of the Human Rights Center]. 2000. Moscow: Memorial.

Zakharovich, Yuri. 1999. "Chechnenskaya voina glazami zhurnalistov amerikanskih izdanii" [The Chechen War through the Eyes of American Journalists]. In Dmitri Furman, ed., *Rossia i Chechnia: Obschestva i gosudarstva* [Russia and Chechnya: Societies and States], 290–307. Moscow: Andrei Sakharov Foundation, Politinfo.

Zaslavski, Viktor. 2001. "Russko-chechenskii konflikt glazami Zapada" [The Russian-Chechen Conflict through Western Eyes]. *Neprikosnovennyi zapas,* no. 2.

Zaurbekova, Galina. 1986. "Osnovnye tendentsii izmenenii sotsialno-klassovogo sostava naselenia Checheno-Ingushetii za gody sovetskoi vlasti" [Main Tendencies in Changes of Social and Class Composition of the Population of the Checheno-Ingushetiya]. In Zura A. Madayeva, ed., *Etnosotsialnye i kulturno-bytovue protsessy v Checheno-Ingushetii* [Ethnosocial and Cultural Processes in the Checheno-Ingushetiya], 19–31. Groznyy: Checheno-Ingush Izdat.

———. 2000. *Separatism v Chechne* [Separatism in Chechnya]. Working Papers in Urgent and Applied Ethnology, no. 135. Moscow: IEA RAS.

Zaurbekova, Galina, and Andarbek Yandarov. 2001. "O nekotorykh paradoksalistskikh tendentsiiakh v separatistskom konflikte" [On Some Paradoxical Tendencies in the Separatist Conflict]. In Dzhabrail D. Gakayev and Andarbek D. Yandarov, eds., *Chechnya: Ot konflikta k stabilnosti (problemy rekonstruktsii)* [Chechnya: From Conflict to Stability (Problems of Reconstruction)], 148–70. Moscow: IEA RAS.

Zdravomyslov, Andrei G. 1998. "Chechenskii krisis i ego znachenie dlya rossiiskogo obschestva" [The Chechen Crisis and Its Significance for Russian Society]. In A. G. Zdravomyslov, ed., *Relyativistkaya teoria natsii* [Relativist Theory of Nation], 109–21. Moscow: ROSSPEN.

Zorin, Vladimir. 1989. *Dnevnik ne dlya sebya* [A Diary Not for Himself]. Moscow: Dialogue Press.

INDEX

Text: 10/12 Baskerville
Display: Baskerville
Indexer: Margie Towery
Compositor: BookMatters, Berkeley
Printer: Maple-Vail Manufacturing Group